MY WICKED, WICKED WAYS

'A document on the Hollywood life far beyond its fan magazine fascination. It describes at length and in many anecdotes the last of the Big Studio era . . . Flynn delivers footnotes to film history that are hard to come by' *San Francisco Chronicle*

'Its greatest distinction is that it manages to pass beyond the conventionally 'frank' to the unconventionally truthful in its portrait of an engaging but by no means overscrupulous romantic extrovert' *Times Literary Supplement*

'An obstinately unabashed report . . . Flynn can be very entertaining – coarse and crapulous, certainly, but never dull – and there are plenty of anecdotes about Hollywood and its Olympians' *New Yorker*

ERROL FLYNN

My Wicked,
Wicked Ways

With an Introduction by
Jeffrey Meyers

First published in Great Britain
2005 by Aurum Press Ltd
7 Greenland Street, London NW1 0ND
www.aurumpress.co.uk

First published by William Heinemann

A catalogue record for this book is available from
the British Library.

ISBN 978 1 84513 049 7

9 10
2011 2010

This book is printed on paper certified by the Forest Stewardship
Council as coming from a forest that is well managed according to
strict environmental, social and economic standards.

Printed by CPI Bookmarque, Croydon, CR0 4TD

To a small companion

COME, ALL YOU YOUNG MEN WITH YOUR WICKED WICKED WAYS,
   SOW YOUR WILD WILD OATS IN YOUR YOUNGER DAYS,
SO THAT WE MAY BE HAPPY WHEN WE GROW OLD.
   AH YES! HAPPY AND HAPPY WHEN WE GROW OLD . . .
FOR THE DAY'S GROWING SHORT, THE NIGHT'S COMING ON;
   WELL DARLING—JUST GIMME YER ARM AND WE'LL JOGGLE ALONG.
WE'LL JOGGLE AND JOGGLE AND JOGGLE ALONG.

ROMANS, 1:29-30—*Being filled with all unrighteousness, fornication, wickedness, covetousness, maliciousness, full of envy, murder, debate, deceit, malignity; whisperers, backbiters, haters of God, despiteful, proud, boasters, inventors of evil things, disobedient to parents.*

ISAIAH, 57:21—*There is no peace, saith my God, to the wicked.*

PSALMS, 32:10—*Many sorrows shall be to the wicked.*

Introduction

In 1958, while living in Jamaica, Errol Flynn hired the ghostwriter Earl Conrad—a literary stand-in—to help him write a scandalous book, guaranteed to offend everyone he knew. From August to October, Flynn dictated and Conrad wrote what later became *My Wicked, Wicked Ways*. According to Flynn's teenage girlfriend, Beverly Aadland (who was surely exaggerating), Conrad was usually drunk, spent most of his time chasing Jamaican women, and did little more than ask a lot of questions. Conrad had an ironclad contract with the publisher, Putnam. Flynn, who had to finish the book in order to get the money to build his long-planned dream house, couldn't get rid of him. "He was basically a door stop," Beverly said, "with a paid vacation." Whatever his faults, Conrad certainly helped Flynn produce a lively, amusing, and extremely successful book—the most entertaining autobiography ever written by an actor.

In his negative portrait of Flynn in his roman à clef, *Crane Eden* (1962), Conrad described the desperate context: "He was broke or very hard up. Crane hadn't had a big picture recently; he was poking about looking for any kind of proposition, bits on television, partnership movie productions, business deals of any kind. These were the movements of an artist in trouble." When his estranged third wife, Pat Wymore, thinking of all the people Flynn intended to libel, asked why he didn't wait another ten years to write the book, he replied: "In another ten years I may be dead."

By the time his book was posthumously published in December 1959, Flynn had virtually killed himself with dissipation and readers were prepared to believe almost anything he said about himself. In life, Flynn habitually disparaged himself, drew fire from others, and often took the blame when he wasn't guilty. On his trip to the Spanish Civil War, he was the victim of malicious lies perpetrated by his pro-Nazi friend, Hermann Erben. Afterward, he became the target of spite against Hollywood.

3

Though he had a heart murmur, tuberculosis, and malaria, he was condemned as a draft evader during World War II. Accused and acquitted of rape in a notorious trial in 1942, he was the scapegoat for a corrupt police force and a hypocritical society. When the historically inaccurate film *Objective, Burma!* (1945) gravely offended the British, Flynn was held personally responsible. In two well-publicized episodes he got into fights with police officers. When they made unreasonable demands and he refused to do their bidding, he was arrested.

Flynn's mythomaniacal autobiography, in which fact and fantasy are indistinguishable, emphasized the lurid and sensational side of his life. He confesses to running from debts, stealing jewels, and cuckolding husbands in Australia, but falsely accused himself of leaving a stranded friend to drown and killing a man in New Guinea. Though he used the title ironically, the public accepted his wicked persona. As Coleridge wrote of Byron, Flynn (who was known as the Baron) was "a wicked lord who, from morbid and restless vanity, pretended to be ten times more wicked than he was."

The carpe diem epigraph supplied the title. Flynn took it from a cowboy folk song, substituting "wicked, wicked ways" for the original "wild in your ways":

> Come, all you young men with your wicked wicked ways,
> Sow your wild wild oats in your younger days,
> So that we may be happy when we grow old.
> Ah yes! happy and happy when we grow old. . . .
> For the day's growing short, the night's coming on.

Flynn's style is witty, his tone ironic, his attitude cynical. As in a relaxed and amusing conversation, he frequently breaks chronology to move forward and backward in time. He begins with a prologue (1953) that describes the personal and financial fallout of *William Tell*. Flynn had backed the film with his own money and lost $430,000. He then recalls his years in Tasmania and Sydney (1909–1927) and in New Guinea (1927–1932), his round-the-world trip with Hermann Erben from Port Moresby to England (1932–1933), his first decade in Hollywood (1933–1943), and his trial for rape. He seems to lose interest in his story three-quarters of the way through, and devotes only 100 pages to the last fifteen years of his life. The final, more introspective section, when he was famous and the facts were known or could be checked, is more accurate and reliable than the early chapters.

A recurrent pattern emerges in the sections on Australia and New Guinea: travel to exotic destinations, criminal adventures, affairs with beautiful women, violent confrontations with deceived husbands—and flight from impossible situations. Although Flynn spends a great deal of time chasing women, he portrays them as stupid and mercenary, predatory and possessive. The dominant themes of the book are his search for extremes of experience and desire to satisfy his intellectual curiosity, dissatisfaction with his acting career, and ultimate loss of self-respect. As he sardonically wrote of his last films, when offered the part of "a once-handsome man, now decadent, a shadow of his former self and who has taken to the bottle . . . I know that must be me. . . . I make more today being a shadow of my former self than I did when I *was* my former self."

The best and liveliest parts of the book are the delicious, potentially libelous passages that his publisher was forced to delete from the paperback editions: Flynn's satiric attacks on his intolerably priggish mother, his first wife Lili Damita, the studio executive Jack Warner, the director Mike Curtiz, his sometime-fiancée Irene Ghika, and his treacherous friend Bruce Cabot. A friend of Lili Damita recalled how Flynn exacted a posthumous revenge on his fiery, uninhibited, and rapacious ex-wife, who devoted her life to ruining him financially. In *My Wicked, Wicked Ways* Flynn describes her intellectual limitations, jealousy, violence, and threats of suicide as well as her shocking behavior in a lesbian nightclub. When his book was received in *Newsweek,* "poor little Lili" arrived at a fashionable Palm Beach party and, her true character revealed, was greeted with frosty silence. There are also some surprising omissions, possibly because Flynn forgot about them: his expulsion from Hobart High School, his celebrated public fistfights with the director John Huston and others, the acquisition and loss of Navy Island in Jamaica, and the filming of Hemingway's *The Sun Also Rises.* To avoid incriminating himself, he left out his sexual relationship with Beverly Aadland.

The theme of impending death, first expressed in the epigraph, "For the day's growing short, the night's coming on" (an echo of John 9:4: "the night cometh when no man can work"), recurs in the last sentence of the book. His four children are in America, his parents are in England, and he's alone with his dogs on his Jamaican estate. He surveys his land and the glittering sea below, and in the last sentence declares: "The second half-century looms up, but I don't feel the night coming on"— which, nonetheless, conveys the sense of imminent doom.

Putnam paid an advance of $9,000. Flynn's English agent, Murray

Pollinger, persuaded the editor of the British newspaper *The People* "to pay £1 per word for a long serial extract (including £1 for each indefinite and definite article); such a sum was unheard of at that time and for long after. . . . To date the sales figures for the British market stand at £230,500, and it is still selling. The paperback edition sales between September 1992 and December 1999 amount to £18,500." The American paperback edition, which had reached a seventh printing in February 1974, has sold more than a million copies. Flynn, who always had ambitions as a writer, published several novels and articles and wrote many vivid and amusing letters. He said "he would rather have written a few good books than made all his films."

Flynn's autobiography shocked and offended Noël Coward, his friend and Jamaican neighbor, who maintained an English sense of propriety. A well-known homosexual himself, he had practiced careful restraint in public. He created witty comedies and musicals that hinted at naughtiness, but never strayed beyond middlebrow good taste. In his frank and reckless narrative Flynn was far ahead of his time, and Coward wasn't ready for his radical self-exposure. "I have at last got round to Errol Flynn's autobiography, which I found painfully irritating," he wrote. "It is indeed as outspoken as it is reputed to be but with a sort of outspokenness which curdles the blood. Such a wealth of unnecessary vulgarity."

The reviews, however, were extremely favorable and critics recognized Flynn's most important work as a masterpiece of its kind. *Newsweek* admired the book's honesty and called it the "confessions of a rake, unsparing of himself or anyone else." The *Guardian* placed it in an exalted tradition and printed an enthusiastic "selling" review: "This is a major autobiography in the tradition of Cellini, Casanova, and Frank Harris. Perhaps it is not the book to leave alone in the house with your daughter. But Flynn was not the man to leave in the house with your daughter."

The critic in *Library Journal,* a book trade publication, acknowledged its transcendent quality: "In describing the drive of his curiosity, his determination to accept all experience, his artistic and intellectual unrest, even his gradual loss of self-respect, the book attains a stature above and beyond its interesting but sordid subject matter." Even the staid *Times Literary Supplement* praised its style, its narrative pace, and its remarkably candid self-portrait: "[It is,] surprisingly, very well written, with a flair of a born raconteur disciplined by something remarkably like the skill of a born writer. . . . Its greatest distinction is that it manages to pass beyond the conventionally 'frank' to the unconventionally truthful in its portrait of an engaging but by no means overscrupulous romantic extrovert." The fantasy and exaggeration, the racy style and tone of Flynn's last testament reveal one of the most charming, engaging, and self-destructive personalities in Hollywood.

JEFFREY MEYERS
KENSINGTON, CALIFORNIA
JULY 2002

JEFFREY MEYERS' acclaimed books include *Edgar Allan Poe, Joseph Conrad, Scott Fitzgerald, Katherine Mansfield, Gary Cooper,* and *Hemingway: Life into Art.*
He has also written biographies of Edmund Wilson, Robert Frost, Humphrey Bogart, George Orwell, and Errol and Sean Flynn. A Fellow of the Royal Society of Literature, he lives in Berkeley, California.

Prologue

Ah, yes, there are many zesty things Errol can tell if he really opens up. . . . He'll be the first male to do so if he does. We'll wager he won't—because in Errol's case, truth is really stranger than the fantastic fiction press agents built around him long ago. . . .

The magazine *Uncensored*, September, 1958.

I particularly detest books that begin something like "Ah, there was joy and happiness in the quaint Tasmanian home of Professor Flynn when the first bellowings of lusty little Errol were heard. . . ." So if you are interested, let's get down to the meat of the matter.

My career with Warner Brothers, two decades of picture-making, ended stormily in 1952. I had a violent argument with Jack Warner before we split. We had been fighting like that since I joined them in 1934. We parted and I said to myself, The hell with them all. I will go to Italy and make my own pictures. I will make a mint and show these guys I don't need them or their studio.

So I took off. I had in mind a certain story on which I figured I might make between ten and twenty millions.

I went into an independent production to make *William Tell*. I wrote the outline of the script myself; I had a scenario drawn, and I went into business with a group of Italians—fifty-fifty. We budgeted for $860,000. I put up half. I had the cash money—all I had—and I joined forces with these sons of Italy. I'll call them that now before I call them other kinds of sons a little later.

I built one of the most beautiful sets right in William Tell country itself at Courmayeur, in Northern Italy, where the Alps run up very high. I built an entire little village, with a stream running through it where we would shoot the famous highlight—knocking an apple off of a boy's head. At one angle you saw high mountain tops, at another a green valley. Hills covered with beautiful verdure rose in another direction. Here I'd have the Austrians attack; they would come charging up there, raging and pillaging. I was going to show the motion picture industry how to do it. Besides, this would be in Cinemascope. Only one other picture, grossing eighteen million dollars, *The Robe,* had been done in Cinemascope, and mine, I hoped, might gross the same amount. I'd teach Jack Warner how to make pictures.

My associate in the making of *William Tell* was Barry Mahon. He and his wife and three children had an apartment in Rome. Patrice and I, and our daughter Arnella, had an apartment not far from theirs.

About a third of the way through the film, the Italians approached me through an interpreter and said they had run out of money.

"How do you mean? I don't understand. I have got $430,000 in this picture. I put up all I am supposed to put up. You must be joking."

Their spokesman gave me a funny smile, which I have never seen on the dome of any Michelangelo ceiling anywhere in Rome. "No, no. We are out of money. You must raise more."

"You must be insane. What is this? I have fulfilled every obligation I have."

Still smiling, he shrugged and said, "Just one of those things."

I stared in absolute bewilderment. "I can't raise any more money. I have extended my credit. What the hell are you talking about?"

The smiles continued: a whole group of nice Italian gentlemen who had just taken me for the longest ride since Marco Polo visited the Orient.

"You must be a bunch of crooks." I kept hollering. "You are nothing but a bunch of bandits, crooks!"

"No, no, no! *Altra mentalidad.*" He was telling me he was not a crook, only he had another type of mentality.

The fellow who coined the cliché that it never rains but it pours needs to be resurrected and given a medal. Just then it started pouring—but good.

The lost $430,000 was only a drop for my bucket.

At just this minute, back in the States, my business manager, Al Blum, died. He had sent me a letter saying, *You owe the government only $18,000. You have nothing to worry about.*

I no sooner walked away from my Italian partners when I picked up the newspaper and read where Uncle Sam assessed me for $840,000. Plus what I had lost.

That tied up every asset I had.

This wasn't enough. My charming ex-wife, Lili Damita—my first wife—who has made a career of pursuing me through every court, bank, note, market operation, legal document and contract I was ever connected with—figured this was a good time to clamp the screw down a little closer. She tied up my house and furniture back in Hollywood, and everything else she could lay her hands on, for back alimony. I thought Al Blum had taken care to prevent that, but he had only taken care of himself.

I was married to Patrice Wymore. Now we were in Rome, flat broke. I had been broke before, but not in a long while. If you are used to a lot of money a sudden change can be very demoralizing.

Following an early policy, when broke, put on your best clothes, if you have any and if you haven't—borrow them, make the tie neater, and go around hoping you never looked more prosperous.

But I couldn't bring myself to go to any of my pals about Rome and say, Listen, old boy, my ass is out. Do you think . . .

I couldn't think of a way to get out of the mess. I felt compelled to stay in Rome. Going back to America owing a million or more bucks was impossible right now.

How could Al Blum have done this to me? He knew he was dying of cancer and he was living it up—on my dough. Everybody wondered why he had a private airplane, two Cadillacs, a house in the country, and a large house in Beverly Hills. Yet everybody supposed—so did I—that he was a successful business manager. I certainly thought so until this news hit me smack in the face. I got word from his secretary that almost his last words were, "Tell Errol I am sorry."

Well, Errol was too—a million dollars' worth sorry, because the Government had me lined up for—but not charged as yet with—fraud. I had never made out an income tax return in my life. I had signed what Al Blum had handed to me to be signed. He had power of attorney. I was cooked, and now there was no Al Blum to rescue me.

But others were about to land on me. There was I walking up the Via Venito, Rome's principal rendezvous, trying to look cheerful and prosperous, and with not enough lire in my pockets to buy my wife a new hat, no way of getting hold of any money to send for the support of three children in America, and trying to smile while wondering what the hell I was going to do to get out of this mess.

I almost felt like passing the hat around. Maybe I ought to use my wiles as an actor. Put a patch on my eye, get a tin cup or lift up a maimed leg and stand on some street corner and see what I could work up.

This went on for weeks. I had an apartment, the rent on it unpaid.

Thank heavens, I had my two cars left: a Mercedes Benz and an English sports car. I didn't have the gas to ride them around but I felt I had an ace in the hole. Small ace, very small hole.

Hanging about Rome was one of my old-time Cuban pals, Pedro Rodriguez. He is a rich, generous nut. A complete utter nut, with sleepy brown eyes and silver-gray hair. He makes a thousand dollars a day from Cuban sugar. He drinks in such a way that you can't take him out, it's hard to be around him, but you love him. Pedro speaks atrocious English, impossible French and incomprehensible Spanish. Yet everyone seems to understand him. It was nothing for him to fly from Cuba to Paris or Rome just to see me for a few days. Fly Europe, have fun, go see Flynn.

I didn't tell Pedro of my misfortunes with the Italians. But he must have sensed something happened. I stopped picking up the tabs at the night clubs (a bad habit I must cure). I behaved moodily. Work had suspended on *William Tell*. I hesitated about accepting Pedro's invitations to go places. All that he could possibly have figured out was that I was in some kind of trouble, but I would never have asked him for a loan.

There was panic in the two apartments, Flynn's and the Mahons'. We decided to cheer ourselves up a bit by putting on a dinner party and inviting some of our friends. The money was low but not so far gone that we couldn't scare up drinks and Pat was a good cook. To the party came Rodriguez and one whom I thought of as an old old pal of Western pictures, Bruce Cabot, who was working with me in *William Tell*.

Bruce and I had roistered and romped in the night clubs of the world together. We had pranked with mutual friends. He was the heavy in many of my pictures, and about the nearest thing to a brother that I had. Maybe that was why I always like to have pals around, like Bruce. "Okay," I said to people, "he is this and that but he will never do it to me." I had loaned him money. I had helped him with jobs and work for fifteen years. I had gone to bat for him even when it meant almost my own neck to do so. He had been one of my buddies around Mulholland House in Hollywood.

Once I was with Bruce when we both chanced to see Maureen O'Hara for the first time. Never did I see a more dreamlike creature.

That flaming red hair, glorious Irish complexion, and beautiful bearing. I said to Bruce, "Isn't she a darling?"

His eyes popped. "My God!"

"Let me tell you something, brother, she is terrific." I gave him a knowing leer.

"Do you know her?"

"*Do* I know her?"

I looked at her from a distance as I said that, my second look. I'd never met her.

"Look," I hissed, "I'm telling you something. This girl who looks so distinguished and ladylike, there is only one way to her. All you have to do is walk right up, bow from the waist, kiss her hand, then grab one of her tits and the girl goes all to pieces."

"No!"

"Yes!"

That did it. Cabot fell. He stood there wetting his lips, contemplating his approach. I egged him on just once more. "You have to do it quick, otherwise she'll pull the ladylike princess stuff on you."

He went over to her. He grabbed that handful and he promptly got the biggest whack over the head I have ever seen a lady deliver.

He tripped and went over backwards flat on the floor.

That was our camaraderie, the way Bruce and I had romped through the years.

He was hanging around Morocco doing nothing when I sent him a wire asking him to come on and play a part with me in *William Tell*. So he came to Italy.

The house party was first-rate fun. I couldn't know what was in the mind of each of my two closest pals, Rodriguez and Cabot.

The next day the Cuban had to leave for Paris. There was a small matter he had to take care of there.

The day after he left I got a cable from the Credit Suisse Bank in Geneva, saying, ACKNOWLEDGE RECEIPT $10,000 YOUR CREDIT.

Dear Pedro. He knew that if he had offered it to me face to face I would have told him to go to hell, due to a greatly overbearing pride.

Then, just when this faith was restored, the other man who came to dinner acted.

I decided to fly up to Geneva on several business matters. The day after I left, two process servers called at my apartment and at the Mahons' place. They seized my wife's clothes and my two cars, and they seized Mrs. Mahon's clothes and their car, even their children's clothes so they couldn't go to school.

When the Italians lowered the boom, Bruce, instead of suing them, thought he could get some money out of me. Maybe he didn't know how broke I was; or didn't care. Attaching my cars was the *coup de grâce*. I couldn't raise any money on them, and had not one other asset.

Cabot went up and down the Via Venito boasting about what he had done.

When I got back and heard of this, Barry Mahon said, "Why don't you go and see him?"

"No, I am afraid."

"What? You afraid of Cabot?"

"Yes, I am afraid."

I was so boiling mad I was afraid of what I might do to him if I saw him. I had to watch myself. I couldn't believe Cabot would do a thing like this to me. No real man strikes at another through his helpless family—especially after he's been befriended for twenty years.

I stayed off the streets of Rome. I stayed away from the Via Venito, the rendezvous street. For there I might bump into Bruce. I said to myself, This is no time for a murder rap.

Under all these tensions, unnerved, broke, I came down with hepatitis. A Swiss doctor told me I was through, that I was going to die— soon.

"Your liver has stopped," he said. "It will go no more."

"No?" I asked. "What happens now?"

"You die." He shrugged. "Maybe not today, maybe not tomorrow, but you die. I am sorry." He then asked, "You worried about something?"

I said I was, slightly.

I crawled out of bed. I staggered to the bathroom. I stared into the mirror. My eyes looked as if they had been dipped in mustard. "You're yellow all right," I muttered. Then, a quite irrelevant, rather ludicrous thought came into my mind: Goddamit, I refuse to predecease Jack Warner!

Somehow I survived. Somehow I was back on my legs, but they were very weak pins. I talked over with Pat what we would do in the future, how we would go on living in greatly reduced circumstances. While I recouped, I stayed away from the spots where I might bump into Cabot, for that was one fever that hadn't broken.

There have been certain people, all my life, who have touched explosive nerve cords inside me. One had been my mother with whom I have had a lifetime hassle. Also, I was afraid to meet up with my first wife, Lili Damita. Afraid in the same kind of way. I couldn't trust myself around her. She had been living off me for many years, ever since our divorce; and she had siphoned hundreds of thousands of dollars out of my hide. I had to ride a lot of horses and wave a lot of swords to take care of her expensive tastes.

Right now, back in America, Lili and her lawyers were dunning me heavily for alimony due her. She was one of a thousand creditors beating around my ears, deafening me, but she was not among the lesser ones.

I flew to New York to talk over with my new lawyer, Jud Golenbock, what I could do about the world having tumbled down on my head. I had been represented by this young Madison Avenue lawyer for two or three years. He had defended someone else in a case and beat me in an action that cost me twenty-five G's and I decided that this was a guy I wanted on my side. After the case I called him and asked him to come and see me. Maybe he thought I wanted to knock his block off. Instead I asked him to take over my absurd life.

When he looked over the whole mess of my finances he almost threw up his hands—which I had done.

"How could you let yourself get into a position like this?" he asked.

How? Having become accustomed to living like a millionaire for twenty years of my life, I simply let others take care of the details of paying my debts. I had the money—let a financial manager handle such matters. I had never even looked at business bills. I sent them to Al Blum. Or I said, "Send the bill to Al." I had been doing that for years. It was a terrible effort for me to keep away from good company, pretty faces, exotic dinners, fine paintings—in order to go over accounts. I didn't understand an income tax form, and still don't. It looked to me like a problem in algebra and I had never opened an algebra book. That's what you hire people for, to take care of such details. Having made forty-five pictures, I was a one-man corporation, and I felt that a business manager should take over on the administration of small details. You have to trust somebody in this world. I trusted Al implicitly.

A week went by while the accountants went over the books. The Government went over them. Jud went over them. Everybody went over them—except me. I couldn't stand the look of them. I had no money. I learned I owed two million.

My lawyer told me that I had made about seven or eight million since I joined up with Warner Brothers in 1934. He said, "Look, if you want to face the facts of life, you're insolvent. In fact, you're lucky you haven't been put into bankruptcy."

"What will happen if I go bankrupt?"

"If you go bankrupt you may be able to pay ten cents on the dollar or something like that."

I thought it over. Somehow the thought of what my father would think entered my mind. I said No, going bankrupt was a form of welching and that I'd have to try to work to pay up in full, although how long that would take me God knows.

He threw up his hands.

I had a vision of going back to where I came from, Tasmania, New Guinea, in ball and chain, like a convict.

The long sheet Jud had before him looked like the financial page of *The New York Times*. It also looked like a miniature of the national debt. "It looks like I have to go on working for the rest of my life to pay off."

I thought for a while.

"No," I said at last, "I won't even consider bankruptcy."

I went to "21" that day for lunch. It is a habit of mine, when you are down and out, go to the best spots.

At the Club a fellow named Ben Finney, a playboy of sorts, called across the room. "Hey Princey"—that's another of my nicknames from *The Prince and the Pauper*—"come over here. What are you doing for lunch?"

As nonchalantly as possible I said, "No, old boy, be my guest." When flat, put on the old front—you know.

We had a halfhearted fight about it. I started with a couple of Jack Roses beforehand. I worked up in my usual style to grouse freshly flown from Scotland, a bottle of Moselle 21, fine vintage. I felt the gloom lifting.

What did he want to talk to me about? He had read in the papers, of course, that I was broke.

"Have you got that Gauguin painting, 'Au Bord du Mer'?" he asked. All of a sudden, daylight!

"You want to sell it?" he went on.

I remembered that Jud had put it in storage, but I didn't know where. It was mortgaged, but for less than full value. But to part with it—

the thought hurt, it was a work of art that somehow didn't count in the mundane field of assets; something that belonged to my heart, my ego, the inner self—for I had long been interested in great paintings.

"I've got a buyer who will pay you $75,000 cash for it tomorrow."

I could feel my palms tingling. "Sorry, old boy, as I love you, I couldn't consider it. You know, it's one of the world's masterpieces."

He said, "This is a firm offer. He's got to have this painting. I've got to have my commission. How much?"

"Well, it's not worth discussing. The price is ridiculous."

Seventy-five grand! A deal like that would solve every immediate problem. "I wouldn't consider it under $110,000 and I'd be reluctant at that."

The day following I closed the deal to sell my Gauguin: my pride and joy, one of Gauguin's finest. It depicted the simplicity of the South Seas. There was a simple man holding the hand of a little boy. But paintings seem to be just loaned to you. The longest you can have a painting is your own lifetime. You stop, but the painting goes on—if it is one that is worth going on.

It was one of the few possessions I really loved. I could stay in front of it, of an evening, especially when alone, and admire it and get a deep, tearful feeling from it.

All of a sudden I was cash ahead, after paying $10,000 commission and the money due on the mortgage.

I didn't go to "21" again. Too expensive!

I ran to Jud's office. "Jud, I got this money. How shall I allocate it? Nobody knows I got it. But for God's sakes, don't leave me with an old hat and a tin cup."

"Don't be too nervous," he said. "Have you forgotten you have a Van Gogh? I can put that up tomorrow and get you another hundred and fifty thousand."

I was shocked. I hadn't included *that* in my thinking.

"Oh no! If that goes . . ."

I still have the Van Gogh as of this writing.

I paid off a regiment of little debts that I had run up, that my wife or ex-wives had run up. A bit here, a bit there. Debts which I thought had been paid off by Al Blum.

With a few thousand dollars as a grubstake I went to England to make some pictures, to start up again.

But when your luck starts running out, it keeps running out.

During the rest of 1952 I made two pictures in England. Horrible flops.

I was tired, and it seemed as though my fate and fortunes were running low. The great debts in the United States hovered over me. My lawyer relayed to me the size and proportion of the pressures upon him for me to fork over money that I didn't have and didn't know where to get.

Ah, screw 'em all, I said. Let 'em chase me around the world.

For the next three years I did little but live on my schooner, the *Zaca,* at Palma de Majorca, Spain. The only real wives I have ever had have been my sailing ships. Up front, on the prow of the *Zaca,* there was painted, appropriately, a rooster, a crowing cock.

I sailed the *Zaca,* went skin-diving, took in the bullfights, tried to live a domestic life with Patrice, and I diapered my lovely little daughter Arnella.

Years before, I had begun drinking steadily, daily—about a fifth of vodka a day, maybe more. Now I extended and deepened this recreation. Why didn't I tire of it? Why did most other things pall on me, but vodka never? Intermittently I played around with the celebrity set at the cosmopolitan centers, or one or two came to visit me on the *Zaca.* I had an occasional brawl in a bar—they were getting less frequent now —and generally I lived the life of a guy who is washed up.

I believed I was washed up, finished.

I had a little kit that I carried around. It was about the size of a medical kit. On it were the words FLYNN ENTERPRISES. Only I knew that inside of it was a tidy bar, with a bottle of vodka, two or three glasses and a bottle or two of quinine water. I had acquired a bible at last and I carted it around with me.

When I went ashore, or called on the beach to see someone, I had my little brief case along. I was going to get security somewhere, somehow, out of something.

There I was, in 1953, '54 and '55 and into '56, Flynn Enterprises moving about Majorca and the South of France, kit in hand, asking myself, How did this happen? What are you doing? Who are you? How can a man live to his forty-sixth or -seventh year and then begin to ask himself questions? Who am I? What am I doing with this medical kit at my side? Where am I going? Is this the way a man should wind up?

Except for the few who were close to me, or dependent upon alimony or support from me, I was now, in the mid-1950's, to the general community a pretty much forgotten man. No pictures were coming out. None in recent years had been sensational successes.

So what? I had my own resources. One thing I always knew how to do: enjoy life. If I have any genius it is a genius for living.

I spent myself to the full, dissipating all that I wanted to, testing how much my constitution could stand, bending where others might break. What the hell is the use? I thought. I can't pay off my indebtedness. I can't go back to America. Can't ride horses like I used to. I'm tired of swinging a sword. Let's drink and go skin-diving. Maybe if I'm lucky I'll go down a hundred feet some day and not come up. I was full up with the whole act of living. Twice in my life I had been close to suicide. Now I was just living, drifting. I went around with a stubble beard and didn't give a damn.

Sitting around on the *Zaca* in shorts, I had plenty of time to contemplate. I had by now made about forty-five pictures, but what had I become? I knew all too well: a phallic symbol. All over the world I was, as a name and personality, equated with sex. Playboy of the Western World. That was me. But what had I set out to become a long time before when I was young and the world opened to me? How far afield had I gone from my early ambitions? Does any man ever set out to become a phallic symbol universally, or does this not rather happen to a man in spite of himself?

The old bromide came back to me, how some were born to greatness, some achieved it, and others had it thrust upon them. I had no greatness, only a deadly fear of mediocrity. But time had set upon me this strange stamp of lady-killer *par excellence*.

How did this happen?

I had my pals, King Farouk, Ali Khan, Prince Ranier, any motion picture pals who might be going my way, such as Orson Welles, Rita Hayworth, and social registerites from the bored Newport and Long Island set. They came and went. I met them at the gambling casinos in southern France. We had drinks and fun. I drifted.

He's broke, they said.

They were right.

He's washed up, they said.

They were right.

Flynn is done.

In Like Flynn? That's a laugh. Out Like Flynn.

So to hell with it. Just open the medical kit, take a drink, go for a swim, diaper Arnella.

I tried to stay interested in my wife, but that was hard. It is hard for me to stay interested in any one woman in the world for very long, no matter how fine she is. Patrice was and is fine, but I got bored. I opened my kit. Another fifth. "Boy, bring me some light Sauterne, I want to clean my teeth." I laughed. My friends laughed. I had pals. They had yachts. We dined on their yachts or they dined on ours.

Months and years drifting. Down and out professionally, but I got my kicks. I got older. I heard them say wherever I went, like Ava Gardner said, "Look at Errol. Look at him. When he was young he was the best-looking thing I ever saw." Ava didn't mean it unkindly. We were good friends long long ago when she was sweet eighteen and the world didn't know her talents and resources.

I was without faith. Full of regret that I could not believe in God. I was upset with people who said to me, "What? You don't believe? You don't have faith? Well if you don't have it, you just don't know," in a very upsetting, smart-alecky tone that many people have. They give it to you in a very superior way. They are in touch with God, you are not! If you don't know, old man, it's your tough luck. I doubt these people. Maybe they don't look at life hard enough and deeply enough. Maybe they let the barriers down at a certain point, and don't resist, and they let something rush in that they call God.

I'm too hardheaded for that. I have been in rebellion against God and Government ever since I can remember. As a result I am tormented, as if I have been missing something that others have. You can have fame, fortune, be an international character, and wonder whether some little guy who has faith has something bigger than anything you have ever had.

But I had my vodka—and had faith in *that*. It came in cases. I got up in the morning and reached. I hawked, coughed around a while, took another drink, started the day.

For four and one-half years I was on the bum.

Rumors were going around, though I didn't know of them then, that I was sick to death, that I had broken my back, that I was drunk and in the gutter, and that I didn't want to work.

In spite of this reputation for disaster, somebody remembered me. Sam Jaffe, a Hollywood agent, came to Palma de Majorca and asked me why I didn't want to work.

"What's going to happen to you?" he asked. "You're living like a beachcomber."

"I'm having a good time. I'm not working and I'm enjoying it." I had been a beachcomber once before, I told him, and it looked like I was going to stick to it.

He shook his head.

I was playing for time and position. I really wanted to get back to work.

A series of cables went back and forth.

I learned that I was wanted for a picture to be called *Istanbul*. I thought the film was to be made in Turkey, but it turned out I must go back to Hollywood.

In the States, people who saw me again on the screen said I looked dissipated. Great! I was tired of being called beautiful, as they had called me when I was younger.

I followed *Istanbul* with some television work. Then came a series of pictures and I was back in the public eye again.

The first break came when Darryl F. Zanuck, whom I hardly knew then, for some obscure reason he has never explained to me thought of me for a juicy part in his *The Sun Also Rises* and all the critics were unanimously very kind, for once. Then, of all people, Jack Warner (remember, I was going to teach him how to make pictures?), my old friend and antagonist, decided I was right for the role of John Barrymore in *Too Much Too Soon* and again the critics leaped into the breech for me, saying I made a good Barrymore and I was welcomed home. Then came *Roots of Heaven*, another one for Darryl. In all of these I played a drunk and a bum. What people believed I was and had become.

Maybe these roles were right for me. I was a natural, I guess. A bum, a rake, a character.

Yet, apparently, all the world loves a comeback.

The magazines began talking about me again. Hollywood is more like its old self, they said, Flynn's In Again. They called it a comeback and they said my new earnings were helping me to pay off my huge debts. That was true. I wanted to owe nobody anything.

More recently I produced, as an interesting side venture, a thing called *Cuban Rebel Girl*. I spent many days with Fidel just before the Batistans quit.

All that is familiar and brings the story up to date and to what seems more or less known about my whereabouts in recent years. And yet what do the people know about me? Nothing.

The wives I have had, the mistresses I've kept, the pictures I've made, the brawls I've been in, the bounces I've taken, my made and lost fortunes, my wicked ways—these are not me. I could not live and believe that these things were really me. Who could live with himself believing himself to be a symbol of sex and nothing more?

What makes anyone think that I am less concerned for the verities of the world than anyone else? Was it all a prank that I went to Loyalist Spain, that I sided with Castro, that I've plumbed the sea depths, and traveled the world?

The search for sensations has played a great part in my life, but there have been other quests.

There is no use telling a story arse backwards. Better begin where it all begins—in the womb—except where, as in my unique case, it so often ends.

PART ONE
Tasmanian Devil
1909-1927

A Tasmanian devil (*Sarcophilus ursinus*) is a carnivorous marsupial known for its extreme ferocity.

MY parents were born in Australia. My father, when he was about twenty-four, was beginning his lifework as a Marine Biologist. He hung around the house of a family named Young, where there were three beautiful young women, Alice, Betty and Marelle. Father was interested in Betty, but my mother, Marelle, nabbed him. He must have been a pushover for Mother. She was twenty-one and full of animal spirits. He was just a tall hunk of scholarship.

My father and mother, after marriage, were on board a ship called the *Aurora,* making a very early scientific expedition to the South Pole. My father shipped as a biologist. The boat was in Australia-Tasmania waters when Mother was found to be pregnant. She was put ashore at Hobart, Tasmania, and my father went on with the expedition.

They strung a bunch of names on me: Errol Leslie Thomson Flynn. I dropped the name Leslie because I had an uncle of that name and we hated each other's guts.

Father settled in Tasmania as a biology lecturer at the Hobart University—a very young man soon to hold a full professorship. Mother began to like the place and they decided to stay there. My earliest years were in this strange cold little land to the south of Australia.

Hobart is a town that nestles at the foot of Mount Wellington. My principal recollection of it is of its apples, its jams, its rosy-cheeked girls. I am happy to note that even at that early age I was pretty observant.

We lived in a little two-story brick house, and there was a courtyard behind us where I spent much of my time. The region was agricultural. A beach, Sandy Bay, was not far away and I was often there, swimming at the age of three.

The beach was of hard brown sand, the water freezing cold. Mother was a good swimmer, and she took me there often. I have never been out of ocean water for very long ever since.

From about four or five I began one long unending scrap with my mother.

As she tells it today—she is living, with my father, in England—I was a devil in boy's clothing. I can only sympathize with her. I can readily understand she had a good case in finding me unmanageable. I wish I could say that time had changed the situation between us. It has not. We have fallen out all our lives.

I have a mindful of memories of these childhood hassles.

Mother was quick to anger and she didn't believe in sparing the rod. She would grab the hairs at the back of my head, pull them very hard, and held in that position, I'd get a whacking.

I don't say she didn't love me. She may have—in her way. I revolted from time to time bellowing, "Every time you come near me you only want to wash me!" That is the sign of a protective mother, I suppose. My resistance to authority led naturally to incessant scoldings and thrashings.

My father was away, engaged in his scientific research. The nearest thing to a man of dash and daring that Hobart might boast was the manager of the local motion picture theatre, and I got in there free from time to time because he and mother were friendly.

He had a glamorous car, the brand of which has long since disappeared from the automobile scene. The outstanding feature of it was a brass horn in the form of a giant python, a contraption running the length of the car. In front, where the noise came out, the snake's jaws were wide open, its fangs showing. You pressed a big rubber bubble and a horrible howling honk emerged. You were frightened into staying on the curb. People jumped back, startled, and knocked each other over when that incredible machine approached.

Mother, in her 1914 motoring hat, her long white veil tied under her chin and flowing in the breeze—laughing gaily—was perfectly beautiful. Stuck in the back seat, it did not occur to me that I was some kind of chaperon, I guess.

I played regularly—or irregularly—with a little girl next door named Nerida. One day we exhausted the interest in bush ranges, which is the Australian equivalent of cowboys and Indians.

She proposed that we play house, husband and wife. She prepared mud pies, I pretended to eat them. The inevitable happened. We went under the porch of Nerida's house and played more seriously at husband and wife.

"I'll show you mine and you show me yours," I said. She was game.

Nerida's mother nabbed us red-fingered, and she promptly told my mother. I got a hell of a shellacking.

I wondered why I should get whaled so, while Nerida, who was older, got off with a You-musn't-do-that, darling.

My mother not only lambasted me, but said, "Now you shall tell your father yourself!"

I dreaded having to do this. It was an afternoon terrible with anticipation, till my father came home. Then, whether from fear or stubbornness, I wouldn't open my mouth.

Mother yelled, "Go on. Tell him what you did, you dirty little brute! Go on! Don't stand there! Tell your father what you were doing!"

My father, who was sympathetic, said, "Now, Marelle, he will tell me in his own time."

"He will not! He will tell you now!"

She flew at me again. I screamed. He stepped in. He was never any match for her, either in words or action, and Mother followed through with a torrent of invective.

This is no place for me, I decided. I'd leave home, get a job.

The next morning I went out of doors, ostensibly to play. I walked off, a long walk, into the farming country. Jobs weren't plentiful. There was a great deal of unemployment in the seven-year-old ranks. I applied at a few farms but was everywhere told to go home.

At night I couldn't go home, didn't even know the way, so I climbed a tree. I settled into the crotch of the tree—at least I was out of reach of any predatory animals—where I spent a most uncomfortable night.

Twenty-four hours passed.

I was ravenous. What to eat?

I saw some cows. They were being suckled by the calves. I thought, That's for me for breakfast.

One of the cows was lying down and I thought, That one looks easy.

What I didn't know was that this cow had no calf, so that when I went to work for breakfast on her udder, all I got was a big kick in the crotch.

Hunger drove me into a farmhouse, and I was given food.

I had two more days and another night on the highway.

On the third morning I hit a farm where the family showed concern. I told them I was out for a job. I even told them who I was and that I had run away. The man of the house left the table while I was eating and went to fetch my father.

After a time I saw Father approaching, looking tall, downcast, worried.

He thanked the woman who took care of me. All he said was, "Come along, son."

We returned in silence.

I had no idea what was going to happen. To my astonishment, when I arrived I saw Mother in bed, as if she had been prostrated. She let out a piercing cry. "Oh, thank God, thank God, you are back! You nearly killed me with worry!"

I felt my father's umbrella poking in the middle of my back. "Go on over," he whispered, "go on over there."

It was a long walk to her bed. She seized me in her arms, showered me with kisses—to my complete astonishment. She had never done that before. Tears streamed down her face. It was bewildering. It ran through my head, Why is she like this to me now, when she was like that to me before?

Was Mother worried about me only because of what effect my absence or death would have on her, her marriage, her husband? I don't know. But it was a greater show of affection than I generally received.

Recently my mother wrote a letter descriptive of that incident, remarking, "He ran away from home when he was about seven and we suffered agonies of anxiety for three days and nights. He was found miles away where he went and offered himself for work at a dairy farm. He asked only five shillings a week as wages, saying that would do him, as he 'never intended to marry.' "

That tells it.

I never have married. I have been tied up with women in one legal situation after another called marriage, but they somehow break up.

Once when I skipped school—a regular practice—I told Father about it. He thought my confession was very honest. "Now go home and tell your mother and I know she will understand," he said. I got a whaling.

At Harvard University there is a distinguished professor, head of the School of Economics. His name is John Glover, my first cousin. He is the son of my mother's sister Betty, who lost out to Dad in the marriage stakes.

John and I lived in the same house at Kirribili Point, Sydney, for some time, and we didn't get along very well. He was studious, smart, well-behaved. He knew more about everything than I did. That must have made me jealous. But I was bigger. I resorted to my usual bullying practice of blackmail. I used to try to force him to lie to get me out of hot spots, but he wasn't good at it. An incident developed, having to do with one of my truancies from school. Someone shook the truth out of him. Again I had to undergo the inevitable hair pulling and slapping.

This time Mother locked me in a back room for two days. I learned then what a prison cell was like. I have hated ever since the prospect of being cooped up.

It was a storeroom, with a board floor, one window, and nothing but a blanket or two and a suitcase sharing space with me. Beneath the wooden floor I heard my friends, the guinea pigs, moving about. That was some slight comfort.

Fortunately, my aging maternal grandmother, Edith, who was about five feet tall, pretty much ruled the house. She was the only one who could give orders to my mother. She stood up on a couple of packing cases to hand in to me through the window some chunks of bread covered with dripping-sugar. A gruesome mess, but I was glad to get it.

Since then my cousin John and I have become good friends. But I remember how he was associated once or twice with the early bitterness between my mother and me.

Mother played the piano. She sang, she danced. She talked three languages, German, French and English. The photographs of her when she was young show a beautiful woman. She was an athlete, a good swimmer. There was much about her that I learned only in my adult years.

Apparently she had theatrical ambitions which she concealed from my scholarly father. Once a motion picture group came through Hobart and Mother was paid to do a swimming bit. The professor didn't know. He was too involved with his laboratory work to follow all her moves or keep pace with her gay, passionate nature.

Yet I have no awareness of having received from her any theatrical motivation. This came to me later on, in New Guinea, by misadventure.

We did have an inside track to local theatricals. My uncle, Oscar O'Thames, was one of the heads of the J. C. Williamson Theatrical Company. Every now and then I got from him a free pass to the theatre to see some traveling show. It was always a gallery seat. One day I looked downward to the stage where there pirouetted a celebrated figure, Pavlova. Her dancing enchanted me. She seemed to me a vision from another world, and I fell desperately in love with her. I think it was from seeing the artistry of this dancer that I first felt an affinity for the world of art. Ever since then dancers do much to me.

The only indication in me for acting was an incident that occurred one day when I was abroad with Mother in the streets of Hobart. One of her male friends came along and commented on how jolly I looked. Mother urged me to acknowledge by bowing. I didn't budge—just kept quiet.

Afterward when she asked me why I was so rude I said, "Mama, I was playing train—being a train—and trains don't speak." That was my first acting bit, a character role.

Another item of Flynniana has it that at the age of two I jangled her nerves one day with a big word. "Evidently you are always at the powder puff." Mother must have remembered it, for it was told to me recently.

For the rest, I recall primarily this continual sore behind of mine.

My young, beautiful, impatient mother, with the itch to live—perhaps too much like my own—was a tempest about my ears, as I about hers.

Our war deepened so that a time came when it was a matter of indifference to me whether I saw her or not.

These brawls with her, almost daily occurrences, did something to me.

Mostly I wanted to get away from her, get away from home.

The rapport was with my father.

He looked Irish. He had red, bushy eyebrows, black hair; he was lean, angular, full of charm, good will, and a certain professorial quietness. He spoke with a clipped British accent, tinged with touches of Irish brogue.

When school finished, I raced home to be at his side, to hurry out into the back yard where we had cages of specimens of rare animals. That courtyard was a fascinating place for a small boy.

Tasmania is the only spot in the world where three prehistoric animals, the Tasmanian tiger, the Tasmanian devil and the animal Zyurus, are found. Father had specimens of all of these in his cages, as well as kangaroo rats, opossums, sheep. I got to know these creatures very well, even the most savage, and I hated it when he had to chloroform one and dissect it. The kangaroo rat in particular was friendly. This animal strayed around like a dog, and it was upsetting to me to observe it being sliced up. Father's experiments were directed at determining the relationship of these animals to the human being. This was a period when Darwin was being confirmed by many biologists. Darwin was my father's hero, and he followed in the footsteps of Darwin and of Sir Thomas Huxley.

To this day there is a very very long account of my father's accomplishments in the British *Who's Who*—with no mention of the exploits of his son.

Through Father's activity I made my first venture into commerce. He bought all the kangaroo rats he could get hold of for Hobart University. I learned to set box traps in the hills of nearby Mount Wellington. He paid a shilling a head.

Occasionally I went with him on a trip in quest of one of the rare Tasmanian animals. We headed for the western coast, a difficult terrain, where there were huge fossilized trees. We hunted the Tasmanian tiger, an animal so rare it took Father four years to trap one. Yet though he prowled in nature frequently, he wasn't essentially an outdoors man. Mostly his work was inside, over books, papers, microscopes, slides.

There were trips into the interior of Tasmania when Father went on his scientific jaunts, along quiet streams up toward Launceton, which was the second biggest city in Tasmania. He looked into out-of-the-way rivers, with microscopes and magnifying glasses, while I ran around ferreting rabbits or trying to catch a fresh-water fish called bream. I tagged along, like a puppy, whenever he would take me.

There was the wonderful fishing expedition when the University hired a trailer, with great metal seines, to scoop up the bottom of the ocean. It was fascinating to see what came up from below: every kind of sea animal peculiar to this region. These investigations afterward won Father remarkable acclaim in scientific circles—the sea spider, the anemone, the giant polar crab two feet in width, scallops, electric eels and electric rays—all these things came out of the steel net. He bottled his finds, exclaiming, "Oh, what a lovely thing! What a beauty! A beauty!" as if it were some pearl or a rare woman.

He was patient when I asked why he cut up some specimen. He'd have a frog stretched out with thumbtacks and he'd split the brain. I peered over his hands, breathing heavily, and he pushed me aside gently and went on with his fine delicate work.

Once Mother bought him a new suit. I admired it enormously, but he ignored it. Yet a day or two later, when the University appropriated enough money to get some new device which would slice the ovary of the echidna (porcupine, to us) to one/two hundred thousandth of an inch, he was delighted. He jumped about like a youngster with a new toy.

I also fancied myself a scientist. . . .

I found out that if you gave a duck a piece of fatty pork, something in its intestinal make-up caused the bird to pass the pork within a minute or two. From beak to exit it was a spectacle you could observe very swiftly.

We had plenty of ducks in our back yard. I pondered a night over this.

It occurred to me that it would be interesting to tie a string about ten feet long to the pork.

Out came the pork, which I then gave to another duck with the same result, holding onto the string that entered the first duck's mouth. In a few minutes I had a half-dozen ducks tied together beak to rectum on this greased string.

I was, in a stroke—and at the age of eight or nine—inventor of the first living bracelet. No scientist discoverer of an antibiotic could have been more enchanted than I.

At once I commercialized. I sold tickets to my friends. The ducks dragged one another around in all directions.

Father came home and witnessed my venture into the world of science.

"You cruel little devil!" He broke his unopened umbrella across my back. I scampered away with a cry of fright and a burst of tears.

"Dad," I said, "you cut open animals all day long in your laboratory. What did I do wrong?"

He looked at his broken umbrella. He saw I had a point. Tears came to his eyes.

It was the only violence I ever experienced at his hands.

So, I was destined never to become a laboratory technician—unless my experience with women can be called such.

There wasn't much room or time for religion in an atmosphere like this. There was church on Sunday but I seem to have no recollection of it. My ancestors in Ireland were Catholic. Legend has it that the priest came around with the hat too often and my great-grandfather, a hard-riding, hard-drinking man, went into a rage and flew, bag and baggage, to the north of Ireland and became Church of England.

By the time I was coming up in Tasmania, with the sea and the prehistoric animals in my ken and the books of Darwin lying about, the mood in the Flynn family was agnostic.

God went His way—and I wound up in Hollywood.

No books were ever bought especially for me, as I recall, and I suppose it was thought that Father's books would do for me too. I think they did. The illustrated books were the most interesting, especially those of the human anatomy, the structure of the skull of man. I lingered over colorful plates of the human female vagina.

Father's reading matter, including Spinoza, Nietzsche and Voltaire, ran smack against Mother's literature. I remember going through the stacks and happening upon a rousing sex thriller called *Three Weeks* by an American writer named Elinor Glyn. There was Michael Arlen's *The Green Hat,* a volume that nestled alongside *The Phenomenon of the Ovaries of the Echidna.* Comic strips from America, *Mutt and Jeff, True Blue Harold,* and the *Katzenjammer Kids,* gave us a picture of the United States. Robinson Crusoe was a figure in our folk lives, and we read *Two Years Before the Mast.*

My mother's people were seafaring folk. She had an ancestor named Midshipman Young. He was the chief aide of Fletcher Christian of *Mutiny on the Bounty,* and had accompanied Christian to Pitcairn Island. Edward Young captured a sword from Captain Bligh and this sword remained in my mother's family. It was handed down and the sword landed in our house in Tasmania where as a small boy I played with it. The tip end came through the scabbard, and writing was engraved on the handle. My father ultimately gave this souvenir to the Naval and Military Club at Hobart where it still hangs on a wall. I could choke him for giving it away.

My mother could stretch a good story, and sometimes when she was in a benign mood she told me of her two ancestors, Robert and Frederick Young, who had a schooner, the *Dainty Belle,* which they sailed to the South Seas to trade. She told tales of "blackbirding," capturing natives and making them work on sugar plantations of Queensland. Apparently Uncle Robert was involved in this practice. My predominating thought was to be the captain of a ship, a sailing ship, not one of those newfangled steamships.

My primary interest became the sea. I listened to anyone who would talk of it, and I relished the occasional trips we took across the Bass Strait to Sydney. So that the two main streams of thinking in the family were very much of this earth: the primordial creatures of the nearly impenetrable Tasmanian wilderness, and the eternal oceans.

Around the water's edge, and only there, I was happy. I used to frolic in the water with such abandon that my father once remarked that human knowledge originally came out of the sea, as well the human himself, "But you look as if you are going from the land back to the sea."

The smell of salt was in our house in the figure of my huge grandparent, the sea captain, who was my mother's father. He was six foot four, and when he wasn't at sea, sailing the *William S. Bowden,* he had brief intervals with us, in which the spray of the South Seas was in our rooms heavily.

I listened to his tales and I eavesdropped when he had old mariners about and they chattered of their travels. Grandpa put a distrust in me of steamers. Smoke pots! he would snarl.

He fought with his short wife, Edith, but she had his measure. She ran the roost, like a little old Bantam hen, defending me against all.

I had a spotted dog of the fox terrier type and Grandfather was as fond of it as I. One day, as I played with the dog, he and my grandmother were having a loud-voiced row, Grandma, in her corner, weighing about ninety-four pounds and standing fully one half inch over five feet, was getting the best of Grandpa, weighing over two hundred pounds and standing a good six-four.

He had a sea chest which he hadn't looked at for many years. My grandmother wanted to empty it out, throw away the junk.

He protested. Snorting, Grandma came out of her corner, rummaging through the box, tossing odd items into a pile intended for burning.

"Look," he bellowed, "now, Ma, don't throw that out. That's a porthole I brought from the Aleutians."

"I am burning the whole damned lot of stuff," she answered. "You don't need it."

"Here, don't throw away that life belt. That saved my life once. I want it!"

"Never you mind! You're still alive, I'm burning it up!"

Grandpa took a deep breath and trumped out of the house, went out on a porch and started reading the Sydney shipping news of his paper. Inside, in the fireplace, the things were burning.

I got down on the floor with my dog. I growled, I teased him, grabbed him by the nose. He bit my nose. I started to bite him back. Then I picked him up, whirled him around the room, and he fell howling into the blaze.

I didn't intend to throw him into the fire. Now everything was there that Grandfather treasured, his souvenirs of the sea and our puppy. The howls of the dog brought him fast.

When he learned what happened—and griped also by his wife's intrusions upon his sea chest—he picked me up, literally with one hand. "Now I'll throw you in the fire!"

He shook me, as a puppy shakes a bone.

Grandma, all of her five-foot high, flew into the picture, started pummeling her huge husband. She shouted for him to let me go, and she made him drop me.

When the situation cooled off I told him I wanted to go to sea with him. "I would love to have you on board," he nodded grimly. "You'd make a fine cabin boy."

Grandma scotched it. She could see the look in his eye, if he ever got me onto his ship.

Yet I was moving closer to water all of the time.

So one day I stowed away on my grandfather's boat. He was well out to sea before I was discovered. He had a choice of carrying me off with him on some long call, turning me into a mariner, or of sailing about and bringing me back to port. He did the latter, taking up much of his time cursing me, and threatening to throw me overboard.

Back home this latest episode resulted in a family conference. What to do about me? Where was I headed for? What kind of evil was I up to? How could I be controlled?

For a while the matter simmered. I went on to school, chafing, raring to be gone around the globe.

My baby sister, Rosemary, had been born two or three years earlier. Now I was twelve or thirteen and I was left home with her from time to time while my parents went out.

I was a tall, skinny boy.

Also I couldn't keep my eyes off girls.

My first affair was with a girl from Burnie who worked for Mother. She was a plump, blond girl, not handsome—but available.

One night when Mother and Father were out, Carrie was seated in the living room reading. Rosemary was asleep.

I hovered around her chair.

I started to make a reconnaissance of her leg.

She kept on reading, as if I were doing nothing.

The reconnaissance went higher—this going on for some time, till suddenly she blurted out, "How much do I owe you?"

"One shilling and ninepence," I said. She would borrow six or ninepence here and there.

"Come on," she said, leading the way to the bedroom.

I followed, a little thunderstruck at my success. From then on I fumbled. I had, of course, absolutely no experience how to go about these matters.

But I caught the hang of it. Oh Carrie! I exclaimed.

Suddenly she bounced into the air. "You damn little fool—you want me to have a baby?"

That canceled the one shilling and ninepence debt.

There were no encores. She managed to keep out of my debt. I had a strange guilty feeling. Maybe she did too. I don't think the family learned of it, but Carrie didn't last very long after that.

It was a long while before I had another experience.

The disputed question—what to do with the incorrigible runaway, the poor student—was suddenly settled by a development in my father's professional life.

He was invited by either the London University or the London Zoo to bring the first specimens of the platypus to England. It was decided I should go with him.

I accompanied him on a steamer voyage of six or seven weeks. The boat had two principal ports of call, Durban and Cape Town, in South Africa. The platypuses, on the voyage from Australia to South Africa, were thriving. They had to have special worms grown for them as their sole item of diet, so great preparations were made to grow the worms on board ship. The platypuses were being waited on hand and foot by my father and an assistant. Royalty never had it better—except for the diet of worms.

Once again—in the interest of science, of course—I goofed. It seemed to me that these valuable species should have something more palatable than worms, and that they were entitled to an *hors d'oeuvre*. How could they possibly enjoy eating worms day in and day out?

So, in Durban, where the ship stayed for several days and where I made a walking tour, I chanced upon a pond loaded with fine-looking tadpoles. Just the thing for a bored platypus, it seemed to me. I put a bunch of them in a tin can, returned to the ship, and fed them to the rare specimens.

Just as I expected, they loved it. They gobbled them right up.

That night two of them were floating, feet up, in the tank.

Father was frantic.

I thought I had better tell him before he cut one of them open and found out the awful tadpole truth.

I confessed. He didn't say a word but the expression on his face was more than punishment.

Three lived and they arrived safely in England. They were exhibited and attracted great interest, scientifically. Father, who was about thirty-six or -seven by now, was acclaimed in scientific circles.

Mother arrived soon afterward, and she and Father located a school for me. It was a junior school called Southwest London College, and it might be the equivalent of a primary school here. It was midway between Putney and Hammersmith.

Father took me to this place himself, enrolled me, and there opened two of the most dismal years of my life.

It was all so horribly cheerless, nothing about but a few empty flowerpots along some window ledges.

There were special entrances for the headmaster and his small staff, and special entrances for the pupils. In front, a special muddy road led dismally to Putney Common. Beyond you saw similar drab private houses, gray and slimy-looking.

The interior was divided into three schoolrooms on the surface floor and three dormitories that were located upstairs. Boys of fourteen slept in one, boys of twelve in another, and the younger ones slept in the third. In each room the lads were crowded in like canned anchovies.

Mr. Burbridge, the headmaster, was a very fat old man, terrifying when he glared at you like a toad, and he had had only about five years of schooling himself.

There was another, Coombs, a young faculty member. I hadn't been there a week when this splay-footed individual wanted to bugger me. I never felt such panic as when I found myself in a corner. Coombs approached stealthily, with an evil and lecherous smile, and an intent of which I had no idea at the time. Yet I sensed something highly ominous.

I knew from the way he stalked me that something wasn't right. He used to put his hand on my knee, unnecessarily. My dreams at night and my waking thoughts were terrorized by the man's presence.

I studied his underslung chin, the sandy hair, his sloppy clothes, and his feet that went out sideways like Charlie Chaplin's. He had the appearance of an armadillo, but his words were soothing.

I had no idea what he wanted at that time, until tipped off later by other students.

Apparently, Mr. Burbridge knew nothing of this, and the boys must have been too petrified to tell him. Coombs kept after me for six months, but I was fleet-footed and learned to stay out of his way and put him off.

The captain of the cricket eleven, a fellow named Burke, a big lad, caught Coombs practicing sodomy with Burke's wicket keeper, a boy of twelve. Burke had enough guts to report the matter to Mr. Burbridge. Coombs left in a hurry.

The assistant headmaster was a wonderful old gentleman aged about sixty, with the picturesque name of Sir Worthbottom Smith, a down-at-heels English aristocrat, a man with a withered arm, who could play cricket better with his one able arm than most athletes could with two. He was reputed to have been a cricket champ with Surrey in his day. He had a long high collar that made him look rather like a penguin and fierce bushy eyebrows, and he always wore a dirty brocaded vest. A strict disciplinarian, still he was a wonderful man.

The standard of scholarship was ridiculous. Though I was backward in many academic respects, I knew that what went on here was inadequate. I already had traveled over half the world, I had been influenced by a scientist father, my horizon was far beyond the walls of this school.

From the outset I had to establish myself among thirty or forty fellow students. They began by mimicking my Irish-Australian accent. I discouraged that rapidly in one or two incidents. I was younger than most, but I was bigger, and rougher too, I hoped. I was regarded as a "colonial," a term uttered with contempt. I resented this very much and it might have given me for a time a complex and a feeling I had something to overcome. "Say, my good fellow, is it true that all Australians are cannibals?" I would be asked. Or, "My goodness, Flynn, is it true that in Australia the women eat their young?" It was a bullying spirit.

A French colored boy from Madagascar became my close friend. Dufresne, his name was, and later he became prominent in politics. He was tough, and together we had the student population pretty much in control.

The main thing, in the mind of all, was the food.

I wondered why I had to thank God for such rotten edibles. You had to mumble a lot of Latin, while your mouth watered and you wanted to eat—even this stinking gruel.

Benedictus benedicat
Pro Christum Dominum Jesum Nostrum,

which I think meant: For what benefits we are about to receive we thank our Good Lord Jesus. Then you went at this thick stuff that seemed to be all gluey bread. The boys whispered to one another, "Nothing has changed since Dickens."

On Sundays we formed into a long line—we called it a crocodile. Two by two by two, a stream of about forty lads, dressed alike with Eton collars and Eton jackets that came down to the waist and striped pants. Then we tramped about two miles to what was called a chapel. In the summer, making this trip, we wore straw hats, in the winter top hats. Each of us was responsible for keeping his clothes clean, down to our knees anyway—below we were caked with mud.

Our unhappy crocodile line would wind itself along this grim Putney Road to church. You wanted to be out in the open air, you could see the other kids playing, and yet you had to march solemnly, like English soldiers, along this ragged footpath, with old witherarm, Sir Worthbottom, up ahead stamping his cane solemnly and moving with what he thought was a proper bearing, none of us daring to break step.

Sunday had one compensation. On that day we got something to eat. It was plum duff which we called Spotted Dog. When we returned from chapel, after listening to the nonsense that was preached there, we had to take off our special Sunday clothes. It was always a race, because then you hurried down to the long board tables on the ground floor, where, if you arrived swiftly, you figured you might get a bigger slice of Spotted Dog. This was an elongated hot dog, like the American hot dog, only three feet long and in proportionate thickness. It was made of suet into a dough, and it was impregnated with parsley and raisins or dried plums. This was the big deal. The rest of the week the food didn't come up to the standard of Spotted Dog.

There were times when I thought father's platypus didn't do badly at all on board ship.

By the time this long wheat-laden baloney was put before us our mouths were well salivated with anticipation. The message from God hadn't reached us; Spotted Dog had. I watched greedily as the headmaster sliced up the long dogs, and if I had a big enough slice, I was ready afterward for a game of cricket out behind the school.

At night, from time to time, Dufresne and I managed to smuggle in some Dutch cheese. This went on for two years, knowing that better food was out there in the outside world, and we dreamed of getting at it some day.

The fact is, after I was dropped into this school I was pretty much neglected by my parents. Father was going great guns in the world of science, coming up with some new little monster out of the primordial past every now and then. Mother had struck up with none other than the Aga Khan in Europe.

Mother and my favorite aunt, Betty, two young beauties not much interested in Tasmanian devils, but with their sights on bigger game, were having a ball in Paris.

My father was back in Australia and Mother was having a small fling with the Aga Khan, who died recently. (The Aga Khan was the father of Ali Khan, who married Rita Hayworth, Rita becoming the wife of Dick Haymes, who married my ex-wife, Nora Eddington.)

I felt my loneliness in particular during vacation periods. When the time-off season arrived, the fellows became excited. One was going to Devonshire where his father had a launch. Two Spanish boys, twins, were returning to Madrid where they'd see a bullfight. Dufresne, whose family lived in the South of France, thought perhaps I might be able to go with him to his home, but nothing came of it and he too left.

Everybody left.

I was alone in school, with the Burbridges and the dubious features of the back yard of the college and the empty dormitories.

Where were my parents? I wished very much I was with them.

I was bewildered.

I tried to make the best of it. I knew the way between Hammersmith and Putney Common and I went into London from time to time. I had, as an allowance, about the equivalent of thirty-five cents, and I couldn't do much with that. I foot-slogged from the school into London and about the great city. Occasionally I took a bus; it only cost a cent. But there wasn't much of a jingle in my pockets.

It taught me a great respect for money—probably the only lesson I learned at this school.

Maybe not a bad one.

While Father was in Australia I don't suppose it crossed his mind that

I was left alone at school. Maybe he thought Mother came to see me or took me out from time to time.

I learned how to be alone. This was preparation for me, I suppose, for long stretches of being alone a little later in the jungles of New Guinea. These were formative years, and I learned to stand on my own two legs.

But it was from this that my first real resentment grew. Not even before, not the runnings away, not the three days in the closet, nor the spankings—but this being alone during the vacation seasons.

I stress now that I have no such feelings left. You write it all off to the past and to childhood. My father was busy, up to his neck in work, and what it amounted to only was that somehow all of this made me hard inside.

In my fifteenth year I was expelled from Southwest London College. I had no interest in study. I played hookey. I was belligerent, restive, lost, angry.

But because my father was Professor Flynn, I could get into another London school. This was Colet Court.

It couldn't last. I was kicked out.

For weeks I was in London, not registered in school. Once more a professional move by my father determined my own course.

We returned to Australia.

I couldn't know that I was coming closer and closer to a break with such sporadic family ties as I did have.

I was admitted to the Northshore Sydney Grammar School only because, again, I was Professor Flynn's son. Not that I could manage the tests and examinations and grades. In an arithmetic class I simply didn't know what was going on.

I was in revolt against all formal schooling. My travels from Tasmania to Australia to England, and back to Australia, had been upsetting to a scholastic career. Outside of reading and athletics I was good for nothing. I had no interest in the dryly presented information of textbooks. It seemed useless to try to catch up with the others.

In some ways I was far ahead of all the boys about me. They may have known the interior of these books but I already knew much of the world.

I was bigger than most. I was an athlete, quite good at tennis, swimming, boxing, and ready to fight, if picked on. I had won the Junior

Davis cup and they wanted to train me for the Davis cup. I had won diving championships. My accomplishments were strictly physical.

My father was supremely patient with me, though I gave him nothing but trouble.

School people couldn't understand the lapse in my learning. They said, "This is Professor Flynn's son. What's wrong?"

He could get me into a school, any school, but nobody could make me study.

I had an insatiable desire to run through the world, and not to be hemmed in by anybody. I hated institutions like schools, with walls and fences.

The world outside of school was more appealing.

I acquired a fiancée. Her name was Naomi Dibbs, and she came from a very correct, serious family, a family that had much to do with the development of Australian culture and politics. She represented the social group that I either aspired to or felt I belonged to. She had to be courted in a reserved way. She was pretty, slender, blond, blue-eyed, my physical type, and she was as naïve about sex as I.

I borrowed some money and bought a small diamond engagement ring and gave it to her. Her family was not entranced with that idea. But Naomi wore the ring, while my uncertain life at school became more uncertain.

About this time Father made an extraordinary discovery, locating a prehistoric fossilized whale deep in the cliffs of a lonely stretch of land in southern Tasmania. It was a find of great interest within the scientific community, and the sensation that accompanied it was stimulating to me. In school I was proud as could be. When the whale residue was brought to Sydney, all the lads went to see it, and naturally some of this scholarship brushed off on me. The find revealed the stage of evolution at which the whale had gone back to the sea as a mammal. It had fossilized bones in its fins that looked like hands and feet, and enormous jaws modeled like those of an alligator. It was many millions of years old.

I preened.

Father returned to England with his rare find, and the whale is now in the British Museum.

The prestige rapidly washed off of me.

I was left alone again in Sydney.

I set records for absolute school indifference.

I wasn't in this school long before I had talks with Mr. Robson, the tall, redheaded schoolmaster whose eyes looked so big behind his glasses. He warned me I was paying no attention to my studies, that I was headed for trouble. He knew my poor record elsewhere, and he cautioned me, for the sake of my father, to attend to school properly.

I only wondered how I could advance my affair with Elsie, the attractive maid, aged about thirty, who worked around the academy at night. There was a window at the rear of the dormitory, and I frequently leaped from it, a considerable drop of about fifteen feet, and met Elsie behind a hedge where there was seclusion.

There was nothing sexual between Elsie and me. Elsie must have thought I was very curious; maybe not. She used to do a bit of grubbing, but I didn't know how to open my fly with a lady present.

Even so, it was much more interesting than algebra. We might hang out around the school by the hedge, or take off for the beaches. We took a ferryboat ride several times. I was having a vicarious kind of nonfruitful affair.

It was fun skipping out, fooling the headmasters, taking off at night after a romantic leap to the ground. They knew I was getting out, but each morning I was back in school on time. The school heads didn't know what to do with me. Expel Professor Flynn's son? It wasn't pleasant to do.

I wasn't the school bully, but the bigger guys made it a matter of cautious principle to lay off me after one or two goings. This is by no means boastful, just a matter of fact. I could handle the biggest boys in school, boys who were two or three years older than myself—even those Australian boys, and that is saying something, because Australians are very tough. I fought dirty, without the English sense of fair play. If I got into a quarrel, I was out to win, not negotiate.

Yet I was always defensive. I don't remember ever picking a fight, but I remember resenting the big boys, the bullies. I always walked way around them. I didn't want any trouble with them because they were bigger and older. But I said to myself, If one of these fellows picks on me, he will know this has been it, because I will never quit. I may be new here but I will take no bull from anyone.

That's about how I have been all my life.

There were certain Australian verses which keynoted me. I got my scrapping tone from a quatrain that ran like this:

> I can strike a line through scrub or pine,
> Or play a hand of poker;
> Or ride a hack or hump a black
> With any other joker.

I got my knuckles hard just thinking of an Aussie folk line such as:

> For scrapping is my special gift,
> My chiefest, sole delight;
> Just ask a wild duck can it swim,
> A wildcat can it fight.

The cock of the walk at school was a very tough fellow named Lindsay. Very big and a year or two older than I. I was frankly afraid of him. He had several bad habits, such as dunking your toothbrush in that chamber pot you had under your bed. When we played at the school games he was usually a little better than me. The boys all feared him. He pushed them and they stayed pushed. He wasn't vicious, just a big boy who tossed his weight around.

Elsie had her eyes on a few boys in the school, Lindsay, myself, perhaps one or two others. She liked it that there was a bit of competition among us to try to make time with her.

Lindsay, jealous that I had a couple of sessions with Elsie behind the hedge, squealed to the school heads. He told them how I got out at night through a certain window. Lindsay was prefect of the dormitories, a strawboss job given to him because he could make the fellows do as he wished. He went to Mr. Wentworth, the housemaster, and suggested that a stop be put to my nightly exits.

They put a sheet of corrugated iron on the ground at the point where I usually landed. One night when I made the leap, it sounded like bells clanging when I hit. Mr. Wentworth was at a nearby window. He shot the window up and told me to report to the headmaster the following day.

I caught hell.

Lindsay was after Elsie. So was I. He had put the screws onto my nightly escapades. I wanted no trouble with him but I could feel it coming. It got around the school that there was bad feeling between the two biggest boys in Sydney Northshore Grammar. I said to myself, If I get into a fight with you, boy, you'll know you've been in one. I'll give you the dirtiest going over I can think of.

By now I felt that Lindsay had about pushed me into a corner, and I had to fight him.

Sure enough, we met not far from the school, by the Paramatta River. He taunted me. He circled around, tongue lashing, goading me to take him on.

We started with routine slugging. Soon we had wrestling grips on each other. The fight became tumble tumble, and now I headed him for the water.

That was my best chance. He was too strong.

I knew the water. I had to get him under water.

He was much bigger, much heavier than me, and he fought smilingly, with a certainty of his own unconquerable nature.

This was disturbing to me. I had to fight now with my anger, work my anger up good, so that I would get dirtier and dirtier and stop at nothing.

We were in the water and he thought he had the best of me because he was on top of me. I moved like a shark beneath him, deliberately turning on my back.

I got him by the throat and down he came, below water.

I knew nothing about wrestling, but in the water I moved instinctively. I stuck my legs underneath his arms. He had big ears and I grabbed onto his ears. I let the breath out of my body.

If I could hold my breath long enough and keep him under water while I held . . . sure enough, the hold I had on him prevented him from reaching my balls. In a dirty fight between men that is the way to clinch it.

With the breath out of my body, I tried to sink, so as to fight under water.

This went on and on, he trying to get loose, and I hanging on like a leech, using my water talents in a fight with a land fighter.

By now we were far out in deep water, not many people around. We were simply and clearly trying to kill one another by any means it could be done.

Each time I came up for air I inhaled deeply. Lindsay didn't know how to breathe in water. He was getting filled up with it.

Suddenly, I was on top of him. I had him by the throat. I held his head under water.

When I felt I had him, a boat came by. The people in it screamed at us to stop the murderous fight.

It must have looked strange to them, with both of us under water most of the time, just my head bobbing up for a quick breath of air.

By the time we got to the bank of the river I had my breath back. Lindsay lay on the edge like a gasping blowfish. The people who brought us in cried out that he was dead.

I was completely exhausted, terrified. My God, have I killed him?

The people were excited, calling for someone who knew something about lifesaving. I knew little of it, but I put my knees right in the middle of Lindsay's back and gave him some makeshift artificial respiration to the best of my ability. Water spouted out of his mouth as from a freshly opened fire hydrant.

Every time I pushed my knee into his back the water gushed from him.

Pretty soon one of the masters from the school arrived and turned him over. Lindsay was breathing again.

I was so totally exhausted I couldn't stand.

After that Lindsay was no threat.

The way I fought Lindsay is about how I have had to battle most of the days of my life. I swore then, and even before Lindsay, I might get beaten up in life, but the joker will know he's been in a fight.

Neither of us was reprimanded for that fight. In Australia they let you fight it out.

A week or two later the headmaster called me into his office. I stared at the cold official face of Mr. Robson. I knew here it goes again. It was like being in the dock just before the sentence.

"Your father is in England?"

"Yessir."

"He is a very distinguished man."

"Yessir. I know, sir."

"You show little prospect of emulating him."

I was silent.

"Your mother—she is also in England?"

"No, she is in France, sir."

"Too bad. Nothing but trouble. I don't know what you need, young man, but, whatever it is, this school has not got it. You are expelled, Flynn, for being a disturbing influence on the rest of the scholars."

I walked out, over me a cold fright.

I headed into the business district of Sydney knowing what I must do. I couldn't tell Father about this. I had now to prove my worth to him. Get work, I said to myself, any kind of work.

I was alone in Australia, not yet seventeen—but from this instant, totally on my own.

Sir Edward Gibbon, the owner of a wool-dealing firm, was a friend of my father's. I told him I was through with school. "Sure thing, lad, I'm happy that Professor Flynn sent you to me."

Of course the professor hadn't, but soon I was behind a counter. My job was to lick stamps and put them on letters.

Another lad named Thomson, five years older than I, worked at the same counter and did the same labor. Near us was a little box labeled *Petty Cash*. We took turns watching it. It wasn't too petty for me. And it wasn't too petty for Thomson.

We discovered that we both shared a passion for the horses at Randwick Race Course, which I used to head for whenever I got a Saturday off from school. My mother, when she was in Sydney, was also fond of that place. There she bet, flirted, and brought home the news of the winners.

Thomson and I tinkled the petty cashbox, and we were off to the races. Our idea was the old simple one. We'd win and put the money back—naturally.

The company fired both of us. I got off easy; it should have been a stretch for us, but because of Dad, Sir Edward's heart of lead melted.

There's no moral to this—except, of course, don't get caught.

Jobs were scarce. Father far, far away and I didn't dare write him. Mother was rarely in my thoughts.

Where to go? Which way to turn?

Thomson and I, commiserating, hanging out together, managed to find work folding political pamphlets and distributing them for the Labour Party. The pamphlets were couched in terms of mild invective against the Government. I suppose it was an early form of Communist activity because we worked in an underground cellar.

We got a feeling we were on the right side, part of a cause.

After a week the job was ended.

Thomson was a tough Australian handicapper, ready to do anything for little reason whatever, with never a shilling in his pocket. He had sandy-brown hair and it stood up like pig bristles on his head, the first fellow I ever knew to have a crewcut, long before its popularity in the States.

For a week we hung about together, both at odds' end, where to go, what to do. Everything I had done so far had ended in swift failure. All was gloomy. How did you survive in this world?

"Look, Flynn," said Thomson, "I know some guys who have got it made."

"Who?"

"You want to meet 'em?"

"Sure."

He took me around to meet the members of the Razor Gang, a crowd that got into the Sydney papers from time to time. They were elusive and the police couldn't locate them. They did their work and they were quick. A slash across the face, grab the loot, and beat it.

There was a strip in Sydney at that time. I don't know if it still exists. It went between King's Cross and Darlinghurst, a rugged district that was called the Dirty Half-Mile. From each side of the Dirty Half-Mile dark alleys sprouted. These young hoodlums, sometimes called the "Woolamallo Gang," hung out in this region. If they caught somebody going through this areaway, they had absolutely no mercy. Come across, digger, or take this. . . .

"This" was their mugging instrument: a cork, halfway through which was embedded a razor blade. The cork held the blade staunchly and you didn't get your hand cut. If the prospective victim was stupid enough not to give up his money, slash, slash, in the form of an x-mark, went the razor, across the face, obliquely down one way, obliquely down the other. The idea was to make a cross on the face, laying it open. A man either came across or was left with plenty of air to breathe.

Thomson ran afoul of the Razor Gang in the very week he and I hung out with these fellows. It was sure as hell death with these boys if you mickied—Australian for squealed. There was some such suspicion of Thomson having done something irregular. After that his head wasn't worth the neck it stood on.

At the end of this week of banditry, Thomson was picked up in a gutter, with all of his throat showing and both cheeks cut wide open. He lost too much blood and never came out of it.

That was enough for me—these boys played too rough. Besides, I was never paid my share of the loot, probably because I was unethical enough not to wield a razor.

I took refuge in Sydney Domain, a big park overlooking Sydney Harbor.

I had no place to go, no money, nothing, and now I got my first introduction to really roughing it in a big city.

The park was closed at night, as I have found public parks to be all over the world. But there were always hobos, tramps, or as they call them in Australia, "swagmen" or "sundowners," around.

I found a cave that was inhabited by three or four of these bums. We would crouch for warmth by a meager fire.

They taught me how, on a cold night, to wrap a newspaper inside your pants to keep warm. The Sydney *Sun* and the Sydney *Herald* stood us in mighty good use for three or four days, lousy reading but warm. They kept out the wind and sometimes before stuffing them inside my clothes, I occasionally read them. I read of the big gold strike in New Guinea.

Gold! Just what I needed.

New Guinea's for you, Sport, I told myself, New Guinea. That vast unknown land to the north.

My latest expulsion from school didn't set right with Naomi, nor with her family. She didn't like my manner of life. Nor did I.

Where was I all the time? What kind of company did I keep? What was going to happen to me?

We fought in a room of her house, tempers rising.

In the high tradition she took off her engagement ring and flung it at me.

Good! Just what I needed!

It missed and went underneath the piano.

Till then I never knew I had lizard blood in me. There was about four inches of crawling space beneath that fixture, but I was lean and angry. I stretched under and grabbed the ring.

I made a dramatic exit, with the right farewells and the right resolves. I'd go out and make my fortune and she'd see, by God, she'd see!

At once I set out to sell back the ring. I needed the money now for one simple thing: escape.

I sold it for about half the money necessary for the fare to New Guinea. The fare was eighteen pounds.

I needed a few more pounds and I went to my uncle, Oscar, and told him I had to get out—fast.

He may have been delighted to hear that I wanted to go to New Guinea, for he gave me the necessary few pounds to take leave.

It was early 1926. I was just seventeen.

From then on I began the wanderings that have never ceased.

PART TWO

The Crocodile and the Sword

1927-1932

N*EW* Guinea is a big body of land. It is the second largest island in the world. Around this mainland there are hundreds of small islands. One of these, the place I was headed for, was called New Britain, but it was part of the general area known as the New Guinea Territory. After World War I, the League of Nations ceded control of New Guinea to Britain. Until 1914, much of the region was under German domination, and Germans owned the plantations and ran the economy of the land. Now Australians were taking over, as part of the loot of the war. And I was on my way.

My boat would land at Rabaul, four hundred miles from the New Guinea mainland. The problem was how to get to the mainland where the gold rush was on. How do you do this with about two quid in your pocket making a not very loud jingle? All I had with which to face this new world was what I stood up in.

On board ship I became friendly with another man named Johnson, who was headed for New Guinea to become a postmaster in the government service. I also got acquainted with a woman whose husband was a District Officer. She gave me a letter of introduction that would be of use when I got to Rabaul.

I had to sleep under a native house on my first night in New Guinea. It was nice and warm there, but the mosquitoes seemed a different and more interested breed than I met anywhere else. As I slept or tried to sleep I worried about my new nice white clothes, which I had preserved carefully because I hoped to get an interview with the Government Secretary and perhaps land a job as a cadet.

These cadets were young men appointed from Sydney by the Government. There were six in New Guinea, of various qualifications. They were embryo District Officers. Whoever had that job was the big wheel of a whole district. It took years to become such a magistrate, and in the meantime they trained the young fellows to go out into the jungle and look to the natives' benefits. I hoped I could talk my way into one of these spots.

I got the interview with the Government Secretary. He was a big joker, heavy set and self-important. I introduced myself, mentioned the name of Johnson, the man I'd met on board ship, and topped it off with dropping the name of my father's eminent colleague, Professor Channery.

"What do you know about sanitation?" he asked.

Sanitation? Why, of course, everything! I babbled and blustered what I had read in my father's books about hygiene, the diseases of the natives, of bacteria, water—jabbered on like a con man. Absurd to ask me a question like that—

I was hired on a probation basis, pending confirmation from Australia, the salary four pounds a week.

My job was to go about in a government car, accompanied by two armed native policemen: we were to travel to the villages and look to the sanitation.

That I did—I dressed in a white suit, wore a white helmet, carried a walking stick, looked very clean, tall and official. I boned up on a pamphlet that told me what to look for among the natives and how to help them. One item showed how to make soap out of coconuts. The Government wouldn't issue soap, but I was to teach the natives how to make it and how it cleaned them and their clothes and destroyed germs. The age-old way to wash clothes was to beat them with a rock against another rock in the river. I got them to make this soap: it was primitively done, yet the process was not much different from the method employed by the soap manufacturers today. And I went after them about other things. Why were the pigs allowed to live under the huts? What was the dead dog doing lying there instead of being buried? Why didn't they dig a deep hole for the latrines? Didn't they know all this led to disease? Of course they didn't, and my job was to teach them.

I lived in a primitive bungalow with three other cadets who were already confirmed in their appointments. They were all very British in manner, and the little hut was rather like a junior league British Army subalterns' quarters in some out-coastal empire spot. Our orderlies stood at attention when we came by and presented arms when we came and went.

Naturally the work soon became a bore. The highlight of my inspection route was a lovely little native swimming hole. I swiftly figured to hell with sanitation, for a while it could wait. I would run over to this place, skillfully camouflage my car in the bush, and dive into that lovely green-bordered water hole for two or three hours a day.

A half Melanesian-Polynesian girl swam there. Her name was Maura and she was divine. She was married to one of the high government officials. Maura was one of the most beautiful women I ever saw: honey-skinned, with freckles, long wavy hair, and a waist you could span with your two hands. Naturally my ambition was to spend as much time spanning it as I could.

She was gay, carefree and, it appeared as the days went by, unhappily married. One day I set out on patrol, but parked the car carefully out of sight and hurried as fast as I could, carrying my swim trunks. There she was, in the water—and I immediately got undressed.

I dove—and came up on the other side staring right into the face of the Government Secretary himself, the man who hired me.

"Flynn," he said, "is this how you conduct your sanitary duties?"

There was nothing to say.

"Report to my office tomorrow at nine o'clock."

With that he turned and went off. I knew I'd had it.

I murmured to Maura that I was only on probation. "That's the end of me for sure." She looked stricken. She felt somehow, she said, that it was her fault. She was sorry.

She said, "Perhaps I can do something. I will tell you what: my husband goes to a meeting tonight. You come to my bungalow and we will figure out something, but you will have to come very quietly. We don't want anyone to see you, do we?"

Sure as hell we didn't, I agreed.

"When you come up the veranda," she said, "take your shoes off, and I will be waiting for you."

"How will I know it is you?"

"Don't worry."

She was splendid there in the sunset. She wore a strange kind of swimsuit which I had never before seen, a filminess to it that showed the outline of her body, highly colored, and it clung to her as if she had been draped into it with a spray gun. Her eyes were big and wide, dark and worried.

I felt grateful to her but terribly depressed. Tomorrow I was finished.

Gloomily I returned to my quarters with my two native policemen. Still they presented arms, in the usual fashion, and I figured that was the last time I would have the funny little feeling of importance I got when arms were presented.

That night I followed instructions. . . .

I barefooted into the bungalow, practically crept inside.

There was absolutely no talk of my situation as a failing cadet. She was in a mood of sympathy, pity, kindness, tenderness. The scent of her! the scent of native tropical flowers. The satin skin, a sort of honey-colored complexion, with little freckles, her soft hair and the softness of her lips. The passion.

One of my most wonderful nights.

The second blow fell. We had lapsed into complete forgetfulness of time—when her husband came in!

After the first shouts died down, he slugged me.

I never had a chance, even though I was in the best fighting form and in the best physical condition. He was big, stocky, enraged. I was swiftly on the defensive.

She tried to get between us and his first roundhouse punch caught her right on the face. She went flat.

I started for him and caught the second roundhouse. I went flat in the opposite direction.

He put the boot into me and kicked in three ribs.

He kept putting the boot on, and as I came to, I could still feel him trying to gouge out my eyes with his heel.

I bit him in the leg, took a great chunk out of the back of his calf, and he let out a scream.

I got up, took a vase, threw it, missed.

He came charging again.

I got out of the way somehow and tripped him.

Down he went. As he started to rise I figured that, since I could hardly stand up by this time, now was the moment to make a dignified exit. I caught him with my knee at just the right instant as he was getting up—right in the teeth—a tremendous whack. Then caught him a second time in the same spot, a smashing whack on the jaw with my knee, and it was all over.

You must remember that Australians fight for keeps and I had learned the hard way. Marquis of Queensbury Rules were not for me, especially if you were caught, on the defensive, and guilty as hell of being the most unwanted type of intruder in the lexicon of men's morals. Having received "the old boot," as we called it in Australia, he lay there prone, hurt, but conscious, and trying to rise.

My face must have looked like it had been caught in a paddle wheel of a steamboat. I felt like that, as if all of me had been caught in that wheel. I ached all over.

I went over to Maura as quickly as I could and lifted her up—but she was out.

I stood there glaring at this guy, and he glaring at me, both of us completely breathless, winded.

He managed to get to his feet, as a drunken man would, but rage stood him erect. I stared at the drooping and smashed jaw. He said, "Get out of here unless you want me to kill you."

"I don't know what you are going to kill me with, but be damned sure you don't miss."

He muttered, "What's going to happen to her?"

I should have left then, but instead I said something I shouldn't have said. "I will take care of her."

"No you won't."

"All right, we'll both take care of her," I said. "What end are you going to take? Top or bottom?"

He said he would take the bottom.

I lifted her head up very carefully, he lifted her feet, and together we carried her in to bed.

"Get some water," he said.

"How the hell can I when I don't know where I am?"

"That's a likely story! What the hell are you doing here if you don't know where you are?"

"I mean I don't know where the kitchen is," I said. "Do something for her. She looks hurt."

"What about me?" he asked.

"What about me? We are all hurt."

Then I said, "Let's go together."

We went to the kitchen, got some hot water and put compresses on Maura.

But still I dared not turn my back on him. I felt the rage still burning in him. He might let fly again any instant.

I put my clothes on, keeping an eye on him. Then I backed out.

Next morning I confronted the Government Secretary as ordered. I felt impossibly low, as if everything was cracked from under me. I figured simply to be fired. But the fellow was wearing an altogether different expression from what I'd expected to see.

Strangely, his face had a rather pleased look.

He opened with a slight smile. "You know, Flynn, I often feel like a swim myself, but I do my swimming on my own time. When I entered the government service I certainly didn't swim on government time. That is why I am where I am today."

I nodded, acknowledging his great success.

"Of course, this is unforgivable, especially as you are on probation. After all, your appointment has never been confirmed. There is no alternative for it, you have to go."

I nodded again.

"But if that were not enough," he went on, "you have to fall afoul of an officer of the government. Have you any explanation for that?"

"No sir. Just what you can see on my face."

"Looks like he gave you a good going-over."

Then he shouted, "If one thing is not enough"—yet there was a glint of amusement in his face—"you have to do this to one of our top government officials, breaking down his door, go bursting in there, and desecrating his home!"

He went on to say that the man had a broken jaw, and that Maura was in the hospital with a nervous breakdown.

"What kind of man are you in the government service, Flynn?"

A bewildered but pleasant feeling came over me, because I could sense something else coming besides dismissal. "You should be summarily dismissed, but instead of that, Flynn, until your appointment is ratified, which should be any day now, I will overlook this—of course, on a promise of proper behavior in the future."

Listening to him, it sounded like a reprieve. Obviously he had a hate on for Maura's husband, and he was delighted to hear of what had happened at the bungalow. All I had to do was stay on, get a confirmation from Canberra, the Australian capital, and I might some day be a government administrator, even a full District Officer— spending a quarter-century of my life in the middle of the fields and the jungles with nobody to talk to. Yet these fellows were heroes, the true rulers of New Guinea, and at the moment, a stay of dismissal appeared a great thing.

"However," he said, "I'm changing your assignment for you. We are taking you off sanitary duty. There will be no more swimming for you for a good while—"

He explained that there had been a massacre at Madang. I was going there, under District Officer Taylor, and serve as one of his subordinates. Four prospectors had been killed and the culprits who murdered them must be brought in.

This was not exactly a sentence to Siberia.

Here he gave me a funny look, as though to say, You didn't expect this, did you, young fellow?

I thanked him and said I would try to do better in the future. Still I couldn't figure it out, beyond the surmise that Maura's husband must have been on the Drop Dead list of the Government Secretary!

He gave me one final direction. I must report on the government schooner leaving from Rabaul, and go to the headquarters of District Officer Taylor.

"One thing more," he said. " I must warn you not to say good-by to the young lady before you leave. Her husband will certainly shoot you, I have been told, even if he has to get up out of his hospital bed to do it."

That was my first experience with an irate husband.

When I entered District Officer Taylor's tent, he was at a table with his three other cadets. Maps were stretched on the table, and Taylor was outlining a campaign. He was a long, tall, thin figure, the Senior District Officer and magistrate of a vast territory. A hollow-cheeked chap, with sunken, gimlet-small blue eyes, and thinnish sandy hair. He had large ears that stuck out like a bat's wings, and he had full jaws that reminded me of a barracuda's. Yet he was the best kind of colonial administrator; he knew the jungle better than any of us—I didn't know it at all—and, as I found out, he could outwalk the best of us younger men.

He explained that he was charged by the Australian Government with bringing in, if they could be found, the murderers of the four Australian prospectors who had been killed somewhere in the interior. We were to round them up, whether or not they had been provoked to murder in self-defense. Right or wrong, this was to be a punitive expedition. The New Guineans were to be shown that they couldn't go around killing white men—a government decision. They were going to be taught a serious lesson.

Taylor pointed his finger at a certain spot on a big map. That was where the massacre had taken place. We had to get there, meet him at a certain time, and fan out from there in search of the guilty New Guineans.

I looked at the map. There, in the middle of nowhere, in the depths of the most horrible jungle thickness in the world, exceeding the African jungle at its worst, was our destination: rivers to cross, mountains to scale, cannibals en route. How the hell did you do it?

"Sir," I asked, "how do we cross those rivers?" I pointed to three rivers that stood between the coast and the point of massacre.

He glared at me. The other cadets stared at me, as if thinking, Who the hell is this guy to ask such a stupid question?

Taylor answered at last, clearly as a bell, "You cross them, Cadet Flynn."

I was about to venture another question, but because of the way they all stared at me, I simply said, "Yes sir. I will be there, sir—" and kept quiet.

It dawned on me that I had no business asking about means of transportation, supplies, routes, methods: just get there, and keep your mouth shut until you did.

The District Officer seemed now to be talking directly to me. "You will be assigned ten native policemen. With these armed men you will complete your assignments." Just like that.

We cadets yes-sirred the chief and left. Outside his tent I met the ten native police who would go with me.

At once we marched to the port where we must take a schooner for a ten-day voyage to Madang. From there go into the New Guinea interior.

The ship was the lousiest, most cockroach-ridden, flea-ridden, copra-bug-ridden schooner, perhaps eighty feet long, with a beam of about thirty feet and a draught of eight or nine feet. She was old, decrepit, the sails all mildewed, the spars too weak for any sudden gale—and astonishingly, on this boat, the Government sent a white woman with two children.

This woman, a Mrs. Anderson, wife of a government official on the mainland of New Guinea, turned out to be a lady of depth and strength, for the hardships of this trip were never intended for females. White women just never traveled on these little inter-island schooners. The crew was only eight or nine Kanaka men. There was a grubby fat captain, my native police and myself—and this woman and her children.

The only toilet on the ship was a rig on the after-end of the stern, a sort of overhang that was covered on three sides, and you sat on this primitive contraption looking down at the water as you did your numbers. As you did, you wondered whether you'd fall in the drink or the rig would give way. This woman took her children there, put them over the side, and they did their business. She herself, from time to time, retired there also while the crew, the police and myself stared in another direction.

She was seasick, so were her children, so was I, so even was the crew; for the sea was heavy and the rickety little schooner behaved like a sliver of wood angling and re-angling through the waters.

Even so I tried to maintain the discipline of my police. I made them show arms each morning at a certain hour to see whether the guns worked, and demanded that they keep their bayonets clean and not let the salt rust the blades.

I think these men felt a little sorry for me. They must have realized I didn't clearly know where I was headed or what I was doing: but I got to know each one personally and won their loyalty. There was nothing like these Melanesians for loyalty, if they liked you. They hadn't been treated well by the Germans, and so, when someone came along who recognized them as individuals, there was this deep response from them.

Once a huge waterspout, high as the Eiffel Tower, came toward us at hurricane speed. The crew and my police made strong mystic passes at it with their knives and bayonets, and chanted and hollered at the tower. This vast fountain kept spinning toward us, and if it enveloped our boat we were done; but when it was close, someone fired a shot at it and all of a sudden it collapsed under the ocean and a great wave came around, and that was the finish of it.

We were a shaken crowd of passengers, but on the tenth day we made port at Madang. We parted company with Mrs. Anderson and her children. I marshaled my men along the beach, checked their rifles once more, and we marched to a crude government station nearby.

I was assigned to a small native bungalow, set up on stilts. My men were given native barracks, and I waited for further orders—which I was supposed to get—before starting on the punitive expedition.

The orders soon came, but from there on in I moved by guesswork, instinct and luck. None of the police knew where I was going. They couldn't read a map, neither could I very well, and I had only a compass, stars and a general notion to work with. My only consolation was my friendly staff of police. They dressed with little caps; they wore small red and black *ramis,* with peaked edges, almost like the modern bikinis. Each wore a belt, and each carried a rifle. They had great mops of fuzzy hair.

With this colorful crew I set out on a trail leading inland. Soon the trail ended and we struck unbroken vegetation. While a bushwhacker up front with a machete smashed through the palm fronds, the weed and the snake grass, we single-filed ahead.

We soon had our first river to cross.

We could see crocodile heads in the water, as the boys rigged up a barge of bamboo. As they perched on this raft, crossing the water, they held their rifles above their heads so as to keep the ammunition dry. We got over. I felt a bit better: somehow the jungle difficulties could be surmounted.

Leeches, horrible slimy things, caught onto you. They would swell up with your blood. For days I didn't know how to handle them. You wouldn't know they were there, you couldn't see them, they'd settle on you gently, and then you saw a blob and you knew you'd been leeched; until you found out how to put a lighted cigarette up their arses to persuade them to drop off.

Day after day we went on, each instant risking getting our heads knocked on rocks, or barely missing falling into some ravine. Small jungle life scampered about making their offensive and defensive sounds.

At night I didn't know enough to set a guard, but fortunately my police did. It was treacherous territory, lived in by Stone Age people, and the whole area was up in arms. It was known now that the Government was doing something about the massacre, that white officers and native police were hunting men.

One night I was tortured with a dream. It was a dream within a dream. I dreamed that I was asleep on two or three sticks of lateral bamboo in a makeshift hut. Actually at the time I was dreaming I was asleep in just such a hut. In my dream a pair of steel claws and a giant jaw had me by the back of the neck. A huge insect which catches birds instead of flies: an insect with a body as big as your fist and legs extending like a giant crab's. In my fitfulness I reached up to my neck and I grabbed onto something that *was* there. I squeezed it and woke up yelling. I had in my hand a crushed rat: he had been nibbling at me, and I grabbed him so hard in my dream his entrails came out between my fingers.

By God knows what chance, crossing streams, going up and down mountains, and with the aid of the compass, the stars and absolute blind luck, we reached the scene of the massacre.

The bodies were still there. By now they looked like feather mattresses that had inflated in the sun and rain, all popping up into the open air and stinking like hell. These prospectors had been innocent of any wrongdoing among the natives, as nearly as we could figure. Men who had been there before them, pillaging from the natives, doubtless taking their women, had made it bad for all whites coming in thereafter. So this peaceful bunch of prospectors bore the brunt of the local rage.

They were Australian-Irish. One was pinned to the ground with six spears. Another apparently made a fight for it, and his body lay some distance from the others; he was full of spears, face down, putrified, his back a pincushion of blades. Littered about the ground there were the men's personal effects—diaries, ink, papers—items that the Kanakas could find no use for.

Within a couple of days the four groups, headed up by the cadets and the District Officer, had arrived, and we set out through the neighboring district to round up the ringleaders, each party heading for a different settlement.

I was assigned to reach a village about two weeks' marching distance away, and my boys and I took off. I wasn't frightened at this: maybe I was too unknowing or involved to feel fear. Maybe it was the confidence I placed in my men, perhaps it was the belief I had got this far and the rest would be all right too.

But when we arrived at the village, nobody was around. Word had been passed all through this neck of New Guinea that government patrols were out looking for certain people, and the natives everywhere disappeared into the high jungles.

We returned to the site of the massacre—another two weeks' passage through the country. My boys' feet were about worn out; they were lacerated, mangled. But I wore boots and tennis shoes and didn't do so badly.

The other parties had rounded up about a dozen suspected ringleaders. They were stockaded until my patrol and I returned. Then all of us, District Officer Taylor, the cadets, the police and the unfortunate captives, marched back through the bush to the coast, to Madang.

Taylor decided to stage a combination feast and public hanging to which all New Guineans in the region were summoned. In the coming days schooners arrived from Rabaul laden with *taurau* (rice)—tons of it—and calico to be dispensed at the hanging. A carrot and club approach: show them we can be tough, show them we can be useful.

A gallows of coconut branches was built, a long platform big enough to hold a dozen men. The natives stood about and watched how the freshly hewn timber was put together in a new kind of construction they had never seen before.

About two thousand came down from the hills and from the little communities scattered about, and they gathered at the gallows scene.

Taylor told me and the other cadets that he hated what he had to do: but he had his orders from Australia and he had no alternative. These people had to learn not to kill white men. But having undertaken it, Taylor did the job thoroughly. When the natives arrived and swarmed around the gallows and the makeshift tables that had been set up for them, they were greeted with the sight of roasting pigs, rice was served, there was plenty of beer, and coconut toddy was available in abundance.

Coming freshly from Sydney, where I lived in a relatively modern environment, a twentieth-century city, it was startling to see this massed display, to realize its remoteness from the urban Australian center. Here were these Stone Age people, perhaps they were even from an age the other side of that, standing about in their special bush dress, mainly their skins, and in their elemental simplicity they wondered at the meaning of it all. They never themselves gathered for big conclaves like this, but the whites had done this. They were curious, festive and animated. They flew at the food and the drink and even were in no hurry for the main event to get started.

Then, under my eyes, the whole thing changed into a genuine political fiasco.

I had to stand at attention with my police behind me, the Union Jack flying high, while the poor condemned captives were lined up on the gallows.

If these fellows had killed the prospectors they were only defending themselves, or revenging themselves, and they may not even have been the original raiders, but they stood on the gallows now with seeming unconcern. You couldn't tell their thoughts or feelings as they waited for the signal for the ropes to be dropped.

As each poor bastard fell and his neck cracked, a great shout of delight went up from the natives. They took it as a show. They didn't understand it at all as an attempt to intimidate and control them. The more a man dangled and danced, if his neck hadn't broke cleanly, the more the people enjoyed it.

One after another the prisoners died, each in his own way: one let his urine go, another lost his bowels, as shout after shout of applause went up—like a successful bullfight.

The impression made on me was altogether different. I was ready to vomit, but I stood at attention trying to hold in my guts, watching the most macabre thing I ever witnessed.

Somehow the terrible day came to an end.

I didn't know it, but while I was in the jungle, I was dropped from the government service. I learned that when I got back to Rabaul.

I had been two months on this jungle mission to teach the Stone Age people control and obedience, adjustment and servitude to a modern civilization.

While I was gone I thought from time to time of Maura and wondered whether I would see her again.

I found the answer to that at Rabaul.

While I was away one of the earliest airplanes to reach New Guinea arrived, a German Junker plane. Maura took the first flight in it. The plane took off, went about fifty yards or more into the air, tried to make a turn, and smacked into a cliff.

That was the end of Maura—a vision before my eyes, an image in my heart, far too beautiful, far too young.

There was a wonderful saloon in Rabaul operated by a Chinaman named Ahsims—who was simply called Sims. It was a big square wooden structure topped by a red roof that you could see for miles. You entered a whitewashed hall and walked to the end of it where you reached the nerve center—the bar. About the long board was everything that the world could yield up: miners, recruiters, con men, thieves, beachcombers, prospectors, planters. There were cubicles at the sides of the room, cubicles upstairs, and two or three phonographs blared music from various points. At the tables men played cards, laughed and fought drunkenly.

As I headed for this joint, I wondered how I could get to the gold fields—still my principal aim. But that took a stake, and I didn't have much. Ahsims, glad to see me, promptly introduced me to a redheaded fellow with bushy eyebrows named Al Tavisher. He and Tavisher had a joint interest in a plantation on a not-too-distant island called New Ireland, part of the New Guinea Territory. Tavisher was one of those Australians to profit by the expropriation of the German properties. With a small amount of money, some credit, and a large debt owing to the government, he was ready to produce copra. Ahsims told his partner I was looking for a job.

Actually I was trained for absolutely nothing—nothing whatsoever. I hadn't even learned how to hold a glass of beer in my hand, had read many books which hadn't prepared me for anything practical, but I had the gift of gab, or blarney, and could either talk my way in or out of a situation, or if necssary, fight my way in or out.

"What do you know about copra?" he asked, as we leaned on the bar.

"M-mh, what do *I* know about copra? Only everything. I've been raised on copra. Spent all my life around copra."

I jabbered like a hen at early-morning rising, how there was nothing about running a plantation that I didn't know. I could handle men, keep books. As for my job with the Government, hell, I had left that, resigned. I wouldn't put up with the way the Government brutalized the natives back there. I hoped he didn't know I'd been fired. That line struck a chord with him and he began telling me about the plantation he and Ahsims owned in Kavieng, New Ireland. Would I like to go there and run it? Would forty pounds a month be all right?

Would it? I grabbed his hand, shook it, told him he had the best plantation operator he could find in all New Guinea. I would do him a favor and take the post, even though it was a long ways distant from this fine saloon. I immediately beat it to the library to see what I could find out about running a coconut plantation. I learned absolutely nothing, only how to crack open a coconut. What I really wondered about was, how do you handle a hundred and twenty indentured laborers?— the work force employed by my fellow Australian.

Desperate for any bit of information on what I could expect in the face of so new and large a situation, I sought out a friend named Basil Hoare, a young Englishman with a first-rate record in World War I as a naval commander. He had come from England and he ran a schooner. To him I stated the problem. What the hell do you do, Basil, with a force of ex-cannibals? Where do you begin?

He was used to working with native labor. "Easy, old boy, nothing to it." Very British manner. "You just get hold of the Boss Boy."

"What's that?"

"On every plantation there is a Boss Boy. You call for him and just say to him, 'Boss Boy, carry on!' "

Basil explained that the Boss Boy knew more about copra than he or I would ever know. "Really, it's easy, old fellow. Just give the Boss Boy the impression you know more than he does—and the plantation will run like a clock."

I took ship for New Ireland and arrived in Kavieng, a town in which the coconut palm is used in scores of ways—palm-covered houses, hats and caps modeled of braided coconut leaf, furniture of the palm stalk—everything touched by copra. The population was picturesque. Most were Melanesian, there were many Chinese, and only a few were white.

From there I made a one-day journey to the plantation called Matinalawa. The whole region was like most coconut islands, low flatland lying close to the sea, the sunlight intense. I occupied a little bungalow near the water, and was delighted to find there a shelf-ful of mildewed books. The Germans who had lived here had left some books in German, French and English. Included were a couple of French and German dictionaries. While it was a hard way to learn a new language, I could have mental exercise, try to improve myself, while away lonely hours.

I called for the Boss Boy. I told him I wanted to inspect the whole labor force. He explained to me that the labor supply had been recruited from two tribes who were hereditary enemies, and he hoped they would get along all right.

The natives ambled in close to the bungalow from all directions of the plantation. Their brown bodies sweated and shone in the hot daylight. I looked over their lean muscularity. Their muscles rippled with the look that the human animal has wherever men live all their days and nights out of doors. Most were as naked as Adam, except for the cloth binding about the head and a twist of cloth or leaf around the loins.

I stood before them, dressed in white, still wearing the white helmet of a government man. I was the only white man within fifty miles. I asked the Boss Boy a few questions, and continued to survey them. Then, taking a deep breath, I tried the magic sesame words: "All right, Boss Boy, *carry on!*"

The Boss Boy called out orders in native, directing them to return to work. They marched off in every direction. I wondered what it was all about—all I knew, I was growing coconuts.

I turned my attention to things I understood better. Close by I heard the roar of the surf. There was reef out there, and sharks would be just beyond the reef. The beach looked beautiful. There was always more to learn about water. I made pals with a playful little dog and we went swimming, while the coconuts grew.

Each morning that scene was repeated. The laborers gathered around my bungalow, with the Boss Boy standing next to me. He carried a stick, to use in case anybody got out of hand. I would boom, "All right, Boss Boy, carry on." Week by week, day by day, the coconut trees grew nuts.

During the succeeding time it appeared to me as if everything prospered. It was wonderful to see the long rows of young palms as they came up. Fowl and pigs were thriving. I even had a good young mare to mount and ride about, lording it over the Kanakas and making it look like I was working and running things.

If I hadn't been so stupid I would have had some fear about the environment, about the men that worked for me.

One evening word was brought to me that beriberi had broken out among them. I went to the barracks area where they lived in palm huts and, for the first time, saw how they lived. I couldn't do much about the beriberi. There weren't enough vitamins in their diet. At the time, vitamins were unknown, but I knew it was inadequate food.

I did notice many cut and wounded men going about. They had been fighting each other. That was how they passed the time at night, these tribal enemies, in individual and group fights, using knives. Now I understood why I had been hearing these noisy demonstrations from their ranks. These were iodine days, and I brought iodine to them and dressed the wounds of the hurt natives. There were no bandages available, just iodine, some permanganate of potash, a few jars of ointments, and I did the best I could as a medicine man.

Thereafter when I heard them brawling I went down among them—bravely stupid, I might have caught a spear or a knife—and hollered at them not to fight. They fought anyway as I looked on, and I would wind up with my iodine ritual.

But they knew how to take care of coconut soil and coconut trees, and I was learning about copra, as coconut cultivation was called.

Time passed, carry on, Boss Boy. Time, while I swam, studied German and French, pored over the damp books, looked out at the sea. I was alone—but not exactly lonely. I was only eighteen and there was too much living I was doing to be lonely. There was monotony, but I had long since learned to be by myself. I didn't like it, but there it was.

I dreamed of Maura dashed to her death in the plane, and looked in my books at the pictures of beautiful white girls.

A Kanaka came running into my camp one day rattling in the local tongue, gesturing toward a distant spot. There had been a salt raid by a mountain tribe upon a seaside community not far off. His description of the horrors excited everyone. I organized a party to go see what had happened.

In packing and rounding up a party of Kanakas to go with me, I made sure to take along a bag of salt. That was what you traded with primarily. The New Guineans of the mountainous hinterland were salt hungry and they'd kill for it. I saw them take a spoonful of salt and ram it down their throats as a hungry American would demolish a hamburger. You could buy anything with a spoonful of the substance and hardly any other currency would be acceptable to most of the natives.

We tramped through jungle thicket for one whole day till we reached this village. Half of the place had been burned. There were charred bodies, guts were strewn all over. Children lay around decapitated. All had their skulls cracked open: the normal custom, for the brains were taken away and eaten. The worst sight of all was where a half-dozen tall pointed stakes had been driven into the earth. Pregnant women had been impaled on these points: the baby on top of the stake, on the sharp point, and the mother's body with the stake right through it. The flies were there in swarms working on the entrails.

I knew I beheld a people of a different mentality who lived and thought as their forebears had 20,000 years earlier. I had to try to deal with them and understand them. What was it? Tribal warfare? Only two things had been carried away, women and salt, and the rest was charring and festering in the hot sun.

On the way back through the jungle trail, about four miles from the massacre, I started at the flicker of a movement in the bush. I took out my revolver. I thought it might be one of the mountain raiders, that a new massacre—of us—might be attempted. I aimed at the bush and was ready to let it go, when of a sudden the shrubbery parted and I beheld a pathetic little creature, a girl, sitting there shaking, expecting to be killed.

She was absolutely exhausted, petrified, and as she looked up at me there was a sort of supplication in her eyes, as if she anticipated death instantly.

One of the boys could talk her village language pretty well. As they communicated, I gave her a long, plaited stick of tobacco, an item that I used in trade sometimes. At first she shrank back, then took a hearty bite. She had some confidence now, and between my bit of local language and the help of the Kanakas with me, we managed to convey to her that there was nothing to be afraid of. We were friends.

Her face lit up, and I realized I was staring at a honey-colored girl of exceeding femininity. She had a perfect figure, and the most glorious pair of breasts you ever saw—the classic ski-jump type, a lovely little hollow, and then the line goes way up into the air and doesn't dip. She was bushy-haired of course, and very lightly tattooed. She wore little except the typical grass skirt, called the *rami*, made of pandora leaves or coconut leaves carefully interwoven. She was barefooted, and I think I liked her very much because she had no ring through her nose.

It was very fashionable among the Melanesian ladies to wear rings of wild boar ivory through their nostrils, but this little one had none, and the natural beauty of the shape of her nose was unmarred.

"What is your name?"

"Maihiati."

I couldn't think what to do with her. After all, those raiders might return. Leave her? To what? To go back to that village where perhaps one of those women on the stakes could have been her mother or sister?

I took another sharp look at her breasts and made the decision. "She comes with us."

We went back, marching another ten miles or so. My first idea was that I should send her to the authorities in Kavieng. They would take her in, since she was probably the only one left alive. They would probably put her to work in a hospital as an orderly or God knows what kind of job.

But when little Maihiati heard that I was going to send her to Kavieng, she had a fit. I gathered from the sort of near hysteria she was in, and from what the boys said, that she would kill herself if sent there. I have listened to many female threats of suicide in my time, most of them phony—most people who are really going to kill themselves don't say much about it beforehand—but I was quite sure Maihiati meant this.

So I decided not to report her to the Government, just to let her work around my place.

I already had a servant in the cookhouse, and I told her to give the girl a job and train her until we could find out what should be done with her.

This child became absolutely like a little puppy. She found my thatched house a haven, and I thought, Why not?

Besides, she was so attractive.

The more I looked at her beauty and desirability, the more I had a horrible feeling of guilt. My father, in a recent letter to me, had admonished: *My boy, always remember a man who has anything to do with a native woman stinks in the nostrils of a decent white man.*

Soon thereafter I wrote back. *Dad, I stink.*

It's true there took place a certain struggle between Conscience and Me. Conscience lost.

The guilty feeling was there beforehand, but the realization, of course, was wonderful. Afterward, instead of any sense of guilt, I felt completely reconciled. I felt that there couldn't be much wrong morally; and I discovered that physically a female is a female the world over.

You might as well accept yourself for what you are. I had already been wondering about the various sets of moral values that we humans put around our emotions, most of them so varying in different cultures and backgrounds.

I came to the conclusion in these formative months in New Guinea that I had certain urges, impulses that were planted in me for ages, and that a relationship with a native girl was possible and desirable. Why should I follow the dictates of people who lived in other lands on the other side of the world?

The conventions of mid-England could not easily hold for a vigorous young white man surrounded by feminine and attractive Melanesian girls.

There was no love in this relationship. It was strictly biophysical. But the little girl helped much to make a man of me.

She had escaped a horrible death, and she was pathetically grateful. She was a wonderful servant and my first steady affair in New Guinea.

Maihiati was little and probably young—though they had no conception of age there—but she was very much of a woman all the same. She was prone to the same emotion as the more civilized woman: a fierce jealousy if any other girls came around. She would pout and sulk until they left, and afterward, she had dark glances of fury for me.

Why me? Why not them? is a question I always asked myself—then and later.

While I raised copra I began writing letters to my father. Many of these, fortunately, he preserved. I must have sounded to him like a thriving young businessman. In a way I was. I consulted him about planting a crop of annato, as I had been advised to do by the Agricultural Director at Kavieng. I wrote:

> I have 500 acres of ground. I don't intend to plant such a large area with coconuts alone, but I don't want to go fooling around with any product that's likely to turn out a dud, so I was wondering if maybe you could have a chat with some scientific authority about this stuff called annato.

I carefully concealed from him the full nature of the latest brawl I was in. Imagine, I confided to him, the other day I was fined ten pounds for hitting a Chinaman who had poor manners and the presumption to call me by my surname without any Mr. or Master before it. I complained to him that the Chinamen around here were coolies and little advanced over the Kanakas. They were becoming increasingly insolent and getting away with it all because the League of Nations recognized them as equals with the white men. I reminded the professor how, when the Germans owned this region, a Chinaman had to take his hat off before talking to a white man, otherwise it was knocked off.

Highhanded arrogance, but in those days that was the way things were in New Guinea.

I never did tell him that what actually happened was that I went to jail.

The District Officer sat on the bench in the small Kavieng courthouse, an austere room, with His Majesty's picture and appropriate Union Jack on the wall in back of him, a dock, and rows of bamboo chairs. I had known the District Officer quite well, but in this situation I had little defense.

This Chinese and I had argued, and I got out of control. Whether it was for the reason I told my father or some other, I don't recall. In the ensuing fisticuffs I fear the Chinese got the worst of it. I remember banging my head against a lamppost, and I made the most of this when I defended myself to the magistrate. He wasn't impressed. "Thirty pounds or two weeks," he said.

"I'll take the two weeks."

The District Officer sat bolt upright. He folded his arms and snarled from the bench, "But Errol, you can't do that! You know we've got no jail."

The law said you couldn't put a white man in with the Kanakas, and the only jail they had there was for these poor natives.

But there was a chap named Tom Price who was in charge of prisoners. So I was placed in his hands, to stay in his house for two weeks, under an honor system, his house having been declared a prison for my particular benefit. Tom and I, and some others, not prisoners, wound up playing poker each night. I maintained as good discipline as I could around Tom's house by avoiding his charming wife. Beyond that I would make no sacrifices. I got out each evening, and finally my jailor wound up pleading with me, "Please, Errol, try to be 'home' by midnight, will you?"

I couldn't afford to be chastened by a small run-in with the law. Life was too exacting, too uncertain in this antediluvian part of the world. Man the barricades, Flynn old man. The Good Lord gave you a fist so you could keep it clenched.

Ahsims came to see how the plantation prospered. On this visit he said, "They been shooting"—and he pointed to the top of the coconut trees.

I didn't know what he was talking about, but I denied it anyway.

"Look," he said, " I know when they been shooting."

What he meant was that they were knocking off the green coconuts to get more copra—a bad practice. The idea, in raising copra, is to wait till the coconuts mature and drop, and not to knock them off before then. However, if you want to make it look good on paper, make it seem as though your monthly output is high, you have your men, with the aid of a long pole and a knife at the end of the pole, cut them down.

After Ahsims spotted this—he was quite right about it—I felt that I was on my way out again. All I could do was raise hell with the Boss Boy.

From then on I began casting about for whatever means of livelihood I might next have to turn to.

On an island about twelve hours away by sailboat there lived two Australians who had also bought up an expropriated German plantation. They were trying to work this land and pay it off. One fellow, "Dusty" Miller, was a down-to-earth type who had conventional interests, manners, and some money. The other was an exact opposite. His name was Simpson and his principal claim to fame was that he had been an actor of sorts in Dublin and I had never met an actor. He had a wonderful vocabulary and a Shakespearean manner. I was much drawn to his phony and imperial style, and catered to it by calling him Simmeaux, accent on the second syllable, which he liked; while I wondered if all actors were like him. From him I picked up a sense of the dash that a man could carry off, but it was with Miller that I entered into a business deal.

I learned of the availability of a new schooner just being built at Kavieng. A Chinese had begun the construction of her, but had died before the boat's completion. I had a little money. Dusty had a lot more. Couldn't we be partners? Freight copra from the small plantation islands to the big New Guinea centers? I told Dusty that by the time the boat was finished I'd have enough money to meet my share.

I went to Kavieng.

My old friend Johnson was now postmaster general of the city. Would he arrange for me to get a contract from the Government permitting me to dynamite for fish? I used the pretext that my workers were under-eating, had beriberi. I needed to supplement their diet, and the waters around my way were filled with fish. If I could get enough fish I could sell it to other plantations too, at maybe three or four pence, and pick up the money I needed to buy my share of the ship. . . .

I got the license.

I returned to the plantation. I hadn't yet been fired, but I had my hooks into a new business now, in case I was; and I entered the strange new field of dynamiting fish for a living.

You learned, you hoped, how not to blow off your arm, as some dynamiters did, by making the fuse of the dynamite plug too short. I had seen dynamiters with arms, heads, ears, knees, elbows blown off because they made the fuses too short and mistimed explosions. I gave myself the leeway of four-inch fuses instead of three. You lit the plug, at the end of which there was a lighted dry coconut leaf, you let her fizz, and tossed it at a school of fish. The plug went under the surface, exploded, and the fish came up, belly white.

I had six neat canoes, each manned by two Kanakas, going for the fish, scooping them up as fast as I exploded plugs into the water. As soon as the fish surfaced, the canoes went for them, scooping them into the canoes. They were weighed, I sold them and got paid. The fish were plentiful, the business risky but lucrative.

I ran into a lot of shark trouble. One big sonofabitch always came around during the dynamiting. He and his tribe would show soon after the fuses blew, as if it were a signal that dinner was served. They hung around the fringes of the area where we dynamited, coming in from miles away. The Kanakas had no fear of them. All that they required of me was to be issued black socks for their feet and hands. The soles of their feet were white, and the sharks might go for something white, perhaps mistaking the *hors d'oeuvre* for the main course, so the socks provided my boys with some protection. They put the socks on their hands and on their feet. Then they'd swim around, catch hold of the sharks, tickle them, jump on them, hang onto their tails, even whack them. The sharks behaved like a bunch of puppies with these fellows, though not the kind I cared to play with.

But this big fellow, the boss shark who came around snooping and led all the others, scooped up a lot of the small fish we killed. The big pig was costing me money. He wouldn't come close to the canoes, but he got to the fish before my boys could, and this was getting me very mad.

I consulted with an expert fisherman, a young Japanese lad who also worked with dynamite. He showed me how to take a fish that was still alive, tie it to the dynamite plug with a longer fuse and throw it out to the far edge where the big shark hung out.

I prepared for mine enemy.

Sure as hell, after we began the new day's blasting this monster, about sixteen feet long, came down the line, his fin lazing over the water. I took one of these not-yet-dead fish and tied it in the way I was told and made the long fuse.

I tossed it way over.

He went for it, scooped it up almost with a yawn and moved on looking for more fish. I could see his passage in the water, because the fuse was right in his belly and the smoke of the fuse was beginning to come out of his mouth.

Once he made a quick spurt, as if he felt he had hot guts; then he settled down, scooped up more fish. He made another spurt. Inside him now the fuse was burning him. He was heading right under my boat. I could see the trail of smoke over the water coming right for my boat, like a damned torpedo. This was completely unexpected.

Underneath the boat he turned around, began another spurt, and then the big sonofabitch exploded. He blew up, went to pieces right under my boat, and blew two planks out of it.

We started to sink.

All of his cousins and brothers, smelling blood, came immediately to the boat. They ate him fast, and there was nothing to be seen of him in five minutes.

After that, when I dynamited for fish, I was the only shark to gobble up the profits.

Maski is a very popular word in the Papuan language. It means I don't care, or I don't give a damn, to hell with it, or screw yourself, anything like that. When the finished ship came off the slips at the dockyard in Kavieng, I christened her by that name, *The Maski.*

She floated down high out of the water like a breasty girl.

Though Dusty and I shared ownership of the boat, we were mortgaged to the rudder to Burns-Philips, Limited, a finance and general enterprise setup with offices in Kavieng and Rabaul and Sydney.

From now on I neglected the plantation. I let the Boss Boy run it. Whenever I returned, Maihiati was there, faithfully waiting for me, convenient and available, but I knew one day soon I'd be leaving her.

I plied the coastal waters between Matinalawa and Kavieng and looked for the copra-shipping business which we thought we'd get. But the planters were holding onto copra because the price was low, and we had to find some other way to make the ship pay off. Burns-Philips, Limited agreed to help us charter passengers; they would act as agents and handle the money till the purchase was complete.

They lined up some passengers to Rabaul. I hurried into Kavieng with *The Maski* and a small crew of Kanakas.

Now it was one thing to run the boat close to the coast, or about Kavieng harbor, and allow the crew to do most of that. It was another to take an overseas trip. I was teaching myself navigation. But how do you steer from point to point on the sea? How do you steer at night from port to port? How do you keep off reefs not even charted then?

I ran for help to Basil.

I said, "Basil, I have a charter to go from Kavieng to Rabaul. I've got passengers. How the hell do I get there?"

He grinned. "Flynn dear boy," he said, "you do the same thing as you did before, only this time you don't call the Boss Boy. You call the boatswain. You just say, 'Bosun, carry on!' "

"Can't you tell me how . . . ?"

"Listen, I can't tell you how to navigate overnight. I've just lost my own boat and I've got enough headaches. Call the bosun. He'll know. Just tell him . . ."

Very well, I'd try it. I knew almost nothing of navigation, nothing of how to be master of a ship. But I had the license, I hired a crew, I was in business.

A couple and their three babies were leaving Kavieng for Rabaul. They signed as passengers on my ship. One baby was in a crib, the other two kids could toddle about.

I stood near the helm, a few feet away from the bosun. I looked outward at the deep water. I held up my arm, poised the palm of my hand seaward, like a knife, as a captain might, indicating the direction we ought to take.

I bellowed, "Carry on, bosun!"

The sails lifted and *The Maski* steered into the green-gray horizon, usually ten days to Rabaul—under a master knowing little of boats or the sea.

For two weeks we went off course, on course, zigzagging our way to Rabaul with not too friendly winds. That wouldn't have been so bad but my passengers soon discovered how green we were. The bosun, apparently, counted on me to be able to navigate, and he didn't know any more about overseas navigation than I. The woman denounced me loudly. The children bawled. The husband stamped up and down on deck saying, "Wait till we get to Rabaul, I'll fix you!"

"Maybe we'll never get there," I suggested weakly.

When we arrived, the male parent went straight to the Port Authority. He reported me as an incompetent, a menace on the high seas, more dangerous than any pirate.

He was dead right.

I survived the protest, and the biggest thing I learned from this was the idea that had been given to me by Basil Hoare, an approach I used all my days thereafter. When you want to get something done, hire a specialist, a foreman, a top man, who knows his business and say to him, "Boss Boy, carry on . . ."

You may have a rough passage, but chances are you'll get somewhere.

For several months, I ran *The Maski* in local waters, carrying passengers, freight, and teaching myself navigation. My principal hangout in Kavieng became the Burns-Philips offices where I dealt mainly with a Mr. Exeter, my principal creditor.

One day, when I walked into headquarters, I was introduced to an

American named Joel Swartz. He was a short man, perhaps hardly above my shoulders in height, but with an ebullient manner. He dressed in sporting khaki, with a white helmet. He had a manner of ease, of being well-heeled and well-traveled, and he was amiable.

Swartz said, "So you're the fellow I've heard so much about."

"Really?"

"Oh, just my way of speaking. I hear you're a schooner captain. You know this country and you've got a good boat."

"*The Maski* gets me there."

"That's just what I want it to do for me."

"Where do you want to go?"

"Up the Sepik."

"The Sepik! That's a long way from here—on the mainland."

"I know, but I have to do it, and you're the man with the boat."

He was pleasant, and I was flattered. Yet the last place in the world I wanted to go was the fearful Sepik River, a human graveyard.

He looked upward at me, smiling, cornering me. "What do you know about head-hunters?"

"Enough to be careful. What do you know about them?"

"Enough to want to take moving pictures of them."

"Moving pictures?"

"Yes, my gear is at the hotel. I've some photographers there too, and I rather think we can meet the question of payment. Would twenty-five pounds a day be all right?"

To me that was a huge sum, and I tried not to show too much interest. Swartz added, "Of course we take care of the provisions, the oil, anything else—"

I appeared to remain unconvinced. Whatever he paid would go to Burns-Philips anyway. They drew their take first, paid me on my return to port.

"Must this be the Sepik River? It'll be rough. You could see head-hunters along other rivers, and even along the coasts."

"No, the Sepik."

"You understand that's an unexplored river. Four days up by boat—nobody's been in farther."

"It has to be the Sepik. We need background for a film we're making. The pictures we shoot are sent back to Hollywood and used in connection with a story filmed there."

At that point Exeter spoke up. "Mr. Flynn will take you, I'm pretty sure. I don't know why he's hesitating." He gave me a look that said, You and Miller still owe us nine hundred pounds.

For the next two months I cruised with film-maker Swartz, his photographers, and my crew, across the waters to the mainland of New Guinea, to the northeast coast where the red, muddy Sepik flowed into the sea. We moved into the broad stream, running against a strong current, *The Maski* able to take the river as we did not draw more loaded than six or seven feet of water.

The Sepik is a monster waterway six hundred miles long. No white man had ever been up the river more than two or three hundred miles and the nature of the river or the land beyond that was practically unknown—and remains little known even to this day. The waterway was heavily populated with mosquitoes, Kanakas and *puk-puks* (crocodiles). We steamed up the river only two days' distance, the camera work going on much of the time.

It wasn't easy to get close-up shots of the natives. As we traveled, the *garramuts,* the tom-toms made of crocodile skin, kept up a steady communication. Outsiders, big magic on the water, beware, the drums said.

When we came in close to shore and tried to get film of the natives, we got arrows instead, real ones, and poisoned.

Here is a letter I wrote to my father shortly after that trip:

DEAR SPORT,
    Thanks very much for D'Albertis' *New Guinea.* Of course I've never been in any of the parts that he writes of, but his description of the Fly River natives corresponds exactly with these bastards of the Sepik River in this territory. They do up their hair in precisely the same manner and wear the same clothes—that is, none at all, except a vine G-string sometimes. From D'Albertis' time till now they've changed very little. They still run away—every blankety one of them—when you get near their village and they still run like hell when they're fired at. Also, if they think it's safe they shoot at you with spears and arrows. In this respect they differ considerably from the natives of other uncontrolled areas who'll put up a good fight until one or two of them get shot. Then they go for their lives. . . .
                                                    YOUR SON

Swartz and I became very friendly and he confided to me that the film his photographers were taking, especially of the mouth of the river, wasn't entirely for purposes of backgrounding a motion picture. The United States and Britain were expecting that one day trouble might blow in from the East, from Japan; and the United States and its probable allies knew little or nothing of the nature of this large hunk of British territory. One of the keys to its possession was this river. Some of the film, the vital shots of the river mouth, were for official purposes. How right he turned out to be!

He asked whether I expected to remain a mariner all my days. I explained that I had no ambition beyond making some money. Soon I'd make a stab at the gold fields. He was interested when I explained there was seafaring blood in my whole line and told him of my seagoing grandfather. I also described the sword we had at home. I doubt, I told him, I could ever remain away from the ocean for very long.

For days I watched the way a motion picture camera lens silently swallowed the landscape. I was aware that, from time to time, one of the cameramen shot me as I took the wheel, or had to get into crocodile-infested waters to shove us off a sandbank.

Once he ceased grinding the scenery long enough to film me at the water's edge, tangling with a crocodile for fun and sport, tantalizing the scaly bastard with a bamboo pole. I couldn't know that later, when the film was run off, my youthful pranks were carefully noted by Swartz and his colleagues.

The trip up the Sepik revived my original interest in the gold fields. I realized that there was no good reason to be in New Guinea other than to try to strike it rich.

When I returned to Kavieng early in 1929, I learned that I was finished at the copra plantation. I had been away too long to please the proprietors. That and the realization I'd never get rich on *The Maski* decided me to head back to the mainland.

I said good-by to Maihiati, but leaving her with many presents. In the interim she had restored contact with some of her tribe and she would return to live with them. But she would go back a rich girl, by prevailing standards.

I had begun, with my first New Guinea mistress, a practice that I was to bring to a fine art later in Hollywood when I bestowed upon wives and mistresses—or, wait a minute—had taken from me, huge alimonies, houses, fortunes.

I sold out my interest in *The Maski* to Dusty Miller, and with a few pounds in my pocket I went by inter-island steamer to Salamaua, on the east coast of the New Guinea mainland.

Edie Creek gold field, discovered two or three years earlier, was a week's march inland from Salamaua. But you couldn't get in there unless you had native labor to go with you to hack out a path, to provide some protection from hostile tribes, and to work the earth when you arrived. From the sale of my share of *The Maski* I had enough money when I arrived to hire eight boys and the necessary marching gear and gold-digging equipment.

Each Kanaka carried a fifty-pound load of produce, chiefly rice, and gadgets for trade. I tried to carry what they did, but they were conditioned to it. I was busy fighting off the leeches on my body all day.

When we camped, the natives of the region came around to see who we were and what we had. As they had spears and preferred a shrunken white head to any other, I had the boys build a waist-high enclosure in which we stayed. Around the enclosure I had them stretch a fishing line from tree to tree in a square or circle, and then I had them tell the onlookers by sign language, or by talking their dialect, that if any of them stepped inside that fishing line they'd be shot. There were too many instances, all of a sudden, of stone axes and clubs hitting you from behind.

It happened once that, while drums were baying in the night all through the jungle and we were holed up, with the fishing line around us, a boy who must have been under eighteen reached for something inside the fishline and the guard immediately shot his hand off. That was the end of that day's trading. We had to go on, and the natives who peered at us from the bush vanished back into the jungle.

All night you'd hear these horrible noises coming at you in the pitch dark, in your little clearing. You heard the bush crackle and you knew they were around. If you found dry wood you'd have a fire going, and it stood out like a beacon, drawing the Melanesian Kanakas for miles around. While they prowled in the dark about you, you tried to sleep, and fought off mosquitoes, leeches, bugs, giant roaches, even New Guinea bats, night bloodsuckers. You'd wake from a few minutes' sleep, light a cigarette, deleech yourself; put the fire on a damned leech and burn him to a bloody pulp. Then back to sleep for a bit and wonder whether that crawly sound you heard a few feet away might be a snake, a cassowary or maybe only a wild boar razorback.

I have seen Central Africa but it was never anything like the jungle of New Guinea.

Each day we climbed these precipitate hills, up and down, then almost straight up again. You could stand on one mountain range and almost piss straight across to another—two days' march away. This was the route to the gold fields.

There were tall tales of a completely different culture beyond a range of mountains into which few men were ever known to have penetrated. When I got to the top of one of those mountains, I saw a vast belly of what they call kunai grass, a high stalk that stands two or three feet above a man's head. I had a little dog with me named Pikis, in New Guinea language "little croc." He had a ferocious snarl and a snap and I loved him. You respected this dangerous small companion with his curly tail like a jaunty question mark.

I didn't understand what was happening to him as we pushed into this grass. He started to drag his hind legs, then he slowed down to a creep. He was always full of energy and I wondered what was happening. At last he stopped altogether, panted heavily for a while, and then died.

Afterwards I learned that two or three feet above the ground where the kunai grass grew there was a poison gas emitted by the roots. The gas hung over the floor of the earth's surface so that poor little Pikis couldn't get his breath.

The Edey Creek gold field was more of a spectacle of men seeking gold than it was of gold waiting for men to find it. Not that there wasn't gold there: there was. I staked out a claim, a plot of soil about a hundred yards square, registered with the Administration, and prepared to get rich overnight.

Within a few days I heard all around the cliché of the gold field. "There is too much New Guinea in the gold," they said, meaning that the earth was thin on gold, thick on soil. A few had hit the real good veins. The others had to scramble and muck through tons of earth for faint glimmerings. "You can find this much gold anywhere in New Guinea," I heard them say. "A man don't have to stay here and take it out where dozens are doing it." Somewhat discouraging.

The gold area was high on the side of a mountain, perhaps eight or nine thousand feet up. At night the tropic region was wintry. By day the natives and the white men chopped at the hillsides like termites, tearing up the soil and panning the earth. Crude living quarters, thatched huts, barracks, makeshift tents, spread out from several central administration buildings run by the Australian Government.

When I arrived with my small band of Kanakas, nobody took much notice. Prospecting parties came and went. Food was scarce, disease was a rule of living. There was no medical attention. Natives died of pneumonia every day.

The big gun of the Edey Creek fields was Sharkeye Bill Park, an old-timer in the gold fields of Australia, who struck it rich. He was in with a partner named Jack Nettleton; and there was this fellow Sloan, a devout Catholic who gave an enormous nugget of gold to the Pope. These were the kingpins of the region, but the rest of the prospectors didn't have their luck.

Around me were some other bizarre figures, now gone, I guess, who had prospected at the Yukon Jack London wrote about. They seemed to be part of a world migration of prospectors who will do nothing else but seek gold. A few had even fought Indians in North America, so they said, and I wondered what sort of a country America was. Others had put up with the rigors even of Siberia. They told tales of the gold fields in all parts of the world, going back fifty years. . . . Now New Guinea was their happy hunting ground.

I was the youngest among them, but I wasn't geared to hold out. My money was running out. My Kanakas didn't like the place. They were frightened at the prospect of dying there of the high cold air. I couldn't pay them, couldn't sell them. I realized I hadn't prepared properly to come here. I had neither the provisions, nor the money, nor the necessary men to work a claim properly. The competition with other prospectors who were better set up was too much. Get out, Flynn. Go back to the coast: try it again later.

The only thing I accomplished on that trip was a fast friendship with a respected prospector named Jack Ryan. Soon afterward Jack was to prove his friendship for me by coming to my aid when a serious charge was brought against me.

My boys and I staggered back to the sea: a shocking, frustrating experience.

Gold is hard to come by—a banality if ever I coined one.

Back at Salamaua, looking for new ways to prosperity, I discovered that the place had a good harbor. I could claim navigator's experience

by now, and I struck up with an elderly schooner captain named Ed
Bowen who had a ship called the *Matupi,* a better boat than *The
Maski.* He needed a right-hand man. I was hired. We were to take a
long trip up the coast to the port of Aitape. You could go inland from
there and reach the territory of Dutch New Guinea.

Bowen said one might find gold there. You could also go into another
business, shooting birds-of-paradise for the beautiful feathers were
then much in demand.

By now the mainland of New Guinea fascinated me as much as the
sea. Aitape, where we were going, was in the Sepik River district. If you
could get into the hinterland and bamboozle the natives into coming
back with you to a plantation or a coastal city, you would be in the
chips. They were strong fellows, good workers, and you could sell them
to plantations or at ports for use in the gold fields. I was a little young
perhaps to go in for slave trading, but it was an acknowledged way to
turn a penny.

"Recruiting" was what they called this form of slave-stealing, and
when you got a bunch of boys in your grasp they were called "indentured laborers." It was one of the main businesses of the rough and
readies like myself who flocked into the New Guinea Territory.

I looked over the scene at Aitape. The coastline looked glum and
unexciting. There was a beach of brown sand. The natives, I noticed,
more than elsewhere, wore wild boar tusks through the nose. The men
laced themselves up tightly with bands, they carried long black bows
and the arrows they shot were four or five feet long. I hadn't seen anything yet that looked more removed from the world of England and
Australia.

Only a few miles in, it was true head-hunting country, but also perhaps gold. There were certainly potential laborers, and the birds-of-
paradise abounded. I had a few pounds, enough to equip a small jungle
party.

I had four shotguns, and my own revolver. A young boy was my
personal servant or "monkey," a little fellow, twelve or thirteen years
old, who carried my personal stuff and was in charge of anything personal I wanted to be done. Native boys loved that job and were very
faithful. This particular one, Tabura, was in charge of making my tea in
the morning. He carried my revolver very proudly. A revolver can weigh
a lot when you are climbing up mountains. Tabura didn't mind. He
carried also my personal knapsack in which there might be some money,
or wax matches kept dry in an empty quinine bottle, my razor, soap,

tobacco, and also wrapped up in watertight wax, old zigzag French cigarette papers. You rolled your own.

For several days we moved steadily northward toward the Dutch border. I was a British subject, so I had no business getting over onto Dutch-owned soil, but it was in this region where the birds-of-paradise flourished.

I discovered that the natives usually deserted their village or else attacked or ambushed when prospecting parties came through. My four guns and revolver should have been enough for any emergency, because you only had to contend with one village at a time. That was because the people here were all *melup,* hereditary enemies. They could never get together; you didn't have to fear a gang-up.

We camped outside one big *campong,* or Kanaka settlement. The men I had seen about hadn't seemed too afraid. They had taken a good look at us and retreated casually. The first night I put out presents, keeping a close guard. The presents were taken. The next night I put them closer to our sleeping quarters—calico, razor blades, some cheap knives. After the third day they started bringing presents, chiefly taro, a root that tasted a little like a yam. They also brought some jungle fowl, very welcome because of our meager supply of bully beef in cans.

Then I found some of them squatting at the camp entrance. I invited them in. I gathered that they were the big men of the village. They were absolutely stark naked: good physical specimens just right for the gold fields. I had no interpreters and sign language had to do. In the distance I saw their women beginning to peer around. That was a good sign.

I rolled a cigarette.

As I did, I noticed they were making much comment. They smoked no tobacco, and had no idea what I was doing. I was sitting on a large rock, getting ready to deal with them, and rolling the butt. I twisted the end, put the thing in my mouth, took out a match, struck it on the stone and lit up. A tremendous shout went up. They fled in every direction. I never could entice them back.

Then, rather suddenly, we hit into a country where the birds-of-paradise were plentiful. Our guns began going to work on them. We made the jungle ring with a foreign sound. Crack! Boom! Down came the birds. The boys went and got them, brought them back to camp, cooked some on hot stones, ate them and preserved the rest in salt. Ladies' hats throughout the world would glow and flutter like the treasures of slowly waving coral reefs in the South Seas. It's lucky for some birds ladies' fashions change.

What we didn't know was that the drums of the natives began sending the news back to the coast that someone was here illicitly, shooting their birds, rumbling the jungle, bringing the usual white man's hell into the traditional paradise.

It is an amazing sight to see a flock of wild birds-of-paradise in these mountain depths. They swoop, a flock at a time, into one tree, with their flowing tails and their colors, gold, and an emerald green that sparkles. The shape and design of this bird is beautiful: a small head, a slender delicate neck, and a leaflike blade coming down to a blaze of color into the body; then a long orange tail that is as long as the body. They fly very gracefully, though not fast, like the flight of a heron. But the noise that comes from these creatures is raucous, dissonant: it breaks through your ears worse than the cry of a peafowl, the worst-sounding of flyers. It shrills through your head, so that something of the beauty of the bird is taken away.

A few days later I got word, through the jungle, that the Dutch New Guinea District Officer was on my trail. I figured he had to be about a day's march behind me.

My boys and I had reached the banks of the Sepik River. There seemed no possible way to get over it. It was broad and turbulent and full of crocodiles. But knowing this fellow was not far behind, I had to think of something.

I had my boys build a bamboo raft. When it was done, we put all of my birds-of-paradise carcasses, preserved in salt, on board. I packed everything else I owned: money, guns, binoculars, rolled tobacco, wax matches, equipment, gear. We knew we would be swept down this boiling current of river, but if we had luck and if we paddled carefully, we might make it across to the other side, about a mile or so downstream.

We shoved off and headed toward the rapids below us, and the flats just beyond that. If we got to the flats, I knew we'd make the other bank. We bounced over the rocks and plunged downstream, hanging on for life. Some of us were in the water and some out. There were jagged rocks beneath us. We went along miraculously for a time, and were getting near the flats when we ran onto a pinnacle of rocks.

The crash split the raft apart. All of us went into the water—my six Kanakas and I—and we were rushed over boiling falls. We landed on the flats—but minus everything. All of it was washed away, birds-of-paradise, feathers, plumage, salt and all.

Washed into fairly calm water, I looked around and counted heads. We were all there.

We struck out for the nearest bank on the other side of the river, putting the Dutch territory behind us. Ahead of us lay the Australian-owned shore.

I was swimming when I felt something I thought was a log hit my leg. Then Yulu, one of my good native boys who had been with me from the outset, let out an awful scream.

The others yelled, *"Puk-puk!"* (Crocodile)

Yulu went down. I never saw him again.

Next moment I felt something smack my buttocks, scraping savagely. I was petrified, but I went into action. I had fifty yards to go. Stroking out wildly, expecting to be grabbed any minute, I made for the shore. The others did the same. All of us got in, except the one who had been seized. I was astonished that little Tabura had made shore too.

I climbed out onto the ground wet, mad, wearing nothing but a bush jacket, broke again, not a speck of salt to my name.

Until then I had never known stark terror. Just a sense of wildness, excitement, even enjoyment of both. But when I got high and dry on the shore and realized that one of my lads was dead—and I came so close to being snapped up too—I started to shake and kept shaking for a couple of days.

We walked, with nothing to eat other than some herbs, to a Lutheran Mission. Through it all my monkey, little Tabura, stayed at my side, jabbering pidgin English, and smiling.

We hung about there and rested up. I got no religion, but we did get some matches, some bread, milk and fruit. Then struggled down to the coast, to Aitape.

Clearly Aitape was no place for me to stay. I was hot. The District Officer could make it bad for me if he wanted to, for there was plenty of evidence that I had gone hunting the illicit plume. The law was, to some extent, sensitive to the pressure of the New Guineans. If the *garramut* told them I had been in Dutch territory, if the Dutch officials wanted me prosecuted so as to make an example, I was vulnerable.

I sought out Captain Bowen and he agreed to take me back to Salamaua. That was a bigger and a livelier port, the gateway to the gold fields, to hotter recruiting activity. You could gamble in that port, meet the sports, the miners, the adventurers, the handicappers, the English "Leave your country for your country's good" boys.

It was when I arrived in Salamaua, a little older, a little more thoughtful, that I developed my first doubts about New Guinea as a place to stay and to wind up in. Some day I had to get out of here—as soon as I struck it rich.

I took a look at where I was and how I was living, roaming from spot to spot, with these primitives all about, looking for gold, bumping and bungling about like a blind bumblebee, hoping for a chance, plunging at a jungle with bare hands. I said to myself, Something is wrong.

I lived on the outskirts in a bamboo-leaf-covered lodging, with no more than a dog or a cat for company. I had a servant to cook whatever I had shot during the daytime. From here I went out on the water in the *Matupi,* or went with bands of Kanakas inland on recruiting trips. Most of the money was in recruiting. You could sell a few New Guineans for twenty to thirty pounds apiece to a copra plantation.

Always, wherever I was, nightfall meant books and a chance to try to connect with the ideas of the world. For I sensed how far a cry all this was from the schoolboy life I had been leading only shortly before. The boys I went to school with were probably still doing their lessons. Now—out of school—an inner need for learning sprang up in me.

I felt ignorant and uneducated. Though I had read whenever I had the chance, now I made the chance. I plunged into reading as if it were my most vital need—and, after money, it was. Father, now in Sydney, sent me reading matter, magazines, papers, books.

It took two weeks for books to reach where I was. When a case of books arrived, it was the biggest thing of all for me. I fondled these books as if I were running my hands through a lovely woman's hair. I waded through Russian novelists, Greek philosophers, French writers.

I had to read by the light of a hurricane lamp. For a time I had one fine lamp called a Coleman. When I was reading, it attracted every goddamned bug in the jungle, and the jungle animals too. As I read I had to contend with the bugs, the lizards in the ceiling, and keep an eye out for big crablike spiders—bigger than tarantulas, they spin webs of fishing line thickness and catch birds.

I wasn't alone, except physically. You couldn't be quite alone with Balzac or de Maupassant, even Robert Louis Stevenson drumming around in your skull. You couldn't be lonely with the poems of the

English school, nor with the beauty of style of that faggot Baudelaire or the other French writer Rostand.

Rostand had the greatest influence upon me. I liked his style. I liked his story of Napoleon II, his *L'Aiglon.* I was able to read him—with difficulty—in French. I had a dictionary at my side and that helped. I was able to grasp the man's romance and poetry.

Now I was stirred by the whole world of the outside, the world of the West: Europe, America. There was a world of culture and excitement up there, but inaccessible, except through print. Whenever I read a footnote that quoted a writer of some other book as having said something interesting, I made a note of his name and the title. I prepared a list of books to order from the Sydney Public Library: Victor Hugo, H. G. Wells' *Outline of History,* and the Greeks: Plato, Aristotle. Sometimes it was hard going. I skipped, muddled and waded. Sometimes I swam well in these works.

Here am I, I said to myself, lost in this jungle. There they are, the primitives. In my hut are these masters of Western style and thought. Is this my chance? I have to make it. I have to find out why I am here in New Guinea, and where I ought to be and who I ought to be.

I think now that the only gold I found in New Guinea was in these books, read at night by hurricane lamp in *campongs,* in bamboo huts, wherever I put up. When I rafted, rowed, sailed, there were books close by. At night when the day's contending with my Kanakas was over with, and the day's wrangling with my colleagues in gold exploration or copra growing, I tried to get the things I never could discipline myself to absorb in the classroom.

I felt a growth of power, a kind of certainty. I'd be able to talk of these men and their works if and when I met people who knew them. I adopted the speech and the manners of the characters I read about, borrowing what seemed useful, for purposes of helping myself to grow up.

One morning, when I woke, I noticed that I had a thick red chin stubble. I hadn't shaved in days. I looked at myself in the mirror. No good, I said to myself. Shave every day, even if there is no one around to see you, even if only the lizard looks down from the branch of any old tree.

If I earned enough money recruiting, I could take another crack at the gold field itself. So I made repeated forays into the interior country.

Once I was with a party of seven boys about three days' march inland. My carriers, going down these precipitous gorges, moved in a narrow, snaky file. There were two boys in the lead with machetes. My other Kanakas, armed with guns, brought up the rear. I was in the middle with my current monkey, a little boy named Ateliwa. He had been with me for months, hanging about my quarters at Salamaua, attending my wants, always smiling, ready to do any bidding.

The exasperating part, as you slogged, was that overhead, from time to time, you saw a huge Junkers plane go by. It made the jump from the coast to an airdrome right at the center of the gold field. A little settlement called Wau had sprung up there a year or two earlier. An enterprising government man named C. J. Levien had hit on the idea of carrying in specially put-together dredges, freighting the parts in by air a couple of tons at a time. A couple of big companies, English- and American-backed, were formed, and they went in for deep mining and alluvial mining. The knowledge that the planes did this one-week trip in about a half-hour made me curse them. My boys wondered why I swore. Also, as I tracked, I lived in dread of getting "Japanese river fever" from a certain bush tick.

I was tiring. I felt malarial, knees weak, head dizzy.

Without a word of warning, spears streamed our way. Ambush! Ateliwa got one right through his belly and it came out low down his back. He writhed to the ground. I jumped behind a tree, with my revolver in my hand. All my other boys, instead of staying there and firing, threw their packs away and ran down the red clay mountainside.

I fired as soon as I could and I hit one of the raiders right in the neck. He dropped, squealing like a pig. I fired twice more, and that was the end of that.

I didn't even feel the poisoned arrow in my foot, the mark of which I still carry.

As soon as I got over the shock I grabbed my knapsack from the dead Ateliwa and hobbled after my boys as fast as I could. They were sitting down in the next clearing, having gone as far as they could run after they had thrown their packs away. Then I learned that one of the other boys had got a spear in the neck and he was gone. That left six of us.

It was dusk and I could hear the *garramuts*. You could hear voices on all sides talking, and they sounded ominous.

It started to rain—with an equatorial madness. We had nothing to eat, not a thing. We were high up and cold. My foot hurt, and I feared infection. My malaria was working in me hard. I was freezing and sweating at the same time.

Throughout the night the *garramuts* dinned in our ears. The crocodile-skin tom-toms kept going, sometimes loud, sometimes seeming to beat softer, as if the tribesmen were trying to make up their minds whether to come and get us. They were letting all New Guinea know that the white invader had shot and killed again.

I stayed awake. I had time to think and listen and to feel fear. Mostly it was the anticipation of what might happen. I could picture myself with spears through me, impaled, de-gutted, as I had seen others in New Guinea.

I decided that the raiders had looted the abandoned packs and maybe that satisfied them. Maybe the firearms scared them. Whatever, their *garramuts* died down and they didn't return.

Shivering and shaking, I passed my most terrifying night in New Guinea.

In the morning the drum sounds ceased.

We struggled down, falling, sliding, cursing, sweating, to the New Guinea coast.

At Salamaua I was arrested and charged with murder.

The word of my fracas with the tribesmen had come back to the coast by *garramut*, and as my boys and I walked into the village, a government man named Hawthorne, who hated my guts, approached and said I had to go with him. I told him I had been raided without warning and had to defend myself.

Behind Hawthorne was the pressure of the missionary folk of certain denominations working hard at this part of the coast. The missionaries wanted me nailed right up. Anything to show the natives they were the right guys. And Hawthorne wanted to impress this group because they had political pull, whereas bums and adventurers like myself, who came and went, had nothing but our nerve.

Owing to the fact that a rough element had come here for the gold hunt, they had built a small jailhouse. From time to time it held a drunken or too adventuresome customer. I was now in this clink, without bail. Salamaua was surrounded by swamp, and the smell oozed into my quarters and stayed.

The word reached the gold fields at once. The news spread elsewhere. A few friends called to see me.

A local physician, Dr. Giblin, and his wife consoled me and offered to do whatever they could. The best visitor was my old friend from the gold field, Jack Ryan. He had come to New Guinea when he was a younger man, about seventeen or eighteen, like myself. Now he was in his late forties. He had brains, a commodity that a man would be better off not having in New Guinea, but he hadn't made it. Every time a fortune seemed in his grasp it skipped him by. I think I reminded him of himself when he, as an adventurous lad, had first come here.

"What happened?" he asked, staring through an interstice of bamboo poles.

I told him, adding that Hawthorne, the man who was pressing the charge against me, hated my type—with some reason. He had accused me earlier of being " pretty young to be a recruiter, aren't you?"

I told Jack I intended to defend myself.

"Murder? Want to be jailed for thirty years?"

"I know what happened out there better than any lawyer."

"That's not enough. You've got to have some legal tricks to get out of a serious jam like this. Say the word and I'll send to Sydney for the right talent."

"God no! Thanks, Jack, but I'll do it myself."

"Then I'll be your witness."

"What did you witness?"

"Natives, Bush Kanakas, for twenty-five years! And I can lie under oath better than any weedy runt you ever met."

Words I was to remember.

I read all the lawbooks I could get my hands on. I studied what Anglo-Australian jurisprudence had to say about the subject. I pictured myself in the role of barrister. I carefully avoided writing to my parents about the fix I was in.

And I nearly destroyed myself.

The Salamauans came out to attend the trial of the young Australian. Prospectors, recruiters, bums, whores, as well as the missionary element, crowded the court.

It wasn't a big courtroom, and the crowd more than filled the ten rows of seats made of the trunks of coconut trees. The District Magistrate sat on a platform elevated about a foot above the rest of the room. There was a dock, a witness chair, a table for the prosecutor, and a table for the defender.

Since I was my own defender, I sat in the seat that counsel ordinarily would occupy.

The prosecutor painted a picture of me as a typical wild, careless prospector. I was unconcerned for the natives, antagonizing them, making it difficult to build good will between the Australian administration and the New Guineans. Common sense required that a depredator like myself should be punished. Show the natives that the Government did not condone mistreatment of the local inhabitants. Show them we believed in fair play, harmonious relations, and we were here for their good as well as our own. Put Flynn away for the rest of his life—right here in the Morobe district—where the natives would see how the white rules punished one of their own who fired at their people with impunity.

I made a brief opening address in which I declared that I had acted in self-defense. The business of recruiting was necessary to the flourishing of Australian interests in the mandated territory, I contended. The gold fields needed labor. I was one of an army of men vital to the needs of the exploitation of New Guinea.

I said that one of the problems of the Australian Administration, and of Western civilization itself, was to lift the natives to the level of civilized living. This was an acknowledge head-hunting country and an advance to a labor relationship would ultimately be helpful to the Melanesians themselves. It wasn't easy. Nobody else had found this process easy. I had never killed anyone in my life, and I had not done so intentionally this time.

I closed by saying I had defended my life out there in the jungle and I would do it here in court!

Prosecutor Hawthorne questioned me about my career in New Guinea. He wanted to know every business I was in, where I had been, how well I knew the natives of this locality or any other locality. He asked me what I paid my boys. How many natives had I recruited for indentured service and what had I earned? I answered and sweated, sweated and answered.

It must have been quite a spectacle for the crowd watching a twenty-year-old dressed in white, carefully shaved, move around in that little dock area, addressing himself to the District Officer, and occasionally trying to look bewildered, yet obliquely glancing at the audience.

I asked the court if I might place on the stand the principal witness for the defense, myself, so that he might tell his story of the raid.

"Consented to," the magistrate said.

I told of our trip inland. I described the little boy who carried my gun, how, without warning, spears had come flying at us, how my gun carrier had been pinned to the ground by spears, how I fired so as to scare off the raiders.

"Did you shoot a man?" I was asked.

"We were greatly outnumbered," I parried. "I might have."

I showed my wounded heel, where the scar was big and evident. I received that before I fired, I told the court.

I put Jack Ryan on the stand. I knew as I questioned him, and as he spoke, that if I got out of a long jail sentence this was the man who would make that possible. Jack was well spoken. He told of his years in the jungle. He said that whatever New Guinea was now, or would become, would be a result of the coming here of enterprising souls who dared the rugged life to bring industrial advance to the region. He wound up his testimony by suddenly saying to the District Commissioner, "What would you do out there if you were suddenly raided and fired on without warning?"

I took the initiative. "Your Honor, I am accused of murder. Where is the body of the man I am said to have killed?"

The law called for a corpus delicti—I hoped—but I couldn't remember.

The prosecution demanded the same of me. Where was the body of my gun carrier?

I produced a witness, one of the Kanakas who had gone on trail with me, and he declared that he knew Ateliwa to be speared to death and pinned to the ground. Likely he was still to be found in the spot where he was killed, for it was the custom of raiders to leave their victims where they fell.

The trial was held up while these crucial points were determined.

They sent an expedition to the scene. There they found the body of Ateliwa, which confirmed that he had been speared to death and that I had, in all probability, fired in self-defense. But they were unable to find the body of the tribesman I had shot.

I got off, but I think if it had not been for Jack Ryan I might have been in jail there until this day.

It is stupid to be your own counsel, I decided. I'd never do it again.

Apparently, as far back as I can remember, I always seem to have needed a lawyer.

I gave myself another piece of counsel. Get out of the gold field region for a while.

About the only note of relief I can suggest, in this episode, is that it was probably the only situation I was ever in where no woman was involved.

I still owned my own claim at Edie Creek. It hasn't been worked. I didn't really know its value and I didn't have the means to get at it. Prospectors entered into all kinds of deals, and just before I left I struck up an arrangement with Mrs. Giblin. If and when I returned, she said, and I wanted to work her claim for her, she would stake me to the prospecting costs. I would work the field and we would split fifty-fifty on anything that came of it.

So as I took a schooner back to Kavieng I had an interest in two plots of mountain earth eight thousand feet up, in dark New Guinea.

Back in Kavieng I caught a "nail in the hoof," Australian for gonorrhea—or black pox, as they also called it thereabouts—and I got a virulent form of the disease. At first I thought it had something to do with my malaria, which was a recurrent malady of mine. I went to a doctor and he told me what I had. He gave me probably what could be the worst treatment a man could get: a series of applications of permanganate of potash injected into the urethra. When my friends learned what I had, I became a sort of hero—but I was terrified.

In juvenile misjudgment I thought I would get rid of it quicker by doubling the dose. That was almost fatal, for I nearly burned out my bladder. I had to enter a hospital and I lay there sick and suffering. I realized I couldn't get correct treatment in New Guinea. I had to get back to Sydney, fast.

I was broke, but I must get the fare to take the ten-day steamer cruise to southern Australia. My partner in *The Maski* enterprise came to my aid. Dusty Miller practically forced a hundred pounds on me. Weakened and upset, I left the hospital.

The night before the ship sailed I got into a poker game with the toughest players in Kavieng: miners from the gold fields and a couple of rich plantation managers, any of whom had much more to gamble with than I.

We played all night. Half of the time I didn't know what I was doing except that I held fantastic cards. Always a wild bettor, in the morning I was ahead four hundred pounds.

This was a fortune. In a few minutes the ship would sail and it was fair of me to quit the game. I picked up my hat and bag and said, "Fellows, see you some other time. If you want revenge, you can see me in Sydney."

In Sydney I entered into prolonged treatment. I wasn't in bed but I received the primitive medication for gonorrhea which prevailed before the penicillin age. It was the most extraordinary torture ever devised outside of the Spanish Inquisition. Youngsters of the present generation, with antibiotics to cure venereal diseases, cannot ever know the enormity of the jump from the early painful treatment to the present chemical cures.

I stayed about Sydney for months, concentrating on trying to get cured. I was told to stay away from alcohol, and that wasn't so hard. I managed to float, a man about town, for a while, without getting work. I saw Naomi Dibbs once or twice, and that curious, reserved nonphysical relationship, as of old, was still there. We even revived our engagement.

But I spent my money too freely and soon it ran out. I had to look for work again. Jobs were scarce. I was still a man without a single training, with no calling, no profession. I had in those days some wit, youth, good looks, charm, I guess, some knowledge of how to work men, but skills? Nothing. My stock-in-trade was a rather baronial air.

I had to switch to a lower-grade residence. I lived in a place called the Sailor's Rest in Woolamallo, at ninepence a night. I was in a dormitory with forty other bums. When you went to sleep at night you had to put your shoes underneath the bedposts. Otherwise you might wake up in the morning and find yourself permanently barefoot. I kept some resemblance to a crease in my trousers by placing them in newspapers between the bed and the mattress. My capital I calculated very carefully. I could remain at the Sailor's Rest for a few more nights before going to the Sydney Domaine, where I could sleep on newspapers in a cave.

Meantime I had to invent some method of eating. The hungrier I got the more ideas came and were dismissed. Then one day. . . . Usher's, a famous hotel on King Street, was generous with their counter lunches: large hams that made you drool; roast beef, cheeses, pretzels. Naturally a customer was expected to buy something, but I overcame this hurdle.

I would saunter in, look around the room haughtily, casually meander over to the bar and buy a pack of Capstan cigarettes, price sixpence.

I would go over to the lunch counter in an even more leisurely manner and help myself to as much ham and cheese as I could nonchalantly swallow.

That assuaged the pangs of hunger. I sat down at a table and glanced at the newspaper. Then I sauntered out, strolled to the corner, and ran like hell over to the Carlton Hotel.

Outside the Carlton was a market where vendors would sell you anything from shoelaces to their sisters. I stood on the corner with the rest to sell my packet of Capstans. "A brand-new pack of cigarettes, cobber. I don't smoke myself." Thus I recouped my capital.

But they got wise to me at the free lunch and I had to stay away from their counter for a while.

For three days I was ravenous. For three full days nothing in my pocket and nothing in my belly.

One day I passed by a shop window in William Street, back and forth, looking at a cutlet in that window. It was surrounded by a few green peas—and many flies. The restaurant was on the side of a very steep hill, and I must have walked up and down that hill about two dozen times in the next three days. Every time I looked in the window I drooled. The meal cost one shilling and sixpence—for the whole plate. Even the flies on it looked attractive.

I got a job as a bottle-smeller. My work was to sit in front of a great pile of bottles and sniff them to find out whether any foreign substances such as kerosene or turpentine had been put in them. If they smelled bad, separate them from the others. This way the factory foreman learned which bottles needed special washing before being refilled with the soft drink. At the end of one day's smelling I had a ring around my nose that gave me the look of a prize bull, but by that time I didn't know one odor from another. Only that the job stank.

After I was paid, my first thought was to go get that cutlet in the window on the hill. My mouth was filled with wishful saliva as I headed for the joint. I had to have it. I had the price in my pocket now. But when I got there it was gone. I stared at the empty window, wondering what they had done with this cutlet. I walked in and asked for it. "Where is the cutlet you had in the window?" The fellow didn't know what I was talking about.

I ordered Australian oysters, probably the most stupid thing you could eat after three days of hunger, several glasses of beer, and to top that off I stuffed myself with tongue sandwiches, lean on tongue, liberal on bread. I swelled up like a football, but by God I had a bellyful and was ready to face the world again.

I resumed calling at Usher's.

There I had a casual meeting with a very big man at the bar. He had huge hands, each big as a ham, and he seemed powerful. He was young, about my age, good-looking, and he talked of his athletic feats. Braggart, I thought, and I didn't take to him. His name was Fred McEvoy. I couldn't know that later, in America, he would become a famous sportsman, destined to a career of marrying rich women, and he would become my close lifetime friend. He had a genius for wringing all the fun there was out of life—a worthy pursuit.

The barmaids at Usher's got to know me, and they turned their eyes when they saw me get my daily helping. One day one of my favorites, a Scotch girl named Alice, who could handle beer glasses like a juggler, called me over and told me someone had been in there looking for me. She had learned that an English company was interested in my gold claim at Edey Creek. Not for the gold that might be in the earth, but because the site was between two large leases belonging to this company, and it interfered with some development they had in mind.

That afternoon I sold my little plot of gold field for the equivalent of $5,000!

I must have celebrated unduly because a day or two later, when I was sober, I discovered that I was the owner of a new yacht called the *Sirocco*. I paid $4,000 for it. I had also paid off some debts, and when my vision cleared I had this ship and several hundred dollars.

The boat was in Sydney harbor. I looked her over and wondered how and why I ever bought her. She was a cutter about forty-four feet long and so narrow in the beam that you could lie across her. The boat had been built in 1881. What the hell could I do with her? She was too big to ship to New Guinea on board some other steamer so that I could use her for inter-island work in that area. There was no cargo space, and her six- or seven-foot draught was too much for the reef-studded waters of the islands.

Not knowing what to do with this new possession, I turned about and did perhaps the craziest thing I ever did. I suppose it is rather lucky that I am alive to tell of it.

I decided that New Guinea might still be lucky for me, figuring that if this deal had come my way, others still bigger might fall to me. Maybe I would still strike gold there too. I ought to go back.

I set out, with three seafaring friends I met about Sydney, on a three-thousand-mile trip to the mainland of New Guinea via the coastal waters of Australia.

For the next few months, all through the spring, summer and fall of 1930, the *Sirocco* crawled up the coast. We stopped every day or two at one or another of the ports. We were short of cash, and we were in all kinds of sea trouble.

My letters to my father, while the *Sirocco* moved northward through the reefy waters of the Australian coast, make strange rereading.

It was around that time when I affected the air of a man of distinction, I suppose, for I addressed my notes to Father as "dear Pater."

No matter. Pater never got dull letters from me. If I didn't ask him for money and excite him that way, I hinted about my latest jailing, or the most recent visit to some house of special integrity.

We reached Townsville on the northeastern coast of Australia:

> "SIROCCO"
> TOWNSVILLE
> 27TH JULY 1930

DEAR PATER:

We're leaving tomorrow morning at 2 A.M. direct to Cooktown, a couple of days there—out to Lizard Island for a day or so and then the pièce d'résistance—Samarai or—in the event of cyclone —Davy Jones' Locker.

I suppose you're wondering what became of us at Rockhampton and how we managed to exist. The answer to the second is that by dint of judicious advertising setting forth the mystery and lure of the Tropics, I managed to recruit a fifth member of the crew and separate him from fifty "ironmen." He has more cash than that, is a hard worker, and can do almost anything he sets his hand to so my conscience is not crying aloud to me in the dead of night.

As regards our stay in Rockhampton, I blush to admit that my lucid intervals were not sufficiently frequent nor of long enough duration to permit of any detailed description of the city. I plainly remember noticing, however, that a pub graces the corner of each street causing such a sameness of perspective to the stranger that geography becomes a very necessary adjunct.

Met bad company there—two of the most wonderful journalists on the local paper. One of them a Red Rag Communist—especially in wine. The other an ex-footman at Government House—among other things both of them very clever fellows and delightful company. Walker, the Communist, was once a member of the underworld—Squzzy Taylor's gang—and a pug of no little renown.

He it was who, in a drunken moment, arranged for me to fight Bud Riley who was in Jimmy Sharman's Troupe. How Sharman came up to me, grabbed me by the hand and told me to be outside his tent the next afternoon at 3 (thus giving me the first intimation that I was booked to fight on the morrow) and to be ready to accept Bud Riley's challenge, how I being at the time prepared to fight Dempsey & Tunney both together (for such effect has firewater on the brain of man) agreed, and how the next day (being in much the same mood) took the biggest hiding in my life but managed to stay the prescribed 3 rounds and collect 5 pounds from the chagrined Sharman, is all too long and a sad story (I couldn't eat for a couple days), but it's a story I'll never forget in all the days of my life and which I'll have to tell you about when we next meet.

We had the J. C. Williamson Chorus out with us on the river. Caused the *Sirocco* to look like a flagship or river excursion steamer. A merry day—with young maidens everywhere from stem to stern.

One of them by the way, a little girl named Ray Fisher, knew you, having stayed at Pressland House a few months ago, but she wouldn't have anything to do with me when she discovered I wasn't a Catholic but was a Protestant Renegade. And when I attempted to instill into her a few of the principles of Agnosticism she regarded me as a thing unclean but promised to tell some beads for me the next morning. . . . Tell them what?

I don't think I'll be able to return to Sydney for a long time because of Naomi. I haven't got the moral courage to write her a straight letter telling her it's no go and in the meantime we're officially engaged in the papers. . . . Of course it's hardly her fault either and although I didn't suggest the married state I just allowed things to drift that way. Now look at the mess! I've been in them before but never to this extent. . . .

Love, from your son,

ERROL

About three weeks later the *Sirocco* arrived at Cooktown, the last port of any consequence at the northernmost tip of Australia. From there we would make the sea jump to the southern tip of New Guinea.

My letters to my father in the New Guinea period are down to about ten that are extant, and this is the one I sent to him as we prepared to head for the New Guinea mainland.

"Sirocco"
Cooktown
17th August 1930

Dear Pater:

We're leaving for Lizard Island day after tomorrow and will probably put in the night there cooking a goat and two fowls I "captured" here—chased the confounded goat for about a mile before I cornered him. The fowls—both of them noble birds—died all unaware of approaching fate until plucked from their perch in the dead of night by the neck—one must live, a Communistic tenet which I heartily support.

I'll certainly send you a cable as soon as we arrive in Samarai wherever you are, but of course, Dad, there's not the slightest need for concern. It's a good time of the year now—no cyclones about—and even if bad weather is encountered, the prevailing winds are all from the south and we can run before them.

As I mentioned in my telegram I shall probably make up toward Dutch New Guinea. From reports I've heard things are bad in Mandated Territory while in the Dutch there is practically no authority at all—a condition eminently suitable to a humble adventurer seeking the elusive shekel.

But one thing I've made my mind up upon. When I've got a credit balance of several hundred I'm going to take myself to Cambridge to study History & Literature—I've been coming to the conclusion for a long time that the most vital thing in Life is to be able to understand something about it. God, what profundity, eh?

All my love and respect, Dad,

from
Errol

We piloted our ship into the rather fine harbor of Port Moresby. We arrived during the rainy season and the whole area was brilliant green. The region seemed beautiful to me and I poked around searching its resources.

About thirty miles from the port the Laloki River flowed through an emerald countryside. I fell in love with it. My partners made their way back to Australia, but I decided to settle there.

With funds I collected from the sale of the *Sirocco* I started a tobacco plantation.

First I built a rather comfortably large house of the local materials, palm and bamboo, in which to live. The lodging was along the banks of the river, and it went up swiftly, with the aid of my Kanaka labor staff. Within a week or two, I was ensconced in a place roomy enough for me to move about in, with plenty of shelves for books, tables and chairs for company, and a decent bed.

Around me, from Laloki to Port Moresby, was a territory plentiful with nutmeg, rattan cane, the okari nut, bananas, mangrove, coconuts, and sandalwood. There were fish in the river, and the natives brought food to my door. For a pence or two I could have the fruit of the region.

Tobacco was not being grown hereabouts. The earth seemed suitable to it, and Australia might be the market. This crop had advantages. You could grow it in a season and didn't have to wait ten years for it to mature as you did with coconuts.

For months I went from daylight till dusk, keen on becoming a planter. It was great to construct things and to watch the place grow under my guidance and management—and ignorance.

I borrowed a government tractor to open up the soil. One of the natives ran it very well, and I watched as the machine moved industriously along the banks of the Laloki.

I wrote feverish letters to my father, telling him of my work, how I built a curing barn, directing the native labor, and how I modeled a furnace to use in curing the tobacco. I had learned about it from books sent to me from America, and from other planters.

As always, when I didn't know what to do, I yelled "Boss Boy! Carry on!" and the foreman of my tobacco workers knew how to direct his men down the long rows of seed beds.

Often I would stop and look at the great field that was growing, with slashes of cheesecloth shades protecting the tobacco beds.

It wasn't easy. Getting a furnace to operate just about turned me gray —figuratively anyway—but it appeared we were going about it the right way, for other planters came around and saw how the tobacco grew, and were good enough to observe, reluctantly, "Flynn, you deserve to succeed, anyway—if only because you're too ignorant to know better."

There was only one thing wrong. I was alone, too much alone, the only white man for miles around, and sometimes I got tired of reading books and was restless.

One day my Boss Boy, Allaman, took me inland a few miles to his village. As we came into the little colony of bamboo- and palm-covered huts a girl ran forward. I hadn't known Allaman had a daughter.

Her shoulders were almost ripe corn and her hair, which wasn't crinkly, reached down to them. She wore a grass skirt, and that was all. Above her *lava-lava* garment, her little up-pointing breasts were so symmetrical and perfect as to have been attached by some means I didn't stop to explain to myself. Her skin was like shining satin, a color of light mahogany, and as I stared at those up-pointing breasts my breath held—or must I resurrect the cliché that my heart stood still? I just stared at her and could only gulp.

I knew I had to buy her.

I had to have her.

Her eyes looked downward to the ground. I didn't realize she was terribly embarrassed and I was also fitful with a shyness I was a long time in overcoming.

I had to have this downcast-eyed little woman, or girl, whichever, for there is no such thing as age in New Guinea. A girl generally matures at about twelve. You can tell such a girl is mature by her actions, her looks. You can also tell she is a woman by the way she keeps the mosquitoes off your back with bush herbs.

Tuperselai!

What a beautiful name, I said in pidgin talk, slowly.

When I bought her off Allaman for two pigs, one fuse of English shillings (called fuse because the bank wrapped them so that they looked like a plug of dynamite) and some sea shell money, I didn't know that she hated me. It appeared that she had a boy friend in the village, a handsome chap, and she didn't want to leave him. But I was some time in learning that.

She was absolutely beautiful, but at first sulky. I could see she resented me very much. She had been sold into slavery to me, for I knew that that was what it amounted to; so I must woo her and show her that I was no harsh owner.

We returned to my tobacco plantation and I set about for the next few days trying to change her opinion of me. A little kindness, a little sweetness, and she softened. After a couple of days, finding I was not the kind of monster she had expected, she shyly drew closer, became attentive in a servant's kind of way.

She could sing, but never gaily; only sadly and lugubriously. She could dance, but her dancing wasn't much. She seemed so tense, her nerves seemed to come out of the ends of her palms. I could see by the way she twisted her hands.

At night when I came back from the tobacco plantation, it was touching to sit down to rest, and she came over to me, kneeled before me and washed my feet, toe by toe. As she did this I would look at her pleading eyes, and didn't feel like reading.

In the evening, sitting there trying to read in the light of a hurricane lamp, lost in Maeterlinck, the writer-naturalist popular in that day, I could feel her presence close by. Then she would come and wash my back with scented bush herbs and water, running her hands softly over my back. I forgot Maeterlinck. Nobody else had ever done this to me and I thought I sensed tenderness beneath her finger tips.

A few days later, as her sense of familiarity increased and I made no move toward her sexually, she took it upon herself to wash my hands between my fingers. She didn't care if my fingernails were grimy, because she knew I had been working. By now her expression changed.

We could look at each other squarely and honestly, and there was an emotion between us. I knew this and she knew this. Though she had been sold to me, what she feared now was that her father might want to take her back to their village.

She was delightful, especially when she took my big paw in both of her little hands, and when she pinpointed flowers in her hair and put shells around her head. Her hips were slender, her legs long. Mostly we stared at each other and spoke in many syllables, each learning word by word the other's tongue.

Tuperselai was almost scentless, a bit like hibiscus. Occasionally, as we hung about our house, or moved by the river, there wafted over us the fragrance of frangipani, and the rich, harsh smell drove me wild. How do you tell a Melanesian, "I want to go to bed with you"? How do you say, "But look, if you don't want to go to bed with me, I understand. Please give me an answer." I had an interpreter—the cook—since I didn't speak the Mutuan language that well then, and I suppose the cook screwed it all up, because I didn't make much headway with the beauty.

How do you tell somebody who doesn't speak your language, "Oh, Tuperselai, you are beautiful and I love the way you put your hand in mine. I like the way we go swimming. How do I tell you that I am filled with emotion?" In the Mutuan language, numbering about three hundred words, there is no such word as "emotion."

Yet in a way we had long conversations, neither of us knowing the language of the other. She caught on to some of my English words. The word "swim." Very good. So down the river we went to swim. She repeated the word "crocodile," and she would make a gesture with her two hands simulating the jaws of the creature.

We swam and drifted in the shallow Laloki River.

Its name meant good-by, and when it twisted and traveled it seemed almost to sigh good-by.

I shall always hear you, Laloki of my younger days: good-by. Is that what you murmured?

We would let ourselves be carried down by the current of the stream, and on the shores, in a secluded nook of shade, at last we made love. I can only say that I don't know whence again my heart pounded so.

The river curved. It went in a strange curve, a bend like a big python. One day Tuperselai let out a yell of fright.

There was a log in the river. I jumped on it and paddled as hard as I could to where she had put a spear through the head of a small crocodile. The creature was five or six feet long, and she had planted the spear right between his eyes.

Tuperselai was enchanted when I looked at the gruesome sight of the blood flowing down the river. She pointed at the still-living croc, shouting and dancing, so that those little breasts jumped up and down. She was like a child as, her two hands clasped together, she called out in the Mutuan language, "There he dies! There he dies!"

We stripped this crocodile and she cooked him that night. He was delicious, like a young tender lobster or crayfish.

Sometimes, as I frolicked with Tuperselai by the riverbanks or lay with her in the soft sand at the shore, I thought I heard or sensed the subtle *gura-gura* mystique of the region. Little people, they said, like the leprechauns of Ireland, who watched out for you. Maybe it was only the eyes of the Melanesian natives spying on us.

Tuperselai and I drifted.

So, in our language of gestures, our smiles, closeness, Tuperselai and I made love and it was a beautiful thing.

I was less alone and soft-aired Laloki River is one of my most precious poetic memories.

I was myself now, and for a while I even turned away from books.

The only conclusion I can draw is that a man and a woman should never speak the same language.

> One ship sails east, The other west,
> By the selfsame gales that blow.
> 'Tis the set of the sails, And not the gales
> That shows you the way to go.

That is just about the inner theme of my life, I suppose. Those lines have often gone through my mind, so much so that I might even have written them.

One day, as I watched the tobacco fields, in full leaf, and wondered whether I'd be able to cure the crop properly and then sell it, a cable arrived from Tahiti, forwarded from Sydney three thousand miles below:

TAHITI

MR. ERROL FLYNN

SAILORS REST

WILAMALOO, SYDNEY

OFFER YOU FIFTY POUNDS ALL EXPENSES COME AT ONCE PLAY PART OF FLETCHER CHRISTIAN IN PICTURE ENTITLED IN THE WAKE OF THE BOUNTY BEING MADE TAHITI. CABLE COLLECT.

JOEL SWARTZ

Swartz had said he would get in touch with me some day! Now here it was! I would be in a film! Suddenly my personal heritage seemed to pay off. Shades of Midshipman Young, who had been companion to Fletcher Christian during the mutiny of the *Bounty!*

I stared at the tobacco field, all my fortune in it, all my labor of several months. The leaves were green. The sun was warming the crop. I could smell the tobacco leaf.

I called my Boss Boy and rapid-talked in pidgin, the language of Papua, made up of German, English and Melanesian words. "Allaman, yufela Big Boss. I go mek ship." I motioned with the fingers of my two hands the number of weeks I might be gone, eight or ten.

"Ai, Taubada."

"Yufela mek tobac job."

"Ai, Taubada."

"Yufela care for him house."

"Ai, Taubada."

"Yufela tek care Tuperselai."

"Yes, Taubada. Allaman tek. Keep for Taubada."

I went into Port Moresby, cabled Swartz, and took ship northward to the famed Tahiti in the Polynesian isles.

For three weeks I worked with Swartz in the picture—without the least idea of what I was doing, except that I was supposed to be an actor. We made much of the film in Maatvai Bay, where a hundred and forty years earlier Captain Bligh had anchored in the *Bounty*.

I was startled to note that I could remember the lines I had to say. I could commit lines to memory and not falter. There were just so many that had to be mastered each day. It was a big discovery in a way.

The experience came swiftly and it seemed to go swiftly. But it was different than anything I had ever done before: so much at variance with digging earth, selling Kanakas the idea of becoming "workers," carrying guns for real in the gold fields.

I had touched on something that the world called an art form and it had affected me deeply.

That was my first movie job and I was never able to convince people of it. When I arrived in Hollywood later and mentioned that I bore this relationship to Fletcher Christian's companion and that I had had my beginnings in a film playing the part of Christian, they looked at me as if with unbelief.

Nor did they believe that I came from Tasmania, Australia and New Guinea. No one believed anything else I ever said about my life and adventures in that part of the world.

The most notable disbeliever was the famous Mark Hellinger, who, when I got to know him in filmdom, would come around to see me just to listen to my stories. He thought I was a magnificent liar, a modern Baron Munchausen, with a wonderful imagination. He would listen and try not to have a spasm.

When I confronted this strange look of incredulity in one person after another in Hollywood, when I saw that they all wanted to believe I was an Irish lad grown up in Ireland and come over straight from Ireland, when I saw that this was what the world wanted to believe, what newspapermen themselves wanted to believe, I thought, let 'em. I'll deny nothing. Someday, I said to myself, I'll tell the whole damned story anyway—if anyone's curious.

I had a hunch that I wasn't going to make any fortune from the tobacco crop, good as it looked. The big problem in New Guinea was to find a market for your produce—whether it was tobacco or anything else. Transportation wasn't worked out well and you had to move things a long distance, which was costly. The Australian Government didn't spend much money on New Guinea expansion.

I had read about stock operations and hatched the idea of floating a tobacco corporation. Get people to buy in on my plantation. Have money to work with. Expand the area of cultivation, find means of selling it. I decided to go back to Sydney and try to interest business-men there in joining with me in forming my tobacco corporation.

I went to the businessmen around Port Moresby, but getting letters of recommendation was tough. I was astonished to read about myself, in one note after another: *To Whom It May Concern:* This gentleman is honest, enterprising, imaginative, and a good man to do business with —*To Whom It May Concern:* I have long known Mr. Flynn and have great confidence in him as a budding financier. I heartily recommend him to any and all businessmen interested in developing a large and profitable enterprise—*To Whom It May Concern:* The young gentleman bearing this letter has done business with me many times and it is a pleasure to say to all to whom he comes, here is a fine character and a substantial citizen—*To Whom It May Concern:* This is Mr. Errol Flynn, mariner, tobacco grower, man of enterprise. He will go far. He has my best wishes in any enterprise in which he invests himself.

Who, me?

I hardly knew myself—even though I'd written them myself.

I gathered together a parcel of photographs of the plantation, a folio full of facts on production and costs, and other pertinent papers into a bundle about two feet high. I would parlay this to a fortune, if I could.

I wrote to my father and commented on this development: *What a scene for me, Dad! inviting hardheaded businessmen to trust their hard-won cash in my hands!*

Actually the businessmen around Port Moresby figured I stood a good chance of floating twelve thousand pounds. If I set up the deal, I intended to work the plantation for about a year and then get out of New Guinea.

Why only a year, Dad? I wrote. *That's what I'm writing you about and it's going to be extremely difficult to explain and make you under-stand that I'm more in earnest now than I've ever been before. I've acquired ambition.*

Yes, I had. I think I acquired it after my trip to Tahiti. The bug of writing or acting, or in some other way leading, was planted in me forever.

One way or the other I was going to get my hands on some money and get the hell out of the South Seas.

The reading I had done must have given me some polish. Certainly it steamed up my ambitions. At the time, I was studying the lives of various great lawyers of England and the United States. I knew that I had certain forensic faculties. My articulation was good. I practiced speaking. I feel that I could have made a good lawyer. I had the appearance, and a courtroom lawyer is also an innate ham, nothing more than a courtroom Barnum.

Beyond these instincts for public life I had political feelings. I was even emotional about them. I was going to be Sir Galahad and clean up every part of the world. There was a touch of the revolutionist about me. It was nothing more than a pipe dream, but idealistically I was on sound ground.

For even way down there, I got hold of the literature of Communism. In that day, 1928 through 1931 or so, there were some big names out of Russia, Radek, Zinoviev, Stalin. The Sydney library even sent Karl Marx to me, and I'll wager I'm one of the few people in the world who ever read that bore from beginning to end. Living as I did in New Guinea by myself, it seemed the only answer to the world's problems. Around me was this paleolithic world that seemed so backward and so in need of some kind of ethic. Marx, it seemed, had the answer. In short, I was one of a breed of the young men who filled the Western world at that time. But now, rereading him, I still find him the dullest sonofabitch you can "opiate" yourself with. How he could have spearheaded such a giant movement in the world was thrilling in my early twenties. Someone, I don't know who—it might even have been me—said, "Any man at the age of twenty-five who is not a Communist has no heart: any man who still is at the age of thirty-five has no head."

I even sent away to Australia for a correspondence course in ballroom dancing. I would take a chair and dance around the room, pushing the chair and trying to get rhythm.

The fact is I was consuming books of all sorts with genuine greed, with more interest than if I had been studying at Cambridge or Trinity College, Dublin. I knew now I had to make another effort to overcome my lack of formal schooling, somehow to make up for my delinquent and disinterested years.

These were my character-forming years—for good or what have you. Many influences worked on me: the savagery of the jungle, my father's culture, my mother's not-too-expert maternal make-up, but certainly artistic leanings.

I was torn between the social patterns of the West and the free-flowing tribal life of New Guinea. There was the impress on me of Melanesian girls.

I read, studied, experimented at mental self-improvement, as in the backdrops I heard always the steady tones of the *garramut* from the hearts and souls of my antediluvian New Guinea friends.

I had arrived in New Guinea four and one-half years earlier. I was now twenty-two. I had reached the end—I hoped—of a prolonged adolescence.

> But [as I wrote my father], if it's been slow it's been good and the consciousness of life I now have is perhaps all the more thorough on account of these years here. Two old friends of mine came over from Edey Creek the other day. One of them, Jack Ryan, is 50 years old. It was he who was mainly instrumental in having the charge of murder squashed against me in the other Territory. The other fellow is the same age and he's going away for good on account of blackwater fever—underground I mean.

I told my father how both these fellows had come to this country at the same age as I, but they had hung on here, always hoping to get to the other side of some hill that always looked prosperous—but they'd never amounted to a damn, even though they were admirable men. Seeing them, listening to them talk about their foredoomed life in New Guinea, hearing them regret they hadn't gotten out when they were younger, threw me into a panic. Would I end up that way? I knew that Jack Ryan would hang on, he'd die here—but did Flynn have to?

I confided to him that I was beginning to doubt the long odds and the big gold strike, or the big fortune in copra or tobacco. There was grave danger I'd fritter away my life here in these strange wastes.

It came out of me, in that letter dated May 24, 1932, what I wanted to be, my secret dream—the one I've never realized—the dream that worked up there inside of me when I read by the hurricane lamp at night, and felt force and energy growing in me, and decided I wanted to conquer—not a colonial land, like some early-day Columbus—but the West, like a man of today:

If you remember, Pater, it's always been my most cherished ambition, if I ever made money here, to do something worth while. I intended to go to Cambridge and read for the Bar, knowing full well that natural advantages suited me for that profession, and realizing I possess one really excellent advantage of an almost congenital knowledge of human nature, which New Guinea has accentuated. Forgive me blowing, but I know it's so.

I hoped to get called up and then try and keep going in the first lean years by writing. I may still be able to do it by going home in 2 years time but if I wait any longer it will be too late and I'll be anchored here for good—or rather bad.

I'm conscious of a lack of education whenever I try to write anything really serious. I eschewed education mainly through my own impulsiveness and a distaste for the grind of the uninteresting parts. But I also missed it because I thought it would be a load off your shoulders financially at a time when you were up to your neck in debt. I suppose it did ease the strain too.

In my present illiterate, almost unintelligent, uneducated condition, my chances of ever doing much worth while in literature are rather negligible. Singularly enough I've never wanted to read Letters at Cambridge—but have always hankered for the Bar, which appeals to me more than anything in life.

It is sometimes permissible to go up to Cambridge without first passing the entrance matriculation. You are given permission to read for it at the end of the first or sometimes the second year. I could probably manage on three hundred pounds a year or less, as my time would be devoted to study exclusively and moreover I could earn a bit from writing as I'm doing now (my income in last six months or so has been twenty pounds—colossal, isn't it? But it could be a lot more if I could write what people like instead of what I like).

Dad, what if I fail here to float this show? I'm getting out, anyhow, of New Guinea, and will try free-lancing in London, if the worst comes to the worst. But this is the crux— Would you put me through Cambridge? A big thing to ask, I know. 3 years at 300 pounds is 900 pounds, and another year in the Inns of Court at something less—a bad investment, I must admit!—on the face of my performance to date. But I know I could get through it if you were prepared to take the risk and make the sacrifice.

For God's sakes, don't think I somehow expect you to educate me and give me a profession as a sort of paternal duty or obligation. I deliberately chose the bed I'm sweltering on at present, and unless you care to make the sacrifice I'm quite prepared to lie on it, unpleasant though it most decidedly will be.

I shall come to England immediately if I fail here. I suppose to analyze my gladness at the prospect of leaving, it would be discovered that Fear lies at the bottom of it—I don't trust my health after seeing so many of my friends taken out of here on a stretcher by blackwater. Good God, you never know who's going next lately— Dad, if you can make this sacrifice I'll try and make it worth your while. I'm no fool and New Guinea, with its enormous variety of queer customers, has taught me more about men than I'd learn in twenty years in a city like London. You never know—I might go far at the Bar if you'll give me the chance to try.

I, of course, never knew at the time that I'd be spending much of the rest of my life in court—not as a lawyer, but as a defendant, and that I was doomed, in part, to a life of the Bar anyway—both Bars.

Whatever Father's reasons, I think he was just simply moneyless. I never went to Cambridge, and he never asked me to come on to England to make a try at becoming another Gladstone.

I had to continue to scrap it out on my own—find my own directions—get out of New Guinea under my own sail—go where the winds would blow.

The winds blew south.

I decided to enter Sydney spectacularly.

I suppose I always had a sense of showmanship. Always. It was certainly present then. I needed to draw attention to myself so as to be able to approach the businessmen and put my solid proposition to them.

I brought eight Melanesian gentlemen savages from behind the Laloki district on board the steamer that took me south. They had never even seen the town of Port Moresby, and knew of the outside world only by rumor. They had seen one or two planes zoom overhead. They had heard guns bark. That was about all.

Yet I got hold of a dwarfish chieftain named Anitok one day, and with interpreters and my pidgin talk, I painted a picture of the great wonders of a land far away. Would he not like to go there with me and see it all and take some of his tribe? *They could go as they were.*

With a caseful of papers of the tobacco proposition, I boarded ship with the Stone Age men who were practically naked except for blazes of color. They wore white egret feathers in their headdresses, flowers behind their ears, and other adornments taken from birds, tree-climbing kangaroos and alligators. Ordinarily their penises were sheathed in some kind of cloth like jock, neatly wrapped, but I decided to outfit them with sailor pants when we entered Sydney.

As we reached Sydney Head and the beams of two lighthouses revolved, my Kanakas stood transfixed. Translucent shafts turned, and they giggled and guffawed when the light bathed them. Their fuzzy hair went straight up into the air.

We arrived at the waterfront and I took them through the streets. I observed the spectacle of them as they watched the spectacle of the city: cars, buses, bicycles, lights. They were astonished to see horses drawing carts. They had never seen or heard of a horse. They jumped up and down and emitted shrieks while the Sydney people stared at them and trailed.

I took them over to the Sydney *Bulletin*. I had been corresponding for the paper for the past six months, sending them news of New Guinea, chiefly of the Port Moresby area. They had even sent me a total of twenty pounds for the articles I wrote. I thought I'd like to work on the staff of a newspaper. I visualized myself as a great journalist. Writing itched in me.

We did get a considerable news story:

MR. FLYNN RETURNS FROM NEW GUINEA
WITH COMPANY OF PAPUANS
He Is Here to Make Stock Flotation in Tobacco

I moved about Sydney with my boys, quite the circus for several days. It would be all I could do to show these fellows the sights just a day or two longer and then arrange for their shipment back to the Laloki district. Fortunately I worked out a deal whereby they would partially work their way back.

I took them to Anthony Horden's, then the biggest department store in Sydney. They ran about the main floor with a tremendous excitement, observing it all—and they themselves observed by the customers and the help. They couldn't believe what they saw and heard: a clock, it ticked, an alarm rang.

We entered the elevator and it was a tense moment. Anitok took a stern grip on my arm. "Taubada, Taubada, we go to Big Master now?"

When the lift reached the third floor and we got out, I told him that Big Master, that is, God, had taken us safely there.

They ran through the toy shop, they stood in awe before the millinery, the *lava-lavas,* the ribbons, the bizarre colors. How universal it is, I thought, for men to be drawn to colorful clothes and personal body adornments.

Anitok made a purchase and gave a clerk his only one-pound note for some cloth. She took the money and put it in a little metal box, then placed the box on a wire over her head. She pulled a cord and the money darted down the line. Anitok asked for the cloth and he couldn't get it yet. He decided he'd been cheated. He raced down the aisle in pursuit of the vanishing change box. He traced it from counter to counter, running as fast as a monkey. The people stepped out of his way. The clerks quit work. He zigzagged for a distance, then lost trace of the flying box. He tried to find his way back to the counter. I had quite a time restoring order, trying to put things right.

I took them to the movies, a Wallace Beery picture. There was much gunplay in the picture. They knew about guns and were delighted when someone was shot. Just like civilized people.

When I got this band of Papuans back on board ship, I settled down to the business of approaching the biggest businessmen in Sydney.

I got nowhere—rapidly.

New Guinea was far away. They knew the handicaps of doing business of any kind there. Nobody yet had worked up any fortune by growing produce in the islands. It was too remote, it was a gamble, they didn't know me, they weren't sure of Melanesian labor.

I returned to the bar in the Usher's Hotel and there was the same bartender. "Remember me?" I asked.

"Sure, cobber," he replied. "What are you looking for now, free beer?"

"No, I'd like to buy you one for a change," I said, and proceeded to tell him how I used to make my living simply by buying a pack of cigarettes from him every day and using the free lunch counter.

"Do you think me and the boys didn't know what you were doing, cobber?" he said. "We got our money's worth just watching you strut in here every day as though you owned the hotel when anybody with one eye could tell your only capital was about a shilling. You think you're the only bloke that's ever been on his ass?"

I think now that that must have been my first public performance as an actor. When people ask me about it, I say that a long matinee run in Sydney was my first real role.

Yet I had one more moment of glory.

In the Wake of the Bounty arrived for its first showing at one of the big theatres. I made it known at once that I was in this picture, playing the part of Fletcher Christian. The Sydney *Bulletin* announced that Errol Flynn, tobacco grower of New Guinea and a former dockyard Sydney boy, just returned from the islands with eight Melanesians who had aroused much interest, was now the center of another novelty.

I called at the theatre and introduced myself. The manager was delighted. Would I not make an appearance on the evening of the first showing of the picture?

"And what is the fee, sir?"

"Well, won't this be good publicity for you and the picture?"

I made it clear I dislike work with no pay.

"Will three pounds do?"

You bet three quid would do.

That evening Naomi went to the theatre with me. The manager made an announcement before the picture was flashed on the screen. He said that Errol Flynn, who would appear as Fletcher Christian in the picture, was here, in person.

I was decked out in a bizarre out-of-date British uniform.

There were only two actors' wigs in Sydney they could find and they stuck one of them on me. It was parted in the middle and it came down in a pigtail in the back, blond, tied with a bow, not like Clark Gable wore in *The Mutiny of the Bounty,* and clapped over my ears so that I reminded myself vividly of an elderly keeper of a whorehouse in King William Street, a little place of some integrity which I was prone to frequent.

And so it was that I made my debut as a motion picture actor.

In a few weeks I was, as of old, back in the Sailor's Rest.

You either slept in your clothes, or on them. It was better to sleep on them, because if you turned them over to the management to hold for you till morning you would get them back deloused, wrinkled, dried, but with a foul grease or soup smell permeating them. As you walked in the streets anyone would know you had spent the night at the Sailor's Rest by the wrinkled, shrunk look of the chemically washed pants.

I tried to keep looking deloused, clean and white. I wore my New Guinea helmet and carried a cane. I held my head higher than ever because my pockets were emptier than ever—a sound policy, I've found.

I tried to move with an air of owning at least a small portion of Australia—and wondered how I could.

I was back at my old haunt, Usher's, snitching more than my fair share of cheese and ham and bread at the counter.

Then I met her, Madge Parkes: statuesque, auburn-haired, married, rich, charming, sophisticated. Age, crowding forty.

I was out of my depth with this woman of the world who had been everywhere, seen everything. Of course, I thought, as I set eyes on her, there is no hope for me here—she is unattainable, way beyond me. But as we chanced to meet in front of Usher's and she spotted me, somehow she had a different view of the possibilities. She moved toward me, sure-footed, without embarrassment, and asked some trivial question about street directions that merely led into animated talk.

She didn't make it obvious, as we met there in the street, but there was a simplicity with which she handled things. "Will you dine with me?" after a few instants of talk about street directions. Then, with a subtly inviting smile, "Do you like dancing?"

We dined, we danced. She was very clever about paying a bill. She wouldn't embarrass you by passing money under the table. It would just be paid. You never knew exactly how she took care of that, but there wasn't an instant when you had to strike the heel of your palm and stammer, "How could I have come out without my money . . ." She was well able to pay, and she did. You walked out of the restaurant or dance place, bewildered but not embarrassed.

We went for a swim, and in her bathing suit she was the most enchanting woman, with a figure such as you would see on a flashy man-appeal magazine cover, and with the air and walk of sophistication and ease. That was what intrigued me most: her ready smile and a charm that only a well-traveled Australian woman can have. But she was far too brilliant, too clever for me. What did she see in a type like me? Of the streets of Sydney and of hell, with a touch of the Woolamallo gang, with an arrogant air. And besides, flat broke.

I never will cease to wonder at the strange rapacity of some women —when they want something. Dr. Kinsey said that a woman only reaches her sexual prime at the age of thirty-five and she goes on flourishing in her love life till the age of fifty-five. I concur. You would think it would be the other way around. That young girls, for instance, in their early twenties, would be at the height of their sexual tempo. No, I'm for Kinsey.

Madge was a living example of this, and she was my first experience with a sophisticated world that I knew existed, but about which I felt fears and uncertainties.

To complicate this sudden and exciting courtship with her, there was, in the background, my renewed engagement to Naomi. This was a relationship on a higher plane than what ensued with Madge. In those days I believed that anyone who advocated long engagements was completely nuts. How in God's name are you supposed to stay at hand's length with somebody you are attracted to without getting down to this business of sex? I suppose it is possible, but it certainly wasn't with me. I only know if I touch the arm of a girl or woman who fires me, I have got to go as far as I can or as far as she will let me. The emotion rises. What are you supposed to do? Just say good night, or have a Coca-Cola, or something, and go home aching from the scrotum up? Nonsense.

With Madge this question never arose. She just definitely made up her mind that she was going to seduce me—period. She made no disguise of her intent.

She showed me a side of life which both terrified me and excited me and drove me completely mad, so that I went up into the sky, high, spiraling, not knowing what I was doing. Then, descending on a soft cloud, and coming back to my senses. She knew how a sweet, kind, or soft gesture could be just right at the right moment. She knew how to place a soft kiss on the side of the cheek when you were still panting, hot, ravenous. She knew what to do with a man—if that is what I could then call myself.

In any case Madge brought it out of me, my manhood. Taught me, started me, woke my understanding of the possible diversity and wonder of the female form.

I felt frustrated, really upset that I couldn't invite her out to the nicest places. Besides, what about Naomi? How do you handle a virtuous steady while you have a married woman on the side? Not easy; my mind was turbulent. Madge had loosed me from clear and responsible moves. Madge knew better than anyone how to excite the senses. Naomi had no idea of this. Madge could get undressed in such a way that you panicked to behold her. Her undressing was a beautiful act; a theatrical performance. I have seen others since, but never till then. The way she slid her dress off, slipped out of her panties in a dancer's gesture, and put out the light at the same time as she took her brassière off—giving me the most wonderful glance in that instant when the light flickered out. I wonder why women always leave their brassières on till the last?

Madge was my first experience of what a real woman could mean.

My father had learned that I was flat. The manager of Usher's called me into his office and smilingly asked me to sign a receipt for one hundred English pounds. I still don't know where he dug it up for me, but it took me no time to splash the lot on Madge. Broke again.

I saw the power of money more than ever. If a beautiful woman gave herself to you, what might you not be able to buy, if you had money, and you could select and choose and move at random through the wide world?

One night we lay in an anguishing tangle of arms and sensation, and I was waking. I sat up in bed and looked down at Madge, her beautiful hair on the coverlet of the pillow: a picture, a dream! A painting of a full woman, and she had been ineffably considerate toward me.

I got up, weak-kneed, and staggered to the bathroom. I knew now that what I had done had destroyed Naomi for me forever. I needed more than Naomi could ever give.

But there was no future for me in Madge either, and I am quite sure she knew it too. It was a mad affair for both of us. And somehow I sensed she was getting the better of the deal. Her demands were becoming nymphomaniacal. This will come as a surprise—but the vigorous, youthful Flynn constitution was beginning to crack and wilt under the strain.

A desperation of purpose and a wildness came over me.

At that moment my eyes lit on the dressing-room table. There, sparkling at me, were a few jewels, big ones, small ones. Some had gold or silver chains, and there were a couple of rings.

One quick thrust, Flynn, and you can sweep up this stuff, put it in your pants pocket and beat it. Hock 'em, make some dough—then bail 'em out and—

I looked back at the bed where she lay, a lovely picture, arms outspread, lovely full breasts.

This is criminal. Not the way to treat anybody. She has been so wonderful, how the hell can you think of this?

But this wrestling with the conscience took no more than a few seconds. I knew it was the most dastardly thing I had ever done. But I must.

Stealthily, I dressed. I scooped up the loot, tiptoed to the door, raced down the staircase like the joint was on fire.

I hurried through the streets. It was nighttime, but I didn't run because I knew that a running man excites suspicion. I beat it back to the Sailor's Rest, wondering how to hide the loot.

I knew enough not to put the stuff in the heel of a shoe. A false heel would be the first place anybody would look. Yet if I were found with the jewels I could go to jail. I could have said she gave them to me—and perhaps she would have if I had asked her to.

I was way way out of my depth.

She had put me into a kind of stew that sophisticated women seem always to have done to me, then and later.

In my cubicle, with barely four walls of plasterboard, I jammed into a small grip the little that I had, primarily my papers of the tobacco plantation and my letters of reference. Then I went for a special shaving brush. The handle was several inches long, and it had at the end a crown that unscrewed to reveal a hollow interior designed to hold a shaving stick. I placed the diamonds in there, put a small end of the shaving stick on top of the diamonds, screwed the crown back on.

If the authorities come around, I thought, and give me a going-over and find this, they are very clever and I've had it.

I had to get out of town right away. Already I fancied I could feel the hot breath of the law after me, sizzling the back of my neck. I felt lousy, despicable—robbing a woman who'd given me a certain kind of ecstasy generously. True, she got what she wanted. But what about the question of principle? Anyway, I consoled myself, it was really only a loan—short or long term, preferably long.

Sure as hell, the law did get after me, finding me on a boat that was set to leave Sydney. Two officers in plain clothes came aboard and got into my stateroom. The ship's captain was at hand, stewards were about, crewmen. There was a hue and cry as the police went through every piece of luggage. They immediately attacked the heels of my shoes to see if they were hollow. They were not. They went through the padding of my shoulders—nothing there. They left nothing to chance.

I stood there with a face, I hoped, scornful, bewildered. I watched them with my eyes going around wheel-like, and developed a sneer to make them feel ridiculous.

But they didn't feel or look ridiculous as they went through the razor, the washcloth, through my socks, shoes, my belt, fingering everything, feeling everywhere for a concealed compartment. I sneezed violently when they handled the shaving brush, hoping to distract them. I had a camera. They took it apart so that it could never be used again.

"Are you two shitheels finished?" I asked. "What do you want to do? Turn me upside down? Why don't you take one leg and you take the other and shake me? I might have them up my arse."

One said, "That would not be a bad idea."

"The first one of you bastards who raises a hand to me, I'll shove him right through that porthole, whether he fits or not."

I had the feeling that if anyone touched me I'd go berserk.

These guys took a good look at me. I must have looked to them like a cornered rat, dangerous to tangle with.

"Come and touch me, one of you yellow-livered sons-of-bitches! But watch yourselves!"

I was ready.

They looked at each other and decided against it, although together the two of them could easily have handled me.

They got off the ship.

I waited till the boat got way out and until it was nightfall. While the ship moved I felt guilty as hell, but now not as much as I should have.

Once alone, I unscrewed the bottom of that shaving brush and looked at the handful of jewels.

I pried open the platinum settings, threw them into the water, one by one by one by one. Here would be a beautiful ring; there would be one of the first baguette diamonds just coming into fashion at that time. The platinum went over the side. No identification—that was my theory, and sure enough I was right. From then on I had a stake.

There was something to be said for being a crook—if you got away with it. I had no illusions about myself, but felt happy. I had left Sydney as a thief, but what was done was done and it was all behind me.

That was the first and only time a woman ever had to pay for what she got from me.

Later, when I began to make hundreds of thousands a year, I hired people in Australia to locate Madge to repay her for the "short-term" loan of her jewels. But the agency never could—and anyway, I still feel that she got the best end of the stick. There should be a moral in this: that having money makes you honest.

I went north as far as the port of Brisbane. That was as far as I could get.

I couldn't sell the stones. I didn't try. That was my dot. If I could get to England, maybe I could convert them to cash.

So again I was flat broke.

I either had to swim back to New Guinea, or start walking.

That was what I did.

I started walking across Queensland, hoping to work my way and hop any available freights to the north coast of Australia.

New Guinea was still my best bet for making a big kill. I hadn't conquered it. Some had. A few had won out there and gone away with a big boodle.

I knew how rich and terrible that land was, its entrails loaded with gold, copper, all kinds of natural wealth, teeming with animal life and ablaze with rich verdure. I must take another flier at that gold, line my pockets, and move up into the big time.

I took a job at well digging in a place called Diamond Downs, in the interior of Queensland. This was a great expanse of near desert in the western side of Queensland, near Central Australia.

Day after day I sweated in the broiling sun as the shafts went lower and lower, looking for water in a land where there wasn't much. During the day I dreamed of nightfall when it was a bit cooler and there might be a faint breeze. When the breeze came it was fainter than that.

For two months we dug, and still no water.

How to get out of here? What was I doing here, digging, in a desert wild, while the world of New Guinea, which still beckoned me, lay to the north? I began to hope for that lucky destiny that I felt always hung over us Flynns, and that so far hovered over me.

I looked out around over the sea of dry earth and stared at the bleak white sky, and hoped wistfully for some kind of rescue.

Then it came.

A fellow named Copley stopped by the site where I was digging. He told me he worked for Jack Stirling, owner of a sheep ranch

eighty miles away. Mr. Jack had fifty thousand sheep, and he was rich.
"By God, I'd like to work for him."

"You would? What are you getting now?"

I told him. It was little enough. He said sheep droving paid better.
"What do you know about sheep droving?"

"Huh-h, what do *I* know about it? Only everything." My expression
looked pained, I hoped.

Copley explained that his job was to herd sheep from the Diamond
Downs region to Townsville, about eight hundred miles away. As sheep
could only travel a few miles a day, the trip would take a long time.
It would be tough finding water, let alone grazing.

"Okay, first let's go see Mr. Jack and have him hire you. Then you
and I take the sheep over-country. Remember, it might take half a
year."

I quit well digging and set out with Copley to Stirling's sheep
ranch or "station," as the Australians called it. It was located in one
of the most desolate parts of Australia.

Mr. Jack turned out to be a big, lean, hard-boned, out-back Australian, a man of the rough, tough shearing sheds. He was fantastically
rich, and sometimes had as many as a hundred thousand sheep on his
ranch. They had to keep going to the coast. I liked the way Mr. Jack
was enshelled, with this big house set smack in that desert spot. But
before I could get to know some sheep, there was work to be done on
the ranch.

At once I was thrown in with a gang of the toughest kind of men in
the world. The only thing that America ever had that would compete
with these fellows was the canallers in the early days of the country.
I'm told these were the toughest, craziest, fightingest breed ever produced in the States.

A sheep shearer, after he clipped the wool off 250 sheep, was
hungry enough to eat it. These fellows hired their own cooks. If the
cooks didn't come up with the right stuff, God help them. It was probably the last job they ever had and the last teeth in their mouths.

I was the newest man and had to begin at the bottom—the bottom of
the sheep itself—literally. I was one of four men in a line, an assembly
belt for sheep shearing. The first man took the young hogget, as a
young lamb was called, and he had to "dag" him; that is, he must
get rid of the bluebottle flies and all the accumulated excreta around
the tail. This he did by holding the sheep in his left hand, and his right
hand went in and "dagged" the sheep. He grabbed a handful of the

sheep's shit, tossed it aside, and passed the sheep on to the man next to him.

The next man was me.

All I had to do was stick my face into this gruesome mess and bite off the young sheep's testicles. Dag a hogget. I had good teeth. I put my nose into this awful-smelling mess, my teeth solidly around the balls of the six-month-old sheep, and took a bite while I held him upside down. My nose was in fur and ordure. I bit and spat out the product into a pile of what they called prairie oysters. We have them in America too: delicious to eat, but not delicious to remove. They said this was the most sanitary way to de-ball a sheep. After I was done, I passed the sheep onto the next man, who put a little coal tar on the same spot for purposes of cleansing and closing up the wound.

The sheep never let out a bleat. You bit, you spat out something like a couple of olives, and passed it on. Every day I had my proportion of oysters. The bluebottle flies swarmed all over me.

At the end of the day I was dripping with blood and sheep's ordure, smelling like . . . well, there is nothing, after that, to compare it with.

I was getting big money: six pounds a week and keep. But my jaws started to freeze up.

And I never did get a chance to herd sheep to the coast, the cards fell so fast.

Mr. Jack's two daughters were coming back from Townsville. The ranch hands were excited. They talked about how attractive the girls were. Both were at school. One was well advanced in a university. They were coming home to Papa and the sheep drivers.

The word couldn't have been truer. They were lovely. Two beauties right in the middle of the vast Australian desert.

On the evening of their arrival I cleaned up. I scrubbed all the sheep ordure off my face, got the smell of the hogget off my thighs, soaked my hands in an excess of soap, prettied myself up as much as I could and managed to make my appearance unobtrusively, but inevitably, before the two young ladies.

The older one, Aline, caught my eye, and I caught as much of her as I could.

She asked me what I was doing on her father's ranch.

"I'm dagging the hogget."

"How awful. I'll ask Father to put you on something else."

Father hardly had time to take me off of sheep's nuts. Aline and I had a swift and flourishing courtship.

The unexpected happened.

Why this should have been unexpected for me then—or now—I don't know.

I was in bed with Aline when Mr. Jack discovered us. He let out a bellow of rage and ran to another building for his shotgun.

"Good-by, darling!" I murmured frantically, slipping into my pants, feeling the sewn-up back pocket which contained my shaving brush handle filled with the "borrowed," so to speak, diamonds, grabbed a shirt and ran out as fast as I could.

I raced in the direction away from the building where I saw Mr. Jack headed.

I ran, and while ordinarily I couldn't go as fast as a horse, this one time I did!

Faster.

I continued to hear the gallop of horses' hoofs behind me for some time.

I just kept going. I broke all Olympic records, but had no official scorer, not even my conscience.

For five and a half days I went on foot across that godawful desert country. Again I had little or nothing to eat. Occasionally I found water at a well under saltbush. My feet were burned. My shoes were torn to shreds in the hots sands of the Queensland desert.

I had no money—but for once I didn't need it.

I reached a railroad siding. There I waited for a train to come along that might take me to Townsville on the coast. I waited all one day. At last along came one of those funny little old Australian trains, this one carrying cattle.

The tracks ran uphill and the trains would slow down, or come to a stop altogether, I figured.

I leaped on. As I had no hat I decided against going up on the roof to ride in the blazing hot Queensland sun. I squeezed in among the cattle. In a corner of the car, with a cow's flanks up against me and lots of cow shit all over, I hung onto the wooden bars.

I might comment that a cow's arse is little different from a sheep's—just larger.

Every once in a while a cow's tail switched around and caught me in the face. They mooed, they shat, they pushed against each other. They resented me and I resented them. But we were both nonpaying passengers, with no right to complain, and I was happy to be on my way.

All went fine till I was about a day's ride from Townsville. The train stopped to take water and the station dick found me and kicked me off.

Lost in this little spot of nowhere, I went into the only establishment that there was, a pub, a ramshackle place that passed as an eatery and hotel.

Once more a kindly female took pity on me.

I presume that even then my face and form were some kind of fortune. I must have known it, for apparently in times of distress I gravitated to females who were more likely to be kind to me than men, I was learning.

This time it was Sheila, the daughter of the hotelkeeper. I got around by the back door and she passed out plates of food to me—secretly.

I thanked her as well as I was able—secretly.

I had nothing else to give her except my devotion and some embraces. I was generous, however.

It wasn't hard to be—she was blond and lusty.

I lay in wait for the next train a day or two, carrying on this fretful fancy with Sheila, not wasting time.

The train I needed came along, and I bade a passionate but weaker farewell to the young lady.

The damned contraption came flying down the hill twice as fast as the train I had been thrown off of. It looked too fast for me, but it was now or never, and I had to make it.

I took a flying jump, grabbed hold of an iron bar that jutted out from a door and managed to get on, clawing to the side and holding on like a fly on a wall while the train barreled on.

The doors opened out. I couldn't get inside, only hang on to these steel fixtures, and feel the earth tearing by beneath me, hear the wheels clatter, and get drafts of smoke into my nostrils from the locomotive up ahead.

This went on and on till I was dizzy. I couldn't hold out for much longer, my gripped fingers told me.

As the train moved into a station, going slower, the trainman, on the inside, flung open the door. I was knocked off the train. I rolled around on the earth a minute and picked myself up. Luckily the train wasn't moving too fast then.

It halted. I took a chance. I went up to the trainman.

"Listen, digger," I said—"digger" is the Australian equivalent of "buddy"—"I'm very hungry, very thirsty and my feet have had it. Can I catch a ride?"

He eyed me. "Why, sure. Come on in. Like some booze?"

"No booze, sir, but if you've got a drink of plain water . . . "

"You look as hungry as a desert rat in a desert drought. Get on." He looked around nervously. "Get on—fast!"

This nice guy—it is amazing how many there are in the world—gave me the first orange I saw in God knew how long, as well as a Dagwood sandwich about three inches thick. He shared his big lunch box with me and I ate till I felt nearly sick.

I rode with this fellow as far as Townsville and told him I was headed for the gold fields. "If I have any luck, sport, I won't forget you ever. Thanks."

Townsville.

This was a sprawling and pleasant city in Queensland. I had been there before, when the *Sirocco* held over in the Townsville port. I had stayed at Her Majesty's Hotel and I hoped they'd remember that I'd been there.

I headed for the nearest latrine to clean myself up and wash as well as I could. My shirt looked awful, my pants worse. But it's no use, if you look like a bum, going into the worst hotel. That was my policy: always go to the best, the odds are better.

I put on my boldest front.

But they did recall me.

I sprang a long story of getting caught in a desert typhoon, getting separated from my horses and having to walk many miles. I had swum a river, foot-slogged it, not knowing where I was, and a whole pack of other lies, which sounded to me fairly convincing. I had actually swum a river, done plenty of walking for sure and some hard train riding, but I had to make this strong. I would like a room, I said, and would they send off some cables?

I cabled two people in New Guinea, Jack Ryan and Mrs. Giblin.

I chewed on fingernails for two days before I got replies.

Both sent money. I heaved a big sigh of relief. I wouldn't have to be a fugitive again, and possibly have to jump out of a hotel window at night.

Mrs. Giblin wired back the most startling news. I had won half of a gold claim!

In the gold fields in New Guinea the Government had several ancient administration buildings where officials issued licenses, certified claims, handled all civil and legal affairs. They built these structures right next to one of the richest claims thereabouts, belonging to two partners named Harry Darby and Hector Wales.

The claims underneath the government buildings were put up for ballot among about three hundred registered miners. I was one of these, and I now learned that my partner, Mrs. Giblin, and I had won the claim!

Right smack in the middle of the gold field she and I won the claim that had been voted on—a three hundred to one chance. Flynn luck. I'd be rich again—couldn't fail—the veins of gold couldn't run out. In the money, boy, this is it!

Once more I was aboard a boat. So much of my time was spent on these Australian and New Guinea waters, it seemed, as I tried to make a fortune. The dream of England was heavy upon me now. As usual, all I needed was money: go to England big style, plush it up at a fine hotel, and start living it up.

I sailed for days to Salamaua, the port that led to the gold fields, and arrived feeling a little like Diamond Jim Brady.

At the pier, Mrs. Giblin, a woman of fifty-five, met me. So did her husband, the doctor. All of us jigged around on the pier like a ballet troupe, only less gracefully, and sang Papuan songs.

She would finance an expedition to go and do the mining. I would try to get the Kanakas, and direct the operations. We'd split whatever we found fifty-fifty.

I no longer had worries about credit. I could get anything I wanted, recruiting equipment, clothes, food, anything. But how was I to get the labor to start working the claim?

Without Kanakas to do the hard work it couldn't be done. I needed about twenty natives—and in a big hurry. All over New Guinea by now, they had learned distrust of us prospectors. It was known that many natives who went to the fields died swiftly of pneumonia or T.B. The gold fields were high. The warm-weather-conditioned natives couldn't take the climate. They'd go do plantation work along the coasts, copra and other crops, but nothing doing on the long, high trek inland.

True, the recruiters often took these Kanakas into virtual slavery. It was called "indentured labor" but it was worse than that, once they signed up and got away from their towns. Being a kindly man, I think, I always saw to my "boys" being well treated. I saw that they had rice and meat and other foods that they never had in their villages. But many recruiters were rougher and tougher, and the young natives never saw their villages again. Back in these home villages they figured, "Our men have been taken away and eaten." So that, after a time, recruiters faced this problem everywhere and couldn't get labor.

In the jungle, where the natives had taken on some of the white customs, they didn't use paper money. The only acceptable legal tender was the English shilling. Traveling through the land you carried a five-pound "fuse," a long package containing a hundred shillings. With these you paid as you went along for food, lodging, articles, whatever. The only other way you traded was with barter items like colored beads, axes, cutllasses. Razor blades came high.

It happens that the English halfpenny, usually called vernacularly a ha'penny, is the same size as a shilling, only it is made of copper and worth only one-twenty-fourth of a shilling. This gave me an idea.

I wanted to get some of the natives who had been touched by just a little bit of missionary influence, just enough to make them know what money was. I knew how dangerous was a little knowledge and I was looking for natives with just the right amount of it but not too much of it.

I thought I knew about where these could be found.

A little below Salamaua was Finchhaven Harbor. Catholic missionaries lived here. I didn't want them to know what I was up to. But I had to operate out of that place.

First I went into the W. R. Carpenter Company store and bought several little kettles. I put in an order for many other things I'd need in the jungle, boots, clothes, food supplies, pots—and I bought a large bottle of quicksilver mercury.

"What do you want with that?" they asked.

"I'll be prospecting," I told them, "and I want to test some samples of what I get out of the ground."

I hired two native boys.

I arranged with my friend, Schooner Captain Bowen, operating the *Matupi,* to take me downcoast, a little below Finchhaven Harbor. My two boys went with me. We carried guns.

Bowen agreed to take me to a river point below Finchhaven Harbor. He would then leave me with a longboat to go up the river with my boys. I was going inland a ways to get a corps of the native labor and would walk them back to the coast to Finchhaven Harbor. There the schooner captain would meet us one week from then. We'd ship these boys north to Salamaua.

—If—the big if—I got the natives lined up.

Gambling on losing a week's time—the worst thing I could lose—we reached the river. For a little way we went with the longboat and then we had to hike. We carried all the gadgets I bought at the department store. For three days we hacked and slogged our way through the bush country to where some mildly influenced Kanakas who knew what money was lived.

I reached the settlement I had in mind. Without exactly saying so, I let it be understood that I had something to do with the Government. I was put up in the Tanhada Hut, the rest house that all villages were required to have to put up government people.

For the next two days I scouted the village: looked over the place and observed some very fine young physical specimens. I made myself as popular as I could.

I gave them my gun—which was against the law—and let them shoot some pigeons and wild pig. Just introducing a little civilization, like the missionaries.

I became friendly with the Luluai, the Chief. That was my man.

He and I had long talks far into the night.

On the third night I allowed him to catch me at a strange rite—a rite which to any ordinary New Guinea eyes, in the dim light of a hurricane lamp, must have looked like a piece of rare sorcery.

I squatted in front of three brass pots like a he-witch.

Incense burned. It made a fine smell which I myself liked. The hurricane light was going. I turned it high. The moon was just after the full.

Three days earlier I had noticed that the tide was nearing the high and the moon was nearing the full.

Now was the right time, just one day after the full moon, for me to do what I wanted.

The Chief came into my quarters. He listened as I chanted in a low voice some kind of sea ditty balderdash, lines I picked up riding the rods, or sitting around poker games, or knocking around with the Woolamallo gang in Sydney.

> "They were talkin' of their shearing
> Down in Jerry Hogan's bar.
> He was a small and weedy shit,
> Like big-shots mostly are . . . "

I glanced briefly at the Chief, a little fellow who was watching me with curiosity.

I said in pidgin tongue, "Sindaun." Sit down.

He crouched.

I waved my hands over the pot in which was the quicksilver. The other pot was filled with copper coins the size of halfpennies. On each piece of circular metal was stamped SAN FRANCISCO FAIR. They were souvenirs, to be worn on the coat of anyone who attended the Fair, or simply carried away from the exposition as mementos of the event. They were exactly the size and thickness of halfpennies and shillings. They had found their way to New Guinea, and I had bought up hundreds of them for a few cents.

I kept on chanting, glancing worriedly up at the starry, moonless sky:

> "Then up spoke Big Bill Jackson
> Who smelt of camel dung,
> And hailed from the wild Monaro
> Where the women eat their young."

I drummed out that ditty with a low pitched cadence. I chanted for a time of Big Bill Jackson and his exploits. Then I said, while stirring the silver, "Mek klir."—Make clear.

I took a handful of the San Francisco Fair copper pieces and put them in the quicksilver pot and stirred them around. I rubbed both thumbs and forefingers on them, and as the silvered coins came out, lo and behold, they were shillings!

I carefully placed the new shining metals on the side, and kept minting money and chanting a sheep-shearing song:

> "So Hogan took the tale up
> Of wild and ridgy cuts,
> How he didn't give a hoot for pizzle
> Or a yard or two of guts. Coo-eee!"

The Chief's eyes bulged. He muttered, "Moni! Moni!"

I hushed him to silence and drew out of my mystic pots a handful of San Francisco coins transformed to bright English shillings. Wonderful new values of grace and color.

At this moment I stopped chanting and said, "Pinis."—Finished.

"Mek tok," he said. That meant he wanted to ask questions.

"Yufela tok," I said.

He said, "Yumi mek talatala."—You and me make friends.

What was it? he asked in pidgin tongue.

I explained that it was the magic new machine from Sydney for making money. "You see with your own eyes? Have I made ha'pennies into shillings?"

He could see with his own eyes as he crouched in the faint light of the lamp. He had a shock of fuzzy hair, whitening. His dark-toned skin was wrapped in a native nightrobe made of glimmering leaf. He was barefooted, about a head and a half shorter than I, and his greedy black eyes glistened as if he saw God.

I said it could be done only after the full of the moon, adding in my now pretty good Melanesian lingo that any other time he could try as he wanted, it was not worth trying, for he would only destroy the magic and the secret formula.

"No bagarimap," I cautioned. —No bugger 'im up.

There was a hush. I tried another stanza or two of the bawdy Aussie lyric that I picked up in Sydney Domaine, or God knows where. . . .

> "So he broke up Hungry Mawson,
>   Way back in Eighty-two,
>   And sheared three hundred sheep that day,
>   Then raped Hungry's daughter, Lou."

And made more shillings. I dropped them at the Chief's side, tempting him to the maximum.

I said, "I leave tomorrow."

"No, Tabauda, wait."

I could not. I had a place further inland where I waited to go to sell this wonderful money machine. I had to be hurrying on as I needed at least twenty good strong boys. I had been promised them at this place where I was going, in exchange for the machine.

"Twenty boy for makeen?"

"Yes."

"Why you go further, Tabauda? I have twenty-two."

I looked surprised. I had counted heads and there seemed to be no more than eighteen.

"It will have to be done tomorrow."

If he could assure me, I would wait, but only till tomorrow.

He looked again at the coins in his hand. He stared hard as if it were revelation. His face lighted. Halfpennies to shillings! The best deal in the world! New Guinea's first millionaire! If you are a chief in New Guinea and you have the machine to make shillings out of ha'pennies, something like a two thousand per cent profit, you got it made—in any jungle.

I said, "Makeen belong U." —The Machine is yours.

I promised him that I would take good care of his young men. They were going with me to the gold fields, they would work my claim. They would have a two-year contract with me, and back they would come to him, home with money in their pockets. Everybody would be well off—and the tribe would prosper.

Sure enough, the next night I made off with these twenty-two young fellows, handsome, healthy chaps. They and the two boys I had with me started for the coast.

I gave a final stern caution to the Chief not to go into business until right after the next full moon. I needed a good head start.

"Mi golong. Bi." —Me go along. Good-by.

That would give me four weeks to mine my claim and make my fortune before all the tribes in this area would hunt me down as the latest white snake needing extermination.

Schooner Captain Bowen was in Finchhaven Harbor with his craft. I was on land with my big party and the missionaries were hanging around wondering what it was all about. I casually built a fire. Distantly in the harbor, Captain Bowen knew that was a signal to send in the longboat.

We began loading my "recruits."

So far, so good.

Back in Salamaua, the hardened recruiters were stunned.

"You mean to say you got recruits from behind Finchhaven?"

"Sure. Why not? The Chief is a distant relative of mine."

"Come on, how did you fix this?"

"Oh, I know a few missionaries, that's all."

I took care of the last detail, the official indenturing of these boys to me for a two-year period. This I arranged with the District Office. Then all of us marched off through the hell of mountain jungle to the gold fields ten days away.

Once more up and down those precipitous hills, once again the leeches, the mosquitoes, snakes, the drumming by night, and the incessant bush.

I figured out one thing that might save my neck as far as the Chief was concerned. His natural greed would get the best of him in a few days. He'd experiment and make up this phony money. He'd write it off to the fact that he had experimented before the full moon was around, then decide he had done it wrong by not following the magic formula.

—So I hoped.

(This is the true story Robert Michener wrote about and Mark Hellinger couldn't credit until he found out the real facts and then laughed his head off.)

Arriving, I set to work. I built my sluicers. My boys started cutting into the face of the ground of the hillside which belonged to Mrs. Giblin and me. We went into the vein which led out from Harry Darby's claim.

I felt yellow with gold. All the boys worked at high pitch. They got up at six in the morning and dug till night. I was so tired by evening that I was even too knocked out for a poker game. I hit the bunk and passed out till the next morning.

On all sides there was this feverishness. The other claims going, just like mine. There is nothing like a gold field to inspire labor and dreams and get you as exhilarated as if you are on dope or something.

We dug and dug and dug, sluiced and sluiced.

We went into the side of the hill deeper and deeper. A trickle of gold came out.

But only a trickle.

As the days went by and we tore up the sixty by sixty foot claim, I knew that this time the Flynn luck was somehow running out. It dawned on me that the rich vein of Harry Darby's claim cut right out and ended on the border of my claim. Nothing there but a few yards of alluvial.

Yet we panned for two full weeks, till the earth was hollow like from a big bomb. I don't suppose we gathered more than a hundred ounces altogether.

I had the new moon hanging over me. Only a few days away.

Down by the coast a chieftain had doubtless found out by now he had been slipped the "moldy fig," as I termed it, and had been rooked —and where were the cherished young men of his tribe?

I pitched in again. Dug this way, dug that. Soon every square inch of my claim had been churned up.

There wasn't a goddamned thing but that hundred ounces.

My boys had knocked out all the greenery, all the shrubbery. The earth lay there upside down like a belly that is inside out. Looking like the entrails of the earth, and all it was—was earth.

It was the second time I was broke on the gold field. Except I still had Madge Parkes' jewels in my shaving kit.

When you are broke on the gold field a cold desperation comes over you. A dream has ended. You think desperate thoughts.

Half of the hundred ounces of gold was Mrs. Giblin's. I'd send it to her, or deposit it in the bank at Salamaua for her.

I'd take what gold dust I had and be gone.

More than ever I knew that my time had run out in New Guinea.

The place was hotter for me than hell was for the Devil. I knew that when my recruiting story came out life would get mighty tough for Flynn, especially if the Government got to know it. The Chief might blow his top, come gunning for me with a tribeful of spears. It wasn't his right to sell me those boys, he could only persuade them.

The old aphorism hung over me, that if you spend more than five years in New Guinea you were done for, you'd never be able to get out, your energy would be gone, and you'd rot there like an aged palm.

I never wanted to run over that five years—and now, four and a half had gone by. The biggest thing in New Guinea was gold, and I had come closer to it than most.

Now what to do? No use trying to sell my claim. Everybody knew it was no good. I signed over half of it, my half, to that trainman in Townsville who befriended me when I rode the rods to the coast.

The last thing was to sell my boys. They were a fine lot of fellows, but they had their bellyful of the gold field. Moreover, they were restless, having heard tales of the other Kanakas who died there. I had no difficulty in getting the District Officer to transfer my contract to a wealthy copra planter who bought them from me at twenty pounds a head.

That is where I stood now: fifty ounces of gold, four hundred pounds, and a shaving brush handle full of a kind lady's jewels.

Yet, for New Guinea, for a young fellow, this was a fortune, a grubstake, a start in the world.

At night, often, when I dreamed a bit before slipping off to sleep, I recalled the curious business I had been in for a short time, playing in *The Wake of the Bounty* in Tahiti.

I might even become an actor. I'd like nothing better than take a flier at that. But how did you start?

That's it, go home! Home where?

Go to England. Get the hell out of here. Leave this damnable jungle forever. You got the money now, Flynn, get out!

England! It roared in me now, and I felt like a patriot, a subject of the empire, of His Majesty the King.

In the succeeding days I made my way to Rabaul.

There, through a government anthropologist named Charles Chimery, a friend of my father's, I swiftly got a passport. I was dressed well when I called to see him at his offices in Rabaul and told him I wanted to see my father.

If he had known why I wanted to get out of New Guinea; if he had known how I bilked that Chief and stole his boys, worked them, and then sold them; if he had known my razor handle bulged with those stolen jewels; if he had known the larceny in my heart and how I felt about what I had twisted out of the guts of New Guinea—he'd have eviscerated me then and there and studied me as a specimen of what a desperate and hard man will do to survive and get on.

But he was charm itself, kindly—and I got the passport.

I had a day or two of waiting in Rabaul before getting away and made a last attempt to secure my finances. I went to Barclay's Bank and arranged to ship off to England my fifty ounces of Edie Creek gold. I'd have that waiting for me when I got there.

While waiting around on the wharf a proposition was put to me by an IDB—Illicit Diamond Buyer. Many of these operated around that part of the world. Their deal enabled you to beat the exchange by converting less valuable Australian pounds into much more valuable English pounds.

It seemed clear to me that I ought to better that four-hundred-pound grubstake of mine. I held out about a hundred pounds for travel, and with the remainder bought illicit diamonds.

I took these lovely little stones and combined them with the diamonds I had swiped from Madge Parkes. I insured them, paid a premium.

I wrapped them in little red wax packages to be held in the ship's safe in the captain's cabin.

For a while I stood on the pier at Rabaul and cooled myself in the gentle trade winds, fragile, laden with unforgettable frangipani scent.

I glanced over the broad, dowdy freighter I was to board.

Then over the gangplank.

An enormous man, much taller than I, strolled the deck. He was huge, blond, hairy.

He appraised me. I appraised him. We seemed mutually curious. But there were no words.

The vibration of the engine stirred the boards beneath my feet.

I walked to the rail and looked shoreward for the last time. I stared beyond, to the hills. They were green and fresh as ever.

One last long look at the port of Rabaul. Without sentiment, without a mood.

Just a look.

The curtain was coming down on New Guinea.

PART THREE
Seven Seas to England
1932-1933

A T once the big man and I fell into the most voluble conversation.

I was astonished at his physical appearance. He was a Hollander. He wore a broad Dutch grin, showing enormous teeth parted. Everything about him was broad. His ears were monsters that stood out about the angle of an enraged elephant about to charge. His face was covered with blond hair, though he wasn't exactly bearded. He wore baggy khaki shorts and heavy leather shoes, without socks. His bare legs and thighs showed the same hirsuteness, so that he looked like a blond, amiable orangutan in a mink coat.

I presumed him to be about fifteen or twenty years older than I.

His name was Dr. Gerrit H. Koets. He had recently been in northern Australia on some medical foundation grant, seeking a solution for hookworm in that part of the world. He was headed eventually for America, taking with him his findings on hookworm, as well as photographs of New Guinea.

He was loaded down with a variety of cameras, medical instruments of all kinds, and a large metal packing case. "The magic case," he called it. It was jammed with all kinds of medicants, with odds and ends picked up in travels all over the South Pacific and South America.

As this was a freighter, with few passengers, we became very close. We discovered that we were adventurers over and under the skin, that we had enormous interests in common—money, women, an impelling thirst for knowledge, and a touch of larceny in our hearts; not necessarily in that order.

At once we set our sights on the captain's wife. Remember, I hadn't laid eyes on a white woman, or hand, in a year or so.

She was crowding forty. She had long blond hair and a mouth full of teeth, any one of which could have been hers. On the starboard side, when she smiled, which was often, there were two beautiful gold teeth. She weighed in the vicinity of a hundred and fifty pounds. Yet she seemed like a woman rare as one from outer space.

Koets and I floated around her, trying to win her favors, her smiles, whatever she'd part with—even her teeth.

139

"This will be easy," said Koets, who fancied himself a Lothario without equal. "Want me to show you how to make her?" He thought that he was irresistible, paralyzing, all-conquering to any female.

I watched his method.

Each morning he stood naked at the ship's stern, absorbing the sunshine—head thrown back, a vast Epstein-like sculpture, grossly misshapen, baring his gleaming teeth fanglike to the sun. He had a theory that sunlight was good for the gums and throat. He stood with his ponderous hairy blond legs and thighs stretched wide apart. His huge flabby belly undulated uneasily with each breath. His entire torso was covered with dense blond hair. He was a heroic sight—except for the incongruously small phallic symbol between his legs. That seemed oddly pathetic to me, wan-looking, especially in the sunlight.

Perhaps obeying some atavistic impulse, he started pounding his enormous chest with his hairy fists. He hollered, "Gorillas do this just before they mate. Urruhh!"

He growled, a Tarzan-like sound, and explained, "Works on all women." He let out another roar. His vast blond eyebrows and the close-cropped hair on his scalp became erect like antennae. A hollow noise came out of his chest, a drumming that reminded me of the *garramuts* of New Guinea.

I stared at him in awe. He was incredulous, but convincing. I believed him. In fact I believed almost everything that he told me.

I now waited for the captain's wife to come over to Koets and lie down and crawl right under him, as he said all women would do.

Koets continued to pound his chest. "Just get it *hard!* They love it! They go mad! Women are sexier and dirtier than men, bless 'em, and far more perverted—never forget that."

He beat his chest again. I looked forward for the captain's wife to come flying down the deck.

She never showed.

His lecture on the female nature continued. "That goes for Buckingham Palace bedroom, as well as for Kipling's Colonel's Lady and Judy O'Grady. They're sisters under the skin—and," added Koets, "foreskin too!"

He burst into a thunderous laugh at his own humor. "You'll find out, pal."

I was willing.

Yet Koets depressed me with his kind of brainwashing or sex therapy. He talked of an ebony Venus in Morocco, a slender vision in

Shanghai, a glorious nymphomaniac in Persia. Since I was practically hairless and built like a stalk of asparagus, I knew that if I tried beating *my* chest a sound would come out like the rattling of dice.

During the next eight days, as the freighter made its way to Manila, in the Philippines, Koets and I walked the deck.

He leaned over the side of the ship. "You see, the tide is going in," he observed.

I argued, "No, it is at the still."

He blinked through his big owl-like glasses. "What's that mean?"

"It's not moving."

That seemed to mean much to him. "Ah, you see, it's like us. We neither move downstream nor upstream. We too are also at the still."

He spoke frequently of medical practice. I mentioned I had had a "black pox"—clap to you. He asked me if I drank much. I told him almost nothing, and he said, "Don't drink at all. Besides that it may bring back your clap, alcohol is the worst killer of all, worse than narcotics.

"Listen, Errol," he said gravely for once, "I would cheerfully kill or poison any bastard who I knew was peddling drugs—any kind. And I would slowly strangle the other killer of the mind, the body, the soul, who openly sells alcohol. It's as criminal as any drug, the only difference being you can buy it at any street corner. As a doctor I'd prefer to see a sign at the corner reading *Your Favorite Cocaine Dealer* sooner than *Your Favorite Liquor Dealer.*"

His real study, he said, was the human being in motion. It didn't escape me that he observed me as a specimen as well as a pal.

The captain's wife arrived in Manila as pure as she had left Rabaul —in spite of Koets's overtures.

"What do we do in Manila?" I asked.

"Whomever we can."

That was the other principal facet that endeared me to Koets: that he loved a dishonest buck better than a legal one. He said that the act of acquiring a dishonest dollar gave him as much of a bang as whisky or drugs gave others. Making a legal buck had no such appeal for him.

The Philippines were beautiful. We were entranced by the sight of little slender mantilla-laced girls dressed in white. For even today they still wear the white mantillas, after the Spanish, and look more beautiful, poetic and untouchable.

We knew that unless we made money we had to cut corners. We took a dingy little hut, Philippine-style, and tried to hang onto our dough. It cost us about two pounds a month for an average-sized room, with a mud floor, a matting over it, no shower and no toilet, of course.

When we weren't around the hut, or barging around Manila looking for girls or a fast buck, we took trips in broken-down little donkey carts over the countryside. On these journeys it didn't matter where we slept—under somebody's house, on a veranda, on the beach.

Besides these economies Koets had another peccadillo. He wouldn't spend five cents without marking it down in a little black book.

It now didn't matter to us when we got to England. The mood was a lark. Adventure. Let the fun come on.

We frequented the places where any betting could be done. Koets was less of a handicapper than I. How much better to win money than earn it by honest labor!

The cockfight is to the Philippines what the bullfight is to Spain. In the Philippines they don't fool. They put a long sharp razor-edged spiked spur in the heel of each cock and let them both go at it. The audience goes in for hot betting. We bought cheap tickets and watched the fighting and the betting.

When two fighting cocks are put into the arena and the bets are down, it is pretty much of an even money go. In the case of an outstanding bird, the odds would sometimes go four to one, but that was rare.

How could we lessen the odds? How beat the Philippine game?

One day Koets flicked his fingers, slapped himself on the thigh. "Eureka!" he growled. "I have it! That's Greek for 'I've got 'em by the nuts!' " he explained.

He pulled me inside our hut and headed for his treasure chest. In one corner of the case was an old pair of socks and a small cabinet filled with colorful phials of drugs, all corked up. In another was a pile of his little black notebooks with expenses carefully enumerated on each page of each book—Dutch efficiency style. Film equipment jammed against one of the walls of the trunk, and in another corner there was surgical equipment. "In case anyone needs a delivery or an abortion in a hurry," he said—"or fallen arches, flat feet or dandruff."

He lifted one glass phial after another. Gleefully, he held them under my nose. "See what I mean?"

I didn't.

"You dope, haven't I told you all about the snake venom that I got from the snake ranch in Rio de Janeiro?"

I still didn't follow.

"Look, have you got a small nail file?"

I had that.

"Now listen carefully—I'll get a chicken and show you what can be done with one of these fighting cocks."

I still didn't get it, but I was getting to know the goodly doctor. We went out, bought two chickens, returned to our little hut.

Still he wouldn't tell me what he had in mind until he started to go to work on the beaks of the two chickens.

In cockfighting in the Philippines, before the birds fight they are momentarily held about a foot apart, then the one on the right picks the comb of the one on the left. The one on the left then picks the comb of the one on the right. This makes them fighting mad, before they are allowed to tangle.

The comb, on a good fighting cock, is generally cut very low. It is a very sensitive part of the bird. It is soft, and if pecked, it may open easily.

"Now watch," said Koets. He serrated the edge of the beak of one of the cocks with the nail file, making it sharp as a pin point. He put three little grooves in the beak, turning it into a virtual fang. He put a dab of snake venom on the beak.

We were ready for the experiment.

I held in my hand the bird whose beak hadn't been tampered with. Koets held the cock with the poisoned beak. I let my bird take a peck out of the comb of the one Koets held. Then he let his bird take a bite out of the comb of mine.

We timed them. How long would it take for the poison in the beak of Koets's bird to affect my chicken?

We put them down and they circled a minute, then flew at each other. In a very few seconds the bird without the poison in his beak toppled over and lay dying. The venom had taken effect.

We ran out and bought four birds. Just ordinary birds which cost us almost nothing. We'd turn them into champs in a jiffy.

Armed with four superb fighters, we headed for the cockfights. We entered our birds and "handicapped" hard.

The odds were always against our birds. They were such scrubby-looking things, but miraculously we won, for Koets had plenty of phials of that Brazilian snake venom in his magic treasure chest.

Koets believed that snake venom had many qualities not yet known to science, curative and destructive. He had hoped to experiment with it—but now he had found the greatest use of all. Snakes never paid off so well before in the history of venomous ideas.

Every now and then we would drop a fight, just for the sake of appearances, but generally speaking, our business was safer than that of the Bank of England.

We moved into another house. We bought new suits. We dressed smartly. That was always important to me at that time. I looked like a dude, sported a cane, and carried a fighting cock under my arm, like a pet poodle.

The place we lived in overlooked Manila Bay. The girls came, the girls went.

Cockfights started at seven o'clock promptly each evening, and sometimes there was a second round of fights at ten o'clock.

It was my job to lay the bets since I spoke better Spanish than Koets. It was his, as the scientist, to keep the birds in fine form, their beaks sharp. We even invested heavily in several brand-new nail files: the only tool we needed.

Bets were paying off so regularly and we were doing so well that Koets was running short of snake juice.

We were doing so well we should have known it couldn't last.

One night I ran around in my usual fashion soliciting bets. *"Si, cuanto, cuanto? Bueno bueno, viejo."* I passed a slip of paper up to somebody prepared to bet. He passed me down his money. I did the bookmaking. I carried a long black bag slung over my shoulders, and in this I held the fine Manila pesos.

This night I was running around, smiling, saying, *"viejo,"* meaning "old boy," to my clients, and placing bets. They suspected nothing. They just thought they had bad luck and we had good luck.

Everything was set. The bets were high.

We were now entering a cock who had won three straight fights in a row. He was practically a contender for the championship of Manila.

I was taking the bets when I felt a hot heavy breath on my neck. It was Koets's. "How much have you got?" he asked.

"Plenty."

"Fine. I've booked a side bet. If it doesn't conflict with your bookings we stand to win ten thousand pesos." At the time that would be about three or four thousand dollars.

The tiers went up, colosseum-fashion, in this arena. A crowd of thousands looked down from their gallery seats.

In their corner, the seconds were handling their champ bird, called The Flower. All fighting cocks have names. Ours was named Strike by Night. The Flower had been well trained for weeks and looked beautiful. He was striped and he was making fighting noises. Our bird was smaller, but looked vicious enough. To look at these two fowl, anyone would pick the other to win.

Because our bird was smaller we got large odds—four to one. It is even possible that a few Filipinos may have suspected by now our endless run of luck. Two strangers and they seemed to know more about cockfighting than the natives.

The fight was ready to start. Everybody was standing in the tiers.

As yet Koets had not placed the venom on the bird's beak. This he learned to do very subtly, like a magician, taking a small bit of cotton wool, which he could hide between his fingers, and placing it on the bird's beak the instant before the ritual of letting the birds peck each other.

Koets cleverly took care of the last detail. The speck of cotton wool slipped into his pocket unnoticed.

The birds were brought together for the bite of challenge before the fight. The handlers held them face to face. Each picked the comb of the other.

They were dropped onto the ground as the handlers went back to their corners.

The whole house was silent as the two birds circled.

Two cocks that had been brought together like that would fly at each other the instant they were put on the ground, or while they were in the air, but these two were wary. They circled far longer than two cocks ordinarily would.

They wheeled, each looking for an opening.

Round and round they went, making of this fight a carousel of slow timing.

All of a sudden the other bird, The Flower, without a blow having been struck, wheeled over dead. There he was, spurs up, in his death throes.

Our Strike by Night went in for a needles kill, jumping on The Flower and pecking at him with no mercy, little knowing that The Flower was already as stiff as the last chicken in the cold freeze.

My back was to the birds. I was still taking bets. I thought something odd was going on when I heard a shout of surprise from the whole gallery. I turned and took a look. The sound got louder. A tremendous eruption from the fans. The officials were excited.

At just that instant Koets's hand sank into my shoulder as if he wanted to take a hunk of meat out of it. *"Alt, alt, rares!"* he called. He looked distraught.

"What's the matter?"

"Don't ask now! Let's get the hell out of here while we're still ahead!"

"What's the matter?"

He held me in that policeman's grip.

"For Christ's sake, let's get going!"

"Where?"

"Anywhere!"

We managed to get out. As we scurried through the streets we had no way of knowing what was happening back at the arena.

We paddled as fast as we could back to our lodging. "All we can take is the cameras and the money," Koets said. "Grab the cameras and let's get to the wharf."

We had in our pockets in Philippine pesos, about the equivalent of $4,000.

We snatched the treasure chest, left all our clothes. We got a horse and buggy cab that took us, via side streets, to the pier.

We didn't know what boat we'd get on, or whether we would get one, or whether there'd be one. We only knew that boats left every hour. East, south, west, north—no matter—just get on something that floated and leave—even if it went back to New Guinea.

We arrived at the pier. Sure enough, a steamer was going out. It was the *Empress of Asia,* a big ancient-looking tub. We rushed up the gangplank, without tickets, only our passports.

For a while we hid in a stateroom. As the boat made ready to leave, we ventured out on deck to take a look at the shore. When the gangplank was being drawn up we saw, on the wharf, an excited crowd of Filipinos. Some pointed at the ship, some at the arena. They were gesticulating, arguing, yelling at the police.

There was no point in nostalgic farewells. We scrammed back to our room, hoping the boat would pull out.

When we felt the motion of the ship we began breathing easier again.

I asked, "Where do you suppose this boat is going?"

"Let's go find out," suggested Koets.

On deck I made inquiries. First stop, Hong Kong.

I gave Koets a jubilant jab in the ribs. "Look at 'em. Still brandishing bolos."

Koets grinned.

"About as close as we'll ever come," I said.

"I didn't know I could run that fast," Koets mused.

He looked around the ship. "Good God!" he cried, striking his head.

"What's up?" I had a sudden horrible thought we had been trailed aboard ship by the Filipino police.

"Do you know where we are?"

I told him yes, on the *Empress of Asia*.

"Yes, but in *first* class!"

The idea of traveling first class was anathema to him. The cost! The mere idea appalled him. He had certain scruples about the wealthy, the mighty, the utilities. Don't pay them a cent more than you have to. Don't enrich the rich. Outwit them, yes; that was reasonable.

"But look," I objected, "we're loaded with dough. We can travel any way we want. In style, old boy."

"And give those thieves the difference? They're a bunch of crooks!" His big broad face flushed. "Not that I mind parting with the money"— he did mind, very much—"but I take pride in doing the world at minimum cost. By God, I'm off. Are you coming?"

No I wasn't. It was only a short trip to Hong Kong. I was going first class—a matter of principle.

"Be seeing you," said Koets, stomping off.

He could find his way about a ship better than a ship's cat. He spent practically all of his time in first class, although paying steerage fare. If you could do it that way, I decided, it made some sense.

When we landed I wanted to go to the best place, the Hong Kong and Shanghai Hotel. Again I couldn't budge Koets. We compromised on a middle-class lodging on the tough outskirts of the Wichai district. The prices, he said, weren't exactly suitable to him, but the place had certain redeeming features. It was four blocks from the whorehouse district.

How to re-invest our large fortune?

I favored the quickest return and the largest profits—the race track.

He looked glum but he was in no position to argue. I had done the booking at the cockfights and we'd made out good, hadn't we?

I convinced him that the horses and even planetary influences were in our favor.

For the next three weeks we played steadily. But those horrible little Chinese ponies wouldn't behave. We went through more than half of the $4,000. We had been working with Shanghai dollars and it sounded like a lot. We had twenty thousand left, but Koets was complaining bitterly because I was doing all the betting and losing.

"Look," I said, "I've been thinking. It's no use fighting a bad streak."

"Shitz," said Koets. He always vociferated that in a spitting Dutch accent. "You can sure fight a losing battle. What's your idea?"

"Macao."

He looked blank.

"Portuguese China," I said. "Not too far from here."

He didn't know where it was and I wasn't sure either. I suggested that we take our capital and go there—the cesspool of the Far East, of the world—and invest it in fantan at one of the casinos.

"Are you mad? They'll skin us."

"Not if we play carefully."

"*If* we play carefully—"

I told him I knew something about the game. I had played it a lot in the Chinese colonies in New Guinea. There I had heard incessant talk of Macao. There was a street called Calle Felicadade—the Street of Happiness.

The name of the street appealed to him. I saw the look of curiosity working up in him.

"Come on, we're certain to win. It's a cinch!"

Next day we boarded the *Fusham,* a small packet that plied between Hong Kong and Macao. For once there was no argument about the style in which we traveled because there was only one class.

While it was well known that Macao was the stinkpot of the East, the games were said to be fair. Only because it would be worth anyone's life to try cheating.

On deck, the second day out, I produced my campaign plan on paper. So much per day as a loss sum, and figure to win every third day. "Then," I said, "with any kind of luck. . . ."

"What if we lose all the time?" Koets wanted to know.

I gave a shrug. "So we're broke again."

"Broke!" he snorted. "My God, what kind of a fool am I with?" He stomped off down the deck, muttering.

Following his big figure along the deck with my eyes, I saw her. . . .

She was leaning over the rail, staring out into the distance. She wore a Chinese-style high-collared, Mandarin-red dress piped with black, in the split of which—quite a conservative split—I could see the beautiful calf and ankle of her left leg as it rested on the bottom rail. Her dress fitted her so that it seemed she wore a fourth layer of skin.

Her profile was beautiful. Her head was held high by the high stiff-necked dress. She wore no hat and her hair was swept back into a Western-style bun at the back—which I hadn't seen before among Chinese women. I stroked her beautiful hair with my eyes.

She seemed lost in thought. I edged down the rail as inconspicuously as possible. Six feet two of inconspicuousness.

I made it about halfway when she glanced in my direction. She gave me such a level penetrating stare with—did I imagine it?—the vestige of a smile for me.

I could detect no other expression, except the unblinking eyes. Her face was strangely long for a Chinese—generally the Chinese face is moon-shaped—although her cheekbones were certainly Mongolian. She was tall, too, by Eastern standards. Must have stood five foot seven.

We both stared out at the sea. How was I going to talk to her? I was thinking. I tried to work up the courage for an approach.

Yet of a sudden this was solved for me. Still looking out to sea, but not addressing me directly, she said, "Will you stay long in Macao?"

"Oh yes, a while."

I quickly moved closer, till we were a couple of feet apart.

"I'm not quite sure how long we will last," I continued. "It depends on my luck."

"Oh," she said, interestedly, looking at me now, "you're going to play?"

"What else do you go to Macao for?"

"That's true." She spoke perfect English. "Oddly enough, I'm on the same business."

"Do you come here often?"

"No no. This will be my first time, but you see I must—" She broke off. Her voice fell.

"Must what?"

"Oh nothing." Her tone brightened. "I have never gambled, but I thought I would try my luck."

"Madame, you find yourself in the right company. I, on the other hand, have gambled all my life. While I can't claim it has got me very far, it's been a lot of fun losing and every so often winning."

"What would you play?"

"Fantan."

"Ah, I used to play that at home when I was a little girl. My father, Colonel O'Connor, was a great fantan player and we had wonderful times at home. But only for fun."

"Colonel *what?*"

"O'Connor," she repeated. "My name is Ting Ling O'Connor." Ting Ling. It sounded like the ring of a bicycle bell.

"Is your father in Hong Kong?"

"No, he's dead one year now."

"Oh." There was a bit of a silence.

"May I introduce myself," I said. "I also have an Irish name. Flynn, Errol." I put it in the Chinese way, inverting the names, though she hadn't done this.

Her mother was Chinese, from Peking, she said. She had two brothers, but they were in the army. Her mother was very sick.

I took a chance. "So you are going to have a little vacation in Macao and make some money, perhaps because you need it?"

"That's right. How did you guess?"

"Shot in the dark."

Ting Ling and I agreed to meet in Macao at the roof casino on Macao's swankiest hotel, the Mandarin House.

Soon afterward she excused herself.

The way she walked was faintly reminiscent of the rear view of a certain lady of the screen who is given to a sideways undulation.

By God, I had to tell Koets about this!

I hastened to find him.

He was intrigued. I could sense his big hairy chest rising to the occasion beneath his shirt. My picture of her beauty roused him. His eyes glistened with interest. But when I told him the full story of her expectation of gambling he asked, "Do you think she's on the level?"

"Of course," I snorted. "I can tell about people. The poor kid must be broke and is going to have a last flicr with whatever she's got left. Wouldn't you do the same?"

"Wonder how much dough she's got?"

There was a silence. It went on for a full minute or so.

"What's the matter with you—in love?" he sneered.

"No. I have another thought," I said. "Though I must say she's about the most attractive girl I ever laid eyes on—you can tell she's a lady."

He let out his usual sardonic horse laugh and he passed an obscene remark in effect that she peed like all the other women, same way, sitting down.

"I don't quite see how that makes any difference," I reproved him. "You have nothing poetic in you—"

I decided to get after Koets when we landed at Macao. I made him buy some clean clothes—much to his disgust. "They only wear out," he said, "and you have to buy more." I told him I wasn't going to have him look like a bum around me, even if we both were.

Once more we argued over hotel accommodations. That infuriated me. I wanted to live high—in my low way—and he wanted to live low anyway. I lectured him about the psychology of living. "Listen, if you are down and getting low on the hip, the idea is always to put on a big front. Now do what I say. Let's go to Mandarin House."

But once more we checked into a cheap hotel. I warned Koets that if matters went well between Ting Ling and me I might check out and just leave him there.

The first night at the casino with Ting Ling was a killer. Stupidly I took half of our capital. That was about ten thousand bucks, Shanghai.

I played cautiously—I thought. So did she. She seemed to know the game very well.

My stack of chips went down. Hers went up. I was sitting next to her and I thought maybe I should change my luck. Beautiful though she was, pound though she could make my blood, I had better move.

Without making it too obvious, I made a change. I went to another table. There I made a big splurge. In no time I was ahead of where I started. I now held about thirteen thousand, Shanghai.

I sauntered back to Ting Ling's side. The piles in front of her had gone down. She tried to look nonchalant. She smiled. She threw out lovely little slender hands, with a shrug, but didn't say anything.

I whispered, "Let's play together a bit."

"All right."

"You like to do the playing?"

"No, you," she said. "My luck is out."

We made a bank. This time I played with confidence. Now her luck was better, as good as mine. Her pile went up, so did mine.

We both came out well ahead of the game.

She was radiant.

I left the croupiers a tip. On principle, I was against tipping them, but I didn't want to look cheap in front of Ting Ling.

We danced. Even with her tight white brocade dress, in which she looked a dream, she was obviously a skilled dancer, and I wasn't.

I could feel that she returned some of the real warmth which I had for her.

I was in a turmoil all evening. There was this thought in the back of my mind. Shall I or shall I not—tonight? Or, shall I play the gentleman —first, that is.

The latter seemed the best course.

I took her to her room. There, at the door, I felt the stiffening attitude of the girl who has to give you the bad news that you mustn't come in. But she hadn't said it.

I bowed. I hoped we'd see each other tomorrow. I thanked her for the wonderful evening.

I kissed her hand, as I had read and heard of it being done.

We were to meet tomorrow afternoon for a swim.

As I said good night it seemed to me that she looked a little puzzled.

It was late when I returned, all elated, to our dingy little room. I looked at the quarters with disgust. Here we were, well on the way to becoming millionaires. Yet there was Koets, like a big, fat conservative, on his narrow bed, and next to his bed was mine. It all looked squalid and beneath our prospects. Much as I liked this fellow, why was he so cheap?

Under my bed was a porcelain utensil. Instead we ought to have a bathroom with a sunken tub, and there should be a bidet of matching color somewhere in the room.

No way to live. Only for peasants. I must move out. I had to keep up with Ting Ling.

I woke him to tell him that on this first night we had a killing. He looked doubtful. "Bad sign that, bad sign. You should never win at first. You should keep wins for the stretch." He grunted, turned over, went to sleep.

I was at the seaside the next afternoon waiting for her. A taxi drew up and she stepped out. She had on a gossamer robe. Under it I could see the full-length bathing suit. For in those days there was no such thing as the bikini, or even the maillot. Her garb was graceful, respectable. She was that way in everything she did, from eating, to drinking, to dancing, to walking, and, I fervently hoped——. The epitome of rhythmic beauty: unhurried, graceful.

Even so, she was wearing incongruous wooden clogs, Dutch in appearance, like some peasants wore then in China.

We got away as far as possible from everyone.

When she took off that gossamer robe I absolutely choked. If before I thought her figure was sensational, she had hidden it in the tight-fitting Chinese dress, crushing in the bosom. The bathing suit didn't do that.

There they were, pointing to the stars.

We swam. We had several hours of lying in the sun. She told me of her family life. She had gone to school in Switzerland. Her father had been of independent means and a regular army man into his twenties. After marrying her mother, he had been forced to resign his commission in a top Irish regiment. He had joined, as far as I could make out, some Chinese regiment of volunteers and he had commanded it for many years. The small pay he got didn't matter because he had enough money of his own to be able to keep the children—the two boys and her—and educate them. The boys, it appeared, had volunteered to meet the Japanese threat from the East. The Japanese were then mobilizing and threatening Chinese borders. It was the beginning of Pan Asia, as it became known—and the Sino-Japanese war wasn't far off.

I told her many of the things that had happened to me since I left New Guinea. She found them riotously funny, so that I began to feel myself a raconteur. She asked me endless questions.

By the time we got a taxi to return she knew pretty much all about me. All but the wicked thoughts.

That week Ting Ling and I spent every waking and sleeping hour together. I could hardly bear to have her out of my sight. After three or four days I got to the point where I was possessive. I hated to recognize the fact that I was jealous. If Ting Ling was gone too long, or if she flashed that dazzling smile and placed her steady eyes on somebody else, even if they were only talking about the next gambling play, I fumed.

At that age I was under the ridiculous assumption that the man went on the make for the woman, not the other way around.

For on the second night we were together in her room, she took off

her panties, gay, gossamer tussah silk, with little quaint designs of
dragons embroidered diagonally across them. At that moment I couldn't
move, couldn't think.

Ting Ling took it in her slender stride. I know now that nothing I
could have said or done or any way that I might have looked would
have made the least bit of difference, as her frail little hand reached out
like the tentacle of a diminutive octopus and dragged me into the sack.
That small, delicate Chinese hand, like a relic of the Ming Dynasty,
knew all there was to know about how to handle my case, and then
and there I decided there was much to be said for Chinese culture.

I will not subscribe to the words of Rudyard Kipling ". . . the cold
hard flesh of the heathen Chinee—" Let me tell you, Mr. Kipling, there
is nothing hard or cold about the flesh of the heathen Chinee.

Or maybe it is just that the unlucky bard of England and India never
ran into anything quite so delectable as the bell-ringing Ting Ling
O'Connor.

Ting Ling and I switched casinos. We went from the top of Mandarin
House to the Street of Happiness. Here was a vastly different kind of
gambling setup. Ricksha drivers, coolies, clerks from offices, players
who were half Portuguese, half Chinese, and others, an absolute
polyglot of the world, were shoulder to shoulder in the stenchlike air
of the Calle Felicidade.

Along this Street of Happiness there were three gigantic casinos.
There you gambled. You could buy or have anything that money could
buy of a sensual sort. You could bet very big or very small.

Ting Ling ushered me into one of these emporiums, Christie's.
Outside you could smell stale earth, the curious stink that permeated
the town. Inside you rubbed shoulders with the flotsam of human
society. A coolie come to make a fortune rubbed shoulders with somebody in a smart sharkskin suit and a black tie. A beautiful girl in a
Shanghai-cut dress sidled up to a big wheel, perhaps even a Kuomintang
general. You would see a priest, of what denomination I don't know,
rubbing shoulders with an amah—a nurse. You could tell she was a
nurse by the black trousers and her special collar. Besides these, pimps,
whores, and from each and all, odors of sweat, odors of perfume.
Overhead big fans revolved and you wondered if they would drop and
decapitate the people. Everywhere handicappers, the chance takers,

looking for the big money quick. At my side walked this dove of a Eurasian beauty confidently guiding me to the fantan balcony.

She and I were in an upper tier where the wager is placed in a basket and lowered down on a pulley. It was accepted below. A note for your bet was put in the basket, and the game started. Fantan is played with a pile of mother-of-pearl counters or buttons, so that it is impossible to guess the amount or how many there are. You gamble with each throw of these tokens. You can double your gamble. You can play from five cents to five hundred dollars or more. A very fair game. It is mostly luck, not much skill.

I was doing well. Ting Ling was holding her own.

Near us stood a tall, distinguished-looking man, well dressed, but a bit bedraggled or harried. He had the face of a European aristocrat, with grayish brown hair and a pleasant whitish mustache, a bit yellow on the bottom, either from smoking or soup. As the game went, he looked on with detachment.

Ting Ling leaned over, said to me, "Look at him. Again he is not lucky tonight. Stupid Englishman. He's been smoking too much, I suppose."

"Smoking what?"

"Opium."

"How do you know?"

She laughed gently, like a whisper. "Haven't you seen behind his ears?"

I looked and saw nothing.

"Those marks. He is a two-elbow man."

"What in God's name do you mean?"

"Look at the things behind his ears. Those are the calluses. He smokes on both elbows because he has a callus behind each ear instead of one."

This time I saw the dark patches.

I asked, "What is that?"

"You smoke opium with your head on a wooden pillow. If you smoke it a lot you get a dark brown callus behind your ear. He has it behind both ears. That means that he smokes on both elbows."

She looked at me piercingly. "Would you like to smoke?"

I was ruffled—but intrigued.

"You never have?"

"No."

"If you like I'll show you."

Did I dare do this? Was I stepping into something I knew nothing of? Of course I was. But the adventure of it, the thought of a new experience—this I could never resist. I never had.

That night we won at fantan.

After the game, we wound our way through the scent of incense. It appeared that this place was also given over to opium smoking for private clients. Ting Ling seemed to know a lot about it.

I expected to be led into some kind of dungeon—for I'd heard the term "opium den." On the contrary, we were guided by one of the operators to a semiprivate room of reasonably ordinary appearance.

I entered and was confronted with a dark blue haze and a curious odor. There were only two people here. Sure enough they were on their elbows. The blue haze seemed to hang over them.

I sat on a soft mat. Ting Ling sat beside me.

A man entered the room with an orange that was cut in half and a lamp which was half copper, half jade. He scooped out the pulp interior of the orange and bored four little portholes into it. I watched Ting Ling while this operation was being done. Her eyes were wider as she looked at the little lamp.

A tiny flame was put in the empty half-orange skin.

The man also had what looked like a tin of English tobacco.

In Chinese Ting Ling had a long debate with him. I figured she was fixing the price.

Quickly a round wooden pillow was put near me. "Lie on your elbow," she panted. "Lie down. Relax."

Ting Ling arranged the pillow with a little impatient gesture, and I was made more or less comfortable.

She herself sat cross-legged, that blue haze around her, like a goddess, enchanted, distant, close, mysterious, all things.

The attendant took out two instruments like crochet needles. He opened the tin box and removed a black treacly substance—opium in the raw.

Ting Ling looked down at it carefully, nodded brightly. "Very good stuff. Very good."

Sitting cross-legged, the attendant cooked this inside the orange and the flame. It bubbled. He mashed it skillfully, delicately, like an artisan.

My eyes followed the work, fascinated.

Here he produced a magnificent instrument. It looked like an early saxophone, but small at each end.

Ting Ling took the freshly prepared pill from the attendant and put it in the end of the piccololike instrument, jamming it in.

She inhaled and held.

I counted. It was a long time.

Very slowly she exhaled.

She puffed very strongly, sibilantly inhaling. In a most truly graceful way she lay down beside me.

Silence.

She lay there staring into the ceiling—that lovely neck, beautiful face. Her figure writhed a little beside me on the mat.

After a time she slowly turned to me on her left elbow. "Now darling" —the first time she had ever called me that—"your turn. You see what I do?"

Surprisingly she lapsed into a pidgin English. "You do same. All same."

I grabbed the instrument and drew on it. The taste was unlike any tobacco that I ever had, but not unpleasant. Certainly wasn't burning my throat in any way.

The man prepared another little round black pill, stuck it on the end of the crochet needle and put it inside the orange. I tried to hold it and go through the same motions as Ting Ling had done.

She seemed to be looking at me with a faraway amusement. "Do you feel anything?" she asked.

"No." I didn't, except that I had a feeling I'd like to open the window.

"All right. Finish that one. Then lie down."

Together we lay side by side, both staring at the ceiling.

Suddenly that ceiling seemed to take on a new dimension. I felt Ting Ling's little hand on my right wrist. "How you feel?"

"Fine."

"You take a little bit more."

She said something in a soft tone to the fellow who prepared the smokes. He prepared another little pill.

The half-orange had grown bigger. Somehow, I don't know, but it seemed that it should be hanging from the ceiling like a Chinese lantern and my eyes were glued to it, fascinated.

I took the next *umchuck,* as Ting Ling told me it was pronounced in Macao.

Lying back, I began to feel a sense of panic. The orange in front of me was no longer an orange. It was a big old lantern, but it was now hilariously funny, because it was doing a dance and smiling at me.

Next thing my mind was clear as a crystal and I saw things as I have never seen them in sober perspective.

My life came before me.

It made sense.

There was this beauty beside me, looking into my eyes with what I believed was true tenderness, even passion.

I stroked her.

A lethargy came over me.

My body came out of my body. There I was on the floor, facing Ting Ling. It was extraordinary how my other body—I had two—hovered above me looking down. There was Flynn, four feet over my head, floating, held by invisible strands of I don't know what, a thing ethereal, bodyless, motionless, relaxed, amused by the whole façade and procession of his life.

Here was my love of my life by my side; so now we were three.

I whispered in Ting Ling's ear with what I can only suppose was the most stupid giggle. "Darling, darling, don't I look strange?"

She looked at me.

I said, "No, no. Me, up there."

She looked up and a strange smile crossed her lips. She said, "Put your head back. Dream."

I did.

I don't know how long it was I led a completely dual life, the one above me watching everything I did.

I was quite in charge of my limbs. As a matter of fact I seemed to have the strength of four men, let alone two.

When I took Ting Ling to another room, I had never known I was capable of such feats.

Today I'm told that the effect of opiates removes sexual desire in the man in inverse ratio to the female who becomes more excited. Dr. Flynn can tell you that such is not the case.

I made love to Ting Ling in ways and manners that I would never believe myself capable of.

Next day I put it all down to a dream.

It was getting so, as Koets prophesied, our bankroll had shrunk.

Playing with or against Ting Ling, the luck kept going and going, until I was desperate.

"Let's quit," he said.

"No, the luck has got to turn. It's got to."

I went to the hotel to meet Ting Ling. She was not there. I said to the room clerk, "Send along a message to her room."

She was not there either.

I went myself to her room. The door was locked.

I returned to the desk and asked for Miss O'Connor. The Chinese desk man looked up surprised. He had seen us together all the week. "Miss O'Connor? She go this morning, catch boat." He resumed with his work.

Catch boat! Impossible! How could she have left without—

I walked glumly over to Koets's scrummy quarters.

He looked at me with a very funny expression I had never seen before. He asked, "How much money have we got?"

"Not much. With a bit of luck—"

He cut me short. "And the pride of the Irish-Chinese—you didn't happen to lend her any money, did you?"

"Yes, but it wasn't a great deal."

"How much?"

"I lent her some every now and then, and she paid it back."

A horrible thought entered my head. I said, "Frankly, something between two and three thousand."

It was really closer to five thousand.

Koets asked, "And how much have we got yet?"

"I haven't counted it."

"Shitz! I knew you were pretty naïve in some ways but I didn't think you would fall for that. You know who your Chinese friend was?"

"What do you mean?"

"She was a shill. She plies that Macao–Hong Kong route regularly on the grab for suckers like you—and me."

"How do you know?"

"I haven't been around this dump a week for nothing. Just ask the manager. He'll tip you off."

"I don't believe it."

"She has a different name and a different set of addresses nearly every trip. The last trip she was under the name of Yok An Lee. She works with the gambling management. Her job is to double the play and break the customer."

I was speechless as Koets continued. "Well, she took me in too at first, I'll admit. But not for as long as you."

He got up and put his arm around my shoulder. "Cheer up, son.

As they say, there's one born every minute. What do we do now?"

I shook my head. I couldn't think. It hurt. I couldn't believe she was just a high-class whore who could teach me the things she did and do with me the things she did and say to me the wonderful things she said—and then dump me—and loot me besides.

"I don't know. Maybe we should go back to Hong Kong. If it's a question of getting stranded when the luck goes out, we might as well be on the beach there. Don't you think so?"

"Errol, my poor friend, let's pack—ahhh, shitz!"

That night we were on the boat back to Hong Kong.

It was one of the worst heart drops that ever happened to me. I actually thought she cared for me.

I also thought there must be something wrong with me.

As usual I checked my little box of—er—borrowed and uncut diamonds with the captain. Win all, lose all, I had clung to this grubstake as the single possession I absolutely would not part with. Never never would I gamble that. This, along with the fifty ounces of raw crude gold that was already there waiting my recovery at Barclay's Bank, must start me in England.

Arriving in Hong Kong, I took my package from the captain, signed a receipt for it, and decided that I must, as soon as we made shore, head for the Hong Kong and Shanghai Bank. It was stupid to carry these stones wherever I went, fleeing as we had to, moving precipitately. Be businesslike, let a big institution geared to handle such matters hang on to my wealth till I was ready to retrieve it.

"Now you are making sense for the first time since I know you," my friend said.

"Koets," I said, "I think I am coming down with malaria."

"Bad, bad, you take liquids."

Doctor's orders, so I retired to the ship's bar for a shandy. That's a lemonade with a little beer in it. The most that I was taking at that time. Malaria makes you very thirsty.

At the bar I tried to forget my illness by conversation with a fellow Australian of great charm. He was so pleasant, so amicable, that I found myself putting a bit more beer than usual or necessary in the shandy. One or two other travelers gathered about.

I was alternately cold, hot, the usual malarial reactions. I took off my white tropic coat, hung it on the back of my chair.

The boat docked. I put my coat back on, got off the ship.

"Let's go straight to the bank," I said, simultaneously putting my hand in my left jacket pocket.

That's funny. I put my other hand in my right pocket. I stopped. Koets was getting on ahead while I was feverishly going through my pockets. Where the hell was that packet of diamonds?—my diamonds! Pants pockets. Both sides. Not there. Back through the jacket pockets again.

Koets returned to my side.

"Come on! Back to the boat!"

Still shaking and shivering with malaria, and now with rage besides, I stormed up the gangplank. Koets hurried behind me. I headed back to the place where I had been sitting.

I put up a big outcry.

"What the hell kind of a ship do you run here! Can't an honest man make port without being stolen from!"

They searched the boat for hours trying to locate my grubstake of hard-earned and hard-"borrowed" cut and uncut diamonds. The Captain came down. Chinese detectives came down. British detectives. One American looked on.

You can't search a boat very easily. It is a big place to go over.

I got off and went barging from saloon to saloon looking for the Australian I had had those shandies with. I recalled two or three other fellows I had been drinking with, and I was willing to find any of them.

I found no trace of anybody.

Koets and I stood on the pier at Hong Kong and we looked at each other, sadly.

We were flat. Absolutely flat. Ting Ling had fleeced me. An Australian countryman had taken me. I had freely spent Koets's stake. We had nothing. Perhaps only a few pounds between us.

"I can sell my medical instruments," he said.

"Don't do that. No, don't do that."

"Wonder where we'll sleep tonight."

"Don't know. I don't know."

"It's a shame there's so much dishonesty."

That split both our guts. The gloom was over. We laughed at ourselves as we always did.

"Anyway," I said, "if I ever get to England there is fifty ounces of gold waiting for me."

"—If the bank don't find some reason to take it," said the dubious Dutchman.

We strolled into the commercial area of Hong Kong, wondering which way to turn next. A huge poster of a young Englishman in uniform pointed straight at me, saying, ENGLAND AND CHINA NEED YOU. *Join the Royal Hong Kong Volunteers.*

"Look at what my buddy is saying," I remarked.

"Yes, plenty trouble. Japs coming here any day now." They were already on the Chinese mainland.

"What about it? Let's join up. What have we got to lose?"

"Only our lives, son."

I pooh-poohed that as of no great importance. "We can eat till we're killed, can't we? They have to give us a spot in some barracks to sleep, don't they?"

"Those Japanese can shoot."

"So can we, can't we?"

"I think we ought to jump the first boat we can and try to work our way—get a steerage trip west. Somehow we could do it. I can always pick up a few dollars with an illegal operation."

I struck a romantic pose. "Look," I said, "we will march with the troops to victory." I was very jaunty. We were walking in a grimy part of Hong Kong, the Kuchai district. I contrasted the glories ahead of us with the squalor of our present position. I even recited a poem having to do with the martial spirit and causes.

He seemed to be considering it. I pressed the idea. "They're not going to pay much, but let's join up. Dying of hunger or exposure is no better than going by a bullet."

He shrugged his shoulders, but he was listening.

I made it vivid, romantic. "Come on, sport, let's go to old Cathay! What do we have to lose? Nothing! What can we gain? Everything, old boy! Loot, rape, plunder. Soldiers of fortune, sport, that's us!"

It seemed to stir him. Especially the rape part of it, especially the loot.

"You can join up as a doctor. I can join up as—"

"Out! No deal! If we go, we go together!"

"Why are you so stupid? You can get a good job as a doctor. I'll be holding you up—"

"*Raus! Raus!* No deal. Together or nothing!"

I loved those spaces over the hill. I always have all my life. What's around the corner? I have got to go and see. Koets had the same mentality. We had had it up and down already.

Like two idealists off on a crusade, we headed for the recruiting station. We'd check the Yellow Peril from Japan and preserve it for the exclusive use of the Chinese.

Actually I still don't know the rights and wrongs of that embroglio. In 1932 we knew that Hong Kong was in danger of being swallowed up. Everywhere there was talk about the possibility of evacuation. How far would the Japanese go? Even so, none of this meant a thing to Koets or to me. Neither of us gave a damn which way the wind blew or which current would take us where. Save perhaps the general objective of reaching the West some day.

Candidly we were thinking of our skins. If it was anything to us it was only adventure, action, the springtime and the nonsense and the villainy in our two souls—if we had any.

We lined up at the dead end of Hu Tung Avenue, where the recruiting barracks were. Inside the low-slung structure, a clammy, horrible-looking fortress, there were hundreds of us. Some had beards, some were clean-shaven, but apparently they were just as much out of a job as we were.

A young, fair-haired English subaltern with a blond mustache, five hairs on the left side of his upper lip, about seven on the right, with a notebook in his hand, followed by a corporal, was trying to get some order. An officer stepped forward and told us what our duties would be. We would go to Shanghai, already under fire, and barricade it before the Japanese had a chance to move in any further.

We were now soldiers.

We were issued a rifle apiece. Ammunition would be given us in Shanghai, because the available bullets didn't fit the available rifles. It would probably be cold in Shanghai, so we were issued greatcoats.

We were marched to the wharf. There we took ship for Shanghai, about four hundred of us, on a small China coaster.

I was a British subject. Koets was an American, and by joining up he had lost his citizenship although this never occurred to him at the time. Americans who enlist in foreign wars are frowned upon. Through all this passage he managed to hang onto his magic steel box containing all his paraphernalia, personal belongings and photographic equipment —and even some snake juice.

Three days later we disembarked. We could hear gunfire. Shanghai was already under siege. It was being attacked on the far bank. Boats anchored in the harbor were under fire.

"This is it, Koets! We're in it!" Now for the loot, the jade, the daughters of the Mings, the treasures of ancient Cathay!

On the wharf we were greeted by another little Englishman dressed in a fancy uniform. He said we would immediately be put in the front line against the Japanese.

While we listened what really engaged our attention was the heavy snowfall all around. The snow was two or three feet deep. I hadn't seen snow in a long time, not since Tasmania. I stood there shivering, wearing that too-small army coat and glad I had it.

"Now," said the little officer, "hand over your guns."

The guns were taken away from us. What the hell was this!

Suddenly a squad of Chinese came onto the scene carrying big heavy shovels and they were going down the ranks handing each of us a shovel!

"Shitz!" growled Koets, lapsing into dialect. "Vat kind of a war is dis!"

The commanding officer barked, "You will proceed to the outskirts of the city and there entrench!"

Koets and I asked what this was for. We were told, "Shut up and just do the job. You are Hong Kong Volunteers."

The next three weeks we dug and dug and dug. First we had to dig away the snow. Then we had to turn up the earth and pile up embankments behind which Shanghai would defend itself. Barbed wire went up. Trenches took form.

The food was not for description. The sleeping accommodations were meant for Chinese beetles.

Treasures of Cathay! I was doing more fast thinking than I had done since I put one over on the Lului chieftain back in New Guinea.

While we dug, occasional bullets were flying over our heads. Some fell short of where we were digging.

For days Koets and I gave each other odd looks, expressive of ideas, schemes, designs.

Finally our feelings burst from us simultaneously.

"Look at your hands," I said, feeding him a small touch of sedition. "Full of blisters! Those hands of yours were meant for operating with."

"You are absolutely right, you idiot, absolutely!"

"Why don't we beat it?"

"Desert?"

"Watch your vocabulary," I whispered.

"That's what it is—but I'm for it. I've had enough!"

For the next few days Koets did the primary scouting. He found a couple of Chinese boys who agreed to take us to a spot on the waterfront nearby where we could get a packet headed down the coast. If we had the money, our passports and a Shanghai Province Permit to get out with, we had a deal.

What the hell was a Shanghai Province Permit?

Koets, whispering to me between shovelfuls of earth, explained that the Shanghai Province Permit might present the greatest problem. It was a small card, rudely comparable to a visa, which said foreigners could not overextend their stay in the Shanghai Province without official sanction, and meaning it was okay to leave before a certain date stamped on it.

We located someone in the Hong Kong Volunteers who had such a permit. I examined it. What I saw gave me hope and an idea.

I looked through my kit of personal effects. Among the papers, receipts, were several Chinese laundry slips. Now to get two of these fixed properly. . . .

I worked over one of them. Down in one corner were the words in English: *Not responsible for laundry left here over six months.* Good, that was the spot to cover with a big British sixpence stamp. I affixed a big blub of sealing wax, with my thumb print on it. Next to that I wrote boldly in thick black ink: OK, ERROL FLYNN. I performed the same operation with Koets's slip, and he signed his name with the same OK.

I forged some Chinese hieroglyphics to it. Then, for the first time since childhood, I prayed, however irreverently, to God. "Look, Sport," I said to Him, "get us out of this Egg Foo Yong."

Koets sold some medical equipment and we now had enough Shanghai to get on a boat.

One evening when, ostensibly, we adjourned to the latrine, we stole out of the barracks.

We hustled down to the waterfront where we met a wizened little fellow who said, like I had heard in whorehouses in New Guinea and the Philippines, "The money, please," with his hand held out.

We were taken on board a bedraggled little packet no more than twenty feet long and perhaps a third of that in the beam. It smelled as if it had been well lived in.

The captain asked to see our credentials, just in case he was stopped en route anywhere and questioned why he was carrying two foreigners. We showed him our papers.

I had carefully stamped this pink laundry slip in a Chinese lettering which meant "Good until December 1933." He fingered that with care, looked at it suspiciously, as Koets shoved some Shanghai at him.

The laundry slip was okay. So were the Shanghai. We could get out of China.

Now for the long jump . . . weeks of travel, all the way to Indo-China.

If we were in luck, our arrow was at last pointing west.

I think I might justly claim to be the only man who traveled through China with a laundry slip for a passport.

> DEAR PATER [I wrote to my father in March of 1933, from Colombo, Ceylon]:
>
> I am on a voyage of discovery. We have seen much of the Orient and I shall have much to tell you of the biology, geography and the philology of these cultures when, as I hope soon, I shall see you. My heartfelt thank-you for cabling the fifty pounds. Pal Koets and I were in a genuine spot when we reached Saigon. We promised the captain of the barkentine who took us from Shanghai that we would have money for him when your cable arrived, but alas, when the money came, we decided we could put it to better use than he.
>
> So we left him to find his own means of returning to China— doubtless a wiser voyager than when he set out with us. You won't believe it when I tell you that a Chinese laundry slip made it possible for us to get out of the Sino-Jap war and off the Asian continent. We have just completed a long trip across Andaman Sea and the Bay of Bengal on board a French boat called the *D'Artagnan*. On board with us were French Colonial Officers. It was a quiet voyage. Before long I will be with you in England. I think I am going to try to make a career of acting when I arrive in London. I feel that that is what I want to do and where I may make my fortune. Give my love to Mother and to little Rosemary.
>
> Respectfully, your son,
>
> ERROL

What I didn't tell Father about the trip on the *D'Artagnan* is, of course, the real story. . . .

She was Japanese and the most spectacular sight you ever saw. I thought she was a dream, out of this world and out of the Japanese world, for she was the most un-Japanese Japanese I have ever seen. Slender, with a twenty-inch waist, and long-legged, which was surprising for a Japanese. Her name was Mayako. She came from Kobe, in Japan, and she was married to a Swiss who was on board with her, a big, rough type. There was a Swiss colony in Kobe, and there they had met and married. Now he was taking her to a sanitarium in his homeland because they hoped to cure her of lung trouble.

Mayako spoke perfect English, perfect French, and she talked German with Koets. Actually her condition was quite grim.

I decided that if she were so ill that she might die, and so young and so beautiful, she certainly should have a fling before passing away. I doped the situation this way: if she was really that ill, she would want one too. I was right.

As usual, I was in first class and Koets was down in steerage. Yet we wound up traveling back and forth between the two levels. This once, though I had passage on the upper deck, I found it advantageous to have a place in the steerage to go to and to bring Mayako.

Her husband seemed to be absent most of the time. She would find it quite pleasant to visit the steerage with Koets and me. My growing affair had been going on with her surreptitiously for several days before we were due to land at Colombo, in Ceylon. If I thought, however, that her husband was unaware of what was going on, I must have been crazy, bemused by that old biological urge.

On the night before we arrived at Colombo, Mayako was below with me in Koets's quarters. Koets was up on deck. She had only a few minutes before given me two beautiful pearls, valuable, expensive black pearls. She said she wanted me to have them as a token of our dear relationship aboard the *D'Artagnan*. I accepted, about the only gift a woman ever gave me, materially I mean. We followed this with a passage of beauty and emotion, immediately after which, who should kick his way through the closed door but the irate Swiss. I was half-dressed. His wife was on the cot, her feet touching the floor, not clad as fully as she would be on the upper deck.

He seized my throat in his two hands. I could feel my tongue coming out and I was starting to go black. I couldn't shake him off, even though I was in good shape, for he was a much more powerful man than I. He was furious, absolutely mad, out of his mind. This is the worst kind of attacker to have to contend with.

As he dug his fingers into my throat, he shouted, "I am going to kill you, I am going to kill you, I am going to kill you now!"

While he said this I tried to pry loose his fingers and get my tongue back into my mouth, since it was hanging down, it seemed to me, about a foot.

I finally whipped him around. I did it by falling on him. I couldn't throw him over my head, he was too strong, but when I fell backward with him, it broke his grip.

He glared at me. "I kill you!" and was ready to lunge again. White-faced, he turned suddenly to his wife. "Get out!"

"Are you mad?" I said. "What the hell do you think we were doing?"

"Don't talk! I am not interested. I am going to kill you!" Both of us very much out of breath, hardly able to talk. I was willing to talk at length, I said, if he would stop repeating himself.

"Look, do you really mean to say that you suspect your wife of ill-doing, of anything wrong? Your wife! *You* suspect her?" Out of breath, I was bluffing, but by this time I figured I could handle men, if not women. I thought I had him stymied. He said, "You'll see!" and slammed the door.

I turned to examine myself in the mirror over the washbasin.

After a minute or so I heard the door behind me crash open and shut. In the mirror I could see him behind me. I turned swiftly. There he was, a revolver in his hand. The sudden realization came to me. This man means business!

He was breathing hard, heavy, with a fixed grin and white face. "I told you I was going to kill you, right?"

Reflexes are very strange things. This was no time to mollify or try to argue it out. He had the gun barrel pointed straight at my scrotum. It went through my mind if I said one more word he would shoot. If I try to argue, he'll drill me.

"Look!" I shouted and pointed out the porthole. At the same instant I flung myself the eight feet of the cabin right at his knees. The bullet went off over my head. It went around the steel cabin like a blowfly over a piece of cheese. I could hear it zinging from wall to wall.

I had to get that gun. I lunged for his right arm and hung on to it. Didn't care what I did so long as I got rid of that. With his left hand he was giving me the biggest pounding I could get on the back of my neck. He was nuts, screeching, completely out of control, but I had that damned gun. Under the bunk there was a little opening about two inches deep. I tossed the gun into that hollow.

I jumped on top of him. Tried to give him the same as he was giving me.

The shot had been heard. In came the French ship's officers. "What's the noise?" they demanded. Mayako, poor little one, was crouched in a corner of the bunk in semitrauma.

Our fighting ceased as the officers demanded to know what was going on. When I told them he tried to shoot me and the gun was under the bunk, politely they took hold of the Swiss and led him away. They also took Mayako out of the cabin. Then they faced me.

"We're coming into Colombo. You'll have to get off the ship. Otherwise we can't be responsible for what this man does to you."

"Why doesn't he get off? He tried to shoot me."

"Yes, that's true, and we think he'd try it again. But after all, he's paid two first-class passenger fares and you have paid one."

The French are very practical people.

You can't argue against economics.

Koets was standing in the doorway, enchanted by the whole thing. Anything out of the normal rut of living delighted him. Nothing pleased him more than to see people at cross purposes. He said once it was like watching bacteria in movement under a microscope. People, when they fought, must be observed the closest, in order to find the greatest truth. So he watched now with clinical interest and a faint smile. I knew that he took great amusement in watching me any time I was in trouble. He wondered what springs prompted me.

We were bounced, Koets and I. Before I went, I insisted that I pay my respects to the charming little lady. My condition for leaving the boat was to bid her farewell under a flag of truce.

Accompanied by two officers and Koets, I knocked on the door of Mayako's stateroom. The Swiss opened it and glared out. Mayako was lying prone, a nervous wreck.

I stared him straight in the eye, and said sternly, "Sir, you amaze me."

He choked. "I amaze you!"

"I wonder how you could treat such a beautiful person as your wife in this manner."

Of course I was full of absolute blarney, ordure and wicked corn.

"Don't you feel ashamed of yourself?" I shook my head reproachfully.

"No, I don't feel ashamed. I don't feel ashamed at all!"

"I just came to bid your charming wife farewell. I'm leaving this ship."

"The sooner you get off the better it will be for you." I could sense his emotions rising.

I went over to Mayako. She was trembling. Those beautiful eyes. Her lovely skin. Probably the most beautiful Japanese girl I have ever seen in my life.

I picked up her little hand, knowing her husband was breathing heavily on my back, kissed it and said, "I hope life will be kind to you. Thank you very much."

My exit, I hoped, was dignified.

Having been kicked off the boat, the thing to do was to push on to Europe. No use staying at Colombo: unfamiliar language, no money around, no purpose here. We looked at maps, made inquiries: the next point to head for was Pondichéry, a port on the Indian mainland.

It was a strange town, under French control, and—like hungry men —we swiftly went to the nerve center to sample its French and East Indian flavors. As Koets always put it, "The heart and soul of any city is its whorehouses. Go there first. Afterwards pay your respects to the Governor, if he will receive you, eat well, enjoy some music, have some fun. But if you want to find out what is going on—definitely, the whorehouse."

We approached a place recommended by one of the ricksha boys. We patronized the ladies, we talked at length with the madam, even dallied with her—often the very best—and as we left the particular salon described to me as the pride of Pondichéry . . .

Our ricksha man was a French-Colonial Indian. He was extra smart, it seemed to me, a little impolite. Koets stood nearby taking pictures of the house where we had been entertained.

I am personally opposed to tipping, unless somebody does something special for you. This ricksha man had done a slight service for us and he had been paid the fair price. But he wanted a tip and began screaming in Hindustani. I tried to make myself understood in French, which he might understand. "What is your problem? I am broke today," some such words as that. He answered me in pretty good French, "But I still have to have my tip."

Koets and I frowned. The man's manners were poor. He was very chesty. His chest was right up against mine, threatening.

I fear I am not the fellow to give the chest treatment to.

When it was clear to him he would get no more money from us, he kicked Koets in the shins. That didn't hurt Koets, because the Hindu had bare feet. But it was poor behavior.

I grabbed the fellow and gave him a waff right where I thought his chin would be. But his head wasn't there.

His head went around and away in a very wily manner. My fist passed over his head. The next instant, there he was, with a knife that shone like quicksilver, and in a single fast stroke he cut my guts from my scrotum to the navel.

I stood there shocked, bleeding in a great gush, with my guts hanging out. The attacker leaped away and was out of sight in the scattering of no time.

I bent over in excruciating pain.

"Stand up straight!" Koets bellowed and grabbed hold of my intestines and stuffed them back in and held them, my belly skin in one huge paw, very red now.

He hailed another ricksha immediately. I was taken to the hospital. As I was being moved off, police arrived, but I was indifferent and losing much blood.

I had sixteen stitches put in this wound and when anyone sees my belly today under the shower or elsewhere they gape, "Some appendix."

Luckily the blade hadn't punctured the intestines, just the skin. A clean-cut rip.

I was supposed to be in bed for two weeks, but in two days I got up. Naturally the wound opened up again, the lymph exploding, and again I lay disabled in that hospital bed.

Koets was angry. "If you don't lie down I'll leave you. Besides that, goddamit, I'll kill you!"

He raged on. "No point in your asking my advice if you don't intend to take it." I said I hadn't asked his advice.

They had to do another job of hemstitching on my belly. After another two weeks of lying there I began to wonder how I would pay them.

Finally I told them I had no money. Besides that, they had the services of the eminent world-famous surgeon and physician, Dr.

Koets. "If you don't realize the importance of this incident in the life of your hospital, then I can't do anything for you."

Up the East Indian coast. Five days in a jammed train that moved not much faster than a man running leisurely. Thirty children in the coach with us. Intolerable heat. A diet of rice. Through the windows, seeing the Untouchables. In the car with us, Untouchables. We ourselves, Undesirables in the land.

A week in Calcutta. Wandering through the city. The dizzying spectacle, the temples, the beggary, the dung in the streets, the wispy Indian girls in their white wrappings. The whorehouses of Calcutta.

Steerage on another French boat, *La Stella,* headed down the Indian coast, through the Gulf of Mannar, due west to Africa. A brawl with a huge black Senegalese soldier on board ship. We were in tiers in the steerage. This huge fellow, sleeping above me, had a habit of coughing, then spitting so that his saliva landed near me. "Look, you bastard, don't spit next to me!" He said, *What!* "You heard me! If you are going to spit, spit three feet to the right or left!" *I will spit where I want to spit!* "You will?" I pulled him out of his berth—a grave error. He picked me up almost as if I were a cat, gave me a whaff over the chin, knocked me out against the wall. When I came to I said, "I have decided you can spit where you want to." Koets held his belly with delight over the incident that lightened our long passage through the wide sea.

Koets guided me to a little room on board ship and asked me to peek inside. It was a captain in the Colonial Army, stark naked, his pale goateed face reflecting death. His legs looked huge as those of an elephant. His two testicles, each big as a basketball, rested on the floor. "Elephantiasis," Koets said. "He's dying." He had been called in as a physician, but he told the officers nothing could be done for the man; he'd be dead in a day or two. After the man died, Koets rushed to me saying, "You know what they found in his cabin? Two and one half kilos of opium! They never paid me for my services. If I'd have known of that dope I'd have kiped it and could have peddled it for thousands!"

Djibouti, the capital of French Somaliland. A brawl with the customs people. I slugged the wrong man, the aide of an important French official. Jail. One of the vilest I was ever in, while Koets rushed to the American Consul and the British Consul to get me out. The British Consul sprang me.

But we were grounded, for our boat had gone on to Marseilles and no other would come for ten days or two weeks. What to do? We were moneyless as usual. "Look," I said, "you realize we are on the threshold of the fabulous kingdom of Ethiopia? You realize this is where the Queen of Sheba was born, where she saw Solomon, and all those historical things? Why don't we go up there?" How do we live? he wanted to know. I asked, "How have we lived so far?"

We arrived in Addis Ababa. Koets promptly bumped into an old classmate from the University he had attended. Next we were in the company of Ras Tafari, the Prime Minister of Ethiopia, posing as big-game hunters. In his personal bungalow—sixteen servant girls, sixteen waiters, a cool, beautiful place. "Where are your rifles?" Ras Tafari asked. Oh, they would be coming to us, along with our carriers, after we explored the hunting possibilities. A week around here, the whore-houses.

England was coming closer.

Yet we were in no hurry. The spell of our wild rollick across the world was heavy upon us. We were sampling the variety of the world.

The Suez Canal. A slow trip along the Red Sea. The Mediterranean. Marseilles.

You got your education about bordellos in the south of France, especially at Marseilles. You saw the most irregular things at small cost. I had to see them.

You are born for peep shows and horror shows or you are not. For example, at Marseilles I saw a braying donkey mounting a French girl, something I can never forget. I saw that, and worse, and it always offended some innate sense, so that I was inclined to laugh at the wrong time, from nervousness. Yet instead of running away, I was held by an irresistible compulsion.

I enter a whorehouse with the same interest as I do the British Museum or the Metropolitan—in the same spirit of curiosity. Here are the works of man, here is an art of man, here is his eternal pursuit of gold and pleasure. I couldn't be more sincere. This doesn't mean that if I go to La Scala in Milan to hear *Carmen,* that I want to get up on the stage and participate. I do not. Neither do I always participate in a fine representative national whorehouse—but I must see it as a spectacle, an offering, a symptom of a nation.

I think I can truthfully say that my behavior in whorehouses has been exemplary. These are about the only institutions I never have been ejected from.

On that trip across the middle of the earth and since then I have found great companionship with these ladies. After they had got through telling you how they became a whore and you listened to the sad story of their lives, you found them the easiest people to level with. There is nobody more charming to talk to than a whore, unless possibly an old lady. These are two types I can get along with, respectable old ladies and whores. They both speak the same language. There is a wider outlook in a whore and a dear, sweet little ancient lady. They look at life just as it is. Both have lost their inhibitions long ago, and they don't much give a damn.

Neither are harsh women. They may be sad, sick, victims, nymphomaniacs, or something else, but they deserve better than any condemnatory term.

The queerest place we were in was in Marrakech, in French Morocco, a male whorehouse. Marrakech is a bizarre place anyway.

I was under the impression I was going to a bordello. So was Koets. Inside we found it was all boys. Big rich Arab sheiks and others picked out their boys from a lineup of dancers. The boys would swing their hips and twitch the wrist. They were homos for that section of old Marrakech who were only interested in young boys. It was all a forthright, blunt exposition of that kind of sexuality in a place approved of in that society. In any other country they would all have been scooped up by the police in no time and carted off to jail. To me that sight was horrible, but as the saying goes, one man's meat is another's poison, and we must remember ancient Greece and the epoch of Pericles, even Socrates.

In eight months we had traveled through seven seas, more than halfway around the world, from the Coral Sea of the New Guinea regions, north to the East and South China Seas, then down to the Anadaman, across the Arabian, the Red, the Mediterranean Seas.

At Marseilles, Koets and I parted company. We did not know whether we would ever meet again.

My heart was heavy. I felt, here is the one person in the world I could really cling to; a wonderful friendship between two men. I thought, Perhaps this is the end of a very deep, deep friendship. He was headed back to some European university to take a postgraduate course. I would make the last coastal jump from Marseilles to London.

This man was the great influence in my life. He showed me in a humorous, bawdy, Rabelaisian, tough, rough way the difference between a man with no soul and a man with one, even though neither of us was sure what a soul was.

He, more than any other, gave me a certain style.

He showed me the difference between cupidity and generosity. He showed me the complete irrelevance of the existence that we humans have while on earth. From Koets I learned to take from this brief span the unimportance of being earnest. I learned from him to laugh at the worst disasters.

PART FOUR

An Actor's Life For Me!

1933-1943

I ARRIVED at Waterloo Station in London with exactly two shillings—thirty cents. Just about the fare from the station to the most fashionable hotel in the city, the Berkeley. After I gave the cabby the fare, there was three cents left. "Keep the change," I told him.

I looked at the imposing entrance.

I stood there dressed in khaki, with a couple of brass dinglets around my neck. I hung onto my small suitcase which was cracking open at several places.

Here goes, sport, take a chance.

I walked inside. I explained to the desk clerk that my luggage was lost in French Somaliland. I gave him a hard sell on who I was, my fortune in Barclay's Bank. I must have done some skillful lying, for to my dismay he put me up in the Royal Suite: three or four bedrooms, a beautiful view of the park. My predecessor in these quarters had been the young King of Jordan.

I was in this room with just about nothing to wear. My shoes were worn and without color. I had no tie.

I ordered a huge meal and signed for it. Now, call Barclay's Bank.

I did. My gold dust had not been cleared through the bank. They didn't seem to know about it. I had better come see them.

I wired my father, who was lecturing at Heidelberg University. AT THE BERKELEY. NEED A LIFT. LIKE TO SEE YOU. There was no answer.

For two days the hotel staff was very sympathetic. Then the management became restive. How to get out of here?

I turned in one of my earliest performances. I came down with a violent case of appendicitis. The management leaped into the breach heroically. They transferred me to one of the most exclusive nursing homes in the West End.

There I lay in bed, groaning, wondering how I was to get hold of money. On the second day of my stay the doctors found nothing wrong with me. There was only one consolation.

My nurse turned out to be a truly lovely girl, aged twenty-two, pretty, efficient, smiling, and dressed in the old-fashioned Florence Nightingale attire.

An English nursing home for the rich is so arranged that the patient's door has a lock on it. The patient can privately entertain friends of the opposite sex.

Dusk settled. Then darkness. I said, "Nurse, lock the door. I wish to tell you something."

She was near, on the small bed, her soft hair next to my cheek. I talked into her aristocratic shell-like ear. I confided my whole story, how I had arrived as I had, broke, desperate, my gold not available, my father not answering my wire. I had feigned illness.

I felt her body shaking beside me, like suppressed tears, I thought. But it became swiftly gales of laughter. She thought it was "frightfully funny."

"I shall help you—" she said.

"You are a darling."

"—On condition that you stay here two more days."

"But how shall I be able to repay you?"

"Don't worry. Daddy's quite rich. But you must stay—or I'll tell on you."

I didn't need such a threat to stay. The food was fine. The personal attention was the choicest. My lovely young caretaker nursed me back into a condition of primal animal vitality.

Yet on the eve of my third day, the night before I was due to leave, she whispered into my ear of marriage. I felt that it was indeed time to leave this haven.

A reply finally came from my father: IF YOU ARE STAYING AT THE BERKELEY WHY DO YOU NEED MONEY?

In the interim my gold dust had cleared at Barclay's. My money, the equivalent of eighteen hundred dollars, was available. I repaid my nurse, but was still in her debt. She feared she was pregnant—and I was supposed to be disabled with appendicitis!

I set about in earnest to get work in the theatre. Not just any job now. But the theatre. Nothing less. The decision I had made in New Guinea to dedicate myself to some kind of artistic calling I now decided to press to whatever end. If I couldn't write, I would act. It would be one or the other.

Weeks of job hunting went by. I foot-slogged it around Leicester Square. London. But I couldn't get my nose into a door without being tossed out. Where did you come from? Who are you? What have you played in?

"I'd like to see the casting director."

"Don't bother us. We have fifty chaps a day like you trying to get a job!"

I had a room, small and inexpensive. Hoard your dough now, boy, this may take time. I traveled the circuit of Piccadilly Circus.

I bumped into an agent, a Mrs. Davis. "Tell you what to do," she said, "take an ad in *Spotlight*." That was the *Variety* of the English stage. "Run a picture of yourself, a list of the plays you've appeared in, give it a try."

I had a picture taken several years earlier, working out in boxer's clothes, trying out for the Olympics. At the cost of twenty pounds I set up an ad with my picture at the top:

ERROL FLYNN
Appeared in *Berea Coldeen*
SMASH HIT!
Appeared in *The Wake of the Bounty*
HIT!
Appeared in *Appleby's Dilemma*
DON'T MISS IT!
Appeared in *The Gorgeous Groom*
GENUINE HIT!

With but one exception they were unknown play titles invented by inventive playwright Flynn. Nobody was taken in. There was no clamor for my services. It got so the doormen at the agents' offices knew me and wouldn't even say hello.

This went on for months. I was drawing on my New Guinea gold reserve.

One day I got a call from Mrs. Davis. She had arranged for me to have an interview with a Mr. Robert Young, director of the Northampton Repertory Company.

In my usual fashion, putting on a front, I invested all of my remaining gold dust fund in an automobile. I had to land this, make it look like I worked regularly. I drove to Northampton, a dowdy, dreary place where they manufactured boots.

Mr. Young was a gray-haired, fine-looking man. He sat in a dingy office. About him were a half-dozen cats. They seemed to listen to the conversation. I hoped he wouldn't ask me to tell him about those plays. But it was my picture, posing as a fighter, that had caught his eye.

"Young man, do you by any chance play cricket?"

I had never played it in my life, except for some piddling back yard running about at school years before, but I gave him that puzzled look as if, how could he ask such an inane question? "Certainly, sir."

"Bowl or do you bat?"

I had no idea what he meant. "Ah, that depends on the captain," I said, stalling.

It turned out that his acting company's cricket team was to play a team from Coventry. They needed an extra man, an outfield or a long-on, whatever those positions meant.

"What about the play? I understand you have a part for me."

"Yes, I see you have had much theatrical experience."

Indeed I had, but not the sort he meant.

"We are putting on a fairy tale. Would you like to play the wicked Prince Donzil?"

I had no idea who the character was but if he was wicked I felt I'd stand half a chance of putting on a convincing performance.

I read the simple child's story. Wicked Prince Donzil, I thought, should look like the Devil himself. I memorized my lines and when the afternoon came for a rehearsal, I appeared on stage in what I thought was an excellent getup. It took me three hours to make up. I cut the hairs off two toothbrushes and put them on my chin. I angled my eyebrows upward, obliquely, in a Mephisthophelean way. I laid the color and the grease on heavily.

The rehearsal was under way. I walked on, with my impressive costume, in time to take the princess away from the hero. Bang! I forgot my lines. I stared at the empty rows, frozen.

Mr. Young's eyes settled on my heavily made-up face. "For God's sakes, what have you got on your face?" Then a tirade. "Take it off! Go away! Get rid of at least two pounds of that ordure. Get off the stage!"

It was my first experience. I have since wondered how anybody gets a start in the theatre.

To make matters worse, we played cricket against Coventry a few days later. Thanks to my ignorance of the game, we lost heavily.

Director Young called me into his office. "Flynn, I am sorry."

My heart was sinking.

"Yes sir, Mr. Young, I did have a bad day. I was thinking of my lines, or I would have played a better game."

"You were thinking of your lines!—and you let Coventry beat us at cricket?"

He was furious. He felt I just didn't fit here. Especially, he said, when I was getting more than six pounds a week. "This is outrageous," he said. "Well, old boy, I wish you luck."

My head was hanging.

"Of course if you weren't getting so high a salary . . . Suppose you were getting something like three pounds a week? Would you . . ."

Would I! I took the cut. I liked the idea of going out of town for another reason, to help in the process of shedding my suddenly too solicitous nurse.

I stayed at Northampton Repertory for a year and a half. I played everything: old maids, old women, chauffeurs, butlers, detectives, burglars. At first I was Williams, generally the butler:

> *Who is that?*
> FLYNN: Williams the butler, sir.
> *Come in.*
> FLYNN: Your car is downstairs, sir.
> *Yes, Williams.*

From being the low man in the company, I somehow rose to the heights, bigger roles, when there were often as many as six people in the theatre: a play called *Yellow Sands;* another was *Once in a Lifetime.* In a third I was a Communist fisherman. Each night the people of Northampton came to see us perform and they would applaud, all six of them. That gave you a great feeling you were accepted, not doing too badly. Later more people came and got to know you very well. When you came on they gave you a hand, they clapped when the play was finished. "You'll get to the West End yet," some would say in the pub over an "arf pint."

That was the big deal. Going from the Northampton Repertory to the big-time shows in the West End of London. If you didn't get there you weren't much. And you never would be until you did get there. There were several acting companies in England—the Birmingham Company, the Liverpool Repertory, and the one I was in. But these rated as "the provinces." It was your training ground, but the beacon pointed to the London theatre. Some of the great names of today's theatre came from the Birmingham Repertory: Greer Garson, Sir Cedric Hardwicke and Sir Barry Jackson. And Robert Donat was the leading light at the time of my arrival in England. Sir Laurence Olivier was already going great.

I got my chance at Shakespearean roles. I had minor spots in *Macbeth* and *Romeo and Juliet*. I played the title role in *Othello*. My performance is still remembered; it was said I made the worst Othello in the history of the English stage. In that role I wore a heavy crimson robe embossed with metal. One night as I performed, the dagger that I reached out for, to kill myself with, got caught in the folds of this robe. I couldn't get it out. At first I thought I'd have to choke myself to die. I decided that the best thing to do was to die of a heart attack. I did, and it made no difference to the audience.

I loved Shakespeare. Once you learned the Bard, his lines stayed in your memory. They remain with me to this day, though I have not played a Shakespearean part since that time. Memory is a strange thing. Though I may have trouble now remembering what happened two days ago, it was never too hard for me to learn lines, except at the very beginning. After that it became a matter of training. You had to learn Shakespeare in a week, while playing two performances a day of another play.

In *Othello* my Desdemona was Frieda Jackson, today one of England's formidable actresses. She liked onions and beer. I didn't drink then and I never liked onions. When she was lying on her deathbed and I had to murmur over her little lips, "Oh thou, my beloved," and the ungentle fragrance of the onion floated up from her, it was hard to be passionate. Nonetheless we both got on in the theatre.

I played Bulldog Drummond, too. I was about to shoot Patterson, the heavy in the play. "I will shoot you in cold blood, Patterson. You are a rat." I pulled the trigger and nothing happened. And I was stuck, so I walked to the front of the stage and confided to the audience, "There is a slight hitch!" They didn't mind.

We put on an American gangster play. An American might have found it hilarious to hear Al Capone played with an English accent. I did the part of a smart, wisecracking American newspaperman. At this time my inflection was a combination of Australian, English and Irish influences.

My literary ambitions forged to the surface. I wrote a play called *Cold Rice*. It was a satire on imperial British India, two pukka sahibs over their "chota pegs" saying interminably, "Drums, old chap, I say, musn't let the ladies know." I even showed at a small theatre in the

Midlands. The central fact of the play was its sharp ridicule of woman-hood. Women seemed to me so stupid, so fatuous, that I had to express it in dramatic terms.

I have been expressing it in the same terms ever since, I suppose.

I managed, in the course of several months, to shake my lovely nurse. The pregnancy fear abated or aborted, I forget which. I put it all down as another part I played: the cad.

Instead, I met Elinor Jocelyn. She was very young, endowed with a beautiful body and hardly a brain in her head.

When we weren't rehearsing, or performing in the evening, we went horseback riding. When we weren't doing these things, we found other pursuits as the saying doesn't go. Once she saved me from getting fired. My salary had gone up to the giant sum of eight pounds a week. The director decided that I might be getting too big for my boots. I was threatened with dismissal, and this girl interceded for me.

The Northampton Repertory had its sponsors, rich old ladies who frittered around in the field of culture and the green field of young men. One of these, a woman of great wealth, had a strictly cultural interest in the drama, and was also endowed with an incredible name. She liked to talk about Shakespeare and the world of the theatre, but had other interests which were anything but cultural. I was invited to her beautiful country house one weekend, and I was stunned to find myself, late in the evening, caught in a bear's hug. She had this half nelson on me. She was so visibly repulsive that I truly felt as if I were being raped. I finally managed to break away, went to my room and locked my door. She made no further sally on my chaste manhood that night. I left her house the following day after a rather desultory breakfast. Pitfalls of the theatre.

I was surprisingly faithful to the attractive Elinor. She had my entire interest at the time, making my last six months at the Northampton Repertory Theatre very agreeable. She was a beginner—at the theatre —and I was seasoned with a year's stage experience when our relationship began. The situation reminds me of a tale apocryphally told by the old character actor who, recalling his young and beginning days, said, "Ah yes! Those were the days we were playing *Hamlet* at Seaforth: myself as the Gloomy One, my wife playing the Queen, and the woman I was sleeping with at the time, I forget her name—Ophelia— Ah, what a cast, my boy!"

All of this came to a head with the Stratford-on-Avon Festival. Actors, playwrights, audiences, gather there and plays are performed nightly. I was selected to appear in two. I had a part in a play by John Drinkwater, *A Man's House,* and also a role in another play: *The Moon and the Yellow River,* by Dennis Johnson, now a well-known playwright. Both shows were selected to go to the West End.

That was the big moment in any actor's life—the West End. The performances were at different theatres blocks apart. In *A Man's House* I played the part of a Roman soldier. In the other play I was an Irish cop. I had to change costumes each night, from cop to Roman soldier, and run for five minutes through the streets, between theatres, so as to appear in both vehicles. One night something went wrong with *A Man's House* and there was a delay. I ran through the streets as a Roman soldier. I arrived at the other show in time to go on as an Irish cop. I went on in my Roman toga.

While the audience gasped for breath at the spectacle of an Irish cop dressed as a Roman soldier, I did the best I could. I cut my speech in half and got offstage as fast as I could.

The shows lasted two weeks. Both flops.

But I was spotted by Irving Asher, then the head of Warner Brothers pictures in England, and his studio manager, Doc Solomon.

They called backstage and asked me if I cared to play a part in a moving picture to be made locally called *Murder at Monte Carlo.* I agreed. It was a quickie, a cops and robbers thing of no consequence, but the film was sent on to Jack Warner.

Warner saw me popping around on the screen with a lot of energy.

There followed an offer of a six-month contract to Hollywood. One hundred and fifty bucks a week. A fortune. They would also buy me a wardrobe. Good. I liked clothes then.

They got me a shooting jacket, riding boots and other English apparel, all of which would be of no earthly use in Hollywood.

It was fashionable in the theatre to leer down at the films at this time. We were the august and traditional theatre, but I didn't look down my nose at the offer entirely. I wanted to see Hollywood. Very well, I'd go for a few months, and return before long to the legitimate theatre in England.

I wrote to my mother and father in Ireland that I was on my way to America. I had a job in films.

None of this meant very much to them. They knew their son. He was trying something else, that was all. This would last a few weeks or months, and he would then probably take up something else.

Vastly amusing, the word went around in Ireland, Errol has a new hobby.

On board *The Paris,* bound for New York, there sailed people who were or were to become famous stars. Going to America for the first time was Merle Oberon, a smash in *Henry VIII,* Louis Hayward, with whom I became friends, and the Russian princess, Naomi Tiarovitch. Probably the most celebrated passenger was Lili Damita. She had been featured as leading lady in numerous money-making films starring Victor McLaglen, Lowe, and others in Europe.

They were not my circle. I hesitated to intrude. I was too awestruck.

Yet I couldn't escape watching the beautifully dressed Damita arrogantly walking the deck. Everything about her was arrogant; and the more arrogant the more beautiful. Did I imagine it, or did I not? Had she given me a few fairly friendly glances?

We were about four days across the ocean when I worked up enough courage to approach this lithe fabulous creature of great animation and ask her to dance. It was evening. I crossed a glass dance floor illuminated by colored lights. It seemed to me the mood and the moment were right. She was seated at a table with the other screen figures.

When I worked up enough guts to ask for the dance she carefully hesitated. She looked about among her friends, eyebrows raised. "Perhaps," she said indifferently. "Come back later."

I slunk back to my table, the longest few yards I ever had to make.

There were two things I wanted to see on my arrival in New York. One was Jack Dempsey's restaurant, and the other was Harlem. That was about all I knew of New York, by hearsay, other than that it had the tallest buildings in the world. I was surprised when a Warner Brothers man met me at the pier. He took me to the St. Moritz Hotel and said good-by to me after I checked in.

I got in the elevator. Who should be in there but the very alluring Princess Tiarovitch. We had seen each other on board ship, but had never spoken. She gave no sign of knowing me. I said nothing. But she said to the elevator boy, "What floor is Room 801 on?" On the eighth, of course, answered the elevator boy. I went on up to the tenth. Did I dare? I kept thinking. Was I a man or a mouse? Anyone with the least bit of sophistication could tell that that was her way of telling me what room she was in.

In my small room I hesitantly picked up the phone and called her.

I was answered by a deep, delightful slightly Russian accent. "Hello. Who is it?"

I rattled as fast as I could. "Look, I do hope you will forgive me, but I was in the elevator with you just now and we were on the same boat. I wondered—er—I wondered if you could . . . "

"Oh, yes. I remember you now. Of course. Would you care to come to my apartment?"

I rushed to my dresser, grabbed a bottle of cologne. squirted it everywhere, combed my hair, knotted my best tie, and was on my way.

It was a large apartment, making my quarters seem a little like a dog kennel.

"I have some champagne. Would you care to join me?"

Would I!

She chatted about the voyage. What was I going to do in the States? . . . Oh, you are going to Hollywood? . . . She would be doing this too. She hoped we might even meet out there.

I hoped we would—fervently.

We went on drinking. We finished a second bottle of champagne.

The picture changed. It hadn't taken me long, at that.

Next she was in my arms—and as I would learn not long after how it would be called in Hollywood—in a fierce "clinch" in her bed.

After a while there were the murmured soft tones of a satisfied male, and little whimpers in Russian from her.

It came time for the second bout.

Suddenly I leaped up with a yell, a real scream of pain. I clutched at my buttocks. It seemed as if I had been bitten by ten scorpions.

I looked down. There was blood on my hands.

I stared at the princess. She had a strange gloating in her eyes, a truly savage look.

She held in her hands a hairbrush with a long handle and very prickly, hard hairs. It looked like a miniature baseball bat, except I am not sure whether the bristles were of hair or of some kind of thin steel.

The princess must have had this brush under the bed or somewhere close at hand. For at the propitious moment of our engagement—to employ a euphemism—she brought it down with all her force on my bare arse.

I stared at her in bewilderment.

She dropped the brush and held out her arms, as if she were finished.

I was! Candidly I was afraid of this woman now. She might get it into her head to whack me in the head next—or some other more sensitive spot.

I backed off. And got dressed in a hell of a hurry.

She said, "Good-by, dear. See you in Hollywood."

It was my first experience with sadism.

The Warner Brothers publicity man, Blake McElroy, reluctantly acquiesced in my wish to see Harlem. We went to several dives. I have never understood the white American reaction to black female pulchritude. It seemed to me that the girls were positively stunning—and in all shades, from dark to white. The dancing I had never seen before, but it was highly exciting, lewd, lascivious.

It was dark in this place. Cigarette haze added to the eeriness. I asked one of the particularly enticing girls for a dance. I turned about on the floor with her for a while, then invited her to sit at our table for a drink. She said she could bring a friend for *my* friend. I said that would be fine.

The drinks had the effect of breaking down my inhibitions to the point where I found my hand on a beautiful thigh. I moved it higher, then higher.

Finally to the highest—and, my God! there I was paralyzed, holding in my hands . . . I didn't know what to do. My hand seemed held to him and shocked like a current of electricity will do to you.

I broke the electric bond.

"Come on," I said to the publicity man. "Let's get out of here." I left a few bucks on the table and we scrammed.

What the hell kind of women were these Americans? John Barrymore told me much the same thing happened to him once.

I went on to Chicago by train. There I was met by Sam Clarke, the Warner Brothers representative. He took me to a sumptuous penthouse which was kept for Warner Brothers personnel. As soon as I met him he burst out laughing. It appeared that he heard what happened to me in Harlem.

Clarke was a fat, amiable fellow, with a balding head ringed by a fringe of curly hair. It was he who came up with the idea that I should be billed as an Irishman from Ireland. He had me photographed as a motorcycle cop. That fitted into the American conception of what an

Irishman fresh in from Ireland should look like and be. You were assumed to be Irish, your name being Flynn.

I had to pose for another picture. In this I had to kiss a female cousin, Maureen O'Toole, from the old sod. She was a beautiful blonde, and the work wasn't hard to do. She confided her name was Susy Goldstein.

That was how I got my start as an Irishman. Nobody knew or cared that my whole life was spent in Tasmania, Australia, New Guinea, England.

From then on, for a long time, nobody believed me when I talked of that background. They didn't want to hear of it. They wanted me to be Flynn of Ireland.

About now I had a curious psychological experience. A mood of incredulity came over me. Was I really in Chicago? Why wasn't I back in New Guinea with the Melanesians, with their Stone Age dress and implements all about me? Where were the bows and arrows? The *campongs?* Was it possible that on one planet two such diversified environments could exist? To which did I really belong? Where was Jack Ryan? What was Dusty Miller doing? Koets . . . Koets? Had I really met such a man? What was I doing headed for some new Edey Creek, where Sutter had been before me? Was this Chicago of the skyscrapers, penthouses and strange comforts on the route? This land of the broad expanses and fantasy of bigness—Was I in it, really? Could it be that I who had just had an honest-to-God true-life experience with a real Russian princess had not long before been with the humble and joyful Tuperselai and the quiet and submissive Maihiati?

Four days later I flew to Hollywood.

It was the beginning of 1935. I was twenty-six now.

I lived in an apartment near the Los Angeles Tennis Club. I wanted to get in as much tennis as I could to keep in shape.

Weeks went by.

I was just a spare wheel on the Warner Brothers lot. I did nothing. One day I got a message to go to the cashier's office and pick up my checks. There were six for me, a windfall. I was getting paid to play tennis.

I made friends with some young people named Falkenberg. Jinx was then only fifteen. She played tennis, so did her mother. I went to their house for meals. Jinx introduced me to a strange American custom,

Coca-Cola with two aspirins. It got you high as a kite, she said. Whatever that meant I wanted to try it anyway.

I haunted the studio, hoping that somebody besides the cashier would remember I was around or alive. Nobody seemed to give a damn.

I bought a little car. Often I went for a spin with a big fellow named Bud Ernst. He was six foot five, weighed about two hundred and fifty pounds. He was a flier, a fun guy. We palled around as I waited for something to happen.

At the studio I lunched regularly with a young unknown writer named Jerry Wald. Sometimes we ate with the Epstein brothers, also unknown writers. None of us had assignments. All of us felt desperation with the seeming indifference of the studio.

Through Wald's director friend, Mike Curtiz, I finally got a part in a picture. I was elated. It was a film with Warren Williams as the lead. In the story, *The Case of the Curious Bride*, a Grade-B job, Williams has shot some unknown person. He has to identify the body.

My part was to be that of the dead body.

I was wheeled onto the set on a morgue table. I lay there, beneath the sheet, holding my breath. If you have to be a corpse, sport, I told myself, be magnificent.

Williams swiftly pulled the sheet back. "That's him all right," he said. He replaced the sheet. I was wheeled out. Some people claim it was my best role.

It was right after my part as the corpse that I saw Lili Damita again. I was on the tennis court at the studio when she passed and called a delightful feminine hello. To my astonishment she was friendliness itself. The incident on board ship was forgotten.

She had come to the studio to meet her friend, Dolores Del Rio. She was wearing a dress of white and plum-colored silk. Her hair was not exactly braided but it was in two loops behind her head. She wore a little beret.

She rustled when she walked. Lili always seemed to rustle; it was one of her wonderful traits. No one could rustle an entrance into a room better than she. No one could seat herself better, on a chair or a sofa or even a park bench, so daintily spreading her skirts.

The hello she called went far into my life.

Would I care to have a drink at her place, the Garden of Allah? What a name! You bet I would.

In a very few days I found myself in an adjoining apartment at the Garden of Allah. Then we shared the same apartment, and needless to say, the same bed.

What began as an affair went far beyond that. We decided it would be a good idea to take a house. We found one with a fantastic view on top of Lookout Mountain.

We hired a couple of domestics, the Flemings. Jim Fleming afterward became my stand-in, and was with me for fifteen years.

Thereafter Lili showed me a great deal of the surroundings. We went everywhere, to Palm Springs, to San Diego, to San Francisco.

She showed me plenty.

In Mexico City we were guests of the Figueroas, an ancient Spanish family. We flew down from Los Angeles on one of those early commercial planes, a three-motor job, which Lili thought was more interesting than any two-motor plane. She said in broken English, "Why you weesh to go ze ozzer way when we can have three motors for ze price of only two? We will go down and stay with Dolores."

But on our arrival we put up at the Figueroas. Lili had known the young and extraordinarily attractive Carmen Figueroa through Dolores Del Rio.

Dolores was one of the most beautiful women I have ever seen, like an Aztec princess, of olive skin, with wondrous eyes. She proposed that we make a visit to the ancient pyramids behind Mexico City. "After that," she said, "I will take you to meet a good friend . . ."

In the vicinity of the Aztec ruins, built before the invasion of Hernando Cortes, I couldn't escape the thought that Dolores herself may have descended from the Aztecs.

She was very artistically minded. It was only natural that an art follower like Dolores would know the world-famous painter, Diego Rivera. For it was to him that she led us, after the inspection of the pyramids. . . .

Rivera had a fantastic home just outside Mexico City, a two-story structure set off by the usual Mexican patio. About the patio was an extensive garden, with varieties of cactus, pot plants, color in abundance.

He greeted Lili pleasantly. He gave me a frown, I think of disdain, perhaps because I may have looked young and immature. I realized he was a spectacular-looking man. You could compare his looks, his face, his full-length appearance to a cross between a walrus, a snipe-nosed pig from Berkshire, and a fish. His big brown eyes seemed about to pop out of his head. I took his right hand; it felt like three stalks of asparagus. It was wet even though it was dry, and I withdrew my fingers wondering if I would be able to wipe them off when I sat.

My excitement increased when in walked Rivera's young wife. What a beauty she was: with long raven hair, piercing eyes, a beautiful mouth, and a figure draped exotically in a Mexican *zarape,* like a bath towel a girl wraps around under her armpits. Only the *zarape* she wore was so flimsy you could see through it, and she wore nothing underneath.

Diego and she made a paradoxically artistic pair.

From the instant of our arrival there was animated talk, but there were so many more sophisticated people here I kept quiet. I was aware of the Master's startling paintings on the walls, on easels, in corners of the room. They were, of course, the controversial proletarian paintings of the Mexican people: peons in the field, workers carrying red flags. All those scenes that made Rivera a Communist symbol in many lands. Rivera was doing no drinking, but the others were; a special drink from the cactus plant in Mexico. If you take enough of it you see a burnt matchstick on the floor and you think it's a log. For a time the painter got off in a corner with Dolores, Carmen and Lili, while I moved about examining his art.

I glanced out a window. Beyond was the magnificent mountain called Popocatepetl. Look to the left, the fabulous pyramids that the Aztecs built. Turn a bit more to the right, close up, and there was a convent across the street. I stared at it, glass-topped, high-walled, covered with the most beautiful flowers: thick stems of bougainvillea, ginger, and the flowery cactus tree. I was dying to look inside those convent walls.

I couldn't get over the contrast between a convent, with its nuns and novitiates, right by this arty Bohemian radical center where, it was hinted, Rivera himself more or less led the Communist movement in the Latin-American world.

Altogether unexpectedly, Rivera left the others. Maybe he wanted to get away from his wife, maybe he wanted to take a piss on the cactus in the garden, maybe he just wanted fresh air. He came over to me and motioned for me to go with him. I felt favored.

As we moved into the outer garden we drifted into a disagreement at once.

"Have you read Prescott?" he asked.

He didn't speak English very well and my Spanish at that time was very shaky.

"You know," he went on, "Prescott—*The Conquest of Mexico*." Oh Prescott, sure. Great!

Here his look became like that of a boxer dog. He had several chins and they seemed to drop to his armpits. A belligerence came over him. His eyelids fell. His nostrils distended to their uttermost. He had set up Prescott in order to knock him down.

"That piratical Englishman! The swine has distorted the whole matter!"

"How can you say that? His was one of the greatest historical chronicles in the world!"

"*Caramba! caracho! chingo!*" Words rudely mellowed into English, "That goddamned sonofabitch Prescott."

"He writes, you paint. He paints too with ink. I think his work will stand longer than yours—"

Rivera looked at me with some interest. I followed through, "When you put down your brush, he will still remain more important than you. . ."

I couldn't have told him any plainer than that, even if I didn't know what I was talking about. I ground my heel into him a bit more, denounced the current habit of the Mexican painters of portraying the downtrodden proletariat by showing some worker holding the hammer and sickle while some wicked capitalist had his foot on the back of the man's neck and stamped his face into the mud. "Why," I asked, "don't you know color is more important?"

His face went from red to white, white to purple, proving what I said about color. I interrupted his change of colors. "The same goes for Orozco and the others of the Mexican school."

Here I made my usual mistake. "Now take Salvador Dali, he is not interested in politics—"

That was as far as I got. He went from red to very red; verged toward apoplexy. "I'll withdraw that," I said. "I think there is no use in our talking of these things—"

"That is true!"

We had a moment's uncomfortable silence.

"Anyway," he said, "isn't it good to get away from them?" He referred to his wife, Lili, and the others.

He stood in front of a cactus bush, breathed heavily, remarked that some people wanted him to paint still life. The thought of it provoked more Mexican expletives. He was the most explosive personality I had ever encountered.

"You were talking about the glories of color. I heard you talking about the color in my pictures, and you are telling me that color is more important than what one has to say. What the hell do you know about color?"

I waited. He asked, "Can you get emotion out of color?"

"Yes."

"More than from music?"

"No."

"Now, Mr. Flynn, I know that you don't know what you're talking about."

"Señor Rivera, isn't it possible that perhaps I could like both?"

He looked at me as if I were some novice in this area—which I certainly was. "Now, I will show you something. I want to show you how little you know. . . . All right?"

"All right."

"You see those little potted cacti? You see this one?"

He pointed to where a lovely Mexican flower had closed itself up like a rose with sunset colors, a delicate pastel shade. "That is how they go to sleep. Amusing, yes?" He said, "Now watch . . . "

He took the cigarette out of my mouth, put it to the flower. Sure as hell, the flower opened. "You see," he remarked, "like women. You have to be tough. Rough. Brutal."

I kept quiet. There was a lot I could still learn about painting, color, women, and men like Rivera.

"This plant has power," he said. "I have carefully cultivated this myself and I take a great deal of pleasure in seeing it growing alongside that convent you keep staring at."

He seemed to be in a lighter mood as he talked of the plant and he even laughed a bit. He asked, "Have you ever *heard* a painting?"

"Heard *what?*

"I said, suppose you looked at a painting and *heard* it play a symphony, would you be surprised?"

I didn't follow.

"Suppose you returned to my studio and you stood in front of one of my paintings and you *heard* it, you heard music coming from the canvas . . . ?"

As he talked he moved from one potted plant to the other, fingering them, pressing them fondly, almost caressing them.

He took from a pocket a few sheets of zigzag French paper, the kind of little tissues you use in rolling cigarettes.

"This plant," he explained, "will allow you to do both. After smoking this you will see a painting and you will hear it as well."

It dawned on me that he was rolling in that zigzag paper the "loco weed" referred to in *The Conquest of Mexico,* the plant called *marijuana* in Mexico, *ganja* in Jamaica, *anis abiba* in other parts of the world, *hashish* in the Far East.

As he took a puff he said, "Look, be sure that nobody besides us knows what we are going to do. I will take you up to the storeroom. You will see paintings there I show to nobody else."

He glanced into the interior of the house, then nudged me in the direction of a side door. We went inside, up a stairs. It was a storeroom for his materials, his paints, canvases, frames. He crossed the room to where there were a couple of big pots of turpentine. He pulled out from under or near them a little can.

The lid opened easily.

I peered in. It contained some brown pulpy material that looked the color of the bottom end of a cigarette holder.

"You can either chew it or smoke it," he said. "This is the same weed the Spanish found here in the fifteenth century. Cortes brought back gold and silver, but he forgot this."

"I will hear the painting?"

"You will hear the color!"

The idea of having sounds translated into terms of paintings, and paintings translated into terms of music . . . a fascinating idea.

I smoked some of it, ate a little of it.

Diego was talking, observing me. I didn't hear much of what he was saying. I was absorbed, waiting for a reaction.

Suddenly I started to sweat. I could feel my extremities going numb, from the elbow down to the hand, and from the knee down to the foot. Felt a strange sense of touch, yet you wanted to touch things, and if you did there was a numb feeling.

Now I felt paralyzed, yet capable of motion.

Over me came the sensation of being suspended in time. All sense of its passage was gone. Everything about me seemed frozen, taut, permanent.

I wasn't certain where we were going, whether among his paintings, or in his garden. Yet we were moving slowly, timelessly. His voice came to me hypnotically. It was getting dark—Mexico—where was I?

I could hear from the convent across the way a girls' choir singing in Latin. Strangely, I could distinguish the peculiar Latin litany. Beyond was the brilliant evening sky, the sun lowering like a great round diver. The pyramids pushed upward into the same red sky. I had the extraordinary feeling that I couldn't cope with this sensation.

Immobile, transfixed, still we were moving, thickly. Once at the studio doorway, looking within, there was a momentary vision: his wife now wore a violently colored robe off the shoulder, and it swept ankle-length. There was a small red bow at the back of her neck around the fluent length of hair; and then the raven mane dipped downward like a black snake to the cleavage of her buttocks. I stared . . . all was exotic, heightened . . . and Rivera himself stayed close by talking talk that only dimly entered into me.

By now too I lost the sense of balance, which was remarkable for me. From somewhere came a cry that dinner was ready.

Food! I shouted to the heavens, arms up, singing, imploring, I sip no sup and I crave no cup, while I cry for the love of a ladee!

Rivera was amused at my disabled reactions; he talked on in a Mexicanized English, directing me into a showroom of pictures, his early works, intended, he said, for the Mexican people.

"Here it is quiet," he suggested. "Listen to Mexico. Look at my pictures and listen to Mexico. . . ."

Whether it was autosuggestion or not, whether it was the suggestive power of a tremendous personality profoundly affecting a young man given so much of his time, or whether it was the marijuana—as some will say it was—I heard these pictures singing: the simple Mexican themes, a woman on a mule moving through a field of cacti, the peasants at their labor, in rhythm: illumination and color and sound in a symphony I could see, feel and hear—but can never translate in words.

No question about it.

Bizarre, I know . . . but I was there.

Lili was a very good sport. She tried her best to keep up with me, although I couldn't get her on a horse. She mounted a horse once and it got away with her. She took up tennis, worked very hard at it. Swimming she never seemed to be able to master. She had a strange kind of stroke which made her look like a little French poodle dog-paddling. It seemed to her foolish to put a bathing suit on that glorious figure, then go in and get both wet.

With Lili I naturally met many of the screen notables I might not have met at this time. I also saw many of the Hollywood beauties. The sight of them stirred me to frenzies of interest and Lili to furies of jealousy.

Through Lili I met Lupe Velez, who played often in Lili's pictures, the director, Cedric Gibbons, and the famous artist, John Decker. I first met Paulette Goddard at Charlie Chaplin's house when he was away. I was overawed by the grandeur of his mansion. The tennis court was excellent. He had a beautiful shower, with spouts that came out from every direction, and the bathroom was as big as a kitchen. I had no idea Charlie was so clean.

Lili had an overpowering possessiveness, like a blanket or an oxygen tent.

I had to be mighty careful not to be caught with any lipstick that wasn't her shade.

We worked at making a domestic life, but there was much variance between us. She could cook beautifully, various French dishes, and she delighted me with that art as well.

What I regarded as erotic love-making in those days came as natural to her as the proverbial duck taking to water.

But the purely animal, ferocious woman-tiger can pall on you after a while. You get bewildered. What else is there? What about good talk? What about cerebral exercise? I had done a world of reading. I had had an early exposure to science. I simply had this other side to me! It needed nourishing too.

A serious discussion bored the hell out of Tiger Lil, as I came to call her (but behind her back). Her eyes took on a glazed look when I brought up anything objective for discussion. Once she exhibited a faint flicker of interest when I showed her an illustration of the hair style and headdress of an ancient Egyptian Queen, Nefertiti. "I will have a hat made like that," said Tiger Lil.

We were poles apart, except in bed. Mentally, woefully inadequate. Sexually, fabulous, wonderfully exciting, beautiful. All this became the source of an irritation that grew and grew. She was bored stiff by any thoughts that didn't bear directly on her day-to-day life. The important thing always was the style of her hair, the color of her shoes, did her bag match her dress, and was Joie the sexiest French perfume or not?

She knew, however, that she was the greatest—bar none, no holds barred. I record it as a fact of any possible interest to future historians.

I do not know where she learned the arts of amour, or whether she was born gifted, but I had the feeling that she performed as if she personally was convinced that she carried with her all the legend, glory and reputation of the French.

We fought. We reconciled. We fought again.

The tremors on Lookout Mountain moved below into the grapevine of Hollywood. Reports went out that the beauteous Lili and the unknown Irishman she was shacked up with were throwing things at each other. Lili did all of the tossing—I did the ducking. I had never raised a hand in anger to a woman in my life.

It chanced that Bud Ernst also knew Lili and he came to the house frequently. With the best of intentions perhaps, he made a suggestion one evening in June of 1935. "Listen, I've got a plane stashed away here. Why don't you two kids make sense? We'll fly up to Yuma in the morning where you can get married." Married! God! Oh—

Lili thought it was an excellent suggestion. My thoughts were gloomy. I had made known my sentiments against the marriage institution at the age of seven, and they weren't changed now, not even by Lili's glorious boudoir art.

Bud poured whisky down my throat to urge on the event he proposed. I got him off to the side. "For Christ's sakes, what kind of a friend are you? What the hell do you think you're doing? You Benedict Arnold!" I had read some American history. "Traitor!"

That night I was determined that the morrow would see no bridegroom. I wouldn't go through with it.

The next morning I summoned the courage to tell Lili. The most awful scene followed. Bottles crashed against the wall. When Lili raged she had to throw things—as on the screen—only these were not breakable props made of cardboard. These were the real fixtures of the place in which you lived. She removed them one by one from their shelves and their tables and they came in rocket succession. What the ancient Greeks wouldn't have given for her at the siege of Troy!

Tears came. Torrents. Then hysteria. I was astonished at such a display from such a slight woman. She was a foot shorter than I. It was from her that I learned that many of these small packages contain potential dynamite.

What was she doing!

I looked on aghast. There she stood sobbing on the window sill overlooking a four-hundred-foot drop. "If you humiliate me like this any more I'll jump!"

I pulled her back, swearing unending love and devotion and trembling.

Later, as I have come to understand better the ways of women, I am able to look upon such antics with equanimity, even aplomb.

She left me with no alternative—either a bullet to my head or marriage.

I put on a front of merriment, joviality, and the three of us flew to Yuma. A very little man married us for two dollars. The greatest bargain Lili Damita ever got. She parlayed that eventually to over a million dollars.

Strangely, things went well upon our return. For a while, at least, there was peace. Neither of us was accustomed to wedlock, and I think we both tried. But I was then an incorrigibly polygamous man. Eventually this arrangement had to explode and shatter badly.

Lili knew everyone in Hollywood. We were no longer living in sin. So, even more people came to our place who wouldn't have before. Actually Hollywood could be just as sanctimonious in its own perverse way as any small town in the Dakotas.

A famous European director on the Warner lot was about to make a picture called *Captain Blood*. The star role had been given to Robert Donat, the famous English actor. Donat had a long-distance quarrel with Warner Brothers and bowed out.

It was decided, by Mervyn LeRoy and Harry Joe Brown, I think, to test an unknown. I don't know how many were tested, but I was one. I tested with a young woman of extraordinary charm, Olivia de Havilland. She was only nineteen then, with warm brown eyes, a soft manner.

It was Jack Warner who had the foresight or the hunch to cast Olivia and me in this film. So many people claim discovering me that I get lost getting discovered. Mervyn LeRoy claimed he did. So did Michael Curtiz. But in truth it was Jack Warner who made the decision. He had the guts to take a complete unknown and put me in the lead of a big production. That took real financial foresight.

While making *Captain Blood* something happened during one of the most violent scenes. I was leading pirates from one ship to another, swinging swords and grappling hooks. Rope in hand, I swung with one hand from one boat to the other, landed on the opposite deck, fought a duel. Suddenly my knees buckled under me. I lay there, shaking, shivering. I knew only too well it was a recurrence of malaria or black-water fever, that it had taken me in the midst of the scene.

This was no time to quit. I asked for a small hot lamp to be placed next to me to warm me, so that I could sweat it out. They had a better idea. A shot of brandy! Someone brought on a bottle of cognac and I gulped it down. I felt hotter, colder—finally better. The restorative, fatal to actors, got me off the ground. I finished the scene. At the end of the afternoon I collapsed.

Next day I received a blue note saying I must see Mr. Jack Warner, the faraway figure way on top. I showed it to a friend who glumly said a white note was bad but a blue—kindly, he put a hand on my shoulder. I was in for it.

The script girl tipped me off. They had rushes of the scene I finished after the bottle of cognac. In the film I was waving the sword about like a Cossack, shouting lines that weren't in the script, and had almost fallen off the boat. A bit of real drunken acting.

The injustice of it! I had given my best for the studio, had come down with fever, and now I was going to get canned? All right, I would tell off this fellow. Warner or no Warner, boss of the big tent or not, he had to be told.

I was led into a plush office, but Warner wasn't there. Be seated, I was told by a prim youngish secretary. One by one I saw people come out of Warner's office, heads bowed, looking chastened. I was being given what's called "the long wait." A smart piece of business designed to cool off anybody and everybody. People kept coming out. I kept waiting, kept getting cooler. The hell I was going to give Jack Warner subsided. "Go in," I was finally told.

I opened the door to a room that looked as long as a bowling alley. At the other end three gentlemen I didn't know sat about a large desk. As I walked forward I heard the high angry voice of the man in the middle, "Listen, Flynn, there's one thing I won't have around this god-damn lot—drinking! I don't drink, my brothers don't drink. Another thing, Flynn, you can't screw around with the broads. Only a bum'll drink when he's working and you can't get the job done if you do, and there'll be none of it, will there, Flynn?"

Jack Warner turned to a fat fellow on his left and he demanded, "Bill, why can't I drink?"

"You can't drink because you got an ulcer."

"That's right," said Warner, glaring at everyone. "That's what it gives you if you drink. My brother can't drink either. And when bums like you start to drink on the set, what are we going to do? Now look, now look——" He banged his desk.

Another fellow on his right, Hal Wallis, the executive producer, sounded a little more reasonable. "Maybe this young fellow doesn't know what this is all about."

Here Warner stood up. He introduced himself, Bill Koenig and Hal Wallis. His face suddenly changed expression. He smiled so warmly I was melted. I had a speech carefully rehearsed, what I was going to tell him, but I'd forgotten it.

He beamed. "How is everything else going?"

"Fine. Thank you, Mr. Warner, and——"

I promised there would be no Flynnanigans.

"Okay, now get back to work. Remember there are thousands of people working for you. They are working for *you*, for *you!* All you have to do is look out the window and you will see five thousand of them."

The thought crossed my mind that they might also be working for him.

I left the office. Downstairs my rage returned. Why, that . . . I thought. *How's everything else going?* That's when I should have asked him for a raise. I was playing this lead part in *Captain Blood* for $300 a week. I could have used a little more; Lili was expensive.

The direction of *Captain Blood* was assigned to Michael Curtiz. I was to spend five miserable years with him, making *Robin Hood, Charge of the Light Brigade,* and many other films. In each he tried to make all scenes so realistic that my skin didn't seem to matter to him. Nothing delighted him more than real bloodshed.

Captain Blood was finished. Word got around the studio that a great picture had been made. Rumor spreads like that sometimes in the industry itself before the public ever knows what it will get.

Captain Blood was acclaimed by the world. It was a triumph for Curtiz, for Warner, even for me, though everybody else was making the loot.

Yet I have no complaint about that. It was a fair, an adequate reward for my services, for the opportunity to have my beginnings. I worked as hard as I knew how. I even suppose that in motion picture history this film has a place too. For the industry has described this film as one of the milestone pictures, as it acclaimed *Robin Hood* several years later.

Overnight I found myself a star. The film made millions for Warner Brothers.

Only Jack Warner's faith in me set off my career—for whatever it has meant to me and to the world, for good or ill—and started me on that road which has so often made the public acquainted with my wicked ways.

Once again I was inactive.

My agent was Minna Wallis, the sister of Hal Wallis. It was that which probably also helped me get my start at Warner's. Minna told me that Metro-Goldwyn-Mayer was going to make *Romeo and Juliet*. This was what I had been trained for at Northampton. No one knew as yet, including myself, how good, bad, indifferent, perhaps one day great, I might be as an actor. You have to have the roles. You have to have the chance to grow. I was hopeful I could get into this picture. I had the English accent, training and manner usually helpful in Shakespearean plays.

The agent sent me to see George Cukor, the director. He was a friend of Lili's. The producer was Irving Thalberg, already a legendary figure in Hollywood. Thalberg had chosen his wife, Norma Shearer, to play the part of Juliet. John Barrymore was to play Mercutio. Basil Rathbone, with whom I had just worked in *Captain Blood*, was Tybalt. Romeo had not yet been cast.

I went to the M-G-M lot to see Thalberg.

It was lunchtime and I browsed around on the lot looking at the sets where Greta Garbo and Jack Gilbert had made their pictures. In the distance I saw someone on a park bench in Shakespearean costume. I strolled by. The man was half asleep.

His eyes opened slowly, like an owl's. He transfixed me with a hard stare. I started to pass on, but he straightened up a bit and cocked his left eyebrow a bit, a gesture for which this man was famous.

"Ah, a glorious day, is it not?" he boomed.

"Magnificent," I agreed.

He pointed to the space on the bench beside him.

"Pray be seated, fellow voyager."

Penetratingly, he went on, "Haven't I seen you somewhere, my friend?—Perhaps in some other life?" It was a tremendously rich voice, of command, music, charm. I well knew who he was.

I told him a little about myself.

"I know who you are. You're the young bastard I saw in the rushes the other day."

I inhaled a familiar scent from his breath. Scotch!

"You remind me of Navarre," he said thoughtfully, frowning. "Do you mind if I call you Navarre?"

"Not at all."

"Glorious country, California," he said. "Too good for these clottish bastards who inhabit it."

I mentioned the Far East, for no known reason.

"Ah, yes, Navarre, what you say reminds me of a place where I was once strangely content—Kualalumpar, Malaya."

"How so?"

"Never shall I forget that whorehouse in Kualalumpar. It was one of much integrity."

I told him of my preference for those of Marseilles and one or two about Saigon.

He gave me a piece of advice. Very solemnly, as if he were reciting a soliloquy from Hamlet. "When you go to a house of joy, Navarre, always take the Madam. The quality is better and the price more reasonable." He exploded with a reverberating laugh.

A voice behind us said softly, "Mr. Barrymore, sir. They're waiting for you on the set."

He rose to his feet, swaying—with dignity, though.

I sprang up.

He took my hand. "Navarre, our talk was most illuminating. We must see more of each other." Off he went.

Subsequently—but not until seven or eight years later—John Barrymore and I became close friends.

I didn't get the role of Romeo. The late Leslie Howard got it.

I was full of ambition at the time. I wanted to create something important. I couldn't forget my training at Northampton, where I had played everything. I couldn't forget that no matter what role I performed, the audience liked it and seemed to like me. Why couldn't I get the chance to play a variety of roles here?

But I couldn't. As the months, the years rollicked on, and as I went from one picture to another, the stereotyped roles I played stamped out of me my ambition to do finer things or to expect to be able to do them in Hollywood. When you're young, a beginner, you have a contract to fulfill, you have little to say about your roles. They are tantamount to legal orders. You're hooked. With time I would lose my inner guts, my belief in myself even as an actor.

I do not know to what extent this stereotyping of me—this handing me a sword and a horse, as they did from then on—led to my rebellions, high jinks and horseplay over the globe, but I think it had plenty to do with it.

I remember fondly the day when I first met John Barrymore; when he got his role in the Shakespearean play and I sought one. Dear John. . . .

I was an hour late to our anniversary party. Lili could not be expected to take a slight like this lying down. It wasn't our wedding anniversary, but it was the anniversary of the beginning of our romance. That was far more important in her logical French reasoning than a date on an Arizona wedding license.

About fifty of our friends were gathered in the apartment of a friend, Peggy Fears, wife of the extraordinary A. C. Blumenthal, friend of Joseph Schenck. Film leaders, my personal pals, Lili's confidantes.

I entered the room after the whole party arrived. I began to mingle when I suddenly heard someone scream, "Look out, Errol!"

Simultaneously there was Lili's voice behind me. "Happy anniversary, darling." At the same instant down on my head came a full bottle of Veuve Cliquot champagne. Consistently French, my wife—it was a fine vintage.

Dazed and blinded by blood pouring out of my head, I rallied for a moment, then pulled back my fist to swing. Knowing I had only one punch in me, I swung hard. Just before blacking out I felt my knuckles connect with a jawbone, breaking a tooth. When I was revived a few moments later, I saw Lili lying at my feet.

Sick with pain, aghast at what I had done, I numbly let myself be led to a hospital.

The next time I awoke it was on the operating table. It had been no nightmare, I reflected, as I sensed the hurt where the surgeon's knife had bit into my scalp.

My God, I thought, I've struck a woman! I told myself, Whatever your faults, you're not the kind of fellow to do that no matter what the provocation. Our marriage? A multimillion-dollar movie production would be delayed indefinitely. The news, made public, that Flynn had beaten up his petite wife might well prove the death blow to my acting career. What really horrified me was the knowledge that I, of all people, had hit a woman. What would my father say? That gentle, kindly man, opposed to violence of any kind.

Actually, very little damage resulted from the incident. The ever-vigilant studio arranged a phony auto accident. The morning papers reported that Lili and I were injured when I swerved our station wagon into a wall to avoid hitting a cat. *Robin Hood* was rescheduled to shoot around me for the fortnight I was out.

Lili was already calling for me to come to her, the doctor said.

After two weeks in the hospital the eighteen stitches healed.

Dr. Frank Nolan, a kindly soul, appealed to me. "Your wife has been asking for you right along. Why don't you go see her?"

"What! And get a few more holes in my head? I never want to see her again."

"Do you really mean that?"

"Yes, nor any other woman. Especially delicate, fragile ones, whose capacity for violence is amazing."

"Certainly you shouldn't feel that way about all women."

"I do." What I believed was that our warfare had gone too far. When I struck her I killed our feeling forever. She had made me do it, but I didn't feel any better about it because of that.

Nevertheless I wandered into her bedroom. There she lay, her head propped up on the pillow like a Dresden doll. Her hair was carefully arranged in the most becoming manner. I looked at her and felt sick inside. She was a figure of pathos. I approached the bed and stood silently and ramrod stiff, not knowing what to say.

She looked up at me with an unhappy mouth. Tears welled in her dark eyes. "How . . . how . . . you, of all people . . . how could you do that to me?"

I stammered, "Do what?"

"My tooth," Lili said. "How could you hit me?"

We made up, of course, but I knew if there had ever been any real love between us, it was badly shattered, perhaps finished.

I sometimes think that in one way Lili and I were somewhat alike. It is possible that she essentially disliked men and that I essentially disliked women. The two of us together could only be an accord of discord, dooming our relationship sooner or later.

I made a couple of pictures at M-G-M. Maybe they weren't world shakers, but I enjoyed working in them. The atmosphere on the Metro lot was friendly and different.

Yet I was unable to get together satisfactorily with Warner Brothers. Even after *Captain Blood* made several million dollars I was only getting about $500 a week, having signed a long-term contract. Try as I did I couldn't get Jack Warner to give me a more reasonable amount, although it was said I was the studio's biggest money-maker.

After endless hassles with Warners, I was assigned to star in a picture in which the third lead was getting paid more than I was. I didn't show up for the first day's shooting.

They called Jack Warner right away. "What's the matter?" he screamed. "Is he sick? Or is he drunk?"

"No," they told him. "He said he'd rather not work at all than work for so little."

Over Jack Warner hung the Damocles sword of the money-making *Captain Blood*.

He thought this over for three full minutes. Then he had a heart attack and was taken to the hospital.

I still did not show up at the studio. The Warners brass were having meetings and fits. How to handle the problem of the upstart who was demanding big star money?

Jack got home from the hospital, but he stayed away from the studio.

Finally we got together. My salary jumped sharply to four figures a week. I was ready to work in pictures.

Through 1936 and 1937 Olivia de Havilland was "the girl" in many of my pictures. She was my sweetheart in *The Charge of the Light Brigade* and in *Four's A Crowd*.

It was around the time I was in the comedy *Four's A Crowd* that I became labeled a swashbuckler. At the time this griped me, but today, what's it matter?

Joan Blondell was my leading lady in *The Perfect Specimen*. I had earlier made my second film, *Don't Bet on Blondes*, with Claire Dodd. There was *Green Light*, with Anita Louise, and *Another Dawn* with Kay Francis; then *The Prince and the Pauper*.

You went from one picture to another swiftly, a month or two or three for the making of each. There'd be a half-dozen pictures "in the can" and you'd be making your sixth or seventh, with the others not yet released. Then they released them, one after another, every month or two, and you found yourself a household word, famous all over the movie-going sphere.

Dodge City with Olivia and *Dawn Patrol* with David Niven. Steady work. *The Sisters,* with Bette Davis.

During the making of *Captain Blood* I had grown very fond of Olivia de Havilland. By the time we made *The Charge of the Light Brigade* I was sure I was in love with her. So that acting in that hard-to-make picture became bearable. It took a long time to produce this vehicle, and all through it I fear I bothered Miss De Havilland in very teasing ways—though I was really trying to display my affection.

Olivia was only twenty-one then. I was married, of course, unhappily. Olivia was lovely—and distant. She must have actively disliked me for the teasing I did, for I sprang some very obstreperous gags. There was the time she found a dead snake in her panties as she went to put them on. She was terrified and she wept. She knew very well who was responsible and it couldn't have endeared me to her. It slowly penetrated my obtuse mind that such juvenile pranks weren't the way to any girl's heart. But it was too late. I couldn't soften her.

Later she told me that she lived in terror of what bit of idiocy I'd spring next. Guess I haven't changed much. Pranksters don't. I must have spent too much of my early life with men. I had a lot to learn about the sensibilities of young ladies.

Late in 1937 I completed the making of a super-costly *The Adventures of Robin Hood*. The first film, I think, in color. Another Jack Warner gamble. There were great expectations for it around the studio. But I was tired. The hard work, the round of social life in Hollywood, my trying personal life with Lili, all this was a drain.

I developed a disgust for the mediocre vehicles to which I was assigned. Beyond that problem, and my efforts to get more money, and putting up with Lili's jealousy and desire to totally control me, I had other urges to contend with.

The sea raged inside me. At night when I fell asleep there was within me sometimes a cerebral mechanism as of the sound of ocean waves lapping at the shore. I had grown up with the ocean pounding on rocks, and it had lulled me to sleep as a boy. I wanted to be out on the salt water again, for one large portion of me was the mariner.

I still had difficulty realizing I was here in the mixed-up world of Hollywood. The pretty women everywhere dazzled me.

Lili was so violently jealous that I suppose she loved me. With my wandering eye, I did nothing to help her overcome her fits of possessiveness. She may even have been impressed by my professional realization which suddenly was exceeding hers. But she had broken so many dishes over my head that when a pretty girl went by I learned to keep my gaze as fixed and glassy as that of one of the guards outside Buckingham Palace—when she was around.

I felt trapped, even asphyxiated by her possessiveness. I had to get away from her. Her bedroom art and her good cooking were not enough. All around me the whole world beckoned. Every structure of society was open to me. I had to see it all, be part of it, have nobody hold me down.

The pressures upon me made me frantic. Maybe I was slightly drunken with my success. The contrast in my living was almost inconceivable. Only yesterday living with aborigines, tramping with white suit, white helmet and boots in the jungle—and now, the whole universe seeing my face on the screen and fan letters by the thousands coming in weekly.

I feared for my sanity unless I could do something about all this pressure. That was the greatest fear of my life. Ever since I was a boy I feared more than anything else losing my mind. Once, in Tasmania, I went with a boy named Charles Rattan to the hospital of which his father was the superintendent. Dr. Rattan managed not only the hospital but the Tasmania Lunatic Asylum. Charles had me look through a porthole of a door. I gazed inside at the sight of poor devils banging their heads on the wall, uttering weird sounds, in strange postures. Shocked, I turned white with fear. The sight became a nightmare that lived on with me in the jungles, on board the ships I mastered. The nightmare followed me to America.

Now I had the curious feeling that I was distended to the point of breaking. Yet I had to keep up the jaunty façade.

Lili's violence was more than I could contend with. She made me melancholy, deeply unhappy with my new-found success. I felt that I could chuck it all and go back on the bum.

You would think that our mutual hospitalization earlier would have brought an end to the violence. It did not. I continued to philander among Hollywood's beautiful girls, and she continued to throw things. Our only moments of peace were when we were in bed. Outside of that there were sparks at every utterance, baleful looks, bottles thrown. Only by great nimbleness of foot did I avoid a weekly fractured skull. I beat it as fast as I could and returned to her presence with all the caution of an Apache creeping up on a paleface encampment.

The boys at Warner Brothers were taking a dim view of this. I was putting too much strain on their make-up department, with my black eyes, puffy lips, cut cheeks. They were hard put to match my face to the previous day's shooting.

Toward the close of 1937 I knew I had had it. Our fights were not only a local scandal but were becoming a national one. The journalists threatened to boycott Warner Brothers if they didn't get at least one scandalous item a day about us. Feeding those fellows was one thing to them, but to me it was something else. It was eating into my heart and spirit. I couldn't stand it much longer. I felt dead creatively. And there was no possible way of knowing how to get out of it.

When I arrived in Hollywood the big stars were James Cagney, John Barrymore, Greta Garbo, Bette Davis, Alan Hale, Norma Shearer, Lili, Charlie Chaplin, and many others. The silent films were gone. So were most of its celebrities, like Fairbanks, Pickford, Wallace Reid, Von Stroheim, Arbuckle. Chaplin, rather eternal, survived all changes. When I was coming up so were a whole flock of other recent arrivals in Hollywood: Niven, Gable, Taylor, Grant, and many feminine stars. Most of us were beginners, with but a few films to our credit. *Captain Blood* had projected me in as meteoric a fashion as had ever befallen anyone. Once I got the salary question straightened out to my partial satisfaction, the vehicles came my way as rapidly as the studio could get hold of screen plays. During the next five years I made about twenty pictures.

I had little choice in selecting them. Just make pictures, make money —and stay and spend the dough. That was the important thing if you once did get a break—to last. Because on all sides there were the handsome and the talented, and they might be as good as you if they had the break you had.

Movie-making was a whole world in itself, a new life, a new relationship between me and others. You collaborated with your colleagues and you contended with them. You made friends, enemies; you had hates and loves. There were those you could work with and those you wanted to kill. How could I know how Olivia de Havilland felt about having to be my leading lady? How could I know what went on in her mind?— that she was sick to death of playing "the girl" and badly wanted a few good roles to show herself and the world that she was a fine actress? And how could she know that I wanted to do something really creative?

The toughest picture I ever made, *The Charge of the Light Brigade*, was filmed, I think, at Bishop, California. Shortly after the company arrived, the hotel we stayed at burned down. Afterward we were quartered poorly, and for the whole five months' period of the screen work, we froze. Warners spent a fortune on the picture, and it was giant hit. But for much of that period of time we huddled around in the cold and the dust, with no facilities, waiting for the action and eating gruesome food.

The action of the picture was supposed to take place in India, in the sweating heat of India. Our costumes were thin, as they would have to be in India to absorb the heat. But this wasn't India. It was California, the cold time of year, and we were in an area and at a height where the cold was numbing. The wind was like a knife; it cut through everything, and it raced through our thin costumes. A cold, piercing wind, not perhaps at the freezing point, but it blew through you—while the illusion was being given that this was blazing Indian heat.

Meantime the hard-boiled Curtiz was bundled in about three top-coats, giving orders. As I was pretty green in pictures I didn't know enough to tell him to give me one of his coats, or to drop dead. He didn't care who hated him or for what. He'd keep us waiting hour after hour sitting on the horses, freezing to death. How all of us didn't get galloping pneumonia I don't know. The only way we could warm up a bit and get some circulation going was to give the horse a spurt and let him turn a bit.

There was the big death scene of the picture. I wanted to do this myself and refused to have a double.

In this scene I was to jump my horse over the Russian cannon, a six-foot leap, with a spear in my hand. The horse under me was as nervous as I was. Picture-making is no easier for horses than men.

They had put a camera under the cannon. The director called "Charge!" and I led the charge of the Light Brigade. My horse took this cannon jump in magnificent style. On the other side, I plunged my lance into the heavy's breast, and that was it. It should have, of course, been done by a stunt man double. It was stupid of me, and stupid of Warner

Brothers to let me do it, but I was really interested in my work at that time.

When the Screen Actors Guild was born, and swiftly grew, it put a stop to conditions such as I experienced in the making of this picture. It moved to halt the more predatory producers and directors from many of their excesses.

As for the treatment of the horses in this film, I myself complained to the Society for the Prevention of Cruelty to Animals.

I hasten to say I have been no angel with all animals in film-making. You couldn't be, and get the action on the screen that the public expects.

Horses have been perhaps the most badly treated animals in the motion picture industry. Especially in the days when these early Westerns were being ground out. A device called "the running W" was used on horses. A trip wire, to make the animals tumble at the right instant. The stunt man, riding the horse, knew where the trip wire was. He knew when he had to get off and all he had to do was take a fall. But the horse would go headfirst, and sometimes get hurt and have to be shot. They stopped this because so many horses broke their legs and their necks, and there were protests by the actors and public.

This gave rise to a wonderful breed of man. This was the stunt man who would train a horse so well that he could ride down the side of a cliff, and at a certain signal, the rider, putting his left foot under the horse, would trip him. The horse knew he would be tripped. It looked just as good, and nobody was hurt. There were some great experts at this, especially an old man, George Dolan, who is dead now. Any time you saw the Sioux going hotfoot for the hero, and you saw the hero turn around and give one unerring shot, bringing down a horse, the redman was fairly certain to be George Dolan dressed in feathers.

To me the most wonderful thing about movies was to see the way people could make animals work. You could see the men behind the camera giving little signals, making sounds, a gesture with the right hand to do this or that. On the screen it looked as if the animal was only looking at the man or woman with whom he was playing the part. Actually he had been watching his trainer.

For *They Died With Their Boots On* we had a wonderful set: long steps leading to the headquarters of General Winfield Scott. I played the part of a young cavalry officer. The plot called for me to soften up the General. I was supposed to have found out what his passion in life was. It turned out to be creamed onions. Good, so I got the creamed onions to him.

I am supposed to be so enchanted at having softened him up that I am to run exuberantly down the steps, jump on my horse, and take off to the wars again.

I had carefully trained my favorite horse to stay at the bottom of these steps.

Camera . . . action . . . The General is happy as a lark with his creamed soup, and I am departing . . .

General, I shall not disappoint you, sir.

Down I go full speed, leaping down this long line of steps; then I am flying through the air, and I land neatly on the back of my favorite horse—

Except the sonofabitch isn't there.

In that same picture death rode at my side one day. I saw luck run out suddenly for a good friend of mine.

Again I was working with Mike Curtiz. I was leading a charge against the Indians, a four-hundred-man brigade of cavalry behind me. We were moving over a long expanse, a plain in the San Fernando Valley. The terrain was rough, mountains were in the background, and a big fellow with a camera followed us in a car as we charged. In a movement like this, you didn't know the terrain, neither did the horse. You hoped to come through alive. . . .

Next to me there rode a young fellow I liked very much—Bill Meade. He came from a well-known California family and had just inherited a million bucks. He had married a beautiful girl and had just become a father. He wanted to be an actor and he had every chance to make it. He was very good-looking, an athlete, an excellent polo player. Always he wanted to ride on my right flank, or behind me.

Bill didn't know it, but I would have cheerfully changed places with him. He could have been the actor, doing these pictures in which I didn't believe, and I would have had his million. He followed me around like a puppy. I wanted to see him get places in films. He had all that the world can offer—except fame as an actor. Now we were riding side by side, after the Indians, and Mike Curtiz after us. . . .

Twice we ran through this charge, but the ruthless perfectionist, Mike Curtiz, was screaming, "Once more!—one more time!—we got to do it one more time!"

All around I could sense fatigue. The cavalrymen in their silver uniforms were tired. There was foam on the mouth of Bill Meade's horse. Inside me there worked up this rage I nearly always felt for Curtiz, that it was time we quit before something terrible happened.

With all these tensions at work, tired horses beneath all of us, four hundred men going slashbang over the plain, noise, the clomp of feet on all sides, whinnying, neighing, suffering horses, swords wildly waving, and the director's voice shrieking above it all—I judged that the odds were bad, that we had overdone, should quit.

But no. The gun went off, the signal for action. . . .

Curtiz eggs us on for this third run across the plains. The weary animals are difficult to control. I can tell from the new, strained sounds they are making how nervous they are. I can hear the camera car going full speed beside us, setting up a cloud of dust to contend with. I know they are filming my profile as I scream out:

"Hell for leather, men! Forward!"

I turn in my saddle and wave the sword back at my brigade. At a time like that you wish you were at the back of the cavalry, not in front, because anything can happen.

Bill Meade moved up alongside. His sword was drawn and he held it in front of him in the cavalry style. He was the closest man to the Indians. Out of the corner of my eye I saw his horse stumble. Like a good horseman, he got rid of his sword and prepared to fall.

He threw the sword about twenty feet ahead. With the momentum of the horse behind his throw, the sword did one of the most curious things. It landed right on the hilt, point upward. As the horse completed his stumble, Meade fell forward toward the ground—the one chance in a million of a thing like this happening. That sword was angled just right for murder. Bill landed on it so that the blade went right through him from chest to the back—right through his lung, not missing his heart.

Fear, and the fight against it, have been with me all the days of my life. I still don't understand how, when I was young, in Australia, I became an expert high diver and almost made the Olympics. I still don't understand how I could get up there, look up at the skies, squint down at the water, and let myself go from ninety feet.

As I got on in screen work the derisive term Fearless Flynn developed. Like calling somebody a show-off. This aggravated me because actually I am more cautiously fearful than most people. I would hear them say, "Just hang out with Flynn. Bravest living white man. He's captured mountains—in the movies." When people were incautious enough to say this to me directly, I found myself in brawls.

In my earliest pictures I didn't know what I was doing most of the time, but stunt man pals always helped. When you're a beginner filled with vim and ambition the last thing you want is to have somebody else do for you what you can do as well. I thought the public would like to see the actor himself at his own daredeviling; they would like to feel that this was no stand-in, no screen-making trickery, but the real thing, a true performance. I didn't understand it when the studio was worried, when they lined my suits with cotton wool and insured me as heavily as they could.

Most of the stunts that people saw in my action pictures I can truthfully say were done by me. I have fought sword fights on parapets, ridden horses over high barriers and deep gullies, and fought with Indians who were real tough stunt men; great boys, always. In *The Adventures of Robin Hood* I did all my own stunts. Dammit, I said to myself, I am not going to be a phony. The reason in back of it was that I had fear and I had to go out and meet my own fear. If I am afraid to do something I move in on it and try to tangle with it and lick it.

Later on I got wise to this business. As I lost interest in the vehicles I was cast in, I let the stunt men take over. Especially if there was swordplay.

Professional actors are the most dangerous people to have a duel with. If Rock Hudson, David Niven or Anthony Quinn challenges me to a duel, we are all in trouble because we don't know how to handle ourselves. We are thespians, not fencers. We come out charging, whirling all around, forgetting the prepared routines of the swordplay.

John Barrymore was that way in *Romeo and Juliet*. When somebody said to him, "You are a dangerous sonofabitch with that sword," he didn't give a damn, just so he would look good.

Anthony Quinn ran a sword through my doublet and I nearly lost an eye, and Tony felt worse about it than I did. I also got a sword tip in my mouth in another joust. You put these things down as incidents of the business. Fencing is rough on the hands. I have had my hands cut up time and again.

There are supposed to be precautions in this swordplay, tips on the ends of the swords, but you can still get hurt. The sides of the sword are sharp; they can cut you up in a thousand bits. I don't mean just a scratch or a cut; you can lose an eye. Especially if the guy comes out slashing like a maniac. That blade can go up, with one slash, and cut you all up.

When the camera starts to rev it is remarkable what happens to actors, so I have always worked with doubles if I could. I never trusted myself with another actor, I don't care who he is. He is always uncertain. A good stunt man, if you know him, you can trust him, and you will come out of your duel with him with your mouth still in front of your face, with teeth still in it, your ear still on the side of your head, and your nose where it was to begin with.

I don't know much about fencing, but I know how to make it look good. You only have to stand still and look forward, your head proud, and let the sword point straight out, you and the sword both unmoving, and it is dramatic. Let the sword point dip two inches, and the gesture can look very clever and dangerous.

Whenever I saw one of these wild actors get a gleam on as the camera started rolling, I would throw down my sword and say, "Let me know when you are finished." Or I would knock the sword out of his hands and throw mine in the air, meaning a clinch.

"Look, buddy," I said, "you forgot that routine, didn't you?"

I'd make sure. "If you want to make a big actor out of yourself and maim me, you are going to do it, but I'll tell you something. I'll give you one more chance to do it right, otherwise I'll slash your head off, and you know I can do it. So continue with this personal routine of yours, and you know what will happen. Now let's be sensible about this thing."

Early one February morning I received a telegram from New York:

ARRIVING HOLLYWOOD MONDAY NOON WITH 1200 MONKEYS
KOETS

Koets! The thought of Koets's coming—only a few hours away—was like a scent of water to a camel in the Sahara. I smelled freedom.

It gave me such a lift that I unthinkingly rushed to bear the tidings to Lili. I had often told her of our riotous days in the Far East.

"Look!" I showed her the telegram.

When she saw the name Koets her mouth fell open. "That pig!" she shouted.

The smile left my face like a wave retreating from rocks. "That pig you refer to happens to be my best friend in the world. Moreover, he's staying here with us."

She looked steadily at me. "All right, Fleen, I'll get his room ready."

I rushed to bear the glad tidings to my pal, John Decker. He was at his easel when I rushed in with the telegram. His face lit up with pleasure and he opened a bottle of whisky.

"What in hell is he doing with twelve hundred monkeys?" Decker asked.

"Who knows? Who gives a damn! He's coming!"

We went back to my house where I expected some kind of argument with Lili.

Koets was there.

"Good Christ," Decker shouted when he saw him. "That's King Kong!"

I hugged Koets as he boomed a greeting.

In the background I could see Lili. She had obviously been conned by his charm, in spite of his incredible appearance. His blue eyes and magnificent voice often melted women.

We talked all day, with Lili listening, and for a long time with Decker about. He explained that the only way he could get to America to see me was to find a good pretext. So he bought 1,200 monkeys. These he would sell to the Rockefeller Institute here for experimentation purposes in connection with the common cold—at a dollar a head profit.

We retired early. But I had to have a private chat with the big baboon.

I entered his room with a bottle of champagne. I kicked him, out of sheer camaraderie, and he woke up.

"How I envy you married men," he said—maliciously.

I told him the truth, how I had to get away from the film factory and from Lili. "Koets, you've got to help me."

Koets sat straight up, put on his thick glasses and his face split in half in a grin.

"We can go anywhere you like," he said. "But there's a hell of a good war going on in Spain—a civil one, the best kind for scientists like ourselves. What do you say?"

When Koets discovered a new war, what was there to say?

I had a lot of sympathy with the Republican government, but I would have gone to either side just to get away.

A couple of fellows in the Warners publicity department agreed to help. They told Lili that I was to appear on an important radio program in Chicago. This went over, except that Lili insisted she would meet us in Chicago.

Koets, Lili and I went to a large farewell party given by Jack Warner. Koets embarrassed me, not because of his appearance, which was abominable, but because he went around asking for autographs. That is strictly taboo in the inner circles of Hollywood. He got them from Gary Cooper, Clark Gable, Humphrey Bogart, Bette Davis. I was upset when he showed me the book he had bought for the purpose.

Only Ann Sheridan was a little impolite about it. His eyes gleamed behind his thick spectacles as he showed me what she had written: *Dr. Koets, I'm the Oomph Girl. Oomph you.*

He was so pleased with that signature he looked as if he had discovered a new antihookworm virus.

The next morning Koets and I caught the plane to Chicago. For some reason the plane put down in a small town a hundred miles from Chicago. I was still drunk from the previous night, and wanted to stay that way. One of my peculiarities is that when drunk I always want to buy an animal. In this little town we found an animal shop that had, of all things, a female lion cub. She cost me $200, complete with collar and chain, and for no plausible reason we named her Wellington.

I hired a taxi. The driver, no animal lover, but mollified by the promise of a big tip on our arrival, agreed to drive us to Chicago. We had to stop frequently as the cub kept taking swipes at the back of the driver's neck.

As my head cleared, Wellington seemed to change into a monstrous beast before my eyes. She was bigger and more dangerous than I had supposed. She now seemed to take up half the taxi.

By the time we arrived in Chicago, nobody was friendly any longer. Koets was hunched in a corner, warily.

We arrived at a hotel where I had promised to meet Lili. I had every intention of breaking the promise. Koets and I walked into the lobby. Behind me, on a chain, trailed Wellington.

I approached the desk clerk, identified myself, and handed him the chain. He hadn't seen what was on it. I said, "Check this. Mrs. Flynn will call for it very soon."

Koets and I beat it.

I have wondered since what the clerk did when he found out what was on the end of the chain.

Lili knew full well I was trying to get away and was using Koets to escape. She didn't know what or where or how, but she was a little ball of intuition.

Koets and I boarded a bus headed for New York. That was the way he wanted it. Save money. The same old peculiarity of his. Don't give it to the railroads, the big hotels, the utilities. Steal from them if you could; hang onto every dime.

I didn't know how to overcome this. It was getting to be the source of a rift in our friendship, now that I had plenty of money. He simply failed to allow the notion to penetrate his Dutch skull that to me money between friends meant very little. We had shared so much when we were broke, why shouldn't we share it now that I had it? He continued to keep his account of every nickel spent, only now it was in a little *red* book.

Warner Brothers had arranged a two-room apartment at the St. Moritz for me, on the same floor where, three years before, I had dallied with the Princess Tiarovitch. When Koets saw the imposing décor, he looked around scornfully. "When will you ever realize that the real benefits of money are to steal it, to take it away from someone who has it?"

I explained that the studio paid for the apartment. His face lit up for a moment. As we haggled, a man from the Warner Brothers public relations office entered. I learned then that Lili was not so easily to be outmaneuvered—she was here in town. Moreover, this publicity director said, I would have to make a public reconciliation with my wife. He pointed out that one of my pictures was playing to large audiences in New York, it was no time for doing anything that would make the public fret about Hollywood high jinks. I reluctantly agreed.

Koets refused to stay at the St. Moritz. He gave me the address of the Municipal Lodging House in the Bowery, where he was going.

Lili was in another suite of the same hotel, a vast apartment. When I got there she was surrounded by photographers. She was dressed in black, her favorite color. Even I was breathless with her beauty. She had that wonderful gay smile. Nobody was immune to her charm. All that we had been through, still the sight of her could charge me and upset me. Pictures were taken so that all would be well in the afternoon papers.

I heard her announce we were going to the theatre that evening.

I turned away from her, made my way to the bathroom. I immediately knew I had to see the house doctor, fast.

It only took him a minute to tell me that I had caught once again the Pearl of Great Price.

Shock after shock! Now I've got the clap!

My wife had trailed me to New York; another lady had given me this gift. Tomorrow I was to go to Spain. It was all too much.

I walked through the streets. It was one of the dark moments of my life. A flood of death-wishing came over me. What next? How much can a young fellow go through? How are you supposed to live? What are you supposed to be and do? What drives you? How do you go from one mess to another? Why do things pile up on you? What is its meaning? What is it worth? What is fame and fortune when you have to fight humiliation and confusion?

I went back to pick up Lili. What lie was I going to tell her?

We set out together from the St. Moritz in an automobile. Halfway to the theatre I could stand it no more. I blew up.

I opened the door of the car and sprang out; then ran like a maniac through the streets of Manhattan.

When I tired of running I hopped into a cab and went to the Bowery dive where Koets was staying.

Koets examined me. He opened his magic box, filled with more medical equipment, mementos and junk than ever it was. He removed a small microscope with which he examined the slide. After a few minutes he announced with a happy grin that I had a minor species of gonorrhea. He was sure he could cure it swiftly.

The next morning we caught the ship that would take us to England.

I was greatly relieved when the big vessel pulled out of New York. I fully expected never to see America again.

Though I was on top, with plenty of money, fame, one of the most beautiful women of the time as my wife, yet I was full up.

I consoled myself. If I am lucky, I may catch a bullet over there and the hell with it all.

Koets came into first class only when he thought he was cheating the Cunard company. I sometimes went into third class to see him and the sixty friends he had already made.

We made plans about Spain. Koets figured he would have to swim a certain river on the French border to get into the country. "They probably won't like us in Spain any more than they did in China or India," he prophesied.

Being a naturalized American, Koets wasn't supposed to become involved in any foreign wars—the same situation as the Sino-Japanese muddle we'd been in—and he could only stay out of the United States for a certain length of time. In 1938 I was still a British subject. It was easier for me to get a permit to enter Spain. I simply went to the Spanish Consul, showed my first book and a couple of magazine articles I had written, and received permission to enter Spain as a journalist observer.

Lili was still hot on my spoor. She had arrived in London and, unable to pick up my tracks, she went to Paris.

Koets and I arrived in Paris and I went to the Plaza Athenée. Just my luck! I might have known she would be there too. Her mother was with her. Mama was typically French, but physically bore no resemblance to her daughter except for a violent temper.

For a day or two we tried to live together again. We stayed in the same suite. But there was a running argument, that bitter, vituperative talk that can twist the guts; when the wits are keen, the language violent and dirty. You do not care. You are hurting each other. You intend to hurt. The more you wound the better it is—and then you feel you want to throw up.

We would make up, and it would be momentarily tender. She would think of something to do, a place to go, some fun.

"I know," she said, one evening, "you must come with me to *Le Monocle*."

It was the last word in French night life. There were many high-class dens, clubs, whorehouses, but none of the caliber of *Le Monocle*.

When you entered the dimly lighted interior, with the large dance floor, the darkened cubicles, the exits and entrances to rooms, corridors, you saw moving about these bulldykes: masculine females, ready to please. All were dressed in tuxedos, like men.

The "King" was about five-foot three or four inches, named Frankie. She had a figure of excellent proportions to go with that appealing height, and a man's haircut. The main difference between Frankie and other women was she liked other women. She dressed better than any man I had ever seen. Suede pumps, replacing the old patent leather pumps, long before others knew of suede in shoes. As you panned up from her feet and legs, a lovely form appeared; her hips snakelike. As you looked a little higher up, the button of her one-button single-breasted coat was no more than an inch and a half above her navel. Up further, her white tuxedo looked flat over a pleated shirt which was finely starched. She affected a butterfly collar, a flowing bow tie, and a white handkerchief, with one dramatic stripe of black in the breast pocket of her coat. Then you settled your view on her face, that delicate face—her over-all effect that of a sophisticated English schoolboy. Her man's haircut looked better on her than on any man. There seemed to be a particular carelessness in it. Close to her I could get the fragrance of her perfume. You could hardly call it Chanel, nor could it be *Carnaval de Venice* and it couldn't be *Rochas,* which hadn't been heard of yet. Yet it was something between a man's delicate perfume and a touch of man's *Fleur de Nuit.*

Mostly it was the attitude, her stance, that compelled attention. Frankie had an incomparable way of putting her hand in her left tuxedo pocket, and with this subtle gesture she looked down her nose, standing or posing with a lofty disdainful arrogance. She had such a distinguished air that you felt like putting a cloak on the ground before her.

She took a shine to Lili at once; amazingly, my wife seemed to take a shine to her.

As I sat at a table, teeth gritting, I noticed that instantly, almost without words, Lili and Frankie were off on the floor dancing in a strange rhythmic silent accord. This left me at the table with several bulldykes, each one looking like a sparring partner for Sugar Ray Robinson, except that they had a bit more upholstery chestwise.

It was a sight to watch Lili and Frankie size each other up. Soft French bistro music, faint lights, no voices raised. Here there were no Americans, no English, and whatever nationalities there were, they knew how to keep their voices down.

I watched Lili now in the darkest corner of the room, still floating with Frankie, but with dancing positions reversed. There was a touch of burlesque about it, but I was too enraged, and ingenuous as well, to wonder if the act was for my benefit. Was Lili trying to make me jealous, enrage me? Today I know she was.

This is no place for a man, I thought miserably.

You could see young ladies necking in the dark corners, in the cubicles, at the distant tables, beneath the dimmed lights. The seats were long, roomy. . . . There was an air over the whole place of an illicit wonder going on.

I could feel my gorge rise. These ladies didn't want a man. Yet in this life, I tried to reflect, everyone, everything is here for a purpose, but I felt about as necessary as balls on a cow.

So I ordered champagne and invited several of the *ladies* to join me in a glass, while I watched the delicate ankles of my wife and the even more delicate feet of Frankie dancing a reserved fox trot. I could see and sense their intricate arm-play, and I felt a terrible frustration.

I knew neither what to do, nor what attitude to take. What does a man do when he is inside a place where men aren't necessary?

The girls lapped up the champagne.

Lili returned to the table. Frankie was wearing a beautiful, rather placid expression as she stood close to me.

Rather impetuously, perhaps to get my morale back, perhaps just as a juvenile reaction, I said to her, "I have got to see what goes on under that lovely pleated shirt—" and reached over and pinched a soft breast.

My arm suddenly went numb.

One of the bulldykes had given me a crushing blow on the wrist, cutting off the circulation. As I held my hand, Frankie looked unperturbed.

Was I in a Lesbian joint or a gymnasium?

I settled back into a temporary quiet, but I was steaming inside.

Lili was now admiring Frankie's fingernails. They were talking girl talk—no doubt for my benefit. Some instinct told me that this talk about nail polish wasn't the same as they'd had before.

I got the bill. Instead of being charged for six glasses of champagne, I was charged for six bottles.

Ordinarily I would have walked out, saying to myself I had been robbed, served me right for being in a place like this. But at this time I only needed one little aggravation to set me off. "You must be nuts," I shouted, "if you think I am going to pay for this. Each of you had a glass of champagne on me, and that's all I'm paying for! That's all!"

At this outburst, Frankie retired with a rather pained look, as if this kind of thing should never have happened.

As she moved off, several heavyweights, attired in tuxedos, busts bursting in female fashion, muscles tensed in male fashion, advanced toward me. There was one who looked exactly like Strangler Lewis, even almost to the haircut, and she-he led the others. This one outweighed me, it was obvious, and I somehow sensed that whether it was a man or woman, he-she could easily handle my case alone. "Look," I proposed, conciliatory but firm I thought, "I'm not paying twelve thousand francs to buy you heavyweight wrestlers more than a glass apiece. I am paying nothing like it. I am paying"—I changed my approach . . . the ladies reminded me of big tomcats cornering a dachshund dog—"I am leaving—"

The big one put her hands on her hips. "That's what *you* think."

I advanced.

"I give you five seconds to get out of my way or I'll knock you down."

The grip she had on her hip stiffened. A couple of her pals came and stood on each side, barring the exit.

If I have any Captain Blood blood, it was boiling now. "Look, ladies or gentlemen, get out of my way. I'm warning you. . . ." Now I felt I could handle the whole crowd—a mistake.

"Out of my way!" I repeated, my last quiet words for many a day. The next thing I knew I was flat on my back on the floor.

I picked myself up, slugging and charging—as screaming and shouting became general in *Le Monocle*. I yelled, batting someone, anyone, "Call the police . . ."

It wasn't necessary. Two cops were right behind me and I'd hit one. They were the protectors of the *maison*. In this instance it was a case of the joint is always right.

Offside there was Lili, her finger to her mouth, looking concerned.

Fighting with tough females and getting the hell lambasted out of me by them and the cops—I was completely out of my depth, I had no way of knowing how to behave. I had lost control. The cops hadn't.

Next thing I knew I was in jail.

It was an old cage, like a large-sized toilet.

They took my shoelaces out of my shoes—so I wouldn't hang myself, they explained. They removed cigarettes, money and matches from my wallet. They left me with my raincoat.

Indignant about this, finding myself powerless, behind bars, I put my shoes outside, as you would in a big hotel. A little later I banged on the door. "You sonofabitch," I yelled to the keeper, "why aren't my shoes cleaned?"

This didn't appeal to the French sense of humor. The French penal system does not call for the guards to clean the prisoner's shoes.

A couple of gendarmes arrived. They shouted at each other, but whatever they said, it meant taking me out of the cell, slapping me around, and throwing me back behind bars.

Lili arrived, talking very voluble French. I peered through the bars and listened.

"Please to forget it," she told the captain. "He is perfectly all right. Just a little out of control. I will pay for the champagne and the bail. Will you please excuse this terrible thing?"

I yelled, "Throw that bitch out of here. If you take her money you are all bums. French bums, you hear me! You are fattening on the—"

This for some reason aggravated the French police again.

All of a sudden I felt I had no fingers. Someone had come along and whacked them as I gripped the bars.

After I recovered, I invoked the American Bill of Rights, national rights, international rights—until some guy came along, up to my cell door. Then I made a terrible mistake. Because I couldn't get at him, I spat in his face.

Three gendarmes came in. They took my raincoat, put it over my head so that I couldn't get my arms out, and while two of them held me a third gave me another going over.

After a while—Lili had put up bail and left the jailhouse—the police said I could go. I picked up my coat, still breathing fire and smoke, still threatening to invoke international law, even phone the Pope.

The sergeant gave me back my shoelaces.

But I had put my shoes out to be cleaned and when they were handed to me, I said, "This is a lousy job you have done. Put the laces back in."

The sergeant ignored that. I demanded my money. I counted it, put it in my pocket. Because I couldn't think of anything else to get mad about, I looked into my cigarette case; the cigarettes were gone. "Who," I demanded, "stole my cigarettes? You are all thieves! I refuse to go until my cigarettes are returned!"

My refusal to go was no great problem to them.

—My feet were off the ground, men were carrying me, I heard someone say, "Put him back in," and they threw me back into the jug again.

It was five A.M. before I got out into the streets.

Roaming the streets of Paris that morning I knew that if I stayed any longer with Lili it could be that I would have to kill her or get killed. I knew this. I could no longer stand the accumulation of insults and lovemaking piled up one after the other.

After the experience at *Le Monocle* there was a deadly silence between Lili and me. I began to pack.

The reasons I wanted to go to Spain were political and heartfelt, but I also wanted to get away from this woman. Otherwise I knew I would destroy her or she would destroy me. She was perfectly capable of destroying me because she was tougher.

Lili knew this was the end. A man who chose to go off to a bitter war instead of remaining with her must be serious.

Koets and I were looking through the one suitcase we were going to share. It was a shabby old thing. As we packed he explained to Lili's mother, trying to have some fun, that he was packing bombs. Actually we put in the suitcase little rolls of film for a Contax camera I was taking to the war. The way they were wrapped, they might have looked like small hand grenades.

All the time we packed there was a running argument between Lili and me. She was getting close to violence and I could see that look in her eyes when she was casting about, looking for something to pick up and throw.

I ran out of the apartment and called for the elevator man to halt. I reached the little cage as Lili came storming through the hall, and managed to beat her down to the lobby.

Then outside, breathless and furious.

I looked up, for I heard screaming. It was Lili standing on the window sill, yelling down that she was going to throw herself out of the window.

Good! Let her jump this time. Wonderful. I shook my fist up at her. "Jump, you sonofabitch, jump!" I was out of control, screaming up at her loudly as she called down. "You promised to jump! Go ahead. Let's see! Go on!"

I felt a hand on my shoulder. I hollered, "You've threatened time and again. Now do it! You are going to make a horrible mess. Jump! Do it . . ."

I looked around, for the hand had got firmer. A big French gendarme was shaking me. He had a white truncheon and he was swinging it energetically, though not at me. "Monsieur, what do you think you are doing making such a scandal in the street?"

I must have looked idiotic, shaking my fist at a little woman perched on a window sill. There was nothing to say. Miserably I could only shake my head. *"Je m'excuse."*

He said, "I should think so. Now, stop this—"

Suddenly there was a crash. A flower pot. Lili had tossed it out of the window. The policeman looked at the crumpled mess of pottery and earth, astonished, and asked in French, "What kind of row is this?"

Heads peered from windows everywhere.

That roused the officer, and he began pushing me. He took my left elbow and pushed me about on the sidewalk, demanding to know what everything was all about.

Where was Koets? I wondered.

"Alors!" The gendarme asked, "Who is that, your wife or your mistress?"

Before I could answer there was a loud explosion under the window of the apartment occupied by Lili's mother. It was my suitcase. Everything I packed in the case, which she thought contained bombs, had missed the policeman's head by inches. The contents now rolled all over the sidewalk and into the gutter: my clothes, shaving gear, the camera equipment, the packets of film; even a jar of caviar splattered.

He looked up. He could see nothing more. Lili had ducked back into the apartment.

Koets came out of the hotel, approached us.

Once more the officer asked, "Is that your mistress?" That seemed to be the crucial point to the officer.

"No, sir, my wife."

"Aw-w-w-," he said very compassionately, now full of understanding. *"Mon pauvre,"* he commiserated. *"Allez. Passez, passez!"*

That was the French way of saying, "If it's your mistress it is bad enough, but if it's your wife, on your way, brother."

Koets and I left Paris on March 26th.

At Barcelona I was surprised to be met by two gentlemen who spoke only Spanish. Neither Koets nor I could speak it well, but I gathered that we were being welcomed.

A man with a car was assigned to us. His name was Pepe, he was from Palma de Majorca. He could speak English. He was a curious example of indefiniteness in the human form. You couldn't tell his age, not even his height very clearly, nor could you decide whether he was good-looking or ugly. Nature hadn't given him a single striking characteristic. Yet he was at hand all the time, like a shadow, and he could drive a car.

As we moved through Barcelona he gave us a running commentary of the city, and the course the war had taken so far. It had been on about two years.

My mood, as we drove, was morbid. I had the feeling I had come to die and it might not matter much if I did. No one would mourn me. I felt unreal, tired, beat up by life with Lili, overworked at the studio. I was inwardly ready for the bullet that I had come to Spain to get.

I had a good grasp on the realities of the war itself. I knew—so did the whole world—that Spain was being used as a testing ground for the weapons to be used later in World War II. Hitler and Mussolini helped Franco. Russia helped the Loyalists. America was playing it neutral.

In the human sense I was for everybody. Why the hell did brother have to fight brother? I knew there were idealists, fanatics, nuts on the Loyalist side. I understood that big money was sentimental to the Franco cause, or outrightly sympathetic. As to my own sympathies, I decided that since the split was a revolution by Franco against the legally elected Republican government, then I leaned toward the Left. There might be a little more idealism and humanity on that side.

Not so with Koets. He was detached about everything except medicine. He professed not to give a damn who killed whom. He would have been quite capable of taking a Nazi belt and bashing the brains of a Communist, and do the same thing to a Nazi with a Communist belt— just to study the reactions of each. Yet he wanted to get into medical work where he would be dedicated to saving life.

Pepe took us to Madrid. We were going there to see a big shot, he wouldn't say who, but it was a top-brass Loyalist. There was steady traffic over the road between the two cities. Supplies, soldiers, messengers, going between the two big cities. You went slowly. Sometimes planes came over.

There were several cars, more or less official, in this entourage, and for the whole journey one specific auto was in front of us.

Once, as we halted to rest, a fellow in the front car, named Jackson, stepped out of his machine and held up a bar of candy. Did I want it? Or part of it? In that instant a bomb landed nearby. Jackson was killed outright. Had I left our car and made a move toward him I might have got it.

That's what I had come here for, but Jackson, who probably wanted to live, was the one who was killed.

I went on to Madrid a little shaken. Lili was somewhat out of my system now. Too much was happening around me.

We arrived in the evening and put up at the Gran Via Hotel.

The next morning Koets's clock struck nine, waking us. He jumped out of bed. As his feet hit the floor there came a whistling noise. The room shook. "What on earth was that?" I asked, going to the window.

I heard the whistling noise again and a large hole appeared in the building opposite. I stared incredulously.

After a few more seconds a third noise sounded and a blast of air brushed past me. A corner of the building opposite blew off and shattered in the street below.

"Shells!" Koets shouted.

We ran down into the lobby. The clerk seemed fairly unconcerned. "That's the Germans," he said. "They always shell at nine o'clock." He went on to say that the building opposite was the communications center. The Germans on the University front were trying to knock it out, being unaware that the equipment had been moved.

I asked him for another room. He suggested one two floors below ours, which was double the price. How about one near the lobby? "All occupied by journalists," he said. Even the basement was full of correspondents.

Another shell burst. "Eight," said the clerk. "We usually get ten." Two more came, putting an end to the morning's bombardment.

We ventured out into the street. There the crowds hardly noticed the building opposite. Two English-speaking youths were examining the hole in the Telefonica with interest. "They're pretty sure to win now," one said. "I bet that fifty shells would knock it in half, but forty-eight haven't so I might as well pay off." He told us about the fighting on the northern front. "I'm an American with the Abraham Lincoln Brigade," he said.

His companion stared at me. "You're Errol Flynn," he said accusingly. "What the hell are you doing over here?"

I said I was covering the war for a couple of magazines. I was trying to be an impartial and fair observer. That seemed to upset them. "You can't be fair with bastards like them," one said.

Pepe showed us a schedule for the day. "First we must get you a Salvo Conducto—a pass. You won't be safe anywhere without one." He said that nothing must happen to gentlemen of our importance. Importance? Koets and I glanced at each other.

At noon we lunched with General von Helmuth. He was more than a soldier of fortune, a brilliant staff officer. He was a member of the upper echelon of the Republican staff, having fled from Nazi Germany. He was an idealist, a man of great reputation, and the world watched his exploits with an inferior army. It seemed incredible that he would want to see us. Of what possible importance could we be in his life?

Two military guards ushered us into an unpretentious building. I saw a man with an aquiline nose, thin brows, thin hair, even thin boots. He bowed Prussian-style. We each muttered something, then sat down at the table. He sat between Koets and me. About twenty other officers were present. The general, to my surprise, bowed his head and said grace in Spanish.

The lunch was difficult, for the general seemed to prefer not to speak German to Koets, and said scarcely a word to me. The food was a tasteless bean soup and a tasteless steak. An officer whispered, "Donkey meat, we ran out of horses."

After the food, the general rose and started to read from a paper. In a monotone, he read of the heartfelt emotions and happiness the Spanish people felt that their hero of the screen and upholder of justice, Errol Flynn, was with them. The Spanish people would never forget this. He didn't mention which part of the Spanish people. I sat there in amazement, trying not to show surprise to be cast in such a role. When he finally came to an end, I stood up and said thank you.

The general said he couldn't disappoint the enemy and he had to get back to the war. We laughed mirthlessly, then rose and left.

"What the hell is this all about?" I whispered to Koets. Why were we getting such special attention?

We went with the local junta to the outskirts of Albacete. The soldiers in our group hailed an elderly priest who was walking over a narrow log, crossing the river. He told them he had been hiding out in a garret for several months. He didn't look very wan. He weighed about two hundred and fifty pounds.

Somebody prevailed upon the military group to give the priest the chance to walk across this log. It would be sporting, he was so fat. He lifted up his cassock and started across in his sandals. The agreement was that if he got to the other side he'd be allowed to live.

As soon as he almost reached the opposite side there was a burst of machine-gun fire. The priest looked as if he had been cut in half with a cleaver.

The handicapper in me was roused to fury and resentment. This was not sporting. I grabbed hold of our guide, Pepe, and yelled, "You lousy bastards! You gave him a chance, didn't you? He got over, didn't he? Why didn't you let him live? Is this the way you fight a war?"

Koets grabbed me by the shoulder and hissed, "Shut up or we'll both be shot, idiot!"

Pepe was afraid that what we had just witnessed might get back to the United States, and he tried to pacify me.

I had been commissioned by William Randolph Hearst himself to cable any stories I could, but I hadn't got around to sending any news dispatches yet.

Koets regarded me with amusement. It seemed ridiculous to him that I should be so upset over the death of a stranger.

We walked into the darkened streets. I cursed the cruelty I had witnessed by the Loyalists with whose general objectives I felt an accord. Suddenly a feminine voice challenged us. "Salvo Conducto!"

Koets chucked the girl under the chin paternally and smiled.

She reached into the top of her dress, between her breasts, and whipped out a gun. "Pronto!" She jabbed him in the stomach with the pistol.

Chastened, Koets dropped back a foot or two, momentarily alarmed. He searched his pockets for the paper she wanted.

I stepped back into the shadows and had a better look while this interplay went on between the two. Amusement was coming back to Koets. He seemed attracted by the girl.

She had dark hair far down over her forehead. A hard line for a mouth. Her figure wasn't bad. But there was a deadly seriousness in her eyes. A little girl playing partisan and being grim about it, while Koets struggled to find his identification.

Suddenly Koets decided to take a second chance. His hairy paw went out to her face in what I suppose he considered a tender gesture.

There was a sudden report. A bullet fired from her gun went through Koets's shirt and grazed his skin.

She started to back up and stumbled on some debris behind her. Koets reached out and grabbed her. He took the gun out of her hands, saying gently, "Do you really need this?"

I emerged partly from my corner under a Spanish balcony. I had been watching the scene like a director studying a set before the camera turns. About fifty yards up the road I heard a shell burst. While I was entranced, the balcony above me, already half shot away by gunfire, collapsed. It gave way from the detonation of the distantly exploding shell. The last I remembered was that curious sight of Koets pulling the girl toward him, and his arms going around her neck affectionately. Then a blinding light as the balcony collapsed and hit me on the head.

I was out.

ERROL FLYNN KILLED IN SPAIN, screamed the headlines.

The incident was reported all over the world and must have made Lili thoughtful.

I awoke in a hospital, the annex of an old monastery. Koets was attending to me, but mostly he was hard at work operating on wounded men constantly being brought in from the battle front.

Lying there on a hospital cot it occurred to me that nothing in this war seriously terrified me. Why was it I had no fear? I didn't understand my own reactions. You heard the sound of shell, mortar, bullets, explosions distantly or close, all the time. Yet I wasn't nearly as bothered as I had been in the old days when my raft turned over in the Sepic River and a croc picked up my Kanaka boy and pulled him under water.

Was I still suffering so badly from the frightening experience of temperamental Lili that, after her, civil war seemed mild?

After a few days, I stood at Koets's side as he operated. He was at his best now, a scientist who worked day and night. He relished it. Men were brought in moaning, with death rattles. Rows of wounded were laid out in the corridors. Koets was a dedicated man. He went from bed to bed, scalpel in hand, operating as best he could with the use of ether. The ether smell filled the hospital. This went on for weeks. I tried to help, but wasn't of much use. Koets was near collapse. He didn't take coffee, liquor or cigarettes, so there was no use offering them to him. But he made me wonder at the variety to be found in human beings. Why was he totally disinterested in the ideological values of the war, yet totally interested in trying to preserve life?

Once a high-ranking officer was brought into the room. His tattered uniform clung to his wounds. He stood there, gray-haired, almost at attention in the shadow of the lamp under which Koets operated. Koets didn't notice him. He was busy working on a man who had a shattered knee.

Koets turned his attention to the officer. They took the coat off and Koets saw that the man's arm was hanging only by a piece of skin and flesh. Koets called for the ether to put the man out and deftly cut the arm off. But the officer had lost so much blood he was near death.

"Remarkable," said Koets. "Can't understand how he stood up." He looked down at the prone figure. "I wonder what the hell he is dying for at this minute." He pondered a second. "Here's a man whose arm I have just removed, and right before our eyes he is dying." He shook his head. His attitude was cold and clinical. He muttered, "Wonder when he last got laid?"

The officer died a few minutes later.

I had seen so much that day I felt I had a bellyful. I wondered what good I was to anyone. How could you get stories like this back to the States? To what end? Just to tell tales of bravery and suffering and belief?

Sometimes Koets mentioned Lita, the girl who had taken a shot at him. They saw each other from time to time when she came to the hospital. He would stop work for a minute or so to talk with her, then she'd be gone. Nights, when he wasn't working, they stayed together.

One evening there was a flurry at the monastery door. Something had to be told to Koets and nobody wanted to do it. Bearers came in, bringing a body. Lita had been raped and murdered. The body was laid on a table. Whoever had done it had used a knife and slit her dress from the neck down. Afterward he had practically slit her in two pieces. The trunk was still bleeding. I thought Koets would crack. I almost did myself. But he didn't. Some bubbles rose in his mouth. One of his big hands took her around the shoulders and the hand seemed to go around her neck in a last affectionate touch. Only from that gesture could I gather that he had some rich feeling about her. Then, like the scientist he was, he snapped out of it. He stared at her remains.

"Remarkable case," he said.

He turned and went outside.

In the days that followed I saw more of the spectacles that only a civil war, with its hatreds and its hopes, can yield up. I saw three nuns ransack corpses for anything they could pick out of the clothes that had been worn. Yet the same nuns carried buckets of human excrement from typhoid patients and cleaned the buckets with their own hands.

Spain had become a bowl filled to the brim with corruption, violence, murder. The young grew old before my eyes. The old no longer wanted to live. I saw homeless people, fanatics, dreamers, the brave and the brash and the stupid. Spain was the dream of a broken home.

While the war waged, domestic life ran along silently at its side. Women fetched water from the well. They carried it home and they washed.

I saw a dead priest hauled out of a cellar. They certainly hated the Church. Perhaps the Church had gotten away from its roots and its reason. There were boards around him, like a sandwich man, and on the board were the words I AM A PRIEST AND A COWARD. I DON'T KNOW HOW TO FIGHT, ONLY TO PREACH LIES. A woman picked up a bucket and flung it at the corpse in fury. Another woman picked up a bucket and struck the first, saying, "He was a man of God."

Sometimes, at night, the air was soft, even beautiful. It was hard to believe, then, that a nation was taking its entrails out and laying them before the world.

A commissar wondered whether I could do real fighting for the cause. They gave me a machine gun and said I must go to a certain point and begin shooting. No more giving revolution a whirl. Get in there and earn your right to be a Loyalist supporter, and to hell with that foreign correspondent stuff.

From my post I could see the fire flashing over the trees and hear the artillery rumbling steadily. My hands were on the machine gun.

I couldn't do it.

I simply couldn't shoot people down. Maybe this wasn't my war after all.

I didn't want to kill anyone. Not for political reasons. I didn't want to fire any guns for uncertain ideas. I had handled weapons galore in pictures, but there was a vast gap between the make-believe of films and the reality here.

I resumed hanging about Koets at the monastery. I helped him. I flitted from hospital to hotel. Pepe stayed at my side. Almost wherever I went he was there. I wondered why. Why wasn't I left alone? What did Pepe want? What did they want?

It was at this time I met Estrella. She was lovely, truly Spanish, with a sense of humor that wasn't usual for a Spanish girl. I had found Spanish girls to be a little ferocious, and passionately, alarmingly sincere. Estrella had long, dark hair, a narrow waistline, long shapely legs, and no knees it seemed. The legs seemed to go straight from the hips down to the ankles. Certainly each toe was a joy to look at. So were her hands. She had an alabaster skin. When she stood up naked she seemed bewitching as a siren. She was young and I hold nothing against youth.

Always, wherever I have been, in no matter what situation, it seems that a woman has finally symbolized my presence. Estrella was my symbolization in Spain.

Now I could leave Spain, start afresh somehow. It was all out of me, the deep melancholy, the flight from Lili, from the studio tension, the death-wish.

I had reached the point where I told Pepe to stay away from me. Why did he follow me around like a puppy? Hadn't he anything better to do in the war than shadow me? I still could not figure out why these people were going to such lengths to treat us well. Why did we get so much better treatment than other war correspondents?

"What do you want of us?" I asked him, after two months had gone by.

"Look, Mr. Flynn," he said. "When are you going to give us the money?"

I looked at him for a long second. Had I heard him right? "The million dollars," Pepe added. "We've been waiting."

"What million?"

Pepe elaborated. "You've brought over a million dollars from Hollywood collected from some of the biggest stars." He mentioned a few names.

I was speechless. I told Pepe that I was flattered that they had thought we were entrusted with such a large sum, but it never happened. I reiterated that I was there for personal reasons and as a war correspondent, an observer. Nothing else.

Koets and I figured we had better get out of Spain right away.

On the way out of Spain I mused at length how the Spaniard could have got the idea I was the bearer of a million bucks. Koets started to chortle raucously.

"What's so funny?" I demanded.

He moved into uproarious laughter. He told me he had set up this idea when he arrived, buzzing the word to the reception committee, but telling them that the money was not available yet, it would be in due course. That was why they gave us a car and a chauffeur-guide.

"What I wanted was a chance to operate, to work and operate, that's all," he said. "The only way I could do it and get by in style here was to use you."

After his thunderous guffaws settled, I said, "Thank you, Comrade Sonofabitch!"

I had picked up a tiny statue of the Madonna and Child. It was about a foot high, slender and delicate. The heads of the Madonna and the Infant were missing, shot off. This struck me as pathetic, ironic, somehow pictorial of the whole scene. It symbolized in a poetic way the futility of civil wars, the futility of wars of any kind.

When I returned from abroad the Knights of Columbus accused me of being a dangerous radical. It happens that in America if you bear the name of Flynn and you achieve some prominence, the Catholic Church is going to get interested in you. Along the line somewhere they found I had no identification with the Catholic Church. I was simply a guy named Flynn. If that was my name, what was I doing on the Republican side?

There were even editorials about me. What was I, an actor, doing sticking my nose into the affairs of another country? Well, a lot of Americans did this. They believed they did it in a just cause. This was an historic moment in the history of the world between World War I and World War II.

I tried to get publication for my impressions of Spain. What I had to say was apparently slanted with Loyalist sympathy, for there was a surprising disinterest among many in high circles and at the most prominent publications.

Before I went to Spain I saw Franklin D. Roosevelt, Jr. from time to time. He had all the charm and good looks of his father. He was a fine athlete; he had a good sense of humor. As a result of my friendship with Franklin, who was about my age, I was invited to the White House from time to time. I had already met the President.

Now, back from Europe and visiting my Aunt Betty who lived in Washington, I was invited to come to the White House for one of their regular Sunday evening social rituals.

I told Mrs. Roosevelt of my difficulties in getting publication for what I had witnessed in Spain. She said it was an outrage that my material had not been published and couldn't get published. She had much interest in what I had to say. I don't say sympathy. But she had much interest in anyone who took up the Republican cause.

The President came in on his wheelchair and he sat at the head of the long table. About were the Roosevelt family, many notables, government people, visitors. Mrs. Roosevelt herself brought in a big platter of scrambled eggs. She prepared this herself and did it magnificently.

The President took one or two old-fashioneds—his favorite drink; but no more. He had such a sparkling gaiety about him and the whole family seemed to be in distinct contrast to the physical condition he was in.

He had more charm and magnetism than I ever found in anyone in Hollywood.

The President seemed to like me. He gave me a fine painting of himself inscribed to me, and he liked to ask questions about motion picture making. When he had a good word to say about my own work, I deprecated what he said.

"Why are you so damned modest?" he asked.

Franklin, Jr. tore into his father. So did James and Elliot. The President had recently said publicly that the borders of America were on the banks of the Rhine and he was being widely criticized for this. The President listened with an amused and tolerant smile as his sons lit on him. It was like a pack of little hounds baying at the old dog. He had an answer for everything.

When he finished handling that, he mentioned that he had just had a dream about this same political question.

"You know," said the President, "I dreamed I was sitting there with Mussolini and Hitler—the three of us. Mussolini said, 'Italy will extend her borders to Abyssinia and beyond, God willing.' Hitler said, 'And Germany will extend her borders all over Europe, God willing.' And I replied, 'But, gentlemen, I am not.' "

I have always resented that the artist should be relegated by the politician to a place with no voice in political or human affairs. The politician and even the press seem to feel that the artist should have a lesser voice than others in public affairs.

It is a little unfair of the world and its leaders to think that we who entertain are marionettes to be tossed about at the end of their string and to be told to do and say what *they* think we should do and say. Authority and philosophy and truth reside in their hands. Ours to entertain; not to reason why—just let *them* continue to make the mess of the world which they have made.

In the history of man the entertainer has often achieved a position in the public mind that perhaps is or is not deserving. He has a stature that in many cases has put him apart from politics and in many cases has put him into politics. Spartacus, a gladiator of ancient Rome, led a revolt of slaves. History still remembers it.

Paderewski, the pianist, became a leader of Poland. Chaliapin could certainly, if he'd wanted to, have had nearly as big a voice as Trotsky in the Russian revolution, but he chose to remain an artist. I am quite sure that if Will Rogers had wanted to run for high office he would have secured it.

In my case, curiosity is a sickness. It gets me into all my troubles and experiences. It got me into Spain and more recently into the Cuban situation. I am quite capable of doing my own thinking and my own living and I don't need somebody somewhere running some jerk organization to tell me what is right and wrong and where my province ends and his begins. My province as a human is the same as yours: it's the world.

Back in New York, I still felt in no shape to resume work. A lot of paychecks had accumulated for me, but I told Warners I was not ready to return to the studio.

Again Lili and I reconciled. I decided I would introduce her to my greatest love—the wide ocean—which no woman has ever been able to compete with for my affections.

My only real happiness is when I am near the sea. Cut off from the beach, away from the sea, I am nervous and I fret. I am never happy in a big city. Only for a week or two of violent living. I have tried it time and again, but it has never worked. My lifeline has always been a boat down by the waterfront.

I had heard of the Caribbean as a world of beauty similar to the South Pacific, which had spawned me. We went to Boston. There I bought a sailboat. You should never rename a boat. I made the mistake of renaming this one. I called it the *Sirocco,* giving it the same name as the one I owned in New Guinea.

I set sails for a trip down the Atlantic Coast into the islands of the West Indies.

In Havana I struck up with a wonderful fellow, tall and good-looking, named Pancho Arranyo, since dead. He typified a Spanish don; his family had been there for centuries, one of the ancient Cuban families. Yet he looked less like a Cuban than any I ever saw. He had a long, aquiline face, startling blue eyes. He was the physical prototype of a man who could have been leaning over the shoulder of one of El Greco's priests. As wicked a man as I ever met, and as is usual with such people, totally charming.

I was fighting with Lili again, so I decided I must get away from her for a few hours or a day. I looked up Pancho.

The Cubans, particularly the playboy-millionaire class there, live a special life. I like it. I quickly learned from Pancho; and the first thing I did was to hire an orchestra to follow me everywhere I went. The musicians were picturesque; toothless, almost clothesless, they wore battered straw hats, gaudy neckcloths, battered shirts, torn unpressed pants through which you could see their thighs, knees, buttocks. But they could sing and strum stringed instruments. "You understand," I said to them in my imperfect Spanish when I hired them, "if you are ever out of my sight or sound, the deal is off, you are fired."

"*Si, si,* Er-r-rol!" They were delighted to be the personal band of a movie star.

I was set. Now for the action. "Pancho, who is that honey-haired beauty over there?" —"Ah, you weesh to meet Mees Gonzalez, she ees from wan of the bast fomilies—"

She was in her twenties, unmarried, her family fabulously rich, and she was untouchable in the Spanish style. You had to pay your compliments from a distance to a woman of this class. I was married, and there was little I could do about it. She was aloof, but friendly, and she spoke fluent English. I learned that she could swim, play tennis. I was attracted highly, for it was rarely that a Cuban girl could do anything athletically. I was always looking for athletic girls, soul mates to do rough and ready things with me on land or sea, like my male pals had always been able to do, but I found few of them. I managed to inveigle her to a lunch: itself a conquest, for anything like a date after five o'clock was looked upon askance, but an assignation for luncheon wasn't so bad.

I took her to a restaurant. I was full of teeth and charm. I put it on like butter. I tried to be like a hero in one of my current hits.

The Morro crab came, hard shell.

I spun what I thought was an amusing story, I was the essence of Gaelic wit—then I heard a pop—it reverberated through my head.

The hard shell!

Next thing, a front tooth popped out of my mouth and landed on the tablecloth. It rolled around indecisively and came to rest plunk in the center of a red square of the tablecloth, and there it was between us. She looked at it, I looked.

She stared at me, I stared at her. The romance was dying under our very gaze.

My tongue went up and found the big space in the front of my mouth—on the face of the man already famous for his toothy smile.

From then I had to finish the story with tight lips. But this is no way to be a raconteur.

So ended the affair before it began.
I ran over to a dentist who put in another phony chopper.
My morale was low. I turned to Pancho for other amusement.
"Ha, Er-rol, I know jost de ting!"

He knew, he said, where the most beautiful girls in the world were. A whole houseful of them. They were not the usual run-of-the-mill ladies of the night, or *putas,* as the Cubans call their whores. The madam, he said, was an old friend, and she would take the finest care of us. He went on, rapturously, to describe the handsomeness and the gifts of the young ladies.

We were already cruising along a quiet street, midafternoon, headed for this place, with my orchestra piled into the back seat. Pancho ran out of vocabulary, Spanish and English, to describe the joys awaiting us—and at that impasse we arrived.

Sure enough, as Pancho said, they were beautiful girls. As we entered, a charming lady came toward us. She welcomed her old customer, Pancho, she was delighted and flattered when she learned who I was—and the next thing I noticed, Pancho was at it. . . .

He had girls under his armpits, girls under his crotch, girls behind his ears, girls under his feet. I was stunned.

Reclining in a bed, thoroughly absorbed, his two hands behind his head, he beckoned. "Come on, Er-rol, get eento theess."

Yet it was the kind of maelstrom I couldn't get into. I looked on with a sort of tearful wonder and envy. You are dressed, the other guy is naked, everybody else is naked. This makes you feel like an awful fool. You wonder what to do.

The orchestra was strumming light Spanish-Cuban airs.

This went on for a time, with me wandering around like a sheepish schoolgirl, unable to get in the act, and Pancho laughing at me. That was upsetting because I was shocked, appalled—yet intrigued. I had the normal inhibitions of a man who has been beset by every possible convention, fear and caution—but the biological nature of me sought always to push through these barriers.

One thing I knew I could do. I could buy champagne. Ah, that's the answer, buy champagne. So the champagne kept coming, the music played, and this kept me off the hook for my nonparticipation. Meantime Pancho continued, the recipient of the infinite favors that a full-scale seraglio could provide. I glanced his way occasionally, drank some champagne, offered it to the madam, poured it for the girls. Once, Pancho tossed the girls off like flies and growled in Spanish about my generosity with the drinks. "He shall not pay! He shall not pay!" The girls recoiled for a minute at his surge of temper—but only for a minute.

It was now about five o'clock. I knew I was in the doghouse with Lili. I could see her pacing the deck of the *Sirocco,* waiting for my return, perhaps with a belaying pin in her dainty fingers. I felt I had to go back if I were to avoid another terrible scene with her.

Yet as I drank I got braver by the instant. This has always happened to me. Only a glass or two of champagne, and I was thinking, By God, if I could get that one with the big breasts and the little feet.

Just then I heard a strange noise outside. A human cry, not altogether unfamiliar. I thought I heard my name.

"What's that, Pancho?" I asked.

He pushed aside the girls, forward, backward, left, right, and went rushing to the window.

"Hah, *viejo*"—which meant "old boy"—"they know you, they love you—"

"Who loves me? How?"

"Leesen . . ."

The noise outside grew stronger.

Pancho, at the window, thoroughly nude, looked down. "They know you are here!"

"Who's 'they'?"

"All you hov to do ees to leesen—"

Then I heard. . . .

"Br-ra-a-v-o-o, Er-r-r-ol *viejo!*"

"Er-r-r-o-l-l, *ven aqui!*"—"Come on!"

The shouting increased. I went to the window and looked below. There I saw an entire girl's school assembled. They were from a convent directly across the road from the bordello. There they were, even the Sisters, all wearing uniforms, and they were lined up across the whole front of the whorehouse. Some of the girls were dancing.

"Br-a-a-v-o, Errol! Bravo!"

I quickly pulled the shade down.

Panic hit me—squarely in the guts.

There had never yet been any bad publicity about me. There had been nothing in my private life that anyone out there knew about. Warner Brothers had no difficulties with me along this line—yet. I was in no way implicated in anything.

This situation was a threat to my career. I went pale. I thought of my father, working sedulously at his experiments in embryology, the scientist disgraced by his errant son. What if he heard that a crowd of schoolgirls in a Cuban convent had declared a holiday and filed across the street to cheer up at me on the balcony—of—of this place.

I turned around to face that rascal, Pancho. "A girls' school!" I hissed. "Look at them!"

He was half doubled in laughter, murmuring, "They love you. They love you. Tremendoos, Er-rol."

Like an Academy Award, only different.

"By God, Pancho, this may be funny to you, but not to me."

I babbled about the dangerous wife I had, but wives meant nothing to him, and he kept breaking through his laughter about how Cuba was honoring me. "You get eet, Errol, they weel spik about thees in de schoolbooks of Cuba heestory—"And he fell back on the bed, lanky legs in the air, and laughed like mad.

"I must get out of this, Pancho."

He was right side again on the bed's edge. "Dawn't be seely. Nawbody cares. Thees ees Cuba!"

"I care!"

I left plenty of money for everybody around and said, "I must go."

I couldn't get out the front way to my cab, not with those girls lined up a block deep. I didn't know the back way, but I knew there must be one, because I'd never been in a place of the sort yet where there wasn't.

I was moving. . . . Cuban houses are built in squares. There is a patio with each. There is a barricade wall between each little home. I knew if I could get up one of these walls between the houses, run across a couple of roofs—I had done this before—I could find a way out. I found the patio.

It had been drizzling a bit. This made wet a rain pipe which I tried to climb. The pipe collapsed and I fell right on my arse flat in the patio again.

It was an eighteen-foot climb, but fear and panic made me try to make the top. I was out of breath, but inspired. Then, thinking I was my own double—I had no stand-in—I actually got up that wall. I made it like a cat, with a long running leap, a pipe, another vine, a crack in the wall—I was up there. I jumped over to a flat roof. I ran over the roof, trying to make the opposite side of this building, where I figured to get down, leap into a taxi, and be gone.

But the Cuban architecture got in my way. I had to keep leaping barricades, the kind they have in these Cuban houses. I swiftly got out of breath. I was dirtied, my white sharkskin suit in tatters, out at the elbows, out at the knees. I must have looked like some kind of assassin.

Suddenly I fell into a kitchen, down down about ten feet, and landed on the floor. My legs sprawled out in front of me, I stared up at a nice fat old colored lady who was cooking.

I looked desperate, I felt desperate, I hurt. "Ps-st—"

She wasn't co-operative. She let out a scream, looked around for help. I stood, I said, "Señora, *por favor*—"

She didn't listen. She dumped her stuff on the stove and ran.

Three little kids came into the kitchen. They screamed. I tried to hush them. They yelled louder.

Abruptly I was confronted by the toughest-looking Cuban I ever saw. He was in shirtsleeves, he had just got up from his dinner, or whatever he was having.

I understood his Spanish more from his tone. "What are you doing here?"

How was I to tell him? "Señor, you speak English?"

"No—little."

"Excuse me, I just want to get down to the street. I have had a bad experience. May I please use your door? I beg your pardon to be here. I am very sorry."

He pulled out a gun.

You must remember that this was just after one of Batista's coups. There was a lot of trouble all over, cloak-and-dagger stuff, and most Cubans were in politics. So, someone falling into his kitchen, looking like me, breathless, would make any householder nervous. He was jittery enough to cock his revolver.

I said quickly, *"Por favor,* no. Please let me get down to the street."

"Who are you, rebel Americano?"

"No—I am in trouble."

"I got trouble too. How you get here?"

"I promise you, just show me the way to the door—"

Here his little daughter, aged ten or twelve, came to my help. "Oh, look, look!" in a highly pitched voice. "Cap-i-tan Blood!"

They all looked. The guy with the revolver stared me up and down; his gun was wavering. Was this true?

"You Cap-i-tan Blood?" he asked.

"Yes."

The little girl stuck her hand in mine. "Oh," she kept saying, delighted.

Here the guy put his pistol away. "You must have dinner—you must—"

No, I couldn't.

Then they said I could go—they'd show me the way.

At last I was free.

At last I had escaped the horrible scandal of being caught in a hookshop across from a convent. The papers would never get it, my father would never learn of it, Warner Brothers would never know.

They led me down the stairs, opened the door—There they all were again—the same people! They had just gone around the block.

Even my orchestra was out there waiting for me.

I had gone through this horrible mess only to run into them again. The howls were just as steady. "Cap-i-tan Blood! Er-rol Fleen!"

So I just took the bows—what else?

I passed through them, signing autographs. The little girl who first spotted me kept shouting, at my side, till she was hoarse, "Er-rol Fleen!" I signed my name for one of the Sisters on her collar.

The last thing I saw, there in the street, was Pancho, literally with his hands on his knees, still howling his Cuban head off. He was enchanted with the whole thing. Endlessly amused by my morality, as if it were some disgrace to be caught like this. How funny, he kept saying, that I was worried what Father might say.

Today, of course, 1 wouldn't care who caught me in a whorehouse. Sometimes I think I would like to end my days in one.

We put up at Nassau for a few days. I took up skin-diving. I went below to see the beautiful underwater sights, and I took with me underwater guns. I went for sting rays with a bow and steel-tipped arrows and shot several big 200-pound fellows. I loved it. The old feeling for the sea was back upon me again. If I could only make Lili like it as I did, but she stayed about the deck, petulant. It was a pleasure to be away from Hollywood. Here was the clean cold salt water, and you could heal yourself of all kinds of inner hurts.

Life photographers shot pictures of me around Miami, having fun in swim trunks. I was surprised to find myself on the cover of that magazine on May 23, 1938: ERROL FLYNN, *Glamour Boy,* it said in white on a black background. There I was, looking eager, young, happy, posed with my chin on my fist, wearing a thin line of mustache, and looking gaily at the world—on top of which, supposedly, I was sitting.

The World's Fair was on at the time, and one of the stunts of the Fair was the burying of a time capsule deep underground, about a hundred feet or so. In this capsule they placed one copy each of a half-dozen or so of the representative United States publications. *The New York Times, Herald Tribune, Daily Worker, Newsweek, Life,* one or two others, I believe. The reasoning was that a thousand years from now, when this capsule was to be unearthed, historians would find these publications and would have a look at what was going on at this moment in time. My picture on *Life's* cover went underground along with the other materials.

My prestige was high in the land at that hour. That issue of *Life* noted the release of my latest vehicle, *The Adventures of Robin Hood.* The critics were kind enough to say that I had replaced Douglas Fairbanks and that only I, in Hollywood, could handle the Robin Hood role in pictures as in my private life.

That picture too, like *Captain Blood,* was destined to become an enormous money-maker for Warners.

The sea was big enough to absorb the irritants with Lili and I was now in good shape physically. My claim of illness must have looked unconvincing at Warners when they picked up *Life* and saw me harpooning fish and skin-diving. They sent their trouble shooter, Bill Guthrie, to see me.

"Am I supposed to see you looking so well?" Guthrie said slyly.

"That's only the sun."

"You mind if the doctor examines you?"

"If he wants to."

"What seems to be the matter?"

"I don't know what it is but every time I put my hand out it shakes. I'm a mass of nerves." I didn't tell him that beyond my genuine need for this period of relaxation, I wanted my contract revamped with more direction rights and with script approval. Others had these provisions and I was determined to have what they had.

The doctor examined me, paid no attention to my complaints, said I was in perfect health. Guthrie's report to the studio was that I was malingering. It was nonsense that I was a mass of nerves due to bad scripts.

Back to work, peace having been made with the studio, I was invited to the holy of holies, the producers' private dining room. I think no actor had ever set foot in there, none that I knew. Writers and directors occasionally dined there, but not actors. There was a long table around which the big wheels were seated. Among them were Robert Buckner, who bore a faint resemblance to me; Henry Blanco, who is still with Warner Brothers; Robert Lord; Jack Warner; and the executive director, Hal Wallis. Jack and Hal arrived late. You didn't exactly jump to your feet and stand at attention when Jack entered, but you sat up straight.

I had to get back to work. As I was leaving, Harry M. Warner arrived. I had never met him. He was another mysterious figure. He did the big-time financing, but generally he kept away from the studio. Harry, who recently passed away, was the boss, outranking even Jack. He looked like a domesticated Australian koala bear. He moved like one too, slowly and cautiously. I suppose he was one of the financial wizards of his day. All I knew about him was that it was said he rarely lost his temper.

He looked at me as he walked by, flanked by two flunkies.

"There he is," he said, pointing a finger at me. I looked back over my shoulders wondering if I had heard right. He was half-turned, addressing me. "So you are back, eh? And you go to a place where they don't like Jews and they won't have Jews. That's gratitude for you."

With that he left me. I stood there, my mouth wide open—you could see all my teeth well down toward my tonsils—and he went inside the dining room. He was obviously incensed.

How he learned I had been to Nassau, I don't know, but there had been a tuna fishing tournament there, and I was interested in the fish and the sport, not anything else. I had heard about anti-Semitism, but it had never seemed to me a flaming issue. It had never occurred to me whether someone was Jewish or not.

A man is a man; if he is a man, I don't give a damn what color he is or what race or religion.

Inside the dining room, Harry worked himself up to a rage and started to rant. "I just saw that goddamn Flynn outside. How do you like that s.o.b.? He treated my brother so badly. Jack had a heart attack when he had the last interview with Flynn; he had to be taken home. The ungrateful sonofabitch. Goddamit. We have more people on the lot than him. What do we need him for? We made him, didn't we? Where did he come from? Nowhere. A lousy Irish beachcomber! We can make him and we can unmake him. By God I can take any of you . . ."

Harry paused for breath. He looked around. "What's your name?" he barked. He pointed at Robert Buckner, a quiet-mannered young Southerner, just hired.

Buckner answered, "Robert Buckner." He was startled to find himself in the conversation.

"What do you do?"

"I'm a writer."

Harry resumed. "Why can't we make this bastard into an actor? For Christ sakes, what's the matter with him? We can take him from nothing and make him into an actor. What the hell! Screw Flynn! This one can make out just as good. We can put a campaign behind this guy here—what's your name?"

"Buckner."

Somebody said nervously, "Oh, he would probably do just the same as Flynn."

Harry glared irately at the writer. "Then screw you too, Buckner!"

That story still ranks high in the folklore of Warner Brothers.

I resumed picture making, *Virginia City, The Sea Hawk, Santa Fe Trail, Footsteps in the Dark,* and I renewed my connubial war with Lili. The pattern of separation and reconciliation with her continued for two more years. Physically I had made a break from her when Koets and I dashed off for Spain. Now I could take her or leave her—and I played the field as I held forth in my own bachelor apartment. Not that Lili accepted this. She watched and pursued me as Javert pursued Jean Valjean.

Lili's screen career petered out. She had been brought to Hollywood in 1928 by Sam Goldwyn to replace Vilma Banky as Ronald Colman's leading lady. Her arrival broke up the Colman-Banky team; and in 1929 there appeared *The Rescue*. The following year she had the lead in *The Bridge of San Luis Rey*. She was in three others pictures that year, including *The Cock-eyed World*, with Victor McLaglen and Edmund Lowe, which was a sequel to *The Big Parade*. The next year she played with Gary Cooper in *Fighting Caravans*, and in two other pictures. In 1932 her picture, *This Is the Night*, introduced Cary Grant to the public. She made only two pictures in the next two years. In the year when I arrived, she played the second lead to Margaret Lindsay in *Frisco Kid*, with Jim Cagney and Ricardo Cortez. The last film she did was *The Devil on Horseback*, in 1936 or '37—a total of about fourteen or fifteen films. Not at all a bad record. But Lili was casting around for independent producers. Or perhaps she gave up the idea of further film-making. Why worry? Her husband was getting around two hundred and fifty thousand a year.

Lili's possessiveness upset our relationship from the start. I have seen this trait wreck more lives than it has helped. Women try to make the man a personal prize. The way I see it, if you love someone, you will love him enough to want to see him free and unfettered. But the feeling that you own someone grows out of the whole archaic, priest-ridden concept of monogamy.

It is not man's natural state to be monogamous. Neither is it woman's. The proof of this is in the well-known rejection of the whole standard by so many people. If this weren't true so much of our modern literature and movie entertainment wouldn't be given over to dealing with this theme and this condition.

We call ourselves a Christian world, we have alleged standards, and we hypocritically evade them. So the divorce courts are full, there is a lot of clandestine contact that never reaches court; we have pornographic appeal in all our art structures—all adding up to a very dubious morality. The Christian concept of monogamy is to me nothing more than a travesty on human nature. It doesn't work, never will.

For myself I will say only that I have tried not to conceal, not to live "a private life" as it is known, and therefore, not to be a damned hypocrite. I cannot skulk around corners or hide in dark alleys or have a mistress stashed away somewhere or a lady who must meet me at a secret rendezvous. I am utterly incapable of being clandestine. To hide in dark corners and behind buildings, or in cleverly arranged apartments in New York or Paris or London, goes against my nature. Let the public guardians of morality do these things.

A psychologist once observed to me, "One of the reasons for the public interest in you as a personality is that there is a certain amount of general male identification with the life you lead. Many men would like to be living as you are doing." I don't know whether this is true, but if it is in some small way true then it is a focus on the dilemma of the national male facing the distaff side of the population armed or underarmed with the strange code he has been given in childhood.

Bit by bit I was permitted on the fringes of the Olympiads. This was a close-knit group to which there was no entry except uniqueness. These were not acting stars. There were no stars at all. Stardom was not the basis of membership. One guy would be a bum and the other would be making $5,000 a week. Mostly they were men of note like Sadakichi Hartman, a half Japanese half German, who had every pulpit preaching against him. He was a complete Bohemian who wrote a book called *The Last Thirty Days of Christ*. He tried to prove that the only really honest disciple of Christ was Judas. It was a view not generally shared. John Decker, the artist, was the center of the club; and secondly, John Barrymore. Decker rated generally as the best artist in Hollywood and one of the best in the country. Gene Fowler, the writer, was a fabulous raconteur and a gifted writer; a figure of great wit and charm, and the kind the Olympiads depended upon for their existence. He and Barrymore were close. Others were Gene Markey, the screen writer; Alan Mowbray, the actor; W. C. Fields, the comic; and actor Thomas Mitchell. There were others, of course, who came and went or were on the edges of the group, and who might be close friends of one or another in the circle.

All of us tried to be profound, or entertaining, or witty. I think we thought of ourselves as essentially philosophic. What characterized us was the range of personal experience which we had each had, physical or mental; something unique or special. One or two might even be abysmal mentally, or bawdy; but outstanding in some particular way.

We met at various houses, but most of the entertaining was in

Decker's old house on Bundy Drive, Hollywood. He had decorated the interior with many pictures, including some that, I suppose, would be regarded by a few as obscene. His place was appropriate for a gathering of oddballs. The house was in a constant stage of siege from their presence. It was doubtless the most unique center of personalities in the community.

Sometimes it functioned as a debating group, a thing that is lacking in society today. Conversation was then the dominant art. There was no radio, no television going at our bull sessions. By and large we thought we were disgusted with politics and politicians. We fought over Roosevelt, either hating or loving him. Very often one or another of us went home feeling mad as hell, for no two of us ever agreed on any one subject. Once I spouted for ten minutes on Sir Julian Huxley, because I knew something of him through my father. They listened, perhaps surprised to hear issuing from me this interest in evolution.

I did far more listening than talking. The only thing I could talk about was my tales of New Guinea. They lifted their eyebrows skeptically. When I told them a lobster reminded me of a baked crocodile I had once eaten on the banks of the Laloki River in New Guinea, I couldn't help but notice the patronizing pained looks. They still thought I came from Ireland, I guess.

People who joined the group or had entree were strange, or strange things had happened to them. Maybe a fellow had been up the Amazon: so they listened to him. I had introduced Koets to them. In a few minutes Koets dispelled any doubts as to his general nuttiness and eligibility for their attention.

One character, the most fabulous bore in the world, had the serious attention of the Olympiads for a time for exclusively that reason. They believed that he was the greatest bore since the mutations that changed the ape into a man. In fact, from this character there arose a subsidiary group which we called the Oh, Shit Club. The idea was to let a bore corner you in any gathering and allow him to tell you the story of his life or to pour out his soul. Our rule was: Let the bore speak for two and one-half minutes. At the end of this time you looked him right in the eye and you said, "Oh, Shit!" Then you walked away. You had to say this and do this whether the bore was a man or a woman. If you were caught lowering your eyes—the others would be watching as you handled the bore—and if you muttered the fatal words as you turned away, you were expelled. You had to do this forthrightly, bravely, and with direct eye-to-eye contact.

We got our kicks.

W. C. Fields held forth about his vaudeville days. Since he and Jack Barrymore were pretty much contemporaries, Jack would interrupt with a story that hinged on one Fields might be telling. Fields was called Claude, for C. He had a gloriously tall and willowy secretary who hovered in the background, serving him, taking care of his needs, anticipating his requirements. He had a hobby of clipping newspapers, taking out bizarre items and sending them to his friends with his own comments such as, *There, you see what a stupid world it is.*

It was a bit of self-flattery for the Olympiads to call themselves by this name, but perhaps the group was entitled to do so. There were few actors among them. Anthony Quinn and myself, both just coming up, were more or less tolerated. Edward G. Robinson, in spite of his interest in art, wasn't admitted. The boys didn't seem to like him, even though he was a very good art collector. They seemed to think that he took himself too seriously.

For a while I teamed up with Decker in something we called the Flynn-Decker Art Gallery. It was in an upstairs studio right behind the Mocambo. There we had exhibitions, for which the usually casual Decker even dressed. He would put on a black stock, a kind of cloth folded high, under the neck, which would make him look very arty.

Out of my association with Decker and the Olympiads came my later interest in art and the purchase of some Van Goghs, Gauguins, and other masters.

Lupe Velez and Lili were more or less rivals. They had acted together in several successful pictures. Lupe, the Mexican spitfire, was as wild as Tiger Lil—but they were friendly, as far as women of that kind can be friendly—the same kind of friendship that a female octopus or giant squid has for another of the same species. There is mutual respect, at least.

Lupe had a unique ability to rotate her left breast. Not only that, she counter-rotated it, a feat so supple and beautiful to observe that you couldn't believe your eyes. Beyond that, her breasts were probably the most beautiful that even Hollywood had ever seen.

Eddie Goulding, the director, was a good friend of Lupe's. He played a trick on her. He told her that I was madly in love with her, that I could think of nobody but her, that I couldn't eat or sleep because of her. She must get in touch with me.

I was asleep after a hard day's work. At about one A.M. the phone kept ringing, and I tossed and ignored it. But finally, so that I could sleep, I answered the damned thing. It was Lupe.

She spoke with a Mexican lilt, used r's plentifully, and two g's or so at the end of each darling-g. She said sweetly into my ears, "E-rr-oll, I must see you, dar-r-ling-g."

I had already seen her rotate her breast clockwise, counterclockwise, north and south.

"Please don't come over, Lupe, I'm dog-tired."

"I'm chust around the block at Chonnie's [Johnnie Weismuller's] house, Er-rol, blease!"

"No, no, Lupe, honest-to-Jesus, don't. I'm tired out tonight."

"Honey—ton't you vurry, I'll be dere in wan meenit!"

I put the phone back in its cradle very nervously because actually Lupe wasn't my type. I thought at first of locking the door, but I had seen Lupe in action. I realized any kind of barricade was no defense against her. Like Lili, she was tough and she had made up her mind. Eddie Goulding had worked her up to a pitch from which there was only one return, for her and for me.

I hardly had time to bite my lower lip with nervousness when I heard the crunch of car tires. That's Lupe in her new Cord, I said to myself. The brake pulled up with an inevitable, even sexual, warning. There was a pounding at the front door. I buttoned up a robe and let her in.

Mark you, don't get the impression Lupe wasn't terribly attractive. She just wasn't my type. I had been through so much violence that I was unable to cope with it any more. In particular, I couldn't cope with women of this type, like Lili. I wasn't capable of being tough and catching a woman by her hair and the seat of her pants and throwing her out of the door.

She bounded up the stairs, into my bedroom.

I protested I was more exhausted than I really was. I took one good look at her and realized I was terribly awake.

She started to undress, singing an enchanting little Mexican song at the same time. In the dim light she was a vision of beauty.

She fell on her knees beside the bed.

For a while we were much engaged. Then her eyes moved. She looked upward at my dresser and let out a little gasp.

There stood the hacked-up figurine of my Madonna and Child from Spain. She stopped what she was doing. I glanced at her, then at the little memento.

At that instant she leaned back in the most religious pose, on her little knees—more beautiful than ever. Her naked little body was itself a figurine of delicacy and ecstasy as she posed in the dim light.

She prayed to the headless Madonna and Child to forgive her for what she was doing.

I watched fascinated as she said a couple of Ave Marias, telling some invisible beads.

Having absolved herself, a smile opened on her momentarily spiritually clothed face—and she again took up the subject of Flynn.

In spite of my separate living quarters I saw Lili frequently. One night she and I went to one of the fabulous parties put on by William Randolph Hearst, Sr. This was a masquerade party. Most figures in history were represented. No Emperor of Rome ever put on a bigger feast, with more music and light or better entertainers. People went around looking like Napoleon, Washington, Moses, Mutt and Jeff, Cleopatra, Donald Duck and even themselves.

David Niven and I decided to be original. We would go as circus yard cleaners—the boys who pick up elephant droppings.

Dressed up in a proper white, ready to clean up the world, we each carried a bucket. On the bucket was carefully printed, in letters not too large—four letters—what was supposed to be in the bucket. Mr. Hearst didn't think it was funny. The photographers gathered around and took more pictures of us merry whitewings than they did of Napoleon or Cleo.

I had fun watching Marion Davies, the most generous, most warmhearted girl you'll ever know. She was a good friend of mine and had influenced Mr. Hearst to let me take that newspaper assignment in Spain.

Lili was not far away, dressed as a Hungarian gypsy. She had heavy bracelets on both arms right up to her elbows.

Near us I saw a smiling face. I walked over to a very attractive girl, introduced myself. She had a wide mouth, a fine smile, a good figure. I learned her name was Eloise Ann Onstott, and I knew of her Social Registerite background. We went wandering.

In Hearst's huge beach place there should certainly be a private rendezvous somewhere. We went past innumerable private detectives who were there to guard the magnate's paintings.

We wandered till we came to the region of swimming pools. We went past one, around a second, behind a third, beyond a fourth. At last, a quiet nook. I was away from Lili. This hot creature gripped me by the arm. The fever of the masquerade was upon us.

We found a little alcove. Above it was a balcony. I looked about. No chairs. Too bad. No chaise lounge. Too bad. Good floor, though—

She had lovely hard breasts and a lascivious mouth. Soft hair. It was dark, but light enough for us to see each other clearly. It was maddening, sudden.

Suddenly I heard the most awful noise. It drilled into my ears with a familiarity which would have normally frozen me, except right now I was so hot. "Fleen—Fleen—Fleen!"

I jumped up. So did Eloise Ann.

"Fleen—Fleen!"

Nearer, nearer. There in the doorway of the alcove was my wife in her gypsy dress. I was doing up my fly. I would have said something but what was there to say?

Lili sprang at Eloise.

"Lili darling," said Eloise coolly. "We weren't doing anything . . . we . . ."

That enraged Lil, who did not come from France for nothing; and not only had she not been born yesterday, but had been born well before she told me she had been born.

She grabbed Eloise by the hair, dragged her out of the alcove and started to beat the poor girl.

I looked up at the balcony. The house detectives were hanging over the rail, looking.

They watched the brawl with gusto. There in the quiet of the alcove Eloise and I had had an audience of fourteen detectives.

Since my return from Spain I had been sharing an apartment with David Niven. I was determined not to shack up with Lili. See her, have her, yes; but have my own life at the same time. I didn't know how close

I was to learning the truth of the old maxim that they quote sometimes, that you can't eat your cake and have it too.

One night Niven and I were invited to the house of Hedy Lamarr. She was married to John Loder at the time. Reginald Gardner and his delightful Russian wife were there, and a few others.

It chances that I think Hedy to be one of the most underestimated actresses, one who has not been lucky enough to get the most desirable roles. I have seen her do a few brilliant things. I always thought she had great talent, and as far as classical beauty is concerned you could not then, nor perhaps even now, find anyone to top Lamarr. Probably one of the most beautiful women of our day. Naturally I wanted to meet her—and subsequently I would want her to play the female lead in my Italian fiasco, *William Tell*.

As we waited for Hedy to enter her living room, David kept prodding me to expect by far the most ravishing creature.

David whispered as she glided in, "By God, she's beautiful, even without the jewels."

"Quiet!"

He wasn't quiet. "See if she will tell you what she told me about how she had to save herself in getting out of Austria."

She had been married to the fabulously rich Fritz Mandel, a munitions magnate. The story was that he used to lock up all her jewels, and he used to lock her up too. Her husband let her wear one or two jewels at a time, but never all together, and the jewels were in his safe all the time. One night he was having a very famous Nazi guest, Prince Von Staremberg, the leader of the Austrian Fascists. Mandel was doing a lot of business with him. Hedy asked her husband if she could wear all her jewels that night because she wanted to impress the prince and so be of some help to Mandel in his business relation.

Her jeweled entrance caused a sensation. From her fingers up to her shoulders in ice, red ice, blue ice, white ice, emeralds, rubies, diamonds. She must have weighed half as much as the late Aga Khan. As the dinner went on, Hedy developed a sick headache and excused herself, just for a moment, to go to the bathroom. But she never came back for coffee.

Next thing she was in America—in Hollywood—jewels and beauty and talent and all.

Now, with Niven prodding me, I didn't know how to get around her to ask her to tell me about her private life, but it sounded intriguing when David repeated, "See if she will talk about the night she couldn't stand it any more and made a getaway."

Hedy and I talked for a while. I started leading up to it in a diplomatic way, and finally got out the words, "Where is Mandel now?"

At which, from this beautiful creature, came the growl, "That son-ofabitch!" She spat and walked off.

In the push and pull of getting my salary upped to what I felt I was entitled to I was prepared not to be afraid of situations. In the Hollywood jungle, it was no trouble for me to say, with a laugh, and mean it, "You can stick this place where the monkey stuck the coconuts!"

If Warners fired me, it meant nothing, and they knew it. I would just go on a holiday: South America, Alaska, back to Australia or England. I saw others in terror because they had obligations; but I didn't have many in these early days. That attitude lasted for years and it upped my income. It was an attitude rarely encountered in Hollywood by the producers. Most people there were Americans. Their future, their career, their life, was in the United States. I was a Tasmanian-Irish bum, and I didn't mind going back to being that. Many times I even longed to get out.

You would have brawls like this:

"We will keep you off work forever. You will never work again!"

I would say, "You think not? I will work whenever I want."

"You will never be able to work in moving pictures."

"What's moving pictures?"

"We will stop you working in the States!"

"Okay, I can drive a horse. I can dig a well. I've done it. Don't tell me you'll stop me working!"

I have always called myself a bum, but as I look on it I have been working just about all my life, even if I have gone on the bum from time to time.

The other stars had the same rows, but few, if any, had what I had to fall back on. I had that crucial training in New Guinea. I had been on my own the hard way, in the hardest parts of the world. I didn't give a goddamn if I had to leave Hollywood; plenty of places left to explore.

In the backdrops of my mind I always had the idea I would get back to the sea and to the islands some day anyway.

So I didn't hesitate to talk turkey with Jack Warner. Like the time I felt he had badly wronged me.

Opposite Warner Brothers is the Lakeside Golf Club which forbids Jews. Naturally a thorn in the side of Warner Bros. The boss didn't like it because the actors would go there at lunchtime and take a drink. One day I was told I didn't have to get back to the set till three o'clock, an hour later than usual. When I returned, an assistant came on stage anxiously, saying Jack was angry and wanted to talk to me. I got on the phone.

At the other end Jack cussed me out about holding up the picture. He was violent. He accused me of being across the road getting loaded. I told him I wasn't late, I wasn't loaded, I had been playing golf, and had been told to show in at three o'clock. He talked back. I raised my voice louder. I called him a sonofabitch. He termed me a few things. "As a matter of fact," I hollered when we ran out of profanity, "I am coming up to see you right this minute. By God, I'll tell you what's going to happen. No. I'll show you, not tell you."

I slammed the receiver. All on stage were like statues.

I ran up to his offices. "Mr. Warner has left. He is gone."

"You sure he's not hiding in here?" My Aussie was up.

The office staff gathered about. They assured me he'd driven off the lot.

"How could he drive off?" I asked. "He had a very important appointment."

About a week later Jack sent me an apology—an unheard-of thing for him. We met again, and this time very pleasantly. I said, "Look, Sporting Blood [my friendly name for him], we had a deal that any time we were in difficulties I could come up to see you immediately. About a week ago I wanted to see you in a hurry."

"You kidding? You think I am going to stick around in my office when you are coming up in that frame of mind?"

"Jack, you broke your word."

"You're damned right I did," said Jack cheerfully.

I will subscribe to no notion declaring me sexually cold. To be quite frank, I think it is the other way around. . . . But when it comes to shooting a scene and trying to do something sexual in front of others, I yield. Can't do it. Never have been able to. It is probably a bromide of public thinking that the romantic male lead is supposed to have an affair with the leading lady. But in all of my experience I can truthfully say that in the course of being polite to them I was actually so distant that I suppose some of these ladies thought I must have been a faggot —of late an appraisal discredited somewhat. Screen loving is such a self-conscious thing for me that I find myself drawing back, growing cold. In fact, I can think of only two, John Barrymore and John Gilbert—not Flynn—who could actually give a literal sexual feeling to a scene with a woman without being self-conscious about it. As for me, there is something in such a private scene that I cannot get myself to do even with the most delightful of leading ladies. What it is I can't explain beyond a congenital shyness, believe it or not. Not only could I not do this on the screen, but after the day's work was over I could not do business in or around the dressing rooms that the stars have at Warner Brothers, or any other studio.

Which brings us to a picture where Bette Davis, at this time the greatest thing in movies, was starred opposite me. It was the Maxwell Anderson adaptation, *The Private Lives of Elizabeth and Essex,* a great love story between Essex and, of course, the first Queen Elizabeth.

I was playing the young Lord Essex, the love of the first Queen Elizabeth of England, and the queen's part was played by Bette Davis. Essex had been younger than Elizabeth I of England, and Flynn was younger than Bette Davis of Warner Brothers.

Now Bette was a dynamic creature, the great big star of the lot, but not physically my type; dominating everybody around, and especially me, or trying to. This drove me off. The normal reticence I feel with leading ladies was even exaggerated in this situation. Something else was annoying her very much: although she was crowned the queen of Hollywood as an actress, she heard I was getting more money than she, and she had been in the business much longer than I. Getting more dough than she earned might have grieved her some, because she was a far better actress than I could ever hope to be an actor—she was a three-time Academy Award winner. It must have struck her as outrageous, I guess, because for one reason or another I had got out of Warner Brothers $6,000 a week, while she was still on about five.

Well, you combine this with an animosity or a hurt that comes from being turned down to an invitation for an afterwork drink a couple of times, and you get a special atmosphere in which something might happen.

There is a time when Essex comes back from Ireland. The scene occurs on an enormous set, with about six hundred extras. When Essex returns, he walks an aisle the length of this set, which is the Court of England, and she is expecting him. She is fanning herself and she is angry. Why hasn't Essex been to see her? But he has a point of view, too: Why hasn't she sent him through Ireland? That is the reason why he has been militarily defeated. He is angry, too, though he is acclaimed by the public. She is furious, because he is stealing her thunder. . . .

So I have this long walk, one of the longest dolly shots I know of in motion picture history, with these six hundred extras around, and I have to approach her and say, *"Your Majesty . . . "*

She replies something like, *"Well, m'Lord Essex, what have you to say for yourself?"*

The dialogue goes on, about like this: *"I have much to say for my-self—but little for you!"*

At which time, in front of the whole Court of England, she is supposed to haul off and whack Essex right over the face, leading to another scene whereby he says, *"Thank you, Madame, that is sufficient."*

This takes a lot of doing on the part of the lead actress. You have this mass of extras in costumes looking on, you have me, you have all the camera crew to worry about, the lights. These things take a tremendous amount of care and technical knowledge on the part of many technicians. The background, the set, the extras, the costumes, the air itself, all must be authentic.

Bette Davis, at a certain point, has to look exactly . . . she must move her head to look exactly like the original contemporary Elizabeth —and being the great actress Bette is, she does, too, she looks somewhat like Elizabeth—striking.

Another thing that contributed to what eventually happened was that Bette's belly had to be pulled in with corsets, to give her the tiny Elizabethan waist, so the poor girl had to draw in her breath while they prepared her, with force applied here and there, and squeezed her inside the stays. This cannot put a girl in good humor, especially if she is at it from six A.M. to six P.M.

We had two portable dressing rooms, neither very large, although hers was much grander than mine. The bosses of Warners figured they would give her a most magnificent dressing room and fix it up with beautiful curtains, and everything else, and pay her less money than me. I personally didn't care if I was on a park bench. Our adjoining rooms were on this vast set, one of the most expensive that the motion picture industry ever built: the Court of Elizabeth of England.

Now picture this. . . .

I put on my armor, it is pretty heavy, and hearing a call to go on-stage, I assume there is going to be a rehearsal. The camera is coming along, I know the dialogue, I know where I am supposed to meet Miss Davis, at the other end of the set—two hundred and fifty feet away—and I take this long walk. But when I arrive there, instead of seeing Bette Davis, I find a stand-in. That seems a bit discourteous, but then, she is a great actress, and I know besides she has the point of view she is the best in the world, and I am certainly anything but an actor: and I have been left to meet this stand-in when I arrive, armor and all, at the end of this long walk. Well, that is nothing very much, I write this off as the business of picture-making.

I went through this long walk a couple more times, each time meeting the stand-in. I played the scene at the end of the walk and the camera movement was fine.

Finally, they called the first real rehearsal, and I must say, that as Bette assumed her place on the throne, dressed as Elizabeth, with great big square jewels on her hands, and on her wrists big heavy bracelets, she was living the part. She *was* Queen Elizabeth.

I started the walk down through the English court. The cameras were grinding, the extras were gazing at me or at the throne, and I reached the Queen, and then there was that dialogue I quoted. . . .

Then, of a sudden, I felt as if I had been hit by a railroad locomotive.

She had lifted one of her hands, heavy with those Elizabethan rings, and Joe Louis himself couldn't give a right hook better than Bette hooked me with.

My jaw went out.

I felt a click behind my ear and I saw all these comets, shooting stars, all in one flash.

It didn't knock me to the ground.

She had given me that little dainty hand, laden with about a pound of costume jewelry, right across the ear.

I felt as if I were deaf.

In front of all these people, I couldn't say anything. Dazed, I was aware that Bette was playing the scene to the finish. I heard the director, Curtiz, say, "All right, boys and girls, we do it again."

If your teeth have been rattled, and your head was ringing, and you felt deaf from the pound of costume jewelry hitting you as hard as a lady like Bette Davis can swing—why, I felt a horrible surge of anger that turned my stomach.

I thought, My God, I have to go through this again! I must talk to her.

But what was I going to say to the great Miss Davis? Still, I made up my mind that I would present myself at her dressing room and ask if I could see her. It was a difficult thing to know how to do—she was such a big wheel—even though I was getting more money.

I intended being very polite. I would say, "Well, I don't know about the camera, Miss Davis . . ."

When my ears stopped ringing and I got over this feeling of anger, I went and carefully knocked at her door.

"Who is it—?" That voice she has, the same onstage and off.

"Bette, it's me—Flynn—er—Errol."

"Oh—come in."

I opened the door. She was in front of the mirror, but she didn't turn around. She just looked into the mirror, dawdled at her make-up, with me behind her, cautiously, like a boy with cap in hand. She continued piddling with her make-up, powdering her face, not offering for me to sit down.

I started to speak. "Bette, I want to talk to you about something . . ."

She shut me up instantly. "Oh, I know perfectly well what you are going to say . . ." in a loud voice, "but if you can't take a little slap, that is just too bad! That's a pity! . . . I knew you were going to complain . . . I can't do it any other way! If I have to pull punches, I can't do this. That's the kind of actress I am—and I *stress* actress! Let's drop the subject. . . . You're ready, I hope. . . ."

I hadn't had a chance to open my mouth.

She said, "Would you mind shutting the door?"

I did.

I backed out.

Having had that blow across the ear, having heard this, and seeing her in front of the mirror, you know what I did?—I went back to my dressing room and threw up.

I had to think it over again, fast, because pretty soon there was going to be another rehearsal.

I found this certain anger accumulating. I didn't like it, so I went back again, and once more I knocked at the door.

"Who is it?"

"Errol."

"Oh, come in. . . ." She said, "Well . . ." and she was still playing in front of the mirror, "what is your problem now?"

"I'd like to figure out this next rehearsal."

"I have told you about the next rehearsal. It is the same as it is going to be in the scene. I cannot do it any other way!"

For the first time, she turned around and faced me. *"I am telling you I cannot do it any other way!"*

This was it.

"I will give you one more chance to try. Do—you—get—me? One—more—chance—to try. You are a great actress, I know it: so certainly you can learn not to hit me with the whole weight of your fist the next time—and if you can't do it . . . *well* . . . *let's—leave—it—at —that!"*

"What the hell are you talking about?"

"Just—what—I—said!"

And I left.

I walked back to my dressing room and threw up for the second time; because I knew one thing for certain: that if she hit me again unnecessarily that way, that in front of all those extras there would be a noise such as this—Thump! Thump!

I knew this. That is why I threw up.

I thought, Oh my God, what a scandal this is going to be, but I am not going to be dominated this way. My life has been hard enough with one woman already, and if women are going to slap me around all the time—that little jaw will have my fist in it.

The second assistant came along and said, "All is ready, Mr. Flynn?"

This is the end of me, I'll do what I propose to do, I'll drop Bette Davis in the guise of Queen Elizabeth of England in front of that whole division of extras. . . . Warners . . . the press . . .

It was one of the hardest things I had to decide. You talk about fear. I knew it then, because I knew I was going through with this. I knew I had to do it. If she hit me, and I knew she was going to, I would have to whack her and drop her—and I believed that if I did, after what I had just been through, I might break her jaw.

All right now . . . the long walk up that aisle, everybody is there, the color is tremendous . . . my own extras are murmuring to me, *"M'Lord Essex, you are back?"*

I am back, and an extra murmurs, *"Quite, he is not in favor with the Queen."*

Far up the line there is Queen Elizabeth fanning herself. . . .

This is about to be one of the longest walks I have ever taken.

Every step was a yard. . . .

I clanked all the way down the aisle in this steel armor. At one point, earlier, when I rushed off to the wars, they had to rig up block and tackle for me so that I could get on my horse, because it was impossible for any living man to get his eyes off the ground and get onto the horse the way I was supposed to. I walked down a stairs, *My dear lady, farewell* . . . an invisible steel wire caught me under the arms, and I was derricked up over the horse's arse, onto his back, then I galloped off in all directions. Now I was jangling down the aisle wearing all that Doug Fairbanks-Flynn armor. . . .

I can see her . . . closer . . . now the rings on her fingers—and every step is leading me rapidly toward the Queen, and I know I have to do it—I know she is going to whack me. She is going to put me in my place, whatever that place is.

I was poised and ready. I knew as soon as I got hit again hard—as hard as I have ever been hit before—harder than even in the boxing ring —just what would happen.

I felt that Bette was quite determined to do it.

I arrived, and the dialogue was developing that leads to the Queen's swipe at the face of Essex.

I braced myself for this hit—and the counterpunch to it. True, I would be disgraced. Me, a man, hitting the world's favorite on the chin was not going to look pretty, but I had to do it. I didn't care.

We went through the dialogue. *Well, M'Lord Essex,* and so forth . . .

I was sort of on my toes. I didn't forget a line.

It came time for her to hit me and I braced myself . . . ready.

She did it in the most beautifully technical way. Her hand came just delicately to the side of my nose, missing by a fraction of an inch. I don't even believe she touched me, but I could feel the wind go by my face, and it looked technically perfect.

Then, there was the rest of the scene.

In other words, she had learned, because she could see in my eyes,

I am quite sure, as I approached, that "Just give it to me, Bette, and you will be as flat as a sardine in a can."

I had to decide this for my own self-respect.

When she did it this time, I didn't flinch an inch. Even though I was expecting the worst.

She said, "I would like to do that again," but the director said that was enough.

I must admit that afterward, for the third time, I went secretly behind my dressing room and vomited again.

You know enough about me by now to understand that I will do almost anything for a laugh, a prank, a bit of fun, the whole idea of lighting up the everyday task of having to work.

Call me a swine, but I got even with Bette in just about the same style . . . and in the same picture.

The Maxwell Anderson play called for a reconciliation afterwards between Essex and Elizabeth. In the story we were supposed to be lovers by this time, and we had to play a love scene. It called for me to frisk around on some steps in the palace, her to lean out and say, "You rascal—" or something like that. She was to push me as only Davis can do it, beautifully, by which time we were to get together very close on the steps.

The director called for me to do something outrageous to the Queen.

This wasn't too difficult. I was still smarting from the thing I had been through. I decided that a strictly unorthodox thing to do around the Elizabethan court in those days would be to give the Queen a playful touch upon her internationally famous pratt, which she could wiggle with the best, if she felt like it, and I wish I knew how often that was.

The idea worked up in me and at the rehearsal scene, when it came time for me to give her the playful pat, I said to myself, Here comes my chance. . . .

I held my hand way out there . . . it must have looked like a piece of ham . . . and it went sailing right through her Elizabethan dresses, slappo, smack on her Academy Award behind. She went about two feet off the ground.

She looked up at me livid with fury, and I said, "I'm awfully sorry. I don't know how to do it any other way. You must forgive me. Tell me if it is wrong or right. . . ."

She was finding her way onto her feet. I said, "Let's run through the technique again. You don't want it that hard?"

"Oh yes!" She was a bundle of contained rage.

I said, "I can only do it one way. I am awfully sorry, I don't know how to do it any other way. . . ."

It wasn't a very pleasant picture to make, for me, that is.

Since that day I have seen Miss Davis many times. When I do she turns her head away.

Once, about five years after this incident, I had the embarrassing moment of going by a table where she was seated, and saying, "Well, Bette, how are you?"

She looked the other way.

That is the only woman in Hollywood I have ever had any histrionic trouble with. No real problem with any of the other ladies at all—as far as I know, anyway. All the other ladies with whom I worked are to this day my very good friends. I have never had a fight with any one of them.

The distinguished Bette Davis is the only one. But, mellowed perhaps, next time we meet—who knows?

I never got to know most of the queens who starred opposite me. Relationships between male and female leads can be startlingly professional, cool, distant.

Such a reaction of reserve is not necessarily limited to me. I have studied the cinema work of my contemporaries and I have noticed that, with rare exceptions, there is a reserve in even the best of actors in playing love scenes.

In one of my more recent pictures, *The Big Boodle,* my leading lady was beautiful Rossana Rory, an Italian girl. She was frightened at the prospect of playing opposite me, having heard that I was a notorious wolf, in my opinion grossly exaggerated boloney. Her father sent her a cable to turn down the offer of a role. We made the picture and she was so disillusioned—or I was so careful—that she popped out with her views in print. "I was very disappointed to find him so shy and uneasy around girls. It was the destruction of an illusion that I have had since childhood."

I would have liked, at kissing, to be a back-bender, but I kissed with tight lips, devoid of passion, no open mouth, not much emotional quality. I usually even stood rather stiffly, bent down and kissed so that my face might be out of view of the camera. Yet it must have had an effect on the audience—because I have been eating regularly from motion picture work.

In approaching these scenes you sometimes thought out the details in advance and tried to carry through during the embrace. At other times you improvised as you acted, trying to be yourself. Both methods. But during rehearsals I wouldn't attempt anything. Where the screenplay called for embraces, or clinches, I handled it this way.

The screenplay read:

HE: *My darling, we have nothing further to worry about. We will be married as soon as possible. Are you happy?* (Embrace)
SHE: (Whispering) *Of course I am, my darling.* (Embrace)

Then we smelt each other's breath—for better or worse.

When I acted it out in rehearsal I would say the line, but instead of embracing, I would utter the word "Clinch."

The female lead didn't have the chance to rehearse that embrace with me. We saved it for the scene that was to be actually filmed: so I found myself frequently uttering these lines and following through with the extra word, "Clinch." The female lead would wind up rehearsing with me the same way, with nary a kiss or a grab taking place.

One leading lady absolutely rocked me. Excuse me for not mentioning her name. I was rehearsing the preceding lines with her. Several times we played it out with both of us, from time to time, saying "Clinch," or "Embrace." Finally this shot had to be filmed.

The camera turned . . . I leaned away so that the camera wouldn't catch too clearly how thin-lipped I was as I kissed her. Her head went back . . . I was not even touching her lips, but I knew that on film this would be an intense kiss. I could see the dreamy look in her eye—the one the public was paying admission to see. Then a surprising thing happened—her tongue suddenly shot down my mouth and down my neck, way down; it felt about a foot down.

There it stayed, I strangling, till I heard "Cut"—and resumed breathing.

Having to work with a variety of female leads, you are in the professional and personal situation of facing, with each picture, a new problem in human nature. I think it was my recognition of this that gave me a certain reserve.

Casting decisions are primarily made by the producer. The director has a say in it, but the final word is the producer's. When you get along in your position in the film world, the actor or actress begins to have a large say in his or her co-star. Then it becomes only a matter of who is available.

I never insisted on anybody to co-star, but I could have. I vetoed quite a few.

The same applies to a director. It depends on his stature in the film industry. If he were a man of outstanding ability and prominence such as John Huston, he would naturally be a deciding factor in who was cast. A man like Zanuck would consult with John Huston in the casting of a picture, if John were going to direct it, and since they could work together very well, there would probably be no disagreement.

But there have been furious battles waged in some cases.

Jack Warner, after I reached a certain stage, was generally open to my suggestions. As a matter of fact, I never had any fight with Jack about casting.

A star does have a lot to say in the casting of the lesser roles, especially if he has to play scenes with somebody. He has the right to say, "Look, I am not compatible with this character at all." Generally speaking, there was, at Warner's, a pretty sympathetic ear. As to the casting of people I was not actually going to play any scenes with, I never made any objection there at all, since I never considered that my business.

Sometimes, of course, a king star could intercede for a starlet and get her a spot in a picture. Some of these "perks" made good. Like Ann Sheridan. I furthered her career, I think, I hope.

Which brings up a mystery I will now unmystify. . . .

It is true that many of these starlets will toss themselves at stars in the hope of getting on with a screen career. This is done a great deal, and a lot of promises are made.

I can honestly say I never made any promises I didn't keep.

But it was funny to watch the goings-on with the starlets who, of course, were as eager to get ahead as a star was to take her to bed.

One famous director absolutely flabbergasted me with his breath-taking approach: "Get up to my office right away if you know what's good for you!"

Films have been done on this theme, dealing with producers' requirements, à la the starlets.

They are often true.

I hasten to point out one thing in such situations as these—certainly as far as I am concerned. People expect you to be vicious and violent about such relationships. You might think that this is what the situation is, or ought to be, or might be, or could be. And that the girls you deal with will have such reactions as this against you.

I found exactly the opposite, with only one or two exceptions. Many relationships have ended in permanent friendships, or at least without animosity. They were not always mutually satisfactory; but they knew what they were doing.

I hope I don't give the impression that polygamy was general. Monogamy also has its adherents in Hollywood, as elsewhere. Perhaps there are just as many monogomous relationships in the theatre as in any other sphere of life. It is only that publicity spotlights the moves of theatre people. The divorce statistics of the country are, after all, national, not local to Hollywood.

I could speak of domestic relationships in the theatre that are permanent.

For example, never in the twenty years that I have worked with Jack Warner, have I known or heard of him making a pass at anyone on the lot.

I can't say as much for myself, of course.

I once played a game of Ping-pong wth Jack's wife, Ann, vivacious, gay, beautiful and eminently desirable. Would we or would we not go to bed? That was the wager.

She was joking—I wasn't.

I won.

She never paid up.

There were other techniques. . . .

Raoul Walsh and I used to gag about this and had a sort of a teamwork deal going. The approach was this:

I would see the girl and then stand stock-still, as if riveted, as if it were the greatest brainstorm in the world, as if here was a vision descended from above. Without saying a word to the girl directly, I'd call out to Raoul, "Uncle, Uncle, quick!"

Uncle was Raoul, and I'd say, as if suddenly struck by a brainstorm, "You see what I see?"

He would look at the young lady and I would follow through, "You see what I mean, sport?"

She would be listening.

Snapping his finger, he would say, "Of course, you're dead right. You mean for the part of the sister?"

Of course there was never any such part; but we would write one if we had to.

And he would do the same thing with me. He would yell out, "Hey, Baron, quick! What do you think?" And I would answer, "But of course—the part of the sister. What else?"

It was pretty good teamwork.

But the girls weren't all so compliant. This was a chance you took, and sometimes it was disastrous.

I often asked myself, was this ethical or not? So what?

But in any case, I don't think it mattered much, one way or the other, and besides that, either Raoul or I could always pay off afterward to the girl, "That lousy producer, he cut your part right down to one line."

We did, in self-defense, always say, "Well, she did play a part." It may have been half a line, but she was in the picture. And that was very often the start of many an interesting career.

All of this operation we called Star's Perks—in other words, star's perquisites. You saw a young lady you fancied and you'd say, "Star's perks!"—which meant, lay off.

Screen writers had perks too. They took the same stare at the girl and pulled about the same gag: "Have you ever done anything, darling?"

She would say, "No, sir."

The writer would then say, "I am writing this next picture. My name is so-and-so. Ah—I can visualize you, and I have a role in mind for you. Come to my office at four o'clock and we will discuss it."

Katharine Hepburn has a story about Jack Barrymore, when she first came out to Hollywood to make *A Bill of Divorcement*. Jack, of course, was the great star, and she was new from the stage, so he sent for her to come to his dressing room. She timidly knocked on the door, and he bellowed, "Come in!"

He was in a robe, under which there was obviously nothing—only himself. "A pleasure to meet you, my dear, I trust we are going to have a very pleasant association. Now, would you like to get undressed?"

She was shocked. "What!"

Jack, an adjustable man, said blandly, "Well, very well, my dear, quite all right. Let's sit down and just talk over the part."

Before I got to Hollywood I had gone along on the assumption that it was the role of the male to pursue the female. I had my occasional successes and my failures. But from the time when the star legend began to surround me, it became different. I discovered that women know far more about seduction than men. At least they know when they want to be "seduced," if one can put it that way.

Not only did I not have to seduce women, but sometimes I even went so far as to say in advance, "I won't put you in a part in my forthcoming picture." Maybe it was the air around Hollywood, the competition among women to get places. It made some of them wild.

My pal Bud Ernst annoyed me by scoffing, "You've never made a dame in your life—you've only had it taken from you."

Not only did I never promise any woman marriage, in order to take her to bed—as I have heard some true seducers do—but I always prefaced my attentions by announcing that marriage was absurd, ridiculous, fatuous.

These warnings to the opposite sex did not seem to have prevented me from becoming "conversant" with them. A star doesn't have to pursue or seduce any woman. What he needs, more likely, is a chastity belt for self-protection, as some of my movie pals will tell you.

Naturally in an environment like this I was like the rabbit tossed into the brier patch. Beautiful gals all about. If the female of the species is more beautiful more often than not, or more deadly, then she helps me to know I am alive. I see and sense the loveliness in ladies even when it is not always there. A woman who might be only pretty to others might seem to me to be beautiful. This is the way I am biologically constructed—slightly blind. In fact, as I look back on my gallery of women, I think it was only Lili who was truly beautiful in the classic sense.

I now had Lili right where I wanted her. I was living the life of a married bachelor. I went my own way, I had male pals around me for sports, athletics, gambling and fun, and starlets for recreation, and the little woman at home.

I received a wire from my sister Rosemary in New York. She was about nineteen or twenty and she had just arrived from England. I had finished a picture, *Dive Bomber,* and was ready for a change. I tried to tell Lili she ought to stay in Hollywood and let Rosemary and me fling around by ourselves.

"Nothing doing, Fleen. I want to meet your sister. I'm going along."

I hardly knew my sister. There had been an age barrier until now, and besides that I had never been around Rosemary very much since my own childhood.

She was now a young woman, and it was different. She was pretty with laughing, bright blue eyes and a tip-tilted nose. She was quiet, conventional, the opposite of me in practically all respects. She could talk French and German as well as she could speak English. She was innocent; yet she was intelligent and poised. I decided to present her to all of my celebrity friends and the socialite crowd.

Rosemary and I went on a round of night clubs. We managed somehow to get away from Lili frequently. Lili could find her own pals, and I found reasons for breaking Rosemary away from her.

One night as we sat at the 21 Club I saw someone at a distant table. I know who she is, I said to myself, that's Amelia Holiphant. Lili had introduced me to her three years earlier.

Amelia was married, beautiful, wealthy, well-educated. No Lili was with me to stop me, so I excused myself to Rosemary and walked across the room.

I shook hands with Amelia, bowed politely to her husband, and in a moment's talk found out enough to be able to get in touch with her.

From then on, I suppose, I neglected Rosemary.

My courtship of Amelia prospered so swiftly that I could hardly believe it. I knew at once that I was in love, genuinely in love. Everything else, till now, had been meek affairs. She was delicate, fragile, with tiny wrists, tiny ankles, a small neck, minute ears. She had a complexion that was indescribable, and it wasn't make-up. She had dark blond curly hair. Beyond these physical allures she had a sense of humor, a musical voice, a lovely feminine magnetism.

After a few secret meetings in Central Park—by which time Lili knew exactly whom I was seeing—we decided we had to get away. We didn't know where or how. She had a child, she had a devoted husband, but she was ready to forget everything. I felt the same desperate need to be with her, no matter what happened.

One morning about 3 o'clock I waited in a cab outside the apartment where she lived with her husband. Her clothes came down in a large trunk. Apparently that is what happens when a prominent socialite abandons home and child and runs off with a star. A trunk comes down first. Then she floats down.

Away we went to the airport.

When we got to New Orleans, I said, "Amelia, we're alone at last. Nobody will ever find us here."

I no sooner said that, in the airport waiting room, than I bumped into Norval Harris. He was the chap who afterward had the misfortune to go to jail when Huey Long was shot. Norval, a well-to-do big shot of the region, was a night club pal of mine. At once he asked me how he could help out. I told him I wanted seclusion. "Norval, I have a wife from whom even a lion would cower. If she learns I am down here I've had it."

Just before we left New York, I had a phone talk with Lili in which I said I'd be home late. "If you zee zat woman again—" she said in her most menacing French accent.

So I had plenty of reason to want secrecy. Norval sympathized. What to do?

Then I hit it.

I told him I wanted to hire a steamboat for Amelia and myself. We'd sail up the Mississippi, and we'd have privacy if I went broke securing it.

"What?" said Norval. "I never heard of such a thing. These ships are built to carry five hundred people."

"I can't help it. Lili may have traced me. The press watches me the way astronomers watch the stars. We've got to be alone."

"How about a small motorboat?"

"The steamboat. Please, Norval."

The price was atrocious. It must have cost me a month's work. In Norval's 22-foot-long, gold-plated custom-built car, conspicuous enough to blind people at a hundred yards, we drove to a quiet place along the banks of the Mississippi.

There she was, the *River Queen,* about a block long, with a high tower, handsome rails, artistically painted, looking like an aged-in-magnolia Southern belle. And for now it was all ours.

I led Amelia out of the car and we went up the gangplank. I was about to return to the auto to gather our luggage when there, at the top of the gangplank, were two smiling reporters. One had a camera and he was shooting me busily. The other greeted me, talking fast about how well connected they were. What about some pictures and who was with me?

I did the first thing that crossed my mind. With all that passion which

I had been reserving for Amelia and hadn't been able to expend on her yet—because we'd almost never been alone in a place where a little expending could be done—I lifted this newspaper fellow right up in the air, as I would a package, and delivered the package over the side of the rail, plump into the Mississippi mud.

I had to get my hands on the cameraman. These fellows are usually not too fleet-footed. They have a tendency to hang around until the camera is knocked out of their hands. I caught this joker about twenty yards from the gangplank and pulled an old Aussie trick on him, stamping on his feet while I pushed him. That doesn't leave a man many places to go.

I grabbed the camera away from him and took out the film. I gave the camera back.

I knew the reporter had the story anyway. He may not have known who was with me, but he could release a story that Errol Flynn, seeking a bit of privacy, had hired a steamboat and crew for himself and a mysterious little lady.

The *River Queen* pulled out.

Five days up the Mississippi on this huge steamer.

Only Amelia and me and the crew.

Every moment was a thing of beauty. We discussed plans for the future, all the possibilities. She might face divorce, she might lose her child. She was wrong and so was I to be doing what we were doing, we admitted to one another, but we couldn't help it. Our only justification was that she said that she didn't love her husband and I told her I didn't love Lili.

The world rolled by.

I never saw a newspaper, nor cared less for one. We saw from time to time, from our stateroom, the shores on either side of the long river. Sometimes the river was muddy, sometimes it seemed to swirl. The shores might be close, or miles apart.

I was in love. I have always loved Amelia and I always will love her. She was, I think, the only woman I had ever truly loved till then.

My affair with her continued intermittently for a year or more. I saw her whenever I went East. But there were barriers. Her husband threatened to shoot me. He even came to Hollywood and surprised me one night at my house, pulling a gun and brandishing it. But he didn't shoot, not having gotten *himself* quite loaded enough.

Beyond the barrier of a husband who was loath to let her go, Amelia was full of certain high-society manners that I couldn't fully cotton to.

A bit of stuffiness, you might say. She was a living incarnation of the ornate salons of her class, of the leisure and the remoteness from the reality of life on the top.

My inability to get together with her in a real way, the complication which she represented in my life, had a deep effect upon me. It sharpened the schism between Lili and me. It made me sense the hopelessness of ever finding a real, a permanent, a workable relationship with any woman. Something—perhaps it was biological—stood between me and a prolonged relationship with even so wonderful a creature as Amelia.

I plunged into picture-making and tried not to figure out the tangle of my relationships. Besides, I now had a new interest: Mulholland House, overlooking the San Fernando Valley.

I designed the house myself. I would make of it a playhouse, a spot for rest, recreation, good living, romping, roistering, and cultured living too.

She went up fast, like the sails of a boat. At the outset she only cost me $35,000. Later, as I extended her and improved her, the total cost went to $125,000. She snuggled on the side of the hill. Inside, in most of her rooms, there were mirrors that brought the beauty of the valley into the house. The swimming pool was almost in my living room. Outside was a riding ring, below on the hillside a tennis court, and a little ways off I had stables for cockfights.

Of course cockfighting was against the law, but we had it anyway on Sunday nights. We had exciting Sunday evenings, I and my cowboy friends, the actors who played with me in the Westerns, and the Hollywood sports who hung around me. In the barn you would have the smell of horses, the smell of fighting cocks, and the smell of cowboys all watching these two game birds peck each other to death. Even my horses loved the cockfights. They peered over their bars at the two birds.

The interior of the house wasn't ornate, but it was beautiful and practical and there was plenty of room. Rooms for guests, rooms for fun, rooms for eating, a room for reading. Leopard skins on the floor, a Gauguin and a Van Gogh on the walls—originals. There were glass cases for firearms. I collected guns but I hated to use them. I had miniatures of boats in cases, under glass, on the wall: schooners, barkentines. Of course there was a bar of my own design. Fancy a house in Hollywood without a private bar. On the wall in back of it was a very special painting of a Mexican bullfight. But I think I liked my den best of all. Here was my desk next to a window where the California light streamed in. There I sat often on weekends, when I barred the doors and I wrote or tried to write. Nearby was a fireplace and wood was on the hearth; and when it was cool the logs burned and the room was aglow.

I thought sometimes: How is all this? I am still in my early thirties and I am sitting on top of the world. Here is my home, out there is the valley, beyond are the people who are writing me all that fan mail. I wonder how Koets is. Whatever happened to Jack Ryan and Dusty Miller? What strange things can happen to a man—and in so short a time.

I had it all figured out, now that the place was built. This was a bachelor house. No woman would live here with me. Not Lili, not anyone else. Sure I'd have them visit me, but this was for me to roam around in—alone. Outside, rolling away in back of the house, was the farm, where there were horses, cows, wallabies, chickens, dogs, cats, everything. Mine. There are some things a man has to have to himself. A busy fellow like Flynn needs some peace sometimes.

When I had arrived in England after my seven-seas voyage across the globe I was surprised to bump into an Australian acquaintance, Freddie McEvoy. I found that in part he complemented me. He was an athlete, a roisterer like myself, and he could be canny too, very. He had his eye out for the main chance and bluntly told me he intended marrying wealthy. With his physique and appearance and his charm and culture I didn't doubt he could do this. When I left England he said he'd make his way back to America sooner or later and we'd meet again. He went to New York and set out on a house-to-house job selling the Encyclopaedia Britannica. It didn't last long; not for him. He dressed himself up, he got out on a few tennis courts in the swankier parts of Long Island; he met people, he fell in with the society crowd, and he began his career as a sportsman and international gadabout.

He was tall, with blond hair, thin, aquiline, rather hawk nose. He had a hard-set mouth and chin, and a pair of piercing blue eyes. They called him "Tiger," a term that, I think, stemmed from the compelling effect of his eyes. His family was from Victoria. They were ranchers. I didn't see Freddie while I first made pictures and not throughout my six-year-long relationship with Lili. But soon after Mulholland was built he returned from Europe, having been pursued there by a fabulously wealthy Standard Oil heiress. I invited him to stay with me. He was a little disconsolate at the time, having had difficulties of a romantic sort. Freddie held the fort all day while I worked at the studio. He brought along with him Alexandre, an ex-Russian royalist manservant who was nuts about betting on horses. Alexandre was given charge of Mulholland.

Strange people wended their way up the hill to Mulholland. Among them pimps, sports, bums, down-at-the-heel actors, gamblers, athletes, sight-seers, process servers, phonies, queers, salesmen—everything in the world. All kinds and all types, as the Lord or Nature composed them. The famous and the infamous, stars, bit players, stunt men and artists. They came by day and by night. Invited and uninvited. The path became so well trodden and there were so many people hanging about some days that at times I had trouble getting into the house myself. I had to go around the back way because the crowd in front would have held me up.

Of course there were pretty girls. The more the merrier. Pals like Freddie McEvoy, Bud Ernst, Johnny Meyers and Bruce Cabot brought them up. I always liked men about me, roisterers, fun guys, rompers. It went back to my New Guinea days, my times in Australia when I roved with a gang, or always had some one guy to pal out with, to look over the girls, drop in at a saloon or even just go for a swim. For some kinds of fun the friendship that two men can have or a gang of fellows can have simply can't be beat. It is a different feeling than what you get from being with a woman, and no woman can replace the gambling-sporting-handicapping air that men together can establish.

One night I returned to Mulholland to find the place more or less peaceful. Nobody seemed to be there. I shouted for Alexandre. There wasn't even any sign of him.

I went in to my bedroom and saw the most adorable girl twins: one was a blonde, the other a brunette. I stared. In the vague light it was like seeing double. What a pleasant intoxication. They were half giggling, half scared, and I wondered who in blazes they were, where they came from, how they got in.

Alexandre suddenly appeared from behind. "M'sier, you call?"

I turned on him in a fury. "You're damn right! What are those two girls doing here sitting on the edge of my bed? Who let them in? Who are they? And what are *you* doing? What kind of a house do you think this is anyway?"

I looked at them again, in all their twin beauty. I yelled as I sat on the edge of the bed, "Now look, Alexandre, if you know what's good for you and don't want to be fired, you get *one* of them out of here!"

Did I say I had Lili where I wanted her?

One evening when I made one of my occasional visits to her apartment, Lili started to get undressed.

I had that old stirring below the navel as she paraded up and down naked. She wore a curious cat-eat-the-canary look. Her tongue was in her cheek—a favorite gesture of hers—and her eyes glinted strangely.

"What do you think of my figure, Fleen?" she asked.

I acknowledged my admiration. Standing there, she was the most beautiful woman of her day, without question.

She picked up the phone and dialed a number. "I want you to talk to my doctor."

I got on the phone. A voice said, "She's in great shape, Mr. Flynn. I want to be the first to congratulate you. And don't you worry. She'll have an easy delivery."

Weakly, I thanked him.

I turned to Lili. She was looking at me, standing there nude, tongue in cheek.

She made a classic remark. "Fleen, you think you've screwed every dame in Hollywood, but now I've screwed you, my friend. You will have a child!"

About three o'clock one morning in Hollywood, during a heavy downpour of rain the bell sounded. The servants were asleep in their own apartment in another part of the house. I went downstairs and answered the door. A bedraggled figure was standing on my porch. I couldn't make out who. I waked a bit as recognition grew. "Jack!"

"Well," said Barrymore, left eyebrow arched, "aren't you going to ask me in for a drink?"

"Sure, come in."

I rushed into the bar and got a bottle. "Say when," I said as I poured. It was a large glass and I poured it about a quarter of an inch from the top, full of whisky.

"Cease," he said. "Soda."

I rushed about and got the soda.

He just waved the bottle of soda over the whisky.

He sat hunched and miserable, like a drowned rat.

"Navarre, have you perchance an old bed I can stay in tonight?" He drank and shook.

That was the beginning. He stayed three weeks. The most frightening three weeks I had since I was in the New Guinea jungle.

He was in domestic troubles and he needed a refuge. My place seemed remote, just right, and Jack dug in. He took my favorite chair, the one I read in at night, and I never got a chance to use it. I never saw him read a book, yet his knowledge was wonderful. He would idly thumb through a book, put it aside and talk, but he must have done much reading at some time because his knowledge was wide-ranging.

Jack thought it was a waste of time to go to the bathroom if there was a window close by. During his visit he took all the varnish off one of my picture windows that overlooked the San Fernando Valley. One day I complained bitterly, "For God's sakes, look at the varnish here. Your piss has eaten away the paint. Can't you do it somewhere else?"

"Certainly, m'lad."

He immediately went to the fireplace and let go there. The smell through the room was atrocious.

He was growing unstable in many ways, and close to breaking up.

One night I heard a horrible scream from the guestroom. "Let me out, you bastard, let me out! Flynn, you traitor, let me out of here!"

I jumped out of bed. My work about now was really going to hell. . . . Because most of the things that happened to him occurred during the night, and I had to get up at about six or half-past six.

Loaded, Jack had lost his sense of direction about his room. Intending to go to the bathroom, he made a wrong turn and walked into a clothes closet. Wandering around in the closet, in the dark, thinking he should be in the bathroom and unable to get out, he was helpless. Suddenly he had felt a tickling at the back of his neck.

He was pounding on the wall and screaming when I entered his room. I let him out and calmed him. "Bats!" he kept exclaiming. "Your house is full of bats!"

I tried to explain to him that the back of his neck had been tickled by coat hangers.

People had learned that Jack was staying with me. Some strangers located my number and telephoned him. He answered: "Yes, this is Mr. Barrymore. Oh really? Are you alone, my dear? . . . You have a

beautiful voice. . . . How old are you? . . . Really, well, well, well.
. . Now what are you doing this evening?"

He wound up making an appointment.

Now a beautiful voice can belong to somebody who looks like a crow. If it is an anonymous voice that is generally the case.

Jack rushed into my bathroom. He put on a magnificent brocaded dressing gown; he powdered himself all over with talcum—he powdered under the armpits, and he even powdered at the crotch. He brushed his hair and cleaned his teeth. He couldn't wait. Like a young boy ready to go out on his first date.

Then up came one of the most awful-looking beasts ever to find her way to Hollywood—with her mother!

I left him there with his guests. I couldn't stand to have my esthetic sense so upset by two such human submonsters in the female form, a form which I worship—as did Jack.

Afterward he cursed me. "You left me there," he accused. "You left me there! You could have at last got rid of the mother."

"I thought you would be safer with the mother."

John and I were talking about the horrors of being found at the corner of Hollywood and Vine with your hat in your hand. What if you slipped so bad you fell into beggary—like many stars? I said, "Why don't we find out how it would be?"

"A hell of a good idea," said Jack.

We made a small wager to see how far we could get as bums. The bet was either fifty or a hundred dollars to see who could pick up the most money in an hour.

Jack's make-up was better than mine. I put on a set of false whiskers, a hat which went down over my face, and a pair of dark glasses and I carried a stick so I could simulate a blind man. Jack wore a horribly dirty sweater with holes in it. He played his part as if he was cold and needed clothes and he simulated a man with palsy.

I took up a stance at a Hollywood intersection where an old woman sold papers. She had been there for years and I forgot that this was her beat. I shuffled along with my toes sticking out of my shoes. I had picked up a few copies of the *The News* and I went into competition with her at her corner. She knew all the cops and got the cops to kick me out. They asked me for a license, asked what I was doing there, and told me to be on my way. I recollected my own experience in New Guinea and knew very well people would fight and sometimes kill each other for three dimes or even three cents.

Jack had also figured on selling papers, but he abandoned that idea and played straight blind man. No cop bothered him and in an hour he picked up a dollar and forty cents.

I was unable to get Jack to talk about himself as an actor. Having been the greatest Hamlet of them all, so it was said, and I could believe it, I wanted to get him to talk about it. How did he feel about Hamlet, Shakespeare, the play, so that he had been inspired to do his kind of performance with this vehicle? I couldn't get him to open up. I discovered that, with all his extroversions, he was innately modest, certainly insofar as his achievements were concerned.

He could talk about Renaissance art, the Wicked Life of Father Barnaby, a hundred different subjects.

He talked shop frequently. He came back home one evening early, full of excitement. He was going to be tested for *The Man Who Came to Dinner*. "I think I can do it," he said.

"Certainly you can. But what the hell are they giving you a test for!" I was infuriated that they were to *test* him for the role. I realized later that Warners wanted to know whether he was on the bottle, whether he was physically and emotionally capable. I protested loudly about the idea of testing John, but the studio probably knew its business.

I knew from personal experience that he could play the role of Sheridan Whiteside in *The Man Who Came to Dinner*. Sometimes, during those three weeks when he came to see me, just for a drink and a night's lodging, I wondered if he was ever going to leave or whether my house would be standing after he went. In some ways he was a ruthless man, with mercy toward none.

Another evening he rushed in with an idea. Same enthusiasm. "Wonderful," he said. "Tremendous. This takes place in 1380." He discussed the parts, the clothes, the role he and I would have, everything.

"You see," he said, "you play my bastard son."

He was sitting on the edge of a table. "Mine is a very small role," he said. "Of course."

"Balls!" I screamed at him. "*You* a small role!"

"Never fear. I shall steal the picture anyway."

"Tell me more," I said.

"I have no more to tell. I just thought this much of it on the way up in the cab."

Jack was very down in the spirit. He was in physical pain. Yet his outer expression was literally lofty. You asked him, "How goes it this noon, Jack?"

"Never a better day, boy," he would answer. I knew then that he was suffering from cirrhosis of the liver, kidney trouble, hardening of the arteries, and other things.

Somehow the three weeks passed and Jack left. I could work again. But it was the opportunity to see Jack in these declining days that made it possible for me, fifteen years later, to play as authentically as I could feel it, the role of Barrymore in *Too Much, Too Soon.*

Freddie McEvoy didn't know how to box, but he was about twice as strong as any man I knew, including me. He had a grip of Australian steel. My only chance in a row with him was to hit him on the nose, which pictorially looked strong and aquiline. Actually his nose couldn't take it. Quite unexpectedly, between his nose and my current ambition to do some writing, I discovered how much he had my interest at heart.

I had just read Thomas De Quincey's *Confessions of an Opium Eater.* I was so impressed with it that I decided I must go through the same thing—subject myself to opium, write about it. I asked a friend if he could get me some opium. He said, "My plane carries a lot of that junk."

He came up with enough to dope half a studio.

I started to take it. Then I tried to write. At first I think I did pretty well. I didn't know my face was growing grayer and grayer by the day. Others noticed my change of complexion. The more I experimented— that's what I called it—the less I wrote. I began to wonder how De Quincey had done it. What I wrote made no sense at all. Maybe this was because I tried to write while taking the stuff. Others wrote afterwards.

I didn't tell Freddie about this. I kept the supply of opium syrettes on a window sill over the bathroom sink.

Each day I worked at the studio. Each evening home for a syrette of opium.

One night I came home, reached into my cache for the daily dose and found nothing. I scrabbled around frantically, wondering if I had, in some stupor, misplaced it.

Freddie opened the door. "What are you looking for?"

"Oh, nothing."

"You stupid sonofabitch. Have you seen yourself lately?"

"What are you talking about?"

"If you want to know where that dope is I'll show you."

He led me into the study where there was a big fire going in the fireplace. "There they are. Now, what are you going to make of that?"

"You bastard. You are a guest in my house. Do you mean to say—"

"Sure, I burned them. All of them!"

I let fly. He caught one right on the nose. I knew just where to tab him. We rolled and rolled around my study. The furniture began to crack up. We almost fell into the fireplace.

"You sonofabitch," I said, "come on outside. I'm not going to soil my place with your blood."

We went outside.

There it was a little better. He would come and try to grab me and I would try to knock him down. If he had got his hands around me he would have finished me, but I was faster.

Finally we were both lying on the ground, mutually knocked out. He was panting. "I'm not going to get up again," he said. "Why should I be knocked down by you? If you are stupid enough to go on with this, nobody can stop you."

Freddie snapped me out of it—the hard way and I dropped the opium before it became a habit. I withdrew in the next few days. I did have something to write about: withdrawal symptoms. These are horrible, and worth writing about. You feel that every single nerve in your body is popping out. There is nothing very new or scientific in pointing that out.

Subsequently I have taken a narcotic now and then, but only on a doctor's advice, administration or prescription.

The only real thing that came of it was my realization of what a good friend Freddie really was.

Freddie and I began underwater spear-fishing and skin-diving, in America, at a time when we knew of no others who were. Swim fins were unknown, we had no underwater guns such as they have now, goggles were still in a primitive stage. Freddie and I went to Mexico and Florida. We chased sharks underwater, fishing as a team. We had a signal system between us, so that we could help each other go for a fish with a spear. Once I put a spear in a hammerhead shark and Freddie put a spear in the same fellow. He just towed us along.

Another time at Acapulco, we were under water, Freddie signaled and pointed in a certain direction. I ran headlong into a giant devil fish, or manta ray. Over me this great white expanse of belly and a big gaping mouth. I went backwards fast as I could. When I came up, there was Freddie by the beach, laughing his head off. I took a poke at him. Boyish stuff, I know, but there was a rough outdoorishness to this, a crude humor, a rugged something that you couldn't get from association with women.

Deep diving has always been a specialty of mine. The first time I did it was in New Guinea, using a pair of crude Japanese goggles made of shell or bamboo, with a piece of glass in it. Then the face mask was invented and Freddie and I rapidly took to this. Instead of the primitive spear, which went through a piece of bamboo and pulled back almost like firing a bow and arrow, the French came out with a wonderful spring gun. Freddie and I went off to Mexico and other parts of the world to fish under water with this new invention. We had ordered this gun from France and I feel pretty sure we were the first on the coast to use it.

Oddly enough, the imaginative Hollywood directors and producers, who knew very well I spent so much time under water, never designed a picture for me to play such a role on the screen. Others who didn't even know how to swim got the underseas stories. I wanted to appear in a film where I might be slugging it out with an octopus or a shark, or experience the rhapsody of the deep, but this wasn't for me in films— only in real life.

Skin-diving took us to Mexico from time to time, chiefly to Acapulco Bay, where the waters are beautiful, the air exhilarating. On one of these haunts I met someone, and as a result of that meeting there has been, since then, more than one international headline.

In a Mexico City bar, as McEvoy, myself and several others sat having a few drinks, we were joined by a beautiful young girl with reddish-brown hair, opaque catlike eyes, a wide shapely mouth and a figure that might have been sculpted. Her name, she said, was Linda Welter. She was demure, she spoke English with just a little trace of accent, and her Spanish was perfect. She was Dutch, and something else, perhaps German.

We were going to Acapulco, we told her. She exclaimed with delight how she had always wanted to go there. (It occurred to me, later, that she probably knew the place better than any of us.) Half-jokingly, I said, "Why don't you come with us? We're going fishing."

"Oh wonderful, when do we leave?"

Freddie, across the table, threw up his hands with a sort of here-we-go-again look.

The following day the three of us flew down in one of those ancient little planes to the miserable airport of Acapulco. We put up at a small hotel where they had little bungalows.

Linda was an excellent companion, a good sport, although she didn't go for underwater fishing, saying there were too many *tiburon* there—she couldn't think of the English name for shark.

She had never been to the States, she said, and that was her next ambition. She wanted a means of getting there, and I was it. It actually occurred to me she might have a chance in films, and I was glad to be helpful.

When we returned to Mexico City she was under contract to me, a six-month contract, which was to be at a starting salary of one hundred dollars a week and expenses.

I returned to Hollywood, and she was to follow.

On the day she arrived, big Bud Ernst chanced also to be coming in from Mexico City. He rushed to my house at once, and reported that on the plane he had met a beautiful young girl with reddish-brown hair, big catlike eyes, and her figure was so-and-so. I should meet her. He was all excitement. . . . At that instant Linda walked in. Bud's jaw dropped as she came over to me.

I got her an apartment not far away, very attractive, very modern. Now came the business of arranging my protégée's future. I thought she was singularly attractive, but she had one long dog-tooth on the left side of her mouth which wouldn't photograph well. It looked like a fang, and in a sense it was.

I sent her to my dentist, Dr. Bill Wallace, and told him to edge off the protruding part of the fang and make it level with the rest of her teeth.

A little later—or was it weeks later?—Dr. Wallace got me on the phone. When was I going to pay him, he asked, this bill was running a little late . . . ?

"What bill? I haven't had any bill from you."

"Linda's teeth."

"What the hell are you talking about? I just asked you to knock off the edge of one tooth—just to file it down. What's so expensive about that?"

"Yes, but I've got a bill here for nine hundred dollars."

"Nine hundred dollars!—She could get a new head for that!"

"That's just about what she has done."

She had had all of her teeth recapped and had apparently told the doctor to send the bill somewhere else so that I wouldn't see it while the work was going on.

Nine hundred dollars was a lot of money in those days. In addition, I got bills from Bullocks, Wiltshire, and other purveyors of feminine merchandise. Where was this going to end?

Meantime, Bud Ernst, McEvoy, Johnnie Myers, Barrymore, Decker and myself had a few conferences as to what her screen name should be. I hadn't yet got around to making a screen test of her, but it was due in time, and in the interim the name Linda Welter didn't seem like good movie fare.

One evening we kicked around possible names. The talk grew heated; each had a different idea of what would sound well. Yet she was my protégée; it was on the strength of my contract she had gotten a passport to enter the States.

I had always liked the name Fortune. I jumped to my feet, pounded the table: "I've got it—Linda Fortune!"

Jack Barrymore let out a hoarse bellow of a laugh. "Navarre, sometimes you frighten me with your blinding brilliance." He laughed again. "Yes, my boy, I can see it now. Linda Fortune—either you have a twisted sense of humor, or, as I say, you are beyond brilliance. How are you going to introduce her?"

I thought for a minute, and I saw what he was getting at.

"Yes," and his eyes lit up as he said, "Miss Fortune!"

I had been associated with various publicity gimmicks with Fletcher Christian of *Mutiny on the Bounty*. I hit upon another name—Linda Christian.

Linda Christian is still a pretty name, and Linda herself, as I see from the papers, is today even lovelier than ever, and certainly she has a wonderful mind. Yet she never quite made it as an actress and I can't understand why, because she has a lot of talent.

If she is called, by various people, should I say "acquisitive," good for her. I started her on the road to fortune. She has more jewelry than Paulette Goddard—and that is like talking about Fort Knox.

Every so often, as the years have gone by, I have seen Linda.

I saw her abroad with her late husband, Tyrone Power, who had amazed me by marrying her. He was a very soft, nice kind of man.

Often, when Ty was about, she looked at me with those big oblique eyes of hers, smiling inwardly, I am sure, for Ty never knew the origin of our own friendship.

I would look at her and murmur, "Smile, honey. I just want to see those choppers. They took their first bite out of me."

She pretended not to hear.

Lili was right. On May 31, 1941, my son Sean was born. As it happens, Susan and I were destined to become close pals and he is now a big fellow about six feet three inches tall who, they say, looks like me but better. Out of this impossible snarl of two volatile people there came something good anyway.

Lili and I made a few public appearances during her pregnancy. Even a few more after the birth of Sean. Cameras clicked. Columnists talked. The intrepid Australian had now entered the sacred precincts of parenthood.

Except that Lili's game was something other. She brought up her heavy artillery, her lawyers in Los Angeles.

She dug in, tougher than the French did at the Maginot Line.

She never had it so good with Sam Goldwyn.

Her real career had begun when she took up with me. Now she was a one-woman army dedicated to taking away my earnings as fast as they came in, and like General Patton I had outrun my supplies, moving too fast.

First she sued for divorce. She had a child in her arms now and apparently the courts figured, "It's only Flynn; she might as well have his money as anyone else."

I loved the idea of having a son. I liked the idea of having children. By accident I fell into the experience of parenthood—unless the same accident happened to me elsewhere without my ever having heard of it —and I was all for it. Let her have the money. I wanted my chance and my time with the boy as soon as he could toddle, which was fast.

I didn't want her around Mulholland House, but Sean could have the place if he wanted it.

When God decided on a policy of bewildering the human race, he created lawyers, to screw up the works.

Any Church can have that quotation free, without requesting permission for its use from my publishers. I just want a copyright on the observation. As possibly the most litigated-against man in modern times, I feel I have the right to speak definitely about lawyers—always a Defendant, rarely a Plaintiff.

California lawyers skinned me properly with the most brutal property settlement ever made and may do it again, who knows?

Lili was to receive alimony from me until she remarried. Naturally with this gimmick, why should she remarry? When, by law, she hooked a permanent meal ticket and a large income. Lili never has remarried, instead, she has stayed quietly in the backdrops of my life living off the sweat of my brow.

She couldn't have afforded to marry, and not even the Vanderbilts and the Astors could pay what this settlement called for. To this day, even if I worked all my life exclusively for her, I could never meet the tax on the tax on the tax.

I had a lot of cowboys around because they worked in pictures with me. They were amusing and good pals. There was "Bear Valley" Charlie Miller. He had the longest mustache in the West, so he claimed, and I never met anyone who could or would dispute it. He wore a sad look, and he loved to bet at my cockfights. He claimed to know the best birds, but he always lost. His wife tired of him and his long mustache and she divorced him on grounds of "mental croolety" as he pronounced it. He couldn't understand being told he was cruel. He told the judge, "Judge, she can whip you and all your goddamn lawyers here in court. What's croolety?" One night when he was drunk we cut off half of his mustache. He woke up and went around with two guns trying to find out who did it. I wore a bemused look.

Buster Wiles, a baldheaded stunt man, could jump two hundred feet into a little pool and come out with as much hair on his head as he went in with. Jimmy Dolgun, a long, lanky Jewish lad, still works as a stunt man for me to this day. And another, Don Turner. I could rely on these guys. They knew they could rely on me too; if they got fired one day they'd be rehired the next. Their salary was good. They were tough, like the men I knew in New Guinea. Sometimes they were sore at me because I wanted to do the stunts in my pictures myself, grumbling it cut out their work. I yielded.

I wanted the excitement of doing these things, until the studio got after me. Insurance companies wouldn't insure a picture if I did the rough stuff. Take when you have to make a parachute jump out of a plane, always a tense shot in a picture. You fall out of camera focus onto a mattress ten or twelve feet below and hope you won't break your back. You may do the jump, or a stand-in may get the work.

Experts in special effects, I liked to have them about. How did they get that way? I was curious for their stories. Like in a hookshop when you so often asked a whore the story of her life and she told you.

I found Hollywood to be a circusland of experts at this and that.

There are people who are specialists with the whip, who can flick a fly or a cigarette out of your mouth—if the camera is properly placed.

Or suppose a man throws a knife at you. This knife is carefully wired so as to take a certain path. You don't want somebody throwing a knife at you and just missing you at hair's breadth, and on the screen this wire has been painted silver so that you can't see it.

There are specialists in every form of danger, like Howard Hill with the bow and arrow, a man who can put out the flame of a candle with his arrow at thirty or forty feet.

You can usually trust a good stunt man, if you know him, but this doesn't always hold. I ran into trouble—but delightful trouble—while making a favorite picture, *Gentleman Jim.* The idea was for me, in the role of the cocky young unknown Jim Corbett, to have six fights on my way to the championship. This was a picture I made with Raoul Walsh while Jack Warner was away. Alexis Smith was the girl lead.

We decided to take advantage of Jack's absence by tossing into the story a lot of whimsy that he might not have allowed. Cracks like, when Jim is reading his fan mail and comes upon a letter from George Bernard Shaw, whom he has never heard of, "Hey, bub, read this. This here one is good. Some bum signs himself George Bernard Shaw, says he's written a play about a boxer. Wants me to play it." That line, in print, mightn't mean much, but on the screen, limning a simple Irish fellow on his way, could have been a laugh. Especially from Shaw fans.

My opponents in the fight game were six well-known wrestlers who later appeared on television. Independent of what they did with me in the ring I had fun on the set bumping their heads together. I would say to Tiny Tim, who was six feet six inches tall, "This guy says you're yellow." He would go over to Lord Fauntleroy, a man whose shoulders were about four feet across, sock him in the back of the neck and drop him. I'd say to Strangler Lewis, "Tiny Tim says you weren't never no champ." Strangler would swing his sledge-hammer fist down on Tiny Tim. Each time these chaps hit the floor, they got up, looked around, found out who dropped them, then went over and clouted the other— as we had the camera going.

There was Abdul the Turk, who made his name riding down Hollywood Boulevard on a camel. I would egg him on to take a clout at His Lordship, who had a shock of glowing hair atop his enormous body. I howled as the behemoths popped each other around the set.

I reached the stage in the film where I waged this championship fight with an excellent and tough fighter, Jack Loper, able enough in the ring to be knocked out by Joe Louis. I suggested a routine to him that would look good on film. He was to throw three punches at me. "Let's get it straight—I'll go down," I said. "Then get up and you throw again. Then I'll step to the left. By this time I will be in the lights." This meant the shot would be complete, with the exchange of blows looking very effective.

Instead, in the first poke he took, he landed on my chin, changed the shot entirely and jarred the liver out of me. I swung an unrehearsed punch back at him. He shot a terrific one to my chin—and I was out for two hours.

Waking up in the first-aid room, I had a talk with Loper. He was remorseful, said it was an accident. Very well, I said, we'd try again. Once more I explained how the blows should land.

Camera . . . action.

On the first punch he lifted me right off the floor and down I went, and again I was hauled off to the first-aid room.

The production manager said, "I think we have had a pretty hard day, haven't we? You must be mad as hell at Loper."

"No, but I would like to have a little chat with him."

Loper came to my side. Tears streamed down his face.

"Buddy," I began, "did somebody put you up to this? Somebody around here that doesn't like me?"

He blubbered with apology. He wept. I was the last one in the world he wanted to hurt.

"I tell you what I am going to do," I proposed. "You know those four corner posts?" He asked where, what posts? "The posts of the ring," I said.

"Yeah."

"I am going to do one more shot with you. If you miss this time I can honestly promise you that that bottle down there"—I pointed to a champagne bottle—"will break your skull and you will never see again. This is my personal guarantee." I told him that when I called out "duck" he must punch over my head.

We were both unnerved. I poured champagne and we drank to the next take.

I warned him once more as we entered the ring. There were only four punches he had to remember. "If you can't remember them without pushing me into those lights or without knocking me cold, I am going to retaliate."

I had to clear up what the word retaliate meant. His eyes opened wide at my translation. "It means I'll break your fucking head in."

By now nice old Jack was petrified. He covered when I hit. He shuffled away from me. Finally to make him come out fighting I did an unforgivable thing. I hit him right in the nuts.

That revived his fighting spirit. He came out, he landed a tremendous one on my jaw, and I went down for the third time. Out!

Three times in one day. I was fed up. A badly beaten actor.

I took three days off.

For once I loved making a picture.

Putting me in cowboy pictures seemed to me the most ridiculous miscasting, but it was successful for Warners. Often, in these pictures, I had to alibi my accent which was still a bit too English for the American ear. I always had to get in a couple of lines which went like this : . .

HEAVY: *Where you from, pardner?*

FLYNN: *I happen to come from Ireland, but I am as American as you are.*

That got to be a trademark in my American films.

There is a difference between the average Western and a big spectacular. A Western was generally batted off very quickly, at a certain price, and for example, no matter what Randolph Scott said or did, the picture sold, like Johnny Wayne's do.

But the big spectaculars, *Dodge City, Virginia City, Silver City,* were made with an enormous budget and created in a very different manner. The studio spared no expense, because they paid off in a big way. Jack Warner knew what the public wanted and gave it better than anyone else.

I felt I was miscast in Westerns, but this was impossible to point out to producers when the pictures were so highly successful. It was most frustrating, it stopped my trying to act. I walked through my roles, jumped on that old horse, swung my legs over that old corral fence. My heart wasn't in it, only my limbs. What was the use? I felt. I couldn't get out of my contract and couldn't get Warners to see me in other acting roles. While I couldn't understand the public buying me particularly, I could understand the Western, the frontier story, as a classic form of national entertainment. It is part of America's heritage, our history. Everybody knows what a Western is about. The title would be enough to tell you, expressive, simple, native, like *Stagecoach.*

I am not denying that the Westerns are wonderful entertainment. I love to look at them as well as anyone. I just wanted to act, to have a chance to play a character, to say good-by to the swashbuckler roles, to get swords and horses to hell out of my life. I itched to turn in a prize-winning job—but they held to making money: box office! box office!

The ruin of creative personalities.

The Nazis invaded the Low Countries. Pearl Harbor was bombed. Hollywood began to make more anti-Nazi and pro-Allies pictures. I was in several of these vehicles, *Dive Bomber, Objective Burma, Edge of Darkness.*

One of the few pictures of which I am proud is *Objective Burma.* Jack Warner wasn't around the studio at the time, so Raoul Walsh and I made the picture, but it was Jerry Wald's baby. I was not the producer, but I had my way with many of the creative aspects.

Sometimes make-believe is not so far from reality as you might suppose. Sometimes make-believe is reality and presents reality better than life itself. Often pictures seem more real than the things they're supposed to portray.

We simulated the conditions of the Burma campaign. We had a technical adviser who had actually been all through the whole British retreat. He was a Britisher, a Major Watkins. He had been gravely wounded there, and Jerry Wald, with his flair for bringing people together, dug him up for counseling on this film.

That picture so delineated the conditions in Burma that even people who had been in the Burma campaign came out of the theatre asking, "What part of Burma was that?" They were dubious, disbelieving, when they were told that was Santa Anita Ranch in California, the ranch of Lucky Baldwin. We built sets there so lifelike that even the experts couldn't tell them from the originals. Warner Brothers took a lot of trouble over location, under very trying circumstances, to make it rough, rugged, tough.

A contribution I made to that particular picture was to introduce the technique of silence. The silence held the suspense. I know it kept the audience on the edge of their seats. A musical score would have ruined it.

The film got a different reception in England. In that country, which gave me my accent and my histrionic training and was my motherland until the time I took out American citizenship, you would have thought I was the representative of the State Department in Washington, telling the British that not only were Americans winning World War II, but that I, Flynn, was doing it singlehanded.

The Lord Chancellor yanked the picture after the first showing—for the English press flipped with rage. Even so, a large crowd was out there, in Leicester Square, to see the picture the following night. Almost an international incident had begun.

In a cartoon in one of the biggest newspapers in England, I was depicted standing triumphantly with the American flag, my right foot on the grave of a British soldier.

Actually *Objective Burma* ended with a shot showing a horde of American planes flying triumphantly over Burma. That might have been good for American morale at the time, but it sure made the English feel bad.

Even His Late Majesty King George VI asked me—later, at a command performance—in a puzzled way, "Mr Flynn, what is this talk that always makes people laugh about you when they mention Burma?"

I hardly knew what to say, all I could think of was, "Sir, apparently the picture proved conclusively that I took Burma singlehanded and it was a pushover, sir."

He laughed, but looked more puzzled than ever.

What I should have said was that the Americans didn't mean to imply that they had won Burma. It was unfortunate that the picture came out when the British were still licking their wounds after a disastrous retreat, and my heroics in that picture, together with the unsubtle point that the Americans were arriving in time to save all, touched a lot of English people on the raw.

But why blame the actor? He does not decide to make a picture. He does not produce the picture or write the screenplay. He is only expected to be entertaining.

Ever since then I have been the butt—often to my amusement—of cartoonists. They usually gag it something like this. The cartoon shows trouble, for example, in Lebanon. A real war is on, and there is a peasant standing nearby who doesn't grasp that it is real war. He's been to movies aplenty and he quips, "Must be a movie company on location here; wonder when Errol will arrive."

My dog Arno, given to me by Robert Lord, a producer, became very famous about Hollywood. Everybody knew the dog. He went with me to the studio, on my yacht, even to night clubs once or twice.

Arno got lost at sea during one of my *Sirocco* trips. I felt pretty bad. I got a call from the Coast Guard saying Arno was identified by his collar. They asked me if I wanted to claim the dog's body. I said no, just send me the collar. I buried the collar in the animal cemetery I had in the rear of Mulholland House.

The movie columnist Jimmy Fidler printed an item saying in effect: *Errol Flynn, whose love for his dog Arno has been much heralded, didn't even bother to go get his body when it was washed up on shore. That's how much he cared for him.*

Just that, but it was enough. Each man mourns in his own way and no one can tell another's feelings.

A little later I went with Bruce Cabot to the Mocambo. As we arrived Cabot remarked, "Hey, there's your pal Fidler."

At that moment I mourned Arno afresh. I walked over to Fidler's table. He saw me coming through the dancers and got up with a smile, ready to extend his hand. I said, "I won't dignify you with a closed fist but—" and I gave him an openhanded wallop, hard. He went over the dance floor.

At that instant I felt a sharp pain in my ear. His wife had picked up the nearest fork and jabbed me with it.

Jimmy brought me into court on a charge of assault. I tried to lighten the proceedings with a crack, "The lady obviously has good table manners. She used the right fork."

Jack Warner was upset because it became a national scandal. You are not supposed to bop the press. Today Fidler and I are excellent friends.

By now, when I walked into Jack Warner's office I could enter without qualms. I even plunked myself down and stretched out my feet. Once, as a sign of bravado, I kicked off my shoes and yawned.

In my incessant balks with Jack over salary, story, direction, the way things were to be done, I had the problem how to overcome his particular charm. He usually threw me by opening up with some funny story. By the time he set the mood, my heat was diminished and I got the worse in the ensuing hassle. One day I decided to get the jump on him. On the way to his offices I passed a fire station. There were fire buckets about. I borrowed one. Before going up I painted on the red bucket in large white letters, TEARS.

I walked in with this bucket.

"Hello, Baron," he greeted me. That was what I was usually called. "Have a cigar? Have a drink?" Always trying to calm me down. No thanks, I said.

His eyes fell on the fire bucket. "What the hell is that?"

I turned it around so he could see the inscription. I said, "Jackson, this is for you and you'll need it after you hear what you're going to pay me."

He burst into a gale of laughter. This time we got right down to business without having to go through his usual jokes, which so often threw me to the point of making me forget what I had come to see him about.

There was one who could tell off Jack with even less hesitation than I, as I learned one day when I was in the presence of Jack and his wife. I can remember Jack's friendship with Anne Warner before their marriage. After came the familiarity, the possessiveness, and I suppose you would call it the deep love of two people. With these wonderful things came this:

Anne had displeased him and he was yelling at her. She gave him that rather wonderful look she alone has—eyes wide. "Jack," she said coolly, "you know where the gates of Warner Brothers are?" That's the white line down the middle of the whole lot. Twenty-two big sound stages.

"What are you talking about?" he said.

"Jack, get this straight. I'll cut that studio lot right down that white line. I'll take stages one to twelve! You take your half, I'll take the other!"

For some people like Jack and Anne there's something to be said for the marriage institution.

Outside his office Jack Warner has an endearing sense of humor and can outcomic most of the comedians I know. I stress *outside,* because inside his office you are confronted with all the ruthlessness of business in Hollywood. That's Jack.

Sometimes he's almost knocked me off my chair laughing, especially the time there was an important luncheon for Madame Chiang Kaishek. This distinguished lady rose to her feet and spoke of the troubles of Nationalist China. At one point she paused, and in the silence Jack's voice came over loudly saying to someone, "Jeezuz, that reminds me. I've got to send my laundry out." I doubt if the lady from China caught the idea, but I almost had a seizure, trying not to laugh.

Greer Garson was the first actress I worked with who was fun and helpful. Many of the other ladies with whom I had been associated either were a bit in awe of me, or else hated me.

But in *That Forsyte Woman,* with Miss Garson, I really felt for the first time that I had a character role. I don't know whether I can convey how deep the yearning is of an actor who has been stereotyped, who has that sword and horse wound around him, to prove to himself and to others that he is an actor.

All those Hollywood years a ghost haunted me: it was the ghost of my young self in England just arrived from that ribald adventure across the world, and working at a whole variety of roles at Northampton for a year and a half, doing everything, anything: playing a father, a butler, a rogue, an adventurer, a clown, a killer, a cop, anything.

I had that single sweet taste far back in England, till someone discovered I could look dashing pointing a sword, and bound that sword to my wrist for two decades.

I worked hard for this role in *That Forsythe Woman.* Now I had the opportunity to show maybe that I could do something else. And it was a joy and a delight to have Greer playing opposite me.

I think that that picture was one of the few worth-while vehicles in which I played.

The popular conception of Greer is that she is a kind of Mrs. Miniver: finely bred, the epitome of English cultured womanhood. She is all this, but at the same time a mischievous imp.

Most people on the lot held her in awe, including the high brass at Metro-Goldwyn-Mayer. When I heard I was to do a picture with her, I built up a nervous reaction which I knew would be fatal.

I had to do something about the nerves that were working up in me. When the time came to meet her I primed myself with about three vodkas. When I was introduced, I adopted an air of bravado, the hearty Australian from the outback. I shook hands heartily, then I slapped her on the fanny. "Hi yuh, Red!" I said.

Everybody froze.

There was a brief pause. Then she went into a torrent of laughter. That broke the ice. Later I told her how nervous I had been.

Making the picture, which was a great success and landed us a command performance in England, there was a scene in which Greer was dressed as a dignified Victorian. She knew the scene so perfectly that I figured a little levity wouldn't throw her. At one point she had to go to a wardrobe room, open the door, take a dress out and start putting it on. When at rehearsals I saw that she was quite at ease in the bit, I got into the wardrobe myself.

I crouched there, like a figure in a waxworks, clad only in a top hat. She went through the scene, as she was supposed to, first singing, then saying, *"Now, Mabel, I'll put my dress on."*

I became Mabel. I screamed in a high falsetto, *"Here I am, honey!"* She jumped and dropped everything.

Greer got even a few days later. We were shooting a scene in a Victorian carriage. I was supposed to be very pompous. I had my gold-headed walking stick between my legs and I played this scene looking straight into the camera, with a stiff grip on the head of my gold cane.

There came a time when I had to open the door and say, *"Now, my dear, shall we alight?"*

We didn't. But I sure as hell did. Because as I touched the doorknob, the electric contact Greer had fixed right in the seat of my pants made me go through the air like a witch riding a broom.

These childish things were good for the studio's atmosphere, I found. They loosened up everybody. They relieved tension. These gags, while they might appear juvenile, did much to lighten the air.

At least for me.

Apart from constant inner qualms about the kind of vehicles they put me in, I was engaged in warfare with my principal director, Mike Curtiz.

Mike was a talented man, probably brilliant, but relentless in his demands. I detested him because he was making me into a stereotype. I disliked comparison to the late Douglas Fairbanks. The worst thing that can happen to you is to be typed after or compared with some insurmountable legend which has preceded you. This was happening to me. Warners was making money off my dashing, slash-bang roles. And Curtiz was the director who whipped me on to such performances.

Our association came to an end at the Warner Brothers ranch one morning on a road covered with huge California tarantulas. The action was all shot here.

Mike had the charming habit of blaming everything on everyone else. As the star I was often given most of the blame.

Curtiz was standing on a high parallel. I was to wheel my horse around and engage in a sword fight with a fellow. This is not easy, even though we had worked out every detail—the horses move, anything can happen. To avoid losing an eye we had guards put on the swords. But during the action I received a cut on the cheek and started bleeding. The scene stopped and the doctor attended to me. To my relief it had missed my eye.

A friend came to me, told me that Curtiz had made him take the tips off the swords. The last straw! I leaped up the twelve-foot parallel to get to Curtiz—I'll never know how.

I grabbed Mike by the throat and began strangling him. Two men tried to pry me off. They succeeded before I killed him.

That was the end of our relationship. I deemed it wiser not to work with this highly artistic gentleman who aroused my worst instincts.

Tensions such as that on the lot led me to create an environment of fun around me in my nonprofessional hours. A corps of actors who worked with me in most of my pictures aided and abetted me in providing the community with a little color—or off-color.

Alan Hale, called the Sarge, and Gwynne "Big Boy" Williams, known as the Corporal, and myself as the Colonel, were a triumvirate of shenanigans pullers. I always tried to keep the three of us together, in pictures and in my private life off the lot. Big Boy was bowlegged and he weighed two hundred and fifty pounds. I worked with him for years. He's a rough, tough Westerner whose face is familiar to millions of movie-goers.

Big Boy had been going with that fireball Lupe Velez, which was another misalliance. There was never a more oddly assorted couple. Once, in the course of an argument with him at my house, she picked up a framed photo of him, beat him over the head with it, broke the frame, and nearly broke his head. She took the picture out of the frame, tore it into two pieces, then peed on it on my carpet. That incident was followed by a bit of additional violence outside of Mulholland House, and that led to the end of their rather poetic association.

One of Big Boy's inexplicable hates—and I don't know the basis—was Orson Welles.

Welles had always wanted to meet John Barrymore. One night, not long after Welles arrived in Hollywood, they met.

Welles wore a beard in those days. Perhaps that is what inspired this dislike of him in Big Boy—to the point where he went into a store with me one day, purchased a great big ham, plastered a beard on it, and sent it to Welles—his way of showing disapproval.

This night several of us were gathered around a table at Mike Romanoff's. Mike's place had just opened. A lot of us came to his support, for he was a very popular figure, a self-proclaimed bum in those days, but a character and a lot of fun. Jack Barrymore, Pat O'Brien, Big Boy and myself were at this table.

For all his enormous size and strength, Big Boy was a hypersensitive fellow, and if he felt he was slighted in any way, tears would come to his eyes and drop into his drinkin' whisky, as he called it. Jack thought Williams was amusing and liked him enormously . . . me too.

Orson made one of his dramatic entrances. He stood at the door, filling it, his beard outthrust like a challenge.

Pat O'Brien glanced over. "Hi—there's Orson Welles."

Big Boy swung around, glaring.

Barrymore, absent-mindedly, for it was late in his life now and he was drinking heavily, looked puzzled. "Orson Welles?" he inquired. "Where's that?" He was under the impression that Orson Welles was some kind of watering place or spa, like Tunbridge Welles, or Baden-Baden, some place where you take the waters.

Pat knew Orson. I didn't. Neither did Jack, neither did Big Boy.

I could feel Big Boy stiffen. Those tremendous muscles went tense against my arm. He took a big breath, filled with dislike.

Pat called, "Orson. . . ."

Orson approached our table. "Hello, Pat." They shook hands across the boards.

Orson was the boy genius of the day. He had everybody's attention. Everybody in Romanoff's looked up to see him at our table, impressed with his size, his bearing and his sudden Promethian reputation. I personally had a tremendous respect for him as a showman, aside from his being a hell of an actor.

Big Boy kept staring at the Easterner rancorously.

Finally, in his low growl of a voice, Big Boy said, with emphasis, "You—stupid-lookin'—bastard!"

Welles' bushy eyebrows lifted.

Big Boy enlarged upon his theme. "In all my goddamn life I have never seen a more hammy, stupid-lookin' piece of blubber than you!"

I, from one side, gave him a jolt in the ribs. Pat O'Brien, on the other, must have done the same, because Big Boy grunted as if an Indian arrow had got him.

Then a fragmentary silence.

Big Boy said, "I would like to try that beard"—as if it were phony. And one big paw came up and pulled it.

The beard didn't come off.

Affronted, Welles took a measuring look at Big Boy, probably one of the most powerful men you could ever find. He growled in that famous voice, "Sir, obviously we had better go outside and settle this."

That tickled Big Boy. "You silly bastard! *You* go outside with *me?*"

Even Barrymore for once was silent, though he naturally enjoyed it. Anything like this pleased the Great Profile.

I thought a helluva lot of Orson's guts at that moment, for he was obviously no match for Big Boy. I hissed into Williams' ear, "Listen, you clunk, shut your trap! Leave the guy alone!"

Big Boy looked at me like a little boy, appealingly, but rebuffed. He decided to take the matter no further.

I got up and said, "Sir, it has been a great pleasure to meet you."

Welles, in ruffled Shakespearean style, decided that there was no point in making any more of it. That night he had all the guts there was in Hollywood.

Alan Hale was the film menace, the most feared character actor in Hollywood. He was such a good actor that if he was with you in a scene he could take it away from you, whether he was standing behind you, beside you, or in front of you.

He was full of tricks.

Other actors of, say, my stature, hesitated to play with Hale because he was so good. Luckily for me, he liked me, so he never pulled any of his scene-stealing with me. He could have stolen every scene, but he didn't. As a picture was being made I'd say to him, "Alan, if you poke your nose behind me, I'll jump on your goddamn instep."

He taught me a hell of a lot.

For example, take the playing of a very intense scene. Now a man in such a scene, who isn't vital to the success of the shot, all he has to do is twiddle his ring, look at it a bit, and the audience's attention is diverted. Alan would go so far as to turn his back and give you the impression he was yawning. That stole a scene easily. You can fix your belt in an interesting way and the attention is diverted to you instead of throwing the scene where it rightly belongs. That is scene-stealing. It is bad manners and Alan—bless his heart—was an expert at it.

I got him and S. Z. "Cuddles" Sakall together one night at Mulholland.

Sakall was a funny old guy. I always liked him for his screwy, mushy personality, but most other actors hated him. He messed up the English language so much that they couldn't get their cues. I let him run on. It was fun to see the effect of him on the other character players. He ran off with many scenes, and that was enough to make him despised by the others.

Hale couldn't stand him. They hated each other and refused to work with each other. To see them together was like a meeting of two prima donnas at a tea party. Naturally I brought them together as often as I could, and on this night Hale hollered, "For Chrissakes, Zakall, ain't it time you learned to speak English? You been here long enough!"

"And for vy I should spik Englich better, ven mitt dis Englich I em makin more vot is you!"

You can work in Hollywood for eighteen or twenty years and not get to know many of its leading figures and not ever meet, more than casually, many of its celebrated stars. People are surprised to learn this. What, you don't know this one or that one? Often I have had to disappoint people by telling them I have never met some notable.

Hollywood studios have been putting out five or six hundred pictures annually for a long time. These pictures have been filled with actors, directed by directors, written by writers, and Hollywood is packed with thousands of people. Only a few dozen reach stardom or international note. Often these artists live in circles of their own. Each may have about him a retinue of aides, secretaries, hangers-on, servants, friends. They work. They have a job to do. It is steady going. They may all gather once a year for Academy Awards and they may then be under one roof, but you don't know them.

In my case, as soon as I finished a picture I ran off to sea, to New York, or South America, any place I hadn't been before. I didn't stay around for Hollywood's parties. While you are working you don't always have the time or the desire to get over the town and mingle with big shots because they are big shots. After you work, you feel like going home to dinner, perhaps do some reading, have a few friends in, then a bath and to bed. I tried to get to bed by midnight, for I had to be up at 6:30 in the morning—and generally made it by 2 A.M. Breakfast, then off to the studio for a day's work. The same round over and over, and it left little time to gad about meeting this one and that one.

But in the six or seven years I had now been here I did get to know more or less many of its topflight characters. I came to know Charles Chaplin rather well. Charlie liked to play tennis, me too, so occasionally I'd be at his house. The outstanding thing to me about him was that while he was gay and witty and charming, unless every bit of conversation centered around him he was deadly bored. He used to have wonderful parties because he attracted the artistic crowds: the most interesting artists and painters. I have seen him go through his steps in the front line of the ballet that he invited to his house.

I was a little better acquainted with his wife of the time, Paulette Goddard.

In that period before World War II I did make the acquaintance of many who, in one connection or another, I have continued to know up to this day.

I can never understand why Sam Goldwyn, whenever he sees me, points at me and bursts into squalls of laughter.

I say, "Hello, Mr. Goldwyn." That makes him slap his leg hard, and he repeats, "Mr. Goldwyn! Haaa—Earl Flinn!"

In Rome, in Sicily, at his famous parties, wherever I have met him this has happened. I have never been able to figure it out. He spots me forty feet across the room, and as soon as he does, this Goldwyn laugh comes out. Not with anyone else, mind you, only with me. With others he growls.

It gave me a complex. What is so funny about me? It's enough to make a man lie awake at night, wondering.

One time at Sam's house I decided I would find out what was so comical about me in his mind, so I sat down beside him and began,

"You know, Mr. Goldwyn——" I only got that far. Again, tides of laughter.

I waited till the latest subsided. "Mr. Goldwyn," I ventured. "There is one thing I've been curious about for a long time. Why is it, whenever you see me, I seem to be some figure of fun?"

This rolled him in the aisle. It was the funniest thing to him, aggravating to me. I said, "Listen, Sam——" His laughing began again . . . I talked louder. "Mr. Goldwyn——Sam——you always seem to find me so funny. If so, why don't you"——he was trying to listen, his mouth half open, still gargling on the latest laugh——"why don't you find a comedy for me that you could make?"

This was the biggest of the lot. He didn't stop laughing——his belly seemed to be hurting. I pondered——what's so mirthful about me?

Because of my desire for fun, gaiety, entertainment, because I am understood to have a sort of humor myself, I sought out, if I sought any particular type, the comedians. I liked to play comedy in the films from time to time. But speaking professionally, I hate comics. I loathe them, hate their guts.

It is no trouble for me to call them to their faces parasitic bastards, and I always will. (That doesn't go for you, Durante.)

Because these comics have, in good part, been living off me for a long time: Flynn jokes. Mention my name, it seems to get a laugh out of a portion of the audience. Like the old vaudeville actors who, to make sure they got applause from the audience, trotted out the American flag.

But individual comics . . . well, there are always exceptions. . . . Jimmy Durante is such a winsome and essentially humble man that *sweet* is the only word I can use for him. He has the warmth of the really great comic as opposed to the aloof snobbery of Charlie Chaplin. Their egos developed in completely opposite directions. One is humble; the other thinks he is God's gift to the world, although you must respect him for his work. It always struck me as a queer paradox that Chaplin, who should know more about humility, having invented the great feet-apart clown, should never have adopted the same humility in his private life.

Jack Benny you have to take as a wonderful guy. I doff my hat to him, because Jack is considerate and kind, although very definite about the job he is going to do. He is a born worrier. He is worried he is not going to be funny at the next performance. I went to Korea with him and I found him the most thoughtful man off stage, and the most self-centered on stage, that you could ever meet: which is good. As to that gag he always plays to the hilt about being a tightwad, he is the most generous guy you could know.

Now George Jessel, there's a different kind of wit. He is the best ad-libber of them all, and even the comics admit this. Another generous warm heart, who for some reason known only to himself, calls me Max Flynn.

But Fred Allen was a man of very little patience. He was intolerant of inferior talent, and as a great natural wit himself, it was rather surprising that he should not have had more compassion for the newcomers: but he never gave them a chance.

Two who used to go stark raving mad at autograph hunters were Bob Benchley and Jack Oakie. I used to pay little boys and old ladies a half-dollar apiece to ask Benchley for his signature, after I had given one. Bob's cheery, kindly demeanor would change. The national humorist would go as red as a turkey cock and he'd shout, "Get out of my way, you little idiotic swine! Leave me alone!" It was well worth the fifty cents to watch him blow up.

Jack Oakie was one of the best-natured men. At one time I knew him very well, but I haven't seen him in fifteen years. Kind, wonderful company, a charming conversationalist, a congenital humorist. But as soon as he was asked for an autograph he also changed color like an octopus, the smile left his face, and he too called the fan everything.

Jack Barrymore took years dying, stalling his exit. Each time he made a recovery his friends, Decker, his brother Lionel, and others gave up. They decided he might really be immortal.

When he finally died, none of us were there.

Repeatedly we would visit him at the hospital as these fatal periods beset him. He would be in a coma, but he managed to come out long enough to ask for a drink or to say something that would at once be repeated all over Hollywood.

He had so much personality that he charmed one nurse after another into bringing liquor to him. They had to keep firing nurses as each new one would decide that this man was entitled to his bottle. Once when

I visited him he explained one of his techniques. He got hold of a bottle of eyewash. He poured the eyewash out and filled the bottle with gin. He would take the top off, put it to his eye, and when no one was looking, switch it to his mouth.

If Jack had found himself alone in the middle of the Sahara, he would have come out with a case of gin.

On the second to the last time he went to the hospital he was in a coma for four days. Everybody rushed to see him. Was he going to pass away or not? His hands were swollen, legs, too, and he was unable to move. Finally his eyes opened, slowly.

He looked up and saw an apparition. This was a nurse noted for being the toughest, roughest, ugliest woman in the hospital. She had shoulders like a wrestler's and a great nose so long she could have smoked a cigarette under a shower and not gotten it wet.

Jack beheld her and didn't know but what he had been consigned to the other side.

He couldn't move. Only his eyes could turn. He said weakly, "God!"

He breathed heavily. Then paused a little. He looked at her again and said, faintly, "Well . . . get in anyway, honey."

In Gene Fowler's biography of Barrymore, *Good Night, Sweet Prince*, the author closes the account of John's death on the night of May 29, 1942, with these words:

> . . . Decker went in to see Jack. He made a sketch of his friend.
> Then, at ten-twenty, Barrymore's breathing no longer could be
> heard across the hall.
> After sixty restless years, he had found the Grampian Hills.

That is not exactly true. He made one more visit on earth before they carted him off to the Grampian Hills.

Jack's body was taken to the Pierce Brothers Mortuary on Sunset Boulevard. There is a big gruesome-looking clock outside which ticks off your life for you.

A group of us gathered at a bar called The Cock and Bull for a general expression of our sadness at the passing of the great romantic. I was particularly sad. I had come to know John pretty well in his declining days and had even felt favored by the three horrible weeks he had invaded my place. With our group was the great and imaginative director, Raoul Walsh, a man with an offbeat sense of humor.

Raoul had once been an actor. He was driving along on a location in the Mojave Desert when a jackrabbit sprang up and went through the windshield. He lost his eye and had to wear a patch afterward. That was the end of his acting career.

Walsh left The Cock and Bull early in the evening.

"I'm feeling badly, fellows. I'm so broken up at John's passing, I'm going home."

"Good night, pal."

But he, Bev Allen and Charles Miller went down to the local undertaking parlor.

Walsh said to the caretaker, "Mr. Barrymore's crippled aunt can't come here herself, but she'd like to have a final look at her beloved nephew. We'd like to take the body to her—just for a while."

Saying that, Walsh offered him $100.

"I can't do it, sir. It's against the law."

"I'll take him in my station wagon and have him back in an hour," Walsh doubled the offer.

Walsh and his friends took John's body out of the back exit of the mortuary in a rough box. They stored the box in the back of the station wagon and drove John to my house.

The entrance to my house was dark. My servants had gone to bed.

They got into the house and brought the corpse inside. They moved my favorite chair in front of the door, so that I would see the chair as I entered. They sat Jack in the chair, propping him up.

I was drunk—sad drunk—when I reached home. I walked in, sad and alone.

As I opened the door I pressed the button. The lights went on and my God—I stared into the face of Barrymore! His eyes were closed. He looked puffed, white, bloodless. They hadn't embalmed him yet.

I let out a delirious scream.

I turned to run out of the house. I intended getting into my car to flee down the hill away from my place, away from myself.

As I got out on the porch I heard voices behind me, from the inside. Out came Walsh and the others.

"Hold on, Errol, it's only a gag."

A gag! I went back in, still shaking.

They took the body back to the morgue. I retired to my room upstairs shaken and sobered. My heart pounded. I couldn't sleep the rest of the night.

It was no way to remember the passing of John Barrymore.

Yet I forgave Walsh. He brought this distorted touch of genius to his films. In his films he always introduced strange little ideas, those touches which are the mark of the man of true talent.

I was with Walsh at Jack's funeral. "Uncle" Raoul took a look at me. He said, "Jack would get up out of that box if he could see who was carrying him."

The pallbearers were the persons he most hated.

One of the consequences of my association with Barrymore and the Olympiads group which circled around him and John Decker was the development of an art interest which was to stay with me permanently.

The first fruit of it occurred when the Nazis went into the Netherlands. A slight black-market operation brought into my possession one of the great Vincent Van Gogh pictures.

It had been owned by a Dr. Gachet, the personal physician to the artist at the time when Van Gogh cut off his ear in the whorehouse. The doctor had received it in payment for his services and the art work had stayed in the Gachet family for several generations.

At the time when Hitler marched, this painting was owned by a son of Dr. Gachet. The son heard that Goering, who collected heads and art, was about to send to his home for the picture.

The painting, called "The Man Is at Sea," was smuggled out of the back door before the soldiers arrived. It was rolled up—a difficult thing to do with a Van Gogh canvas because he laid his paint on so heavily—and smuggled out of the country.

I do not know how. Probably God doesn't know either. But it went to Uruguay. From there it went to New York where it landed in the hands of an art dealer named De Orio. He knew that I was looking for art masterpieces, but they must be the very finest, the best of a Master's work.

The word was relayed to me that this canvas was available. I bought it.

I took it back West with me to Mulholland House. There I hung it and invited a few people in to see it.

The connoisseurs say that this Van Gogh was done during the artist's most creative, turbulent period. The picture has always been emotional to me because of its reality and symbolism.

I too had been at sea in my youth, in one way, and destined to be at sea intermittently ever afterward. I was also at sea in my effort to find out what things meant.

I am still at sea.

In August, 1942, I received my naturalization papers. I was an American citizen. The country had been good to me. It had given me wealth and an international reputation. I was grateful. While I didn't like what I conceived to be the mediocre character of some of my pictures, or most of them, still I was in, I was making them. Others would have liked to make even these Westerns, quickies and box-office films.

I was surrounded with lovely women. I had a beautiful house. I was finished with Lil—I thought. Why complain?

I couldn't have it better.

PART FIVE

Head Hunters of California

1942-1943

O_N this particular night, late in 1942, I was alone in my Mulholland study.

My valet Alexandre came in trembling like an autumn leaf. Two men are at the door, he said in French. They had shown him some official papers, also a policeman's badge.

"What do they want?"

"They say they must see you."

I laughed. "What the hell are you shaking for? They're not here to see you. Go on, let them in. . . ."

In came two dicks. They were in plain clothes but I could have told, on the street, a hundred feet from them, they were police. Plain-clothes men usually look more like police than uniformed cops. You get to be able to make a fine distinction like that after you've had your share of contact with these necessary gentlemen. They were quite pleasant. "Come on in, gentlemen."

Have a seat, I said. Did they want some coffee, or drinks perhaps? They said yes, they'd have coffee.

I didn't know then never to talk to *two* policemen if you are alone. I know it now. Two coppers will outweigh anything you have to say.

After a minute or two one of them said, "Mr. Flynn, we have a very serious charge against you."

What had I done?

"Well, your accuser is in Juvenile Hall and we've come to take a statement from you."

"What's it all about?"

A pause. Then, "Statutory rape."

My smile disappeared in a hurry. Rape? I didn't know what statutory rape meant. I didn't know the difference between statutory rape and rape.

Rape to me meant picking up a chair and hitting some young lady over the head with it and having your wicked way. I hadn't done any of these things.

"I don't know what you're talking about."

"It concerns a Miss Betty Hansen—and we are holding you."

311

"I've never heard of her. Betty Hansen? Who is she?"

"She's a teen-ager and she's been picked up for vagrancy. Among her possessions we found your phone number, and she has claimed that you had sexual intercourse with her on a certain date."

"Where was this supposed to have happened?"

"We're not supposed to tell you, Mr. Flynn, but it happened at the house rented by your friends, Stephen Raphael, Bruce Cabot and Freddie McEvoy."

This was a big rambling place, with a tennis court, owned by Colleen Moore, of silent films. The sporting crowd foregathered there to bet on tennis matches, to swim, play cards, Ping-pong, poker—amusements practically always instigated by Freddie. It was a bachelor's house, rented by famous and/or moneyed bachelors, and it was a place I frequented. Usually it cost me a lot to go there. My friends took my money like Jesse James robbed a bank; they were skillful card players, congenital handicappers. In any case there were always lovely girls around.

But for the life of me, I couldn't recall any Betty Hansen with whom I was supposed to have gone to bed—whom I had raped.

"What am I supposed to do?" I asked them.

"We'd like you to come down with us to Juvenile Hall and identify the girl."

"But I don't know any such girl."

"Well, look," they said, "we just want to clear this matter up. It might be nothing, it might be something, we don't know. She says that you were all playing tennis. She seemed to know everybody at the house there, all your friends. She gave a detailed description of the act."

"What did she say?"

"She said she could even describe you. You got undressed but you kept your shoes on."

"Good God! Tell me, what does she look like?"

"She described you as sitting on your chair, then you took her upstairs and—"

All of a sudden a picture flashed before me, and I saw again the scene that was behind this horrible accusation. I could remember somebody sitting on the edge of my chair. Many of the girls had sat on the edge of the chair or around it. I recalled this particular one being overfriendly and I recollected getting up out of the chair.

"You don't mean that frowsy little blonde?—Is she a frowsy little blonde?"

"Yes, that's the one!"

Those were the worst words I could ever have said, because eventually they were repeated to her, and, being feminine, she naturally resented this description. Also, as it turned out, she had been threatened by the authorities with four years of detention in Juvenile Hall, and with these two things, she would swear to anything—and she did.

"Look," I said to the two dicks, "I must call my lawyer right away."

"You don't need a lawyer."

When you hear a cop tell you that, brother, always get the lawyer!

"This is my house," I said. "Sit down. Have another coffee, or drink, whatever you want!"

My mind was in absolute turmoil.

I called up Robert Ford, a young Irish lawyer just beginning his practice. He was the son of a famous lawyer, a fine guy, a guardian of my interests.

"Bob, there are a couple of boys here, from . . . " I turned to them and asked them where they were from. From Downtown Los Angeles Police Department, they said. "That's where they are from, Bob, Downtown Police Department. What am I to do? They want me to go down to Juvenile Hall. They say I screwed somebody. I know I didn't. It's very late and I don't know if you're in bed, but if you are, Bob, I don't give a damn. Get out of it! Get on down there. They said they'll arrest me if I don't come under my own steam."

It was late at night, but down we went to Juvenile Hall. That was a long ride, done in silence now, no more fishing from them, no more biting by me. Why I should have been called upon at this hour I don't know; they could have waited till the daytime, but I discovered then that there is sometimes a narrow line between how crooks and police find it necessary to work. Get the guy when he's tired—his mind isn't with it.

As we entered Juvenile Hall, I asked, "You won't mind waiting till my attorney gets here?"

"Oh, he's here already, waiting outside."

Bob took over from there.

"What's the charge?" he asked, inside a gloomy-looking office.

They told him. He wanted to know what was the idea of their bringing me down here.

"Under the law," they explained, "the accuser and the accused must confront each other."

They brought in a girl, dressed in some kind of uniform which they put on kids unfortunate enough to get into this kind of place. At once I recognized her as the one who had indeed sat on the arm of my chair. To my utter astonishment. I said, "It can't be!"

I mean she was gruesome-looking.

They said to her, "Will you repeat the charge?"

She hung her head and said, "Yes. He took me upstairs." She talked in a low, monotonous voice, as if by rote. "They had been playing tennis, then they played some cards. He took me upstairs, undressed me, and then he—he—he—" She ran out of words. "You know what I told you," she said to the police.

Bob Ford asked, "Did you put up a fight?"

"No, no. Why should I?"

They turned to me. "Well, what do you say about this, Mr. Flynn?"

"Utterly untrue. Certainly I met her. True she was at the house. I don't know how she got there."

Actually I was thinking very fast. I did remember that there was a young fellow called Armand, somebody who was more or less in charge of inviting girls to this house for the boys who were living in it. I am not suggesting that this was a den of animals. On the contrary, it was mainly devoted to sports, and gambling, but it was a bachelor's house and "ladies" rarely object to visiting a bachelor's house in Hollywood.

The officer said, "That's all."

The girl was led out.

I drove home with Bob. "How did I get into all this?"

"Did you or didn't you?" he asked me.

I said no.

"I believe you."

The Los Angeles District Attorney's office apparently decided that they had a very weak case against me on Betty Hansen, but having leveled this charge they got a bit frantic. They dug up another girl whom I knew, a certain Peggy Satterlee, and my lawyer phoned me to get set for a second charge.

At two o'clock in the morning they went to the night club where this girl was dancing, brought her down to headquarters, and by whatever means and through whatever threats they used, they got her to tell of her meeting with me a year earlier. It had taken her a year to discover that she also had been raped by me. Now there was no question that I knew this second young lady very well, and I did not deny it. Peggy Satterlee had been out on my yacht, the *Sirocco,* for a weekend.

If you meet a young lady who, in fact, invites herself for a trip on your yacht—"I'd love to cru," she said, in the vernacular unknown to yachtsmen—knowing in advance full well what the risks are, who the hell asks her for her birth certificate, especially when she is built like Venus? And if afterward she tells you she has had the most wonderful time in her life, who has been hurt? What is all the fuss about? Why international headlines? Who approaches a prospective sweetheart by asking her to whip out her birth certificate, or driver's license, or show a letter from her mother? Naturally I had no knowledge of how old she was, nor did I know the difference between rape and statutory rape.

Statutory rape as it is now defined is actually a nineteenth-century improvement on an older law designed to protect infant girls against degenerates. The law is quite clear. If you have had carnal knowledge of a person or persons under the age of eighteen, you can go to jail for five years or more, whether or not—and this is important—she consented. It doesn't matter if you had no way of knowing she was under eighteen, or even if she actually tells you she is over the so-called age of consent. Broadly interpreted, it could even mean that should a powerful girl under the age of eighteen knock down a man, sit on his chest, put a knife to his jugular vein, and say that if he didn't overpower her she would cut his throat, he could still get five years in jail for doing as ordered. That would be stretching the law, but that is actually what the law says.

While this hadn't happened to me, they could definitely prove that Betty Hansen was underage—she was seventeen. Yet to this day nobody knows for certain how old Peggy Satterlee was; although it appeared later, from a driver's license she owned, that she was twenty-one.

So here I was faced with four charges of statutory rape, two on each count, and scheduled to go before the Grand Jury two days later.

The District Attorney's office lost no time in giving the story to the newspapers. It caused, at once, national, even international, headlines.

Errol Flynn Charged with Rape

I didn't sleep much in the period before the Grand Jury session. I tried to imagine what effect my troubles would have on my father, who was Dean of the Faculty of Science at Belfast. What would my mother, my sister, think of it?

Crowds swarmed around the courthouse. The people were strung out in front of the place, and I wanted to shrink into the ground with shame. The mere idea of force or rape was unthinkable. Who had to hit somebody over the head with a chair, or trip them up, or smuggle them across a border? On the contrary, where was my baseball bat to ward them off?

Women banged on the doors of Mulholland House like icedrops in a hailstorm. I had to bolt the doors against them. I had proposals of marriage every day. I got letters from women setting up dates, hours and places where they would be waiting for me, ripe and ready, and they didn't wait for a written reply. They went ahead with their plans and when I wouldn't show up I suppose they were disappointed. But this wasn't New Guinea, where I was alone with palm trees. I was a big Hollywood star, and female flak burst around me all the time. So what the hell was this charge of RAPE?

Somebody was out to put the screws into me. Who was it? What was it?

Still I held my head up, I must go into this with a fairly dignified demeanor. It came back to me how, as a younger man, I had set out to acquire a dignified look, the manner of a man of means, of stature and pride, how I had deliberately squared my shoulders, stood erect, held my head up imperially, and practiced moving about with a certain hauteur—in the belief that you can make yourself what you feel, what you want to be, that if you act great you may become great. Now I needed this force again, needed to see over the heads of this crowd, of this situation, and face it with an air of courage, even if I didn't feel confident inside.

The girls told their story to the Grand Jury. I told mine. Freddie McEvoy gave evidence supporting what I said about my knowledge of the Hansen girl—and the Grand Jury was swift about it. They saw something stank. They promptly returned what is called a "No True Bill."

This meant they believed me; not the Prosecution.

So—rather quickly—it was over with.

Freddie and I went back to Mulholland House. The load was off my mind. We celebrated my acquittal by opening a bottle of champagne. Freddie said, "Christ, you're lucky, pal."

Still it had been turbulent, and I tramped around my place loosing profanity at the walls, at the mystic forces that seemed to have been out to get me. It was all a goddamed torture, and I hollered, "To hell with Christ!"

Freddie, a devout Catholic when he felt like being so, shouted back, "That's blasphemy! Don't say that. You will be sorry."

"To hell with God too! This is a crooked thing!"

I couldn't sleep. I stayed awake, hanging around the fireplace, wondering why I had been singled out for this business.

Maybe I shouldn't have cursed God.

Freddie had gone to bed, so had Alexandre. I was alone, stewing over the incident, when the phone rang. My number was unlisted, so I presumed some friend was calling.

"Hello."

The voice at the other end said, "Hello, Flynn?"

"Yes, who is this?"

"That don't matter. Listen, Flynn, you got a lucky break—"

"Lucky break about what?"

"You know about what—downtown. You got a lucky break."

"That's a matter of opinion. Anyway, what's on your mind? Who are you?"

"I am not identifying myself," this man said. "But I will tell you something. If you know what's good for you—" Then he asked, "Do you know Jack Warner?"

"Of course."

"Well, just ask Jack if he knows Joe. Just say 'Joe.'"

"Joe. He must know a million Joes. Why should I?"

"Just tell him Joe called you. If Warner only knows what's good for him and if you know what's good for you, you will just drop a little thing called ten G's at the corner of Melrose and La Cienega."

"Repeat that, will you?"

"Okay. I'm telling you now, if you think you have been hit, don't wait. Get ten G's down there, or brother, you will never know what really hit you. Today is Monday. I will give you two nights to get it there, otherwise, brother, on Wednesday you will have had it."

I figured I was talking to some crank, so, before hanging up, I said, "Oh sure. Ten thousand dollars? How would you like it? In nickels or dimes?"

"Okay, wiseguy, I guess you don't know what's good for you. You'll find out."

"Why don't you go to hell?"—And I hung up.

I paid no attention to this. I figured it was just some crank.

I supposed I was a free man. The charges took only a few minutes for the Grand Jury to throw out. In cases like that, where the Grand Jury has refused to indict, perhaps not in a hundred years has the District Attorney's office gone any further—although under the law, the District Attorney could proceed.

That mysterious telephone call couldn't have hit the nail more on the head.

On Wednesday the District Attorney's office announced that they were going to override the Grand Jury's decision and proceed against me on the same charges.

Everyone was flabbergasted—the studio, my lawyer, my friends. When I heard about this I was holding in my hands a cablegram from my father. He had indulged in a bit of whimsy. He had learned of my acquittal, and he cabled: HOW WAS IT ANYWAY?

When this new announcement was made, Bob Ford quickly realized that he shouldn't handle it himself. "This is very serious," he said. "There is only one man for it—Jerry Geisler. I'm going to retain him if I can."

"Bob, do what you think best."

Geisler had a wonderful reputation. But he did not come cheap. I was told that when Geisler took the case of Busby Berkeley, who was charged with manslaughter for being drunk and killing three people, it cost Berkeley a fortune to have Geisler defend him.

Geisler agreed to take the case.

I was taken down to the police station and fingerprinted.

I found myself sitting on a long bench next to a fellow, and at once he gave me the lowdown on jail conditions in the vicinity.

"What are you here for, Errol?"

"Rape."

"Ahh, that's nothing."

"What are you here for, brother?" I asked.

"Kidnaping. That's ten."

"Ten what?"

"Ten years," he said, "but of course I'm innocent."

I turned to a colored fellow sitting on the other side of me. "What are you here for, pal?"

"Murder, but of course I'm innocent."

Then he asked me. "What are you here for?"

"I'm innocent too, chum."

Bob Ford was in another part of the courthouse trying to arrange bail. Jerry Geisler was in conference with the District Attorney's men, and my colleagues with charges against them continued chummy with me. One guy said, "Errol, don't get down to Lincoln. They don't give you a break down there. The County Jail is the best. You can't get it better, kid. For Christ's sake, a guy lives well here. The boys get a break. And they ain't a bad bunch of guys . . . "

"Who?"

"The wardens. Who else? They're all crooks, like us—"

Jesus! I thought, am I one of the "boys" already?

This same informant went on. "Of course the best thing can happen to you, you are sent to the Honor Farm. There it is fine. You are out in the sunshine. All you have to do is try to get a rake, and scratch up something."

I listened appreciatively, wondered whether I had influence enough left around town to get a rake. He went on, "You ought to be able to make a rake job, Errol. Don't get none of them shovels. Jesus, you've got to dig! I have blisters on my hands—"

Somebody else cut in. "Nah, nahnah. A soft spot's the dispensary. A big shot like him, he could get into the dispensary maybe. Another soft spot is the library. Jesus! That's a good idea. Try and make the library, Errol. Sit down on your ass and you read."

On all sides I could see and feel nothing but disaster. The idea of books cheered me up a little, but not much.

They took me up to the top floor to measure me. If I went to prison, I was going to have a nice striped suit, one that fitted me well, and if I tried to make a prison break, maybe a coffin.

What nobody knew but Freddie and myself was that I had made up my mind that I would never let them send me to jail on this deal.

I had made arrangements to have a two-motor Beachcraft sitting out at the Burbank airport, because I knew I could get out on bail—and if the thing looked bad, unbeatable, I was going to leave the United States forever. I would head first for Mexico . . . and from there . . .

Jerry Geisler never asked me whether I was guilty or innocent. Not once in the next five months of trial operations. Maybe he was afraid I was, and didn't want to know it. But at the outset, in my first talk with him, I told him of the mysterious telephone call I had, and I pointed out to him that things had happened just as the guy on the phone predicted they would.

All that he said was, "Very interesting." Nothing more.

Geisler, with his own special genius, discovered by talking with the District Attorney's office, knowing downtown politics, looking into the present and recent political picture in Los Angeles, that there appeared to be a whole political force at work to get me—men with their own axes, ambitions, motives.

He didn't tell me what he uncovered, but he did tell Bob Ford. He discovered the following:

The previous District Attorney, Buron Fitts, had been the protector of Hollywood's big names in squashing any kind of complaints. The big studios naturally supported him generously in his political campaigns: so much so that he had been in office three terms, and that was an almost unheard-of thing. Since he had made three terms, it looked likely that he might win a fourth, so the big studios supported him in a race against an opponent, John Dockwiler, called "Honest John" Dockwiler. The studios, while they made large contributions to Fitts' election, had only made small token ones to "Honest John's" campaign, which was worse than giving nothing.

But in a landslide victory Fitts was knocked out, and "Honest John" moved in. He brought in with him, of course, a lot of sub-district attorneys who had to make their reputations. They had won the hard way, and they had vengeance in their hearts. They said, "Okay, instead of getting any preferential treatment the first guy of your lot who gets in trouble has had it. Watch."

I was the first guy.

Soon after the "Honest John" administration came into office these moves against me began.

Moreover, after this began, I had a very strong feeling—which by now was widely shared—that I was being railroaded for some unknown reason. I couldn't figure it out. At that time neither could anyone else.

But supposing there is a big political force, with its own objectives, out to get someone, out to make an example, out to get revenge for some party politics? You still have to do what Jerry Geisler had to do: you have to conduct your defense on the basis of the actual charges, the merit in the case, the specific counts. You couldn't try a political grouping. You might see and understand that this "throwing of the book" at someone was a consequence of internecine local politics, but a defense had to be conducted on the basis of the actual complaints.

I had never been in trouble in Hollywood. But I was known as a roisterer. I was vulnerable, an ideal scapegoat.

For what went on trial, there in the Los Angeles Courthouse, was my personality and above all my way of life. Certainly it was a much more complicated thing than has ever been presented by the press, the magazine writers, the clowns who joke about me on radio and television, and the fellows around saloons who tell salacious stories.

Bear in mind that at this time although married, I was technically a bachelor, a man living alone. I had no evil practices. I did no one any injury. I wasn't even drinking much. I would have champagne around and if people wanted it they could have it, and I'd take a bit with them, but that was it. I was thirty-four, in my prime; women liked me, I liked them; nobody got hurt. I thought, Let's have fun, let's live by the sunshine, let's swim and play; let's make love, let's cruise in the Pacific, let's have pleasant parties, gay chatter; let's work, let's make pictures, let's entertain the people, let's be artists, if we can.

This was my balls, my way of living, breathing and exulting in this short swift act called Creation. Am I supposed to live as other people? Are they supposed to do what I do? Do I have to be made over into their image, and they into mine?

A man who is so overwhelmed by willing females has a special problem. Bud Ernst ribbed me unmercifully, saying it was the girls who were taking me—over and over again—and that I was incapable of "making" them. In fact he provoked my manhood by this, for it was true. My problem was not to get girls into my life, but to get them out—once they had "had" me. A strange story, of course, and one perhaps that men all over may envy, but it has been true, and it was why I got into this scrape of the five months that shook the world's glands.

There has to be something wrong with any man who says he is not interested in the company of the opposite sex. I am a man who likes female company. I always have and I always will. But I like having wonderful, gay people of both sexes around. I particularly like to have youngsters about, reminding me of how life is always renewing itself. In brief, I like people. I like to enjoy the thrill of living every day, every hour of the day, for we are here only this once, and let's feel the wind while we may.

For months the case drifted, with postponement after postponement. Geisler wanted and needed time. He had to prepare his defense the way a general plots a campaign. He told me later, "The whole secret of my success is preparation. You cannot go too far with preparation." He dug up everything he could on the young ladies; he maneuvered, he studied the law.

These delays seemed not to disturb the prosecution. They liked the big newspaper play. The new prosecutors were getting known about California.

But the press, remarkably fair to me, began to ask questions. What is going on Downtown? Who is out to get Flynn? Why has this specific actor been chosen for a going-over?

Hollywood's morals had often been criticized: now it seemed the incident had appeared which was to set off the whole question of the cinema capital's morality. This was the exterior look of the case as it loomed; but in back of it was simply this local political hassle, a payoff deal to get even with the big studios for not coughing up properly—Dockwiler, and a few prosecuting attorneys out to make their names over somebody's dead body.

During this period I neither heard from my people in England, nor did I write to them. Perhaps at most a single letter, to let them know my troubles continued. I only felt an uncontrollable sense of shame and involvement when I thought of them. Later I heard that they were stunned at the news of the revival of the action, but helpless. Beyond that, Belfast was being bombed heavily: so that my problems may not have been so noticeable in that community.

Lili was by no means out of my hair, though we were divorced. She began about that time an unceasing battle—continuing into the present—to take me financially.

Being single I could—and when I wasn't working—stay in my room and think or walk the floors. I could go out alone on the Mulholland property and walk with my anger and confusion, and I did.

The word "swordsman" had a double-edged meaning now.

All over the country people didn't know or care about the difference between statutory rape and rape. There prevailed in people's minds somehow the thought that I had forced these girls, made them surrender to my wicked way by getting them to do something they didn't want to do. Headlines never said or explained the statutory aspect of the charge; only they used that anciently harsh word which men and women all over the world despise: *rape*.

The war against Nazism went onto pages two and three, and my case covered five and six and seven columns of front-page space in papers all over the land. In New York—I have always been sensitive to the mood of the people there, the life of the press, and the cultural world located there—in that city the tabloid papers shot their circulation skyward. People came out, I was told, in queues each evening at eight o'clock to get the papers, to read the latest testimony.

The war effort seemed dragging to many. Government was embarrassed by the incessant calls for the opening of a second front. Everyone seemed to welcome something light and racy to keep their minds off the recent exposures of the horrors of concentration camps, to make them forget the terrible progress the Nazis appeared to be making all over Europe. Our troops weren't doing too well in the South Pacific.

In this international crisis of morale, in the democratic camp, the little forgotten isle of Tasmania came through.

I got to know the courtroom bailiff, Jack, very well as the trial dragged on. One day, while waiting outside the court, one of the tallest men I ever saw, long and slender like a telegraph pole, passed by, dressed in the uniform of the Salvation Army. He was being propelled by a guard. As he went by I did a double take. A midget woman followed him: he was so high, she so minute. I said to Jack, "What's going on here?"

"Section 288(a)."

"I am up on Section 288," I said, with a cozy sense of familiarity.

"Yes, I know," said Jack, "but this is Section 288(a) of the California Penal Code."

"What's that?"

"Any man that places his lips to the private parts of one of the opposite sex is hereby liable to ten years."

He went into details, told me something of the case of the State of California versus Harrison. "Something like yours," he added.

"What do you mean?"

"Look up the Harrison case, Errol. What happened between these two: the little girl is a midget and he is a Salvation Army guy, and they caught 'em. That's all I know."

"Who was doing what to whom?"

"Oh, I don't know . . . It's your turn now, Errol. Go on in."

I looked it up, too.

It appeared that there was another old Spanish law in the California Penal Code which has never been changed. Twenty-five years earlier a man named Harrison was out to get rid of dirty politics in Los Angeles County, and his political opposition decided to frame him. They dug up this old law when they supposedly got something on him. They burst open a window and took a picture of Harrison in bed with his wife, making love to her in what the law said was an abnormal way. The case went to trial, a judge was bribed, Harrison was ruined—even though the alleged offense was *with his willing wife*. It seems to me that that was their God-given business.

I reached the conclusion—a position I hold to this day, in the space age—that the trouble is: the California Penal Code hasn't come into the Union yet. Out in that State, King Phillip, or somebody, is still telling them what to do.

Jerry Geisler dressed immaculately, but in a plain way. Here was a man with force, but with no overbearing personality. His power lay in his latent strength. He kept his forces in reserve, for his work in court. To me he always seemed a bit distrait, which may have meant only that he was concentrating on the job: he wore a faraway look and usually he went about with a nice smile. He wore dignity as some wear fine clothes; and he had a high-pitched offbeat voice with charm and command to it. You couldn't easily define his mentality, except of course, as the legal community knows, he almost never loses—*almost*. He advised me beforehand, "Bear in mind that the District Attorney's office will say, 'This man is an actor,' and they will expect the jury to discount your testimony because you are trained as a performer." To this Geisler had his own answer. If and when this arose he intended saying—and he did—"Hasn't this man the right to his day in Court—as any of us?"

The trial opened. Inside the court all seats were taken, outside there was a jam of humanity. On one side of the room sat the press, by and large friendly to me, so friendly that I couldn't fully understand it. Geisler had advised me to co-operate with the press, and he talked to the newspapers freely. My legal help was limited to two men: Geisler and Ford. The prosecution had a battery of eight attorneys headed up by a prosecutor named Cochran.

Some not surprising instinct guided Geisler into selecting a nearly all-female jury: nine out of twelve of the "good men and true."

Prosecutor Cochran put Peggy Larue Satterlee on the stand. She was a beautiful girl. Her upholstery was sensational. Her waist was a lovely molding. She had long, dark, silky hair, and could have passed for anywhere between twenty and twenty-five.

Yet when she came in, I hardly recognized her. They had put her in bobby socks, flat-heeled shoes, and *pigtails*. She could have looked like my kid sister. My heart sank when I beheld her. Migod, I thought, she looks like a baby. Yet a week or two earlier she had been in a chorus dressed scantily, to say the least.

While Peggy gave her testimony I sat at my desk, listening hard and concentrating on a pad of paper onto which I wrote notes. Occasionally I looked at her or at Cochran—a furtive glance—and I seemed to need the actual physical warmth of Geisler on my right and the young Irish lawyer on my left.

Cochran asked her to tell how, nearly two years before, she had yielded to me on board the *Sirocco*. We were cruising to Catalina, a weekend jaunt, she said, and I had kissed her at the companionway of the yacht. Then, she said, she had gone into her stateroom, and I followed her.

Then came the juicy dialogue that the newspaper boys—and the public—were waiting for. The White House must have been a little grateful to have the war news taken off Page One and some of the fire deflected elsewhere.

Question: Who kissed you?
Answer: Why, Mr. Flynn.
Q. What did you do?
A. I went to the stateroom and went to bed.
Q. What happened then?
A. In about ten minutes there was a knock at the door. At the same time Flynn walked in, clad in pajamas. He asked if he could talk to me. I said it was not very nice for a gentleman to be in a lady's bedroom, especially if she was in bed.
Q. What did he say?
A. "If you let me get in bed with you, I won't bother you. I just want to talk with you."

Then, she tesified, I was intimate with her.

(At just about that time, when Peggy said it wasn't very gentlemanly of me to call at her bedroom, Warners released *Gentleman Jim*. A lot of merriment went around all through the country and elsewhere. Because I had a certain very apposite line of dialogue at the close of that picture. Alexis Smith, the girl, is almost in my arms and I say to her, *"How could I marry you? You are a lady."*

She says, *"I am no lady."*

Gentleman Jim slaps her, grabs her in his arms, kisses her and says, *"I am no gentleman."*

The wartime public was thrown into mild hysterics over this. In some parts of the country they even had to throw out this last line so as to prevent anything too raucous happening in the theatres.

Peggy also testified that on returning to port we were standing at the rail and she remarked how beautiful the moon was. "He said it would look much more beautiful through a porthole."

Apparently, she testified, we actually looked at the moon through the porthole. We went below, she said, I took a yachting outfit off her, and we had another session.

Question: How did you feel about this?
Answer: I was just plain mad this time, instead of scared as before.

I don't have to defend myself as I recount the trial. My lawyers did that and the jury arrived at its decision. Nonetheless the trial was an

American drama, and Jerry Geisler produced much of it as he handled the young ladies and the legal opposition.

When he cross-examined Peggy, employing a soft voice, and not at all the harsh accuser, he said, "Miss Satterlee, I am a little bit mystified. I have here a picture. Is this you?"

He showed her the picture.

Yes.

He made a clucking sound with his tongue two or three times, as if expressing surprise. He didn't show the picture to anybody in the court except her. But he said, "What a difference! Tell me, do you always dress like this?"

"Like what?"

"In bobby socks and pigtails?"

"Sometimes, if I feel like it."

"That's all."

Yet the effect on the jury must have been fantastic. They could only have wondered, "What has he got there?"—a picture she admitted was herself.

Peggy was smart, very smart. She stuck to her story. She described in minute detail how I lured her into the after-cabin and, as she said, pushed her onto the bunk.

In other words, she did not admit consent.

She was implying a knock-her-down-drag-her-out rape.

I pushed her up onto the bunk, she said, where I forcefully took her. Meanwhile I said to her, "Darling, look out the porthole. You see that glorious moon?"

That remark followed me around for years: Oh Errol, look at the porthole and the glorious moon. I rather suppose that that expression has become the dividing line of my life—everything that went on before the porthole and the glorious moon, and everything that has gone on since.

Geisler began his attack. He brought out a picture of the *Sirocco*'s interior, and he drew a counterpart of it on a blackboard. He asked Peggy how high the bunk was. She indicated a height not much above the knees. Geisler proved that the bunk was at least five feet off of the floorboard. He wondered, before the jury, if I had enough strength to get her up there forcibly, or whether or not she had enough strength to resist being put up there or enough strength to get down.

This kind of testimony went on for days. Yet slowly, steadily, the talented Geisler convinced everybody that these two young ladies knew what they were doing, that they were ambitious to become show girls, they knew and understood the risks of visiting a famous bachelor's house, or yacht, in Hollywood.

Thereafter Geisler battered down Peggy's claim of intercourse without consent.

January 1943 ended. The trial moved into February. Day after day the law dragged us all into this court. Those poor girls were pawns in the local political wrangle as much as I was. They were being drained and wrung out and so was I. There, in back of all this, was an age-old political pitch: a threatening of the big studios, someone getting even with them, saying, "You didn't shell out enough dough to us for the protection you want from an administration, we'll show you, we'll teach you not to buck us." There was my head on the block because Warners and the other studios had not picked the right political horse to back, hadn't paid off right.

Letters poured in from all over the world. One would say: *That is an outrage. You are being swindled by two gold-digging girls. They ought to be strung up.* Another said: *You lecherous swine! You ought to be hung. I hope they send you away for twenty years!* But few people then, and not even now, know how plaintiff and defendant were both caught up in a political whirlpool: how corruption, money, power, graft, stood in the rear, symbolically and actually, and ran the show.

But they didn't run everything.

I still had some will left: quite a lot of it, in fact, and some of that I directed to a very lovely-looking redhead who occupied a cubicle in the lobby entrance of the City Hall. Day by day I passed by her and watched how she sold chewing gum, cigarettes, cigars. It was easier to look at her loveliness than to stare into the wilderness of the mob that hung about the courthouse waiting to get a look at me. As I walked past there'd be shouts of "Attaboy, Errol." "Let her go, kid!" "You got 'em whipped, Errol." I hoped some of that would rub off on the jury. I listened to these cries of encouragement but glanced over to the cigarette counter at this slender girl with the lovely complexion, the bluish-green eyes that slanted up at the corner.

I didn't get a look at her figure for quite some time. Finally I stopped and bought some cigarettes. I stared beneath the lovely complexion and spotted just enough freckles to make it interesting. I craned my neck a bit over the counter, and saw that all was well. She had about a nineteen- or twenty-inch waist, hips to go with it, and slender ankles and wrists. All my life I have been partial to slender ankles.

The case was drawing near to its close. I would either be sentenced to jail or not. Under the law there was no such thing as a suspended sentence or a fine. None of these nice amenities. You either had it, or you hadn't. I had no intention of going to jail. My two-engine plane was out at Burbank, waiting, so that if I got a bum rap, I'd get out there, hop in, and leave America and my screen career forever. Meantime, the redhead behind the counter interested me to the point where something had to be done. . . .

I had a friend, Buster Wiles, a baldheaded fellow aged about twenty-nine, a stunt man and a daredevil—one of the best in movies. He had a Tennessee drawl, very thick, and he had a sense of humor and more charm than most cowboys or stunt men. I knew I had to meet this girl; it might be my last companionship of the sort prior to a flight over Mexico or, if I couldn't make it, a long spell in the clink. Apparently I hadn't lost my faith in the opposite sex. But I didn't have enough guts to make any advances myself, so it was Buster into the breach.

He charmed her into agreeing to come to Mulholland House for "tea" —which would turn out to be a slug of champagne. She was invited to come up with a girl friend, just to put her mind at ease—and up she came.

I had to go about this very slowly. She had read the papers like everyone else, and I had to watch my technique—do no rushing whatever. I treated her with what I can only now think of as exaggerated courtesy. I even greeted her with a hand-kiss on arrival and the same hand-kiss upon her departure. Very bad manners, of course, since she would presumably be a virgin. In the Kissing-of-the-Hand Department, you only kiss the hand of married women. I skipped this point of protocol, knowing she would never know the difference. I was rewarded for my gallantry with a shy simper.

Having decided to take things slowly—bear in mind this was in the middle of the double statutory rape trail—it took me about a week to advance the hand-kissing stage up her arm. However, I was careful not to make the deadly proposition, or at least not to rush it.

There was a certain precaution that I took before all of this. I carefully checked her age. She was eighteen, safe ground. Her name, it turned out, was Nora Eddington.

What I didn't know was that her father was Captain Jack Eddington of the Los Angeles County Sheriff's office.

Betty Hansen had her day in court.

It was now February 15th. I understand that throughout the nation the newspapers were feeling the pinch of a newsprint shortage, partly because of the war effort and its needs, and partly because their pages were being filled with extra columns of testimony at my trail. I may or may not be joking about that.

Geisler had the seventeen-year-old Betty on the stand and was most kindly and sympathetic toward her as she began her testimony by identifying herself as a drugstore clerk. He was almost fatherly as he led her to admit that the prosecutors had stressed to her that she could be held in Juvenile Hall for four years if she didn't testify properly. All this he brought out by indirect cross-examination without even seeming to try, and it appeared to me that what he said was having its effect upon the jury.

He examined her about the alleged act, almost as if he were her lawyer, not mine.

Q. What did he do when he came into the den, as you call it?
A. He told me he was going to take me upstairs and lie me down.
Q. Then what did you do?
A. We went upstairs.
Q. Then what did you do?
A. We went into a little bedroom off the big bedroom where there were two twin beds. He sat me down on the bed and told me he was going to put me to bed. I said I didn't want to go to bed and that I wanted to go downstairs around with the others. Then he said, "You don't think I'm really going to let you go downstairs, do you?" And then he got up and went into the big room and I heard a click and I don't know if he locked the door or not.
Q. Then what did he do?
A. He came back and he started to undress me. I thought he was just going to put me to bed, like he said.
Q. What did you have on?
A. I had on slacks, a blouse, brassière and teddies. He took off everything but my shoes and stockings. Then he took off his clothes, all but his shoes.

Q. Did he have on socks?
A. No.

(Right then they had released *They Died With Their Boots On*. The press had a circus with this testimony.)

Q. Then what happened?
A. Then we had an act of intercourse.

Geisler tore into her at this point. He was out to show consent. Hadn't she been going around saying that Flynn was good-looking. Hadn't she been playing up to Flynn?

A. Yes.
Q. But you didn't mean to play up to him all the way?
A. No, I didn't.
Q. You thought you'd played up to him far enough when you let him remove your clothes?
A. Yes.

Geisler said, "You say that Flynn removed your slacks. Didn't you want him to take them off?"

She hesitated a minute. Then she made the remark that may have endeared her to the grammarians but not the jury:

"I didn't have no objections."

Through all such testimony I sat with clammy hands. I felt I was growing grayer by the day. Downstairs, in the lobby, I had a new-found redheaded friend, but this wasn't enough. The unrevealing face of Judge Stone was always before me, and I prayed for the day when this horror would end.

There were technical delays; twice they tried to throw off the jury one man who spoke out of turn. The prosecutor wanted to get him bounced, but Geisler didn't want a retrial, knowing the kind of cost and misery involved, so he blocked those motions. Naturally the politicos in and around the D.A.'s office would have liked this case to drag on for years while they stayed in control.

Betty Hansen said I had locked the door before getting undressed. Geisler set out to prove that there was no lock on this door, or that it wouldn't work. The prosecution sent sleuths around and they found evidence of steel scrapings on the floor, proving somebody had tampered with the lock. Actually I am pretty sure somebody had. It was none of my doing. But it caused a great outcry when they brought in these steel scrapings and swore they found them under this supposed lock that wouldn't lock. That was a dark day. It looked as if my legal help had somebody go out there and frame this thing.

Another time there was an incident that sent everyone in America to their dictionaries. Somebody, in testimony, used the word "crumpet," which I think is an English cookie. But this was construed as strumpet, which is a different kind of cookie. There was a debate in court over whether the girls were crumpets or strumpets, and there was a spill-over of this row to the press, which sent everybody skedaddling to Webster's to see what he had to say.

In the midst of all this I had a the-show-must-go-on stint to do. I remember working with David Butler, the director, on a film called *Thank Your Lucky Stars*. Warner Brothers convinced the stars that it was their patriotic duty to do this picture for nothing. Each of us had an act to provide. We were not to get paid and the proceeds were to go to the Hollywood Canteen. We all thought this was a good idea and everybody kicked in with a performing bit. The film made a lot of money, some of which the Canteen got. What Warner Brothers hadn't told us was: since it was their distribution, they were getting a big chunk of the proceeds out of the bottom drawer—through distribution. And while the motors spun out at Burbank, and the trial raged on, I had to fit in some time to go and do this number, sing and dance and try to look gay and carefree.

A song-and-dance routine, when, to pile on the contradictions, I had never been a song-and-dance man. David Butler was astounded. He said, "I don't see how you can do it." I still don't.

One day the judge ordered the jury to consider the evidence and come in with a decision.

The jury was out about four hours. I looked out into the streets. The way the crowd was massed outside reminded me of a mob scene that Cecil DeMille might have been filming. Would I be thrown to the lions or not? Would the old Spanish statute, of another day, hold for Hollywood in 1943?

As the jury filed back in I felt myself go numb. There were four counts and each had to be read out.

I felt Jerry's hand on my leg, gripping me like an eagle grasping a rabbit. He didn't know or wasn't sure what was going to happen, any more than I, but this was his way of showing his feeling for me, and his gesture took away some of the numbness.

I heard voices.

"On the first count—Not Guilty." Jerry's hand gripped tighter.

"On the second count—Not Guilty." Again his hand tightened.

"On the third count—Not Guilty." He gripped so hard that I felt the circulation had stopped in my leg.

"On the fourth count—Not Guilty!"

The courtroom broke into cheers. Judge Stone didn't even try to quiet them. He let the outburst go on. When the noise inside court settled, I heard a din from the street.

I got a strange choked feeling, a stopped-up emotion that seemed to hold on. I couldn't talk: only sit there and gulp and choke and try to smile at Jerry.

I wasn't wearing a hat, but I touched my hair—to the ladies—as if I were wearing one.

When the air settled, Judge Stone congratulated the jury on what he considered a fair decision. I was grateful to hear that, and grateful for the applause in the court.

It left an enduring scar but also another kind of emotion: the thought that the common sense of people will always prevail. I might have been as guilty as hell—under the law, that is—but in the world of day-to-day common sense, where the ebb and flow of existence can't always be measured to the dotted i and the crossed t of living, everybody knew that the girls had asked for it, whether or not I had my wicked ways with them.

Besides all this there was nothing that the prosecution could bring out to show that I had in any way been unfair or unclean. I think in the public's mind nobody objects to making love, providing it is in a decent way. The public hasn't anything against sex per se: but if it had been brought out that I had been perverted, salacious, sexually offensive, why then, no matter how innocent I might have been, I would have gone up. Nothing like this could be brought out.

I supposed that Jerry Geisler was going to charge me a hundred grand, as he did others.

On the contrary, his fee was only $30,000. It cost, of course, another $20,000 for expenses.

Subsequently I saw him from time to time. In my ledger, a wonderful person and one of the great attorneys. He claimed that of all the witnesses he had, I made the best. What he meant by that I still can't figure out: maybe he meant I made the most skillful liar under oath?

There was a sequel to my costs of the defense.

After the five months of hell ended, I began to nurse a grudge. Warners, for whom I had made a lot of money, had not helped. They had been neutral, like Switzerland. I figured they should have stepped in to my support, instead of staying on the barrel.

I asked Jack Warner for an interview. Because there is something personal about this, I said, I want it in a very private place. So the talk took place in a projection room, a place a little bit bigger than a telephone booth. Hal Wallis, who was the big producer for Jack at the time, was present. By now I was as cagey as an old crab in a trap.

"Jack, I am coming right to the point. This has cost me, apart from all the misery, $50,000 in cash, which I didn't really have and still don't have—and I feel that Warners should help."

He laughed. "That's a hell of an idea. What makes you think that? You are off, aren't you? The public still wants to see your pictures, don't they? They want to see them even more than before."

"That is very fine for Warners. It's not much good for Flynn. After all, I don't get a piece if my pictures get bigger."

"Oh, yes you do. The public thinks you're great."

"I am talking about money. I think Warner Brothers should kick in."

"You are out of your mind! Why should we—for Christ's sakes! Is that what you came here about?"

"Yes, I will tell you why. I got a telephone call—" and I repeated the conversation I had one night at Mulholland, early in the case, when somebody tried to shake me down.

I told Jack. "Joe said that you would remember . . ."

Jack Warner said, "Joe who?"

"That's what he said you would say. 'But you just tell Jack it's the Joe that went to him for ten G's.' You remember that?"

Jack's expression changed.

He turned to Hal Wallis thoughtfully. "Hal, you know something, the Baron has got a point there; he has got a point; he has got a point. We ought to do something for him, Hal."

This is the way he did something for me. He loaned me $50,000, at 6 per cent interest.

So it cost me more money in the end.

I never got back the costs of the trial. I had to pay back that $50,000, plus the interest.

Ostensibly I won the case. The people had vindicated me. There was applause for the verdict, and the crowds thronged into the theatres to see my pictures and get a double laugh: to laugh at the film fare and to enjoy seeing the man who gave them so much entertainment over and beyond the call of picture-making. A new legend was born, and new terms went into the national idiom. . . .

A GI or Marine or sailor went out at night sparking and the next day he reported to his cronies, who asked him how he made out, and the fellow said, with a sly grin, *"I'm in like Flynn."*

I picked up some letters that I had written to my father from New Guinea many years earlier. I asked him to send me a few of those letters, I wanted to look back at what I was in the lonely jungle of the deep Pacific, and compare myself with what I was now, and see which figure I liked better. At that time I wanted so much to live. In October of 1931, I wrote to him from Laloki Tobacco Plantation where I had just built a furnace and concrete firebox inside a tobacco-curing barn. I thought I built this very well and I said: *This one is all right though and should still be here in two hundred years time, barring earthquakes. It is a depressing thought to consider that at the end of that period of time I shall most probably not be here to enjoy the fruits of this labor.*

At that time I regretted I wouldn't be around two hundred years later—that was how interested I was in living.

But now, sitting around Mulholland, those first thoughts of death, destruction, and suicide began to occur within me—which would not early or easily or perhaps ever vanish. I no longer had such an interest in living. I didn't give a damn, in fact. Much of the will to live had gone.

In a way I had conquered the forces of life—rather young. I had fame, fortune—and Nature had given me a unique physique. I had even had luck!

I had everything—ostensibly.

And yet I knew I had lost. I knew that I could never escape this brand that was now upon me: that I would always be associated in the public mind with an internationally followed rape case.

A FTER the trial I found myself relatively ostracized locally. I was thrown on my own resources again.

I slid back to where I was years before at Laloki. I pulled out the books. I closed the doors at night. I brightened the reading lamp and I plunged into history again. I reread Gibbon's *Decline and Fall of the Roman Empire*. I decided the Roman Empire had stood for a long while. Maybe I would too, after all this died down.

While I wasn't treated as a leper, uncertainty prevailed as to what would happen with my career. I didn't know then that the congenital disease of America is that Americans buy success, and almost nothing else.

I put on a house party. I thought I ought to start living again, seeing people, find out who my friends were. I did.

Mulholland House was loaded with flowers, liquor, lights. I invited just about everybody in the community to come to my house for an evening of fun. I invited all the big-shot producers, stars, directors and writers.

Along about the middle of the evening I realized practically nobody was coming. A handful of people showed, perhaps a half-dozen.

Orry Kelly went around the house laughing to beat his head off, slapping his thigh and saying, "Stella Dallas had a party. Nobody came to the party."

When he said that for about the sixth time and split laughing each time, I called up a studio where they had beautiful models. I had them round up about forty and rush them over. They blew in, the prettiest mob of young ladies you ever saw. They drank and mingled with the few guests.

I got roaring drunk, while Orry's words kept going through my mind. *Stella Dallas had a party. Nobody came to the party.*

I had tried a social comeback too blasted soon.

The thing had to be done in the American way. I had to have a picture that was a big success. I had to make with the box office in a huge way before my Hollywood friends would recognize me again.

Okay, do it their way.

That is exactly what happened.

My place had always been an open house to my pals. They came around, as loyal as ever, and party life resumed on an even bigger scale at Mulholland.

I did take some precautions, putting in several devices at the approaches to my place. If somebody stepped through the gate uninvited, all of a sudden fifteen floodlights would shoot on. The guy would be like a frozen steer wondering what the hell he'd stepped into. If a lady checked in, she was requested by a neatly printed notice on the door to have her birth certificate:

> LADIES: Kindly be prepared to produce your birth certificate and driver's license and any other identification marks.

One of my pals scrawled after that, *Preferably on your thigh.*

Sometimes I saw Nora Eddington, but it was, so far, a sporadic romance. I was pretty damned careful to check Nora's age. I had dark intents, but she was a withholding type.

While I believed I would be an object of scorn and derision, it didn't turn out to be that way at all. On the contrary, the whole country seemed to get amusement out of it. I expected to be an object of ridicule, but the opposite surprisingly happened. My box-office appeal went up, and with one or two box-office successes I was completely restored in the Hollywood community.

But it now had a rampant character. Public appearances were absolute hell. I would sweat a week before I agreed to open a Red Cross drive. You couldn't easily turn down requests such as these. You were bombarded with such demands, very very mandatory. Peremptory demands: appear here, there; and if you had been six people you couldn't get to all the places they said you must be. Before each of these events I would get a hollow feeling in my stomach. I didn't know what I would say, what I would do a week in advance.

When you showed up, you were manhandled. You might have six cops protecting you, and you and the cops would get overwhelmed. At one event in South America, people broke barriers. The police and I found ourselves trampled upon, so that I wished I was in something relatively mild like a Mike Curtiz production. My suit was torn to shreds. It got so I never wore a handkerchief, one lost that in an instant.

At Fort Myers, Texas, where I appeared for a polio benefit, I was met by a howling mob. President Roosevelt was there, and others of importance. I felt I was some kind of interloper, the way I was stealing their thunder, without intending to do so. They rammed at me, pulling my ears, trying to kiss me—men and women both—my pockets looted or torn, or my shoelaces pulled off and my shoes removed. Everybody wanting a souvenir. A mob hysteria that made it hard for me to keep my dignity. All the time I wondered Why? Because I had made some pictures, because I was freed of a rape charge? What the hell kind of national heroes do they have in this country?

The worst thing one could try to do was run from such a mob. Then I got tripped. Once when I was tripped and was trying to get up, I wished wholeheartedly I could sink back into the obscurity from which I never should have emerged. I believed that in my heart. It was all very well to see naked Ubangis in Africa, or the Aitape head-hunters of New Guinea doing strange dances, letting out shrill cries, patting themselves on the ass, but who would expect to see such demonstrations in the big cities of America? There was very little difference in the human behavior: the screeches, the howls. It made me wonder whether we have progressed very far from the so-called primitives when I saw such manifestations of mass hysteria.

In one way it was flattering. Yet I had the feeling there were scientists, idealists, even politicians who did more for society than I had done. Why was this adulation falling to me? Didn't they know what I thought of myself?

Every dog has his day. I had mine. I came in, I think, just at the point where the mass hysteria, the *curiosa Americana* about movie stars as public figures, had already become part of the national folklore. Gable, Cagney, Raft, Barbara Stanwyck, Bette Davis, Joan Crawford, Spencer Tracy, a number of others. A new court of St. James, off Catalina Island. Duke Wayne, the Earl of Grant, Lord Cooper, the Marquis of Cagney. We replaced Jesse James and the Dalton brothers in the national affections.

In back of all this there was a fellow inside myself who would say to me, "You are an impostor, Flynn. In real life you don't do any of the things you do on the screen. You are no more capable of that kind of action in real life than a choirboy."

Maybe that is why, in my private life, I went ahead, consciously or unconsciously, to live such a life of reality instead of just portraying it all the time.

All I know is: this is a different world than it was before the cinema. Before that time I would have stayed forever a bum; and the people who now are deposed monarchs and ex-kings and ex-princesses, they are often the bums today, and I have been living the kingly life.

One day I called my valet. "Alexandre," I said, "I want you to put this monogram on each of my suits underneath the handkerchief pocket."

"Why?" he asked.

"That is a good question," I said. "Why? That is what I want to know and I can't find out why. So I want this monogram sewed onto all of my suits."

I had drawn a squarish question mark, thus:

$$\text{?}$$

This, my own confusion, became my trademark. My own questioning of myself. Why? How does a man become what he becomes? Whom does he become? I do not know. I didn't know then.

But it pressed on my thinking so much that I felt I must carry this symbolism to gratify my own curiosity or torment, or to make people think.

I still wear a question mark beneath my handkerchief pocket on all of my suits. I am still wondering *why*.

I was now fair game.

Weird letters came to Mulholland claiming I was the father of this child or that. I used to get one very embarrassing letter from a place I never heard of called Little Falls. The lady would give me the news of "Little Errol." How he was getting along. "Why don't you acknowledge him? He looks so much like you." I had never been in Little Falls and I never dawdled with anyone who hailed from there. I started to keep a file of blackmail letters: threats, accusations, claims, knocks. I never read the fan mail telling me how much they loved me or how great I was: but these knock and blackmail letters were funny. Now the stack is three feet deep.

About six months after the rape case, two elderly people came to my business manager and said I was the father of their grandchild. My manager said the child was a cute little girl. "These people are going to be a nuisance. Why don't you take a look at the kid?"

His advice was about the worst I could get. But I was curious, so I went down to his office. Two elderly, apparently sincere people presented a small child. The business manager said, "All they want you to do is to take a look. If it's yours they know you'll do right."

All they wanted was $1,750 a week.

I walked around the exhibit. I knew there could be no resemblance to myself in the little girl except that she had two arms and two legs, but—you never know—

It was explained to me that I had taken the girl home in an open car, but with the top down at the time, and a dog in the back seat. She lived at the corner of a crowded Hollywood boulevard. There, in the front seat, at this busy intersection, I had had relations with her.

I said to myself, I am lucky if I do not wind up with the national title "Hard Way" Flynn.

The studio heard of this. I was persuaded, so as to avoid bad publicity, to settle this nuisance for about two or three thousand dollars.

But on my honor, I am too large a man for any front seat of even a 1959 model—and this was back in the mid-1940's.

A particularly good pal of mine is Hedda Hopper, the famous columnist, but our friendship was not cemented until the night I gave Hedda a good swift kick in the pants in public—and I think I may well claim to be the only one in my profession to have done so. Maybe you have to give somebody a kick in the pants sometimes to gain a friend. Whatever the immoral, this happened when I was taking Nora about and hadn't yet married her.

Hedda printed something about Nora which hurt. I can't remember what it was but I phoned her immediately.

Hedda said, "Hello, dear." That dear stuff fouls up the whole entertainment profession. Dear, darling and dearie. The knife is never far behind these three d's.

"Listen, you bitch, what do you mean by saying such and such?" I protested. "You know damn well it isn't true. You should have checked your facts."

"Keep your head on, honey." Hedda laughed. That maddened me more. "It must have hit home, eh?"

"I'm going to sue you."

She laughed even louder. "I couldn't think of anything nicer. If you do, I might get syndicated even wider." That was true.

"Okay, kid," I said. "There's only one thing for me. The next time I see you, look out. I'm going to kick you right in your fat prat."

It wasn't fat, I might add.

I was dancing with Nora at the Mocambo a few days later. Nora pointed to a woman behind her who, she said, was laughing at her. That did it.

I went over to Hedda and her partner, and when Heddsie's rear was turned, gave her a good one just where I promised. She let out a shrill sound and her hat flew into the air. She looked surprised.

I said, "You see, honey, I told you I would."

Hedda's humor never fails her—but for once it took a bit of time. Had it been anybody else with less of a good nature than she has, I'd never have taken the chance.

In Mexico in 1944, Nora and I were married and my first daughter, Deirdre, was born on January 10, 1945.

I got Nora a house in Hollywood. There she lived her life and I lived mine at Mulholland. This was the only way I would be married to anybody: separate house, separate lives, separate people.

I had a life to live, pictures to make: *Desperate Journey, Northern Pursuit, Uncertain Glory, San Antonio, Never Say Good-by, Escape Me Never, Cry Wolf*. The career went ahead, with better or worse stories. Mostly I walked through my pictures. I had my dissatisfactions with the vehicles, but I had huge expenses now that had to be met. I had to keep working.

Occasionally I would have Nora up to Mulholland for a weekend. She swiftly picked up the Hollywood ways. She learned to pal out with the screen people, go to the right places, she no longer talked like a Hollywood high school girl. She had learned to roll with the punch that had rocked her from obscurity into the circle of so-called Hollywood society.

I hired Nora's stepmother, Marge Eddington, a lovely birdlike little woman, to oversee Mulholland House. Marge spent much of her time there while Nora stayed in her own house.

Candidly, life with the Eddingtons, Nora and her stepmother, provided no pattern for the human race on which to model itself in any effort toward fashioning the perfect home.

One day I asked Ann Sheridan, on the lot, what she was drinking. It looked like tomato juice. It was, but it had vodka in it. I took up vodka drinking. Vodka has no odor. Nobody need know you have had it, that's the theory. Of course alcoholism is one of the slowest though most certain forms of suicide.

I still retained my looks, but avoided looking at myself in the mirror. I knew what I looked like. I had no vanity about my face, my build, my features. I even became disdainful of this—my stock-in-trade.

Inside I was smarting, terribly wounded from the scar of the rape trial. I knew now I would never get over it. Perhaps this was, in part, because the press began to take a fantastic interest in me, in everything I did, and they were always looking for a certain type of story— strictly sex. It wanted to report any and all activity and relationship I had with women. It seemed to think it wonderful and colorful copy. The boys and girls had been good to me in the rape case, damned good, so I decided to roll with the punch. Never meet the press unless there's something sexy to offer along with the drinks and learn to laugh at yourself first.

I was in New York, accompanied by Freddie. While there I was on a radio show. There is always a group of fans outside waiting to get your autograph or say hello. As we came out Freddie and I noticed an unusually good-looking redhead. I returned to my hotel and this redhead was already there with an autograph book. She had a charming smile, and besides, she was outside my apartment. When you are pursued that much, give in.

I invited her in.

I hired her as a nurse-secretary and sent her to a nearby shop to buy a smart white uniform. On one side of her white cap was embroidered the word NURSE, and on the other, SECRETARY. I decided to have her about to provide color—so that nobody would be disappointed.

This was absolutely platonic and she had no duties outside of upsetting my friends. Her job, when people were about, was simply to walk up to me wearing the NURSE hat and take my pulse, put her lovely red head down by my breast and listen. Then make notes. All this to be done deadpan, while I watched the expression on the faces of my friends.

Freddie had her services when he took a bath. Her job was to scrub his back. He loved a bubble bath and always had a small rubber toy duck floating in it.

Sadly this design for living broke up when the girl's boy friend came to the apartment and raised much smoke, demanding that his fiancée get out of this impossible situation with two such characters—and this ended the nurse-secretary deal.

The press watched me like hawks to find out who I was going with next and what the shenanigans would be. I fell into a pattern of obliging them.

There was a press conference at Mulholland. This time I meant to regale the lads and lasses of the Fourth Estate. I was now definitely going along on the line, "If I've got the name, then give me the fame."

While the boys asked me questions, I nonchalantly sat on a settee talking deadpan. Freddie was in the room.

Two beautiful young twins, in their early twenties, walked into the room stark naked. The boys stared.

The reporters pivoted their heads about as the naked girls walked chatting together, from one room into another as if nothing was happening at all; as if they were here because they were part of the Flynn retinue. Actually I didn't know these girls at all. They were models hired to do just this—this once.

"What the hell is this, Flynn—a gag?" one of the reporters asked.

"Gag hell. These are just a couple of my girls, ready at a minute's notice."

The girls casually walked back into the room again and went on into another room, not even looking at the reporters.

These boys looked stymied. Though I think they realized later I was satirizing.

Smarting under the growing legend of myself as blood brother to the god Phallus, I didn't let on. I smiled more broadly. I gave a good performance as the guy who just doesn't give a damn.

It was growing on me that I had had a hard time with ladies—to employ the term in a liberal sense—all my life. There had been no consolation from or with my mother. Lili had nearly destroyed me. Two women, pawns in a big political game, had been used to try to destroy me. Women I never knew accused me of siring their children. I was candidly disillusioned with the opposite sex, much as I needed the female of our species, biologically speaking.

It might surprise people to hear there have even been months, ladies and gentlemen, months at a time, when I was a celibate. If women are going to dominate me all the days of my life—that thought hammered through my mind often, resentfully.

This led me to make an experiment that confirmed my thinking.

Curious about what women discuss when they are by themselves, or what they might talk about in the specific atmosphere of the "can," I bugged the ladies' room at Mulholland. During a party, while the men were in one room and the women were where they were, their words came to our ears.

My God, what I heard! The things I learned about myself and my friends were astonishing.

These lovely ladies came out with the frankest talk. They said what they wanted to say when they thought they were alone. I couldn't figure why the ladies' toilet bred such confidence, one woman for another, but it did. I learned more about myself in ten seconds—the time it took to to put a toilet seat down—than in a year any other way.

And such language!

Any notion that a woman's mind is nobler, purer, higher, more decent, cleaner, or anything else gentler, or superior, to a man's is pure delusion.

What goes into the human mind, male and female, is no more or less than what is all around us, and the female mind takes it in and digests it and handles it and works with it just as the male mind does.

I claim, without any chest beating, that I can tell a woman's motive, if she is pleasant to me, almost within an hour. I have a pretty clear picture of what she is out to get. They have a better survival mechanism than their brothers, and if, as a matter of fact, this is a world of the survival of the fittest, women will certainly survive.

This business of a woman's mind being a mystery is a lot of crap to me.

Perhaps I have had a special kind of experience with women. Perhaps because women have often been aggressive with me, taking the initiative, openly wanting to hang my scalp on their belts, perhaps because of this type of experience I have been able to get an insight into feminine nature denied to others.

You can read all the books, articles, stories, that indicate women want and need "attention"; that this is one of the main things they expect and need from a man. Nuts. If there is one thing they like better than personal attention I'd say it was this: The man who for a woman fits the bill is the one who pays the bill.

We are all dependent upon some love and affection, no matter what form it takes. And I am not denying the part of love, warmth, human feeling in personal relationships. It is there, it is real. I am just saying that in the war between the sexes dollar bills change hands.

A sorry conclusion, but that has been my experience. It goes for wives, mistresses, ladies of the street—all of them. You may think they love your deep dark eyes, or your little beady red-rimmed eyes—whatever you have—but that is the conclusion I have come to—they are as interested in dough as they are in what they eat, wear and where they live, because they are one and the same. That may be only human and it may be right or wrong, but thinking that women are out for some rare romanticism is bull. I have had mistresses who put the bite on me from early morning till late at night, and the following day there were enough new purchases lying about for me to open a drygoods store. Wives want houses. They call it love but it spells h-o-u-s-e.

In the theatre the play's the thing—in real life the thing is the play.

I yielded, with a smile, to the now complete legend of myself as a modern Don Juan. There was even talk about the studio of my playing the part of the Don in a film—and a couple of years later I did.

But when I read the press I shrank. I was afraid to pick up the daily paper for fear there'd be a story in it about me, another of those humorous snide ones about the great swordsman and the swordmanship he did on the lot and off. Those yarns made me wince.

The reputation of being a great ladies' man produced certain effects on me when I was in the presence of women. I was afraid of this name that I had and, with most ladies—this will come as a surprise—I was hesitant lest I seem the forward, the aggressive person I was by reputation.

Gradually I moved into a condition of despondency that was similar to the panic and self-loathing I had when I escaped Lili and ran to the Spanish Civil War.

There I was, sitting on top of the world. I had wealth, friends, I was internationally known, I was sought after by women. I could have anything that money could buy. Yet I found that at the top of the world there was nothing. I was sitting on the pinnacle, with no mountain under me.

Over and over, in my mind, I saw those days in the courtroom. I couldn't wipe away the scenes. The headlines still blared. The word "rape" went through my thoughts. I now knew that everything in my life dated from before that event and after it.

Two and a half years had gone by since the trial, but the effect of it was as fresh as if it had just happened.

My principal emotion was that I was hoaxed by life, that I had become something other than what I set out to be. Now my name was simply associated with sex. I was a male Mae West, as it were. Me, Errol Leslie Thomson Flynn, son of the respectable biologist, student of Darwin, lover of culture—and nothing that I had wanted had happened. Instead I was in a swamp of Flynn jokes, dirty stories, snide innuendoes.

I had wanted to do something for people, for the human race. As a young man in New Guinea, despite the sharp practice I engaged in, I had also this other side to me—contradictory as it might seem—where I sought causes. Darwin and Huxley were my gods. The great Britons were my symbols. Lord Nelson my hero.

What was I doing with a sword in one hand and a garter in the other?

I knew that if and when my true condition was understood abroad I might, I would, be considered a figure of pathos.

How did I ever wander so far afield of my youthful ambitions? What would have happened if I hadn't met the movie man Swartz and taken him up the Sepik River and later played Fletcher Christian in a moving picture made in Polynesia? Would I still be a bum in the land down under? Would I have gone on and educated myself and made something of myself in England?

That which I had, my big house, my yacht, my bank accounts, seemed hollow. None of these could take the place of self-respect, which I had lost.

I know that many who have a hard time making five thousand a year will find it strange when I say that I was indifferent to my income of $200,000 a picture, that it meant little, that I was filled with self-disgust. They will say, "Waste no time feeling sorry for him." Nor do I ask anyone to feel sorry for me.

I am only explaining why I was ready to blow my brains out. The rich and successful can do this, for their reasons, as the poor can do it for theirs.

I walked through my pictures without interest. Beyond the personal humiliation that stayed with me as a consequence of the trial, there was a constellation of factors that made my professional guts drag.

I wonder if you can imagine what it might mean to one who believes that given the chance at good and great roles, he might be able to act, say, like a Barrymore—but never to be given the chance. Only to be given those sure-fire box office attractions—entertainment pictures that often didn't even entertain—action, action, action.

I felt used. Used by the studio. Used to make money. Used by the press for fun. Used by society as a piece of chalk to provide the world with a dab of color.

You don't get the feeling of being a man if you believe the world is treating you in that kind of way.

But I didn't run the studios. Producers run them. The money departments of the studios decided what pictures you made. If a stereotype makes money, keep the stereotype alive. Don't make a switch. Don't experiment, don't pander to an actor's whim that he might like to do something special, different. Keep the sword shiny, shoe the horse and turn Flynn loose on a new one.

I hoped for a few good pictures where I might have the chance to really act, to do something great—that this opportunity might help me to redeem myself for what I had become and for what I was known as. But there was no chance. There was always a schedule to be filled— scripts that came my way from the producers. Do this next.

At this time I worked in several pictures with a director named David Butler. He was an actor who became a director. He sensed my disinterest. He knew I didn't like my roles, and he adopted my own attitude about getting through a film. "Well, Flynn doesn't care. I don't care. Let's get the picture done."

My disinterest showed in my screen portraiture. Your inner spirit, no matter what character you are playing, shows. The camera is that powerful. If you have a world on your mind and on your shoulders, if you are distracted, you cannot concentrate as an artist must. Moreover, I was playing youthful and virile roles, cowboys and swordsman roles, and such parts require gusto and genuine inner interest—such as I had felt at the time I was making *Captain Blood* and *Robin Hood*—but I no longer felt that way. My second-rate feelings came across in the finished product. Even my screen laughter was different, not really mine. You can then easily get a reputation for being a poor actor, a mediocre performer. I knew this, yet I couldn't control it.

All I could do was become more disconsolate.

All my life the one thing I feared the most was mediocrity—and my whole living effort was to oppose ever being or becoming a mediocrity. I did not wish to live in a mediocre way, nor to be regarded artistically as a mediocrity. This to me was the cardinal sin, to be middling was to be nothing.

I had the feeling that I was slipping into professional mediocrity. This alone was enough to make me suicidal. Better to kill yourself, Flynn, than have them say, "He can't act. He never could." Yet everything that was happening to me was destroying my gifts of feeling, which you have to have in order to act.

Feeling was the one thing I had been robbed of in the Los Angeles courtroom.

I looked back ten years. There had been a period after *Captain Blood* was made when I was living with Lili. I had so much belief in the validity of creation that I decided to write a book. In a few months I wrote *Beam Ends,* the story of a five-month boat trip from Australia to New Guinea—a documentary account of the trip I made there with the first *Sirocco* when I was about twenty. The book made no great impact in the field of literature, but it answered a need in myself.

It dawned on me now that I was beaten as a writer too. That dream had been shattered. I had chosen to be an actor, to make big money, to become famous, and I had put by a deeper yearning to write. Had I made a mistake? Right now I admired the writers around Hollywood more than I did the actors. I had only added another stone to my pile of confusion. Nothing I dreamed of had matured.

I was placing figurative bullets into my soul and it was only a matter of time before I'd try real ones.

I wasn't much of a parent. I had a son and daughter and I hardly knew them. I was stretched between two homes in Hollywood. I was no success at a matrimonial life. I doubted I was any genuine help, as a parent, to either of my children.

A few people around me knew that I was in great personal distress. About this time Sheilah Graham, in a dispatch to the New York *Journal-American,* wrote:

> Errol Flynn is far from being the happiest man in the world at this point. Not only is his domestic life chaotic, but he has to make a Western as his next movie and Errol is fed up with Westerns. He doesn't want to be the rich man's Roy Rogers.

Nobody knew how seared I was but myself. They liked me as I seemed to be. Mr. High-Jinks of Hollywood, funboy, playboy, handi-capper de-luxe, fast with his mitts in a bar, clever with the ladies, the world at his feet, and always something funny to say.

My smile got broader and broader, so broad that one night I went to a dresser in my bedroom at Mulholland and took out a gun.

For hours I sat on the edge of my bed, in darkness, my hands gripped to the handle of the revolver. I sat, thought, felt little, but couldn't bring myself to raise the gun to my head. Very well, no hurry. If not tonight, then tomorrow night.

Like an automaton I went through the motions of work the following day. Home again at night. I answered no phone calls. I ordered that the house be barred to all. I retired to my room again. Once more I drew the gun out of the dresser, again sat on the edge of the bed, utterly dejected.

I turned on the lights. If I shot myself with the lights on I wouldn't miss. That was one thing I didn't want to do, to have a fiasco. I heard of a lot of failures. I looked into a mirror. I could see myself aim that way. A good way not to miss.

I got fully dressed. I went into the yard behind my house. I put up a tin can a few feet away, so as to see whether everything would work well. I aimed carefully, pulled the trigger. There was a click and nothing more; no sound, no bullet.

I thought, My God, if I got the guts to do it and a click came out, it would be horrible. Would I be able to do it again?

I went into the house and fell into bed. A second night of failure.

I had told two friends who were thinking of doing this, "Think it over, and in the morning you'll feel different."

I was telling myself this each night, trying to tell myself there were good and sufficient reasons to go on living.

The third night I tried taking a few drinks, maybe that would help me to get up the necessary guts. I sat on the edge of the bed with the muzzle of the gun directly in my mouth, pointed at the roof of my mouth. I sat that way for quite a while but couldn't bring myself to pull the trigger. Disconsolation went through me in waves, giving me mo-mentary urges to end it, but there must have been a stronger life force in me than I could emotionally or intellectually resist.

It left me with a sense of abandon. I didn't give a damn what I did, where I went, what happened to me. I said to myself, Nothing matters now, do as you damned please, you will get it some other way. Go out with a flash and bang sometime, at sea, in a plane, or doing some daredevil stunt, anything—but don't drag your nuts, Flynn.

Instead of killing myself I bought a new boat.

I would go down to the harbor and take a look at the *Sirocco*. She had an evil memory for me now and I decided to get rid of her. I had made a mistake, one of the gravest errors a mariner can make, in changing her name. A mariner doesn't kill a dolphin, shoot an albatross or change the name of a boat. I had never been superstitious—but look what happened.

I told myself in getting rid of the *Sirocco* that she was too wet for the sea, yet I have a sneaking hunch that I had paid off for violating one of the rules of the marine world. Sirocco is a wind that blows across Northern Africa. It is the wind that is said to drive men mad. In the French Foreign Legion they have a saying, "He is suffering from *le cafard*," a form of madness that the Legionnaires are apt to get when the wind blows in a certain direction. I had had this yacht with the dangerous name and a great upheaval had occurred in my life.

Without a boat I felt like a bachelor. I got a craving for another. I said to myself, if I get another it will be smaller than the *Sirocco*.

But then I came across a picture in some yachting magazine showing a dream boat called the *Zaca*. She had belonged to the banker Templeton Crocker, of San Francisco. She had been around the world twice and Dr. William Beebe had written in his books about her. She had been pressed into war service. They mounted two 20 mm. guns on her, fitted her with a complement of about thirty-five naval men, and she patrolled offshore of the Golden Gate Bridge in San Francisco as an enemy submarine detector. She would patrol under sail for thirty days at a time—

When I talk about a boat, all of my esthetic sense is as alert as when I describe the shape and coloring of some new young lady, for my boats, if anything, are probably fully as important to me as flesh and blood. . . .

When the war ended, the *Zaca,* now painted a navy gray, was dismasted and put up for sale. Surplus operators bought the ship first and I bought it from them. I employed an experienced mariner, Kingsley Hayward, to look over this boat and see what shape she was in. He went under water, along the sides, examining the keel before I bought her, and he pronounced her condition good. I had her repainted, re-rigged, remasted. I was working at the studio, and from time to time I went up to San Francisco to see how Kingsley was doing with her.

She was draining my pocketbook. I spent fifty thousand to fix her up, but at last she was a dream ready to sail the seas.

I did one other thing. When the boat was finished I said to myself, Let her be a symbol of what I have come to represent. I'll fly a crowing rooster for my house flag and let us crow over the world.

In the months that followed the overhauling of the *Zaca* I took her out frequently. I took on a larger crew. I changed motors, I got acquainted with her. A boat is like a horse. Every ship has her own personality, the tricks she does, the foibles she has. Several times in this period I nearly lost the ship—and my own life—in many water safaris. At last I felt I knew this lady and could command her.

My mother and father made a trip to the United States to visit me.

Before they disembarked at New York harbor, they were interviewed by the press.

The reporters remarked on the physical similarity between my mother and me.

"What do you think of your son's fame?" they asked.

Mother minced no words. "Errol was a nasty little boy," she said.

A Warner Brothers public relations man rounded up the press and appealed to them not to print my mother's quote. They were good fellows. The incident was forgotten.

There were two grandchildren in Los Angeles to occupy my mother's time. Sean, now five or six years old, and little Deirdre.

I had other plans for my father. I proposed to him a trip to the Galapagos Islands, six hundred miles west of Ecuador, in the Pacific. This was where Darwin had prospered. For me and for my father it would be a sentimental journey, recalling for us our times in Tasmania and the days when I went into the field with him as he quested for strange items of marine biology.

We made up a big party. All of us would go to some little islands off the coast of Mexico; then a few of us would go on to the Galapagos. We lined up Professor Carl Hubbs of the La Jolla headquarters of the Scripps Institute of Oceanography. Nora was with us. I invited John Decker. We had on board as a seaman Wallace Beery, Jr., who was seventeen.

When we got to Acapulco, Nora had to leave ship for she was pregnant again and the ocean was too rough an experience. She returned to Los Angeles, while Father and I moved in on these Mexican islands. Father was delighted at what he discovered. He came upon five species of pool tide fish, the existence of which, he said, had been unknown. In deference to the host, he named the new types Zacy, Erroli and Nori.

Few boat trips are altogether successful. John Decker had left the ship before Nora did. He couldn't get along with her. He quit at Acapulco, returning to Los Angeles alone. The Beery boy got a harpoon in his left foot. We operated on board and pulled him through that mishap.

Father returned to Los Angeles with his biological finds and Professor Hubbs went with him. Other Hollywood friends joined the returning party. Instead of sailing to the Galapagos, I changed my mind and set course for Cocos Island and spent a week on a strange, haunted sea mountain.

We sailed the *Zaca* through the Panama Canal and entered the large waters of the Caribbean. I knew it was a dangerous season to be in this part of the world. This was the time—it is so each year—when the wind torrents form mysteriously and terrorize the islands.

But I didn't give a damn. Caution was now less a part of my nature than it had ever been.

There are days at sea when you can laze along under full sail . . . lazy days and nights. These make up for the hard times on the water. Then you can think and feel and wonder why you're here. Or, on the dogwatch. I always made it a point to take the dogwatch. It wasn't necessary on the *Zaca*, but I felt it to be good for self-discipline. I kept the watch, like the others, the night watch or whatever trick befell me. On that four-hour stretch, given a quiet sea, you can really be alone with God and the universe, you being one little speck on the sea.

You can look at the stars as you never can on the land, wonder and reflect. Your thoughts seem to gain a different dimension. Here is the boundless sea, three-quarters of the earth's surface is water, and you are on it, a tiny speck. Your thoughts wander to the edge of eternity. At times like these I felt like the early mariners and explorers, because if I was out of radio contact, I was in no different situation.

There is nothing like lying flat on your back on the deck, alone except for the helmsman aft at the wheel, silence except for the lapping of the sea against the side of the ship. At that time you can be equal to Ulysses and brother to him.

Through the Panama Canal, I put in at Venezuela for a few days, then headed for Cap-Haitien. The balmy weather we had been having took a change for the worse. The barometer began to fall alarmingly. I wondered what we were in for and got busy on the radio. I could not pick up any messages.

The waves rose.

I shortened sail and got ready for a blow.

Down went the barometer.

That night something hit, the like of which, having spent all my life on or around the sea, I had never experienced.

For four straight days we were on the edge of a hurricane.

The storm sail, a heavy piece of canvas stretched between the masts, went the second day. The force of the wind ripped a streak down it, and it flew into two pieces with a sound like a 20 mm. gun. The wind howled through the rigging. You couldn't stand upright. You had to crawl or fight your way foreward or aft. Even with the motors at full speed, we couldn't keep our head. The waves became mountainous. The boat's prow would plunge underwater, go down, take the green sea, and somehow we'd ride out the next giant roller.

It needed two men on the wheel to hold her. Each time she took a sheer, there was danger of capsizing, or being overwhelmed by the great seas. The force of the wind, I estimated, was between ninety and a hundred miles an hour.

To slow us down, I put out heavy anchors weighing many tons. Yet unbelievably, those two huge pieces of metal skipped along the surface of the water as if they were bait being trolled! It was uncanny to see those two huge irons surfacing in the wake, sometimes just below the water, sometimes partially out of it.

At night there were no stars. The sky was black. The ocean black. We might have been flying through the air. We sped and were pushed like a sliver, strictly in the hand of fortune.

On the second day I lost track of where we were. I had no idea as to our position. On the third day we were more at sea than ever, with no radio, nothing but guesswork to go by.

On we hurtled.

Nothing warm to eat or drink. The galley was out, having shipped a big sea, and we had neither time nor means to make repairs. We were on cold tack.

My man Pedro, the ablest seaman, nearly lost his life to sharks during one act of trying to retrieve a foresail which had fouled forward in the dolphin-stricken sea. He was in the water, with sharks slashing at him and at the dragging sail, till we pulled him back in.

On the fourth day I was sure that we had to run aground somewhere. I could not make out the nature of a curious body of land that rose from the sea. Harsh cliffs, volcanic-looking, stern and ragged of edge, loomed at us.

The *Zaca* moved wearily along the edge of this giant gray land which seemed to rise high into the clouds. What was it? Where were we?

Suddenly the sky cleared sharply. Winds howled the clouds out, and a powerful sun illumined the greenest hills I'd ever seen. Far away, down the coast, we saw a spot that seemed like a center, perhaps a port. We headed that way.

"It's a port," someone announced. "A port."

We headed in, five miles, two miles, one mile. We saw a few fishing craft near shore. Definitely here was a port city. But on what continent?

We sailed in over green seas, entering a sunny harbor. The sky was blue. The ocean was still swept and hastening, but we had licked the hurricane and we were alive.

We must have made a strange-looking sight as we reached shore. There was curiosity as to who we were. They knew it was a craft blown in by the wild wind.

I stepped onto a wharf. People gathered around. I was recognized at once. "It's Errol Flynn!"

They were black. They spoke beautiful English. Who were they? "What is this place?" I asked.

"Jamaica. This is Kingston."

"Jamaica?" So that was it.

The newspapers of Jamaica made quite a fuss about my having been blown in there. I was interviewed and told the story of our trip and of being lost at sea, and I was besieged for a time with the usual autographing procedure. Consuls visited me. Abe Issa, proprietor of one of the big hotels and a town father, came to see me.

For a day or two I rested at his hotel.

My crew began making repairs with the aid of shipwrights of Kingston.

I received many letters from Jamaicans inviting me to their homes. I didn't know what to do about this, there were so many. I liked in particular one letter that came from a man named Joe Blackwell. We had a mutual friend in Ireland. Would I not be his guest and let him show me around?

Joe Blackwell picked me up at the hotel one day and he drove me across the island to where he lived.

Never had I seen a land so beautiful. Now I knew where the writers of the Bible had gotten their description of Paradise. They had come here to Jamaica and then their words had been set down and they have been read ever since.

Most of it is an incessant rolling and unraveling hill. One might say Jamaica is all one hill which rolls into millions of unceasing shapes for a length of 144 miles and crosswise for another 50 miles, rising to five or six thousand feet. Everywhere there is a blanket of green so thick that the earth never shows through. Jamaica is peopled primarily with dark-skinned people, perhaps ninety-five per cent. They are well-spoken, courteous in the English manner, and they have been English subjects ever since the English swiped it from the Spanish in the seventeenth century.

I knew that once more I had found Laloki. Here I would come and here I would stay. This would be my base forevermore, two or three months a year, or five months a year. It reminded me of all of the beauty of the Polynesian Islands, but it had the civilizing features of the West. And the women were black, but comely.

Joe took me to his house to meet his wife. She hadn't wanted to see me for she was ill. Joe confided she had large painful boils on her behind. But when I arrived and met this pale-faced girl with the dark, intense eyes and beautiful teeth, and a laugh like the sound of water tinkling over a waterfall, we fell into the most animated conversation. I had come from one end of the earth and she lived here, at the other, and yet it seemed that we had whole worlds to speak of.

I can only say for Blanche Blackwell, who not long afterward was divorced from Joe, that she and I became the fastest friends to the point where I thought of proposing—while still married to Nora—but I feared a rejection and perhaps a difference in our relationship. Blanche and I formed an enduring friendship amazingly platonic.

In fact I believe, with all my strange ways and life with women—
with my love for them and often my bitterness toward them—with all
this, I say there is no true friendship like that between a man and a
woman, especially if platonic.

I left Blanche and Joe, knowing that I would return to this greenest
of all islands. Here I would buy property and settle. Here I would
try to salvage myself. All around was the sea, fine tropic foods, rare
sea foods, a wonderful region for skin-diving. And sun, wonderful
year-round sun.

After thirty-seven years of wandering I had found my Grecian isle.

My second daughter, Rory, was born in March of 1947. When that
happened I began to think I was living like an idiot. Here I had two
lovely children by Nora. So I made a belated proposal if ever I made
one. I asked her to live with me at Mulholland permanently, for the
sake of the children if not for ourselves. By now neither of us had any
love for the other. But maybe we should try to make a go of it. I
offered to give her Mulholland, in her name, which she might as well
have taken, since afterwards Lili got it for back alimony.

I was beginning to think of the children more than of myself and
more than of Nora, but I was too late. She was now friendly with a
man she wanted to marry. That was of some concern to me because
her friend had a lot of children of his own. Nora wanted to take over
his children as well as have the custody of ours.

We had a down-to-earth talk.

I said, "If you are in love with this guy, that's fine. I wish you all
the happiness in the world. What can I do for you?"

She burst into tears. "You can't do anything more for me than you
have done. You took me from nothing and made me something and you
have been so generous. I want to divorce you and I won't take a penny
from you. I am going to walk out of your life. You can see the children.
We can share them."

My marriage to Nora drifted on into 1949. During that time I tried to
get acquainted with my children.

A man as involved as I have been with the world's intricacies—and
my own—doesn't have as much of a chance to be with his children as
he might like. My particular life is not the usual one where a man, after

an eight-hour day, comes home in the evening and spends time with his wife and kids.

My course has been different, and I don't really know what it is to watch a youngster grow steadily from infancy to childhood to adolescence.

Still, I have diapered my young. With one of my kids, Sean, by Lily, now aged eighteen and old enough to be a good companion, I spend as much time as I can. We meet frequently at airports, railway terminals, and we go together to one place or another.

Sean, from early childhood on, came around the studio sets when I made pictures. Nora would bring Diedre and Rory up to Mulholland, and sometimes my three youngsters were about the place for days and weeks at a time. I staged parties for them—big circuses, I must confess. They had the run of Mulholland Farm, animals to play with, room to romp in, and I tried to keep them amused.

We had tremendous fun one day because I couldn't get to work in the usual way. This was one of the few times it snowed heavily in Hollywood. All the roads were blocked from Mulholland to the Metro-Goldwyn-Mayer Studio where I was working on *That Forsythe Woman*. The kids were excited over the big snowfall and we were looking out the windows at the white scenery.

Telephonic communication wasn't disrupted. I called the studio and suggested an unheard-of measure to get to work. They thought it a bit strange and asked time to think it over. They called back and said it was not a bad idea: so a helicopter was sent to my house.

The helicopter, a hazardous thing to fly in those days, arrived and landed in front of my breakfast table. I said good-by to the family amid much gaiety and stepped into the machine.

I was promptly whisked through the air to the Metro lot where I reported only a half-hour late for work. Otherwise I might have been stuck on my mountain top for three days.

When Clark Gable heard of it—and the publicity that chanced to result from it—he said, "Goddamn, there he goes again, that haywire Flynn."

Some of us had an informal film-exchange club. Cary Grant had his own library. Gable had his. I'd switch my pictures with Gable, and he'd send over some of his for the amusement of my youngsters. Or Abbott and Costello. Their comedies went big with Sean. I'd send over a swashbuckling item for kids, and they'd return a comedy.

Robin Hood nearly got worn out, it was borrowed so much. This went on week after week. The children would invite their pals, families would gather for these private showings.

Bud Abbott and Lou Costello were very good friends of mine. They were having a feud, I don't remember what about. A day arrived when the Costello family were to show an Errol Flynn picture.

The family—the kids, Lou and his wife, Lou's mother—some other elderly ladies, were all seated in his projection room. Such nice sweet kids. They were all properly seated, waiting for the man on horseback to make his appearance and wave his cutlass around, when of a sudden this altogether different picture started to unreel.

It was a pornographic film, about as obscene as could be devised! It went on and on.

They were so paralyzed with shock, Lou couldn't push the button to halt it.

Finally, somehow, they got the film switched off.

At once Costello accused Abbott of doing this deliberately. This didn't help their business relationship at all. In fact it led to trouble with both of their wives. Not only did the comedians stop talking to each other, but now the wives were not talking to either their own husbands, the other husband, or the other wife. An awful impasse.

I don't know who got each to thinking the other was to blame.

They both called me and said, "Wait a minute! Are you pulling gags again? If this is your idea of a gag—!"

I explained to both that I had nothing to do with it. A chauffeur of one of them had come up and borrowed *Robin Hood*. I was sorry, I told them both, if the old ladies fell out of the chairs.

I swore on the Koran it was not I.

With so many mouths to feed—and in the manner to which I had accustomed them—I had to keep at the last, as the shoemaker puts it. I prepared to go to India to make *Kim*, having been loaned to Metro-Goldwyn-Mayer.

On my way there I passed a few days in New York. It is astonishing how I cannot get out into the streets without something happening.

I was walking about with a young brunette. She had been rather kind to me and I wished to do something in return. I walked into a prominent jewelry store, and there was Lili, in the same old tired attitude, her tongue in her cheek, eying the girl I was with.

"Hello, Fleen, buying jewelry?"

I said, "Seems we are on the same mission. You are buying it for yourself, I am buying it for somebody else."

I felt entitled to the crack since Lili was making her purchase with my dough.

Graham Wahn, a good friend and public relations man for Warner Brothers, escorted me, on behalf of Warners, to a formal occasion in Manhattan, prior to my leaving for India. We left my apartment early in the evening, took a taxi, and as we moved off, a police car came alongside with two cops in it.

One officer said, "Get over to the curb!"

The other asked, "Are you Errol Flynn?" I answered that I was. "All right, get over to the curb and sign this."

It was an autograph book. I said, "We're in a horrible hurry, fellow."

"If you know what's good for you"—tough as he could sound—"sign it and shut up!"

We pulled over to the curb.

Graham, ordinarily a very serious, very respectful man, said, "Why, you goddamn New York coppers, who the hell do you think you are, the Gestapo? What kind of Fascist action is this?"

They bristled at those words.

I said, "Jesus, you made us pull over here and practically at gunpoint. Hitler wouldn't do this."

This must have aggravated them for they told our cabbie, "Go on down the 8th Precinct!"

The hackie knew better than to get into trouble with tough cops, and at the station house he kept quiet. We kept asking what we were arrested for.

Nobody could tell us. Nobody had anything to say.

"What the hell are we here for?" That was me. I made a move to get out of the station to get my lawyer.

One of them pushed me toward the sergeant at the desk. That was all—a shove on the back—and the Australian came up. I turned around and stamped with all I had on his instep.

It was a grave mistake. Gentlemen, never get tough with a New York cop. Never do it, no matter how right you are. As this guy swung at me, I ducked. I still had my foot on his instep. I swung at him—and that was the last I knew.

They beat me right in front of the sergeant. They nearly knocked the top off my head. They battered me up and tossed me into a cell. But not one of them hit me in the face, luckily—but that's about the only spot they missed.

By the time I came to—on the cell floor—I was ready to take on anyone. Rage at injustice is common to better and lesser men than me. I said, "Listen, any of you bastards come in here, you'd better come in by twos and threes!"

I went on yelling, completely out of control. I must have looked drunk as hell. I wasn't—I was just enraged.

Meantime Graham phoned my friend John Perona at El Morocco to come bail me out. At first Perona thought it was another one of my gags, but he came at four o'clock in the morning, black hat and all, bearing $500.

By this time I didn't care who came. I was raving. Graham said the sergeant in charge was prepared to let the charges drop.

"What charges?"—in as loud a voice as I could summon.

"Quiet, quiet, Errol, let's get the hell out of here. . . ."

"Bunch of Nazi Gestapo bastards," I kept on. "What kind of a country is this?"

As I went out I walked backwards. Nobody spoke. I was waiting for somebody to say something, for I was certain I would have been thrown back in. I would have fought like a wildcat in a bag.

The next day I was brought up before a woman judge on a charge of assault.

But who assaulted whom?

I was asked, "Do you think you can go about New York picking fights with police?"

I pleaded not guilty and explained that these gentlemen of the police force had forced my taxi over to the side of the road for an autograph. . . . Which they both denied.

"He was disturbing the peace," they lied under oath.

I was fined $50. For what? What peace?

I paid the fifty, then I had to humble myself and make an apology. "Officer," I said, "I apologize for my action." Almost choking on the words.

Then I hissed right into his ear, "If I ever catch you alone, you yellow bastard, I'll beat your brains out." And I smiled.

"What?"

"You heard me. Just don't go out alone, sport."

The local press made much of this, giving the impression that I had, without reason or provocation, kicked a cop in the shins.

In order to plot any kind of mischief, you have first to be interested in the person you are going to hoax. The best gag must always be played on a pal. It is no use hanging it on somebody you don't like; that's not interesting. But to upset a friend—ah, that's different.

We were making *Kim* in India. Paul Lukas, who had recently won the Academy Award for his performance in *Watch on the Rhine,* is an irascible man who can get sore quicker than anybody I know and with less reason. But we have always been very good friends. Paul is a Hungarian and a formidable actor. He has an overbearing manner with almost everybody, so I decided I would try to do something about this.

He was cast as the Lama, a choice role in this picture, and he was coming in from Los Angeles, flying over the South Pacific—a tremendously long flight—to Karachi and Bombay.

For a week before his arrival I rehearsed a beautiful young Anglo-Indian girl in a rite involving special religious pillars, the ancient pillars of all India. I named her "The Flower of Delight," and her role on this occasion was to be president of the Paul Lukas Fan Club of India, which we figured Lukas didn't know about and which of course didn't exist.

I went out to the customs office at the airport and involved and coached the Chief Inspector. With his bandolier across his chest and a big gun on the table before him, he looked pretty ominous. There was a corps of soldiers about, with drawn bayonets, turbans, khaki overcoats. For about fifty rupees I persuaded one of them to let me borrow his uniform for a half-hour.

With a beard, colored turban topping my six feet two, and some dark make-up, then one quick look in the mirror in the men's room, I saw that I looked very much like one of the Sikh guard, regular fixtures of the airport.

All was ready.

Lukas got off the plane and entered the airport customs office. Immediately, the Inspector asked Lukas who and what he was. Gracefully, Paul replied that he was an actor, and possibly with as much grace, if a little less modesty, mentioned he had just won the Academy Award—which naturally the Inspector had never heard of.

What was the reason for his coming to India?—To make a picture, he explained.

"Ah—you paint."

"No. A motion picture, a movie."

"Ah, what picture?"

The name was "Kim."

At that moment the Inspector leaned backward and loudly asked, "Are you a good actor?"

Lukas—he had been through a lot—loosened his tie and faintly admitted he was indeed a good actor.

At this cue the Flower of Delight rushed in and fell on her knees. "Mr. Lukas, Mr. Lukas, my hero! At last!"

He did a double take and looked downward studiously, for her Pillars of Wisdom were showing—and they were as luscious as all the coconuts ancient India had ever seen.

The Indian girl sputtered out her lines about the fan club.

Lukas said, "Yes, yes. Thank you very much!"

She grabbed hold of his right leg and groveled. "I can't let you go." She kissed his knee.

Lukas tried to shush her but she refused. "I am alone. My mother has gone to the market with my father. My two sisters are not in the house. You must come and stay with me!"

Lukas will never duplicate his triple take.

All the while he was under cross-fire by the Inspector: Where had he come from? What about this passport photo which didn't seem to resemble him?

I paced up and down close by, rifle on my shoulder. Once, when he looked around at the kneeling and emoting Flower of Delight I gave him a rough shove in the back and whispered something in double talk Hindustani.

Lukas seemed to get smaller. I loomed over him. Now he was attacked from three directions: the Flower of Delight at his pants cuffs, the Inspector from the front, and the rough tough bearded Sikh giving him the elbow.

Each time the Inspector yelled, "Take that woman out of here," I threw her out. But as rehearsed, she came back. Her performance was marvelous.

Lukas was foundering fast. His tension was almost visible like marks breaking out on the chart of a radar screen, and I felt he'd had enough.

So the third time I shoved him roughly, I allowed my turban to fall to the floor and took the beard off at the same time.

Paul gaped, speechless. Rage replaced any possible Academy Award performance he could conceivably have put on at the time. He screamed like a wounded panther and to everyone's astonishment grabbed his hat, dashed it on the floor and began jumping up and down on it like a human yo-yo.

Sometimes these things backfire.

I made the mistake of leaving a solid amount of money on the Chief Inspector's table. He had played his part magnificently. I believe in actors being paid.

The Inspector glowered. I had touched his Indian pride. "Are you trying to bribe me?" he barked.

"What? Good God no!"

"You *are* trying to bribe me! Stand over there!"

He pulled his gun toward him, his hand properly around the handle and the trigger loop. "You are in India! Our country! What is this?" His finger stabbed accusingly at the rupees.

I didn't know what to say. I stammered, "Just to thank you very much."

"That is not the point! Don't you know better than to bribe a government official?"

"Would your—er—you gentlemen care to put it in your Christmas fund?"

He said, *"We—do—not—observe—Christmas!"*

I was in deeper.

I was there for another hour, trying to double talk for the policemen's fund—any kind of fund—so that I could get out of the place.

Later I told Lukas how the thing boomeranged. He was mollified. Today he regales any listener with his very different version of the incident.

I had not been to India in fifteen or sixteen years, not since Koets and I bummed our way through that exotic land. It was good and it was strange to return there. This was on such a different level. Now I met the leaders of India, the maharajahs, the great newspaper publishers, the Brahmins, the politicians.

Often as I sat in the company of these notables I thought of how I, as a young man, lean, half-hungry generally, sometimes wearing only shorts, my only pair of pants hanging up to dry after I'd washed them, had barged about in the market place of Calcutta looking for action—feminine, that is.

I ventured to tell this one night to the Maharajah of Bundi. This is a state just below the famous Rajput, where live the fighting warriors of northern India. I sat with him at an elaborate table he had prepared. At length he ordered brought to the table two small phials of a rare drink that he told me had been in his family for a century. The phials contained crushed pearls and fine specks of gold. The liquid in these ancient bottles looked amber. It was the same as Cleopatra was supposed to have served Mark Anthony, or was it the Queen of Sheba whose delicate hand served this to King Solomon?

Anyway, said His Highness the maharajah, this was a fabulous aphrodisiac. I told him I didn't need it on my first trip to India, nor on this return occasion, and I hoped not to need it if I ever came back a third time. "There is no imminent fear lurking around the mattress," I added.

I drank of that aged liquor and wondered what it would do for me. It tasted sweet, too sweet for my taste, but I liked to see the gold flecks and the pearl specks wander around in the amber fluid as I held the bottles up to the light.

Whatever this stuff did for old Sol or Mark it did nothing for Flynn; just a flat calm.

Aphrodisiacs? You may have them. I have tested them all, in India, in France, in Spain, in Mexico: Cantarides, or as it is known, Spanish fly; a little cocaine on the end of the penis; a certain root found only in Santo Domingo which they sell at Ciudad Trujillo, which is supposed to excite the male and female when it is drunk. Actually I defy anybody to tell me there is any efficient sex stimulant.

There is only one aphrodisiac—the special woman you love to touch and see and smell and crush.

I left the maharajah later and went into the streets looking for a cool glass of beer.

I put on my false nose.

I have always carried with me two false noses. They alter my appearance so that I can sit down and read a newspaper anywhere and be unrecognizable.

It is one of the bugbears of being who I am that I have lost my anonymity. I have often missed it. The right to be your own private self is as important as the right to speak your mind. So, in various centers of the world, in Europe or in Asia, when I traveled for my own recreation or went to make a picture, I made experiments while disguised.

Parenthetically, here's a tip to all criminals, cads, crooks and cons—· you can't change your eyes. You can change your hair, shave it off or part it differently, or wear a wig. You can change your mouth by angling it and setting it differently, thus concealing the normal cast of your mouth; or do a little cosmetic work and alter its shape. But the dead giveaway is your nose. This is the one feature in the human face that can give you anonymity.

I had a couple of noses made up in plastic and rubber so that I could turn my nose to left or right, or turn it up at the bottom and reveal wide nostrils. Wherever I put on these false noses I was able to get away with it. People see you with a distorted nose, they turn away quickly, saying, "Poor guy—must have got in some trouble to have a nose like that."

In Paris, Rome, London, Calcutta, Rio de Janeiro, I have put on my false noses. I could stand at a street corner and watch the world go by and the anonymity was blessed.

I wore a pitch-black beard when I got back. It looked pretty shoddy, as if somebody had taken my head and dumped it in mud.

Thinking I must get to look like myself again, I shaved the beard. Not that I am too fond of the face beneath the beard.

I have been tired of this face for a long time.

I look at it as little as possible—even when I shave.

When I go to the bathroom I look at the can, not the mirror.

I feel that this is a face, not like Helen of Troy's that launched a thousand ships, but only has launched millions of tickets.

Therefore it is not what I like to see.

I would like to have a façade behind a façade, and therefore I especially dislike my face.

I never did like it, even when it was "pretty." I liked only what I hoped was behind that face, and wished for and longed to be. . . . I liked what I thought I was inside, not what I appeared to be from skinside. . . .

I have often thought, Supposing I had been a little dwarf with short fingers, with crooked legs, perhaps with a hump on my back. Supposing I had been so ugly as to have people revolted and repelled by the sight of this individual Flynn. What would have happened to me then? Suppose a little cripple had come out of the womb, with arms and limbs askew, I wonder what kind of fight I might have put up in life. I wonder if my spirit would have been the same?

Prior to self-misuse—and I worked hard at that—they said I was beautiful—a strange appellation for a man. But I have always felt that my face and appearance did not reflect the real self, and that my face obscured it from view. Growing up in the shadow of an intellectual and distinguished father, Science was in my breeding. Curiosity was in my every reflex, and curiosity was my principal addiction. The curious man inside me wandered over the world in quest of life's answers; but my face stood in my path. True, it became my fortune—but it turned me from the things I wanted to be.

I learned indifference to the looks that so many women of the world have found so engrossing.

Glamour? Beauty?

No wonder I have punished myself and put lines in my face and a map of experience on my forehead. It is some consolation to hear people say, now, that the years have given me at last the look of a head that might have something inside it.

That's why I like a picture of me that was printed in *Esquire* a couple of years ago. My face was wrinkled, the brow was hard lined; a bit bewildered still, but the look of an experienced man.

Back in Hollywood, I resumed picture-making and batting around with my special pal, McEvoy.

Freddie and I were delighted one evening at the Mocambo to see an attractive brunette tangling in a brawl with an equally stunning blonde.

We went as close as we could get, because these girls were putting on a round-by-round brawl, and neither letting up. The blonde on top one minute, brunette on top the next. They bit, scratched, and took good wrestling holds.

"Wonderful, isn't it, Freddie?"

"Excellent."

The girls were separated and we went back to our table. Just then a friend rushed up to me and asked, "Errol, you were there. What was it all about?"

"Damned if I know. I don't know either of them and don't give a damn. All I know is that when they were on the floor with their legs up in the air I could tell which one was the blonde and which was the brunette."

At that instant I looked around. There was the brunette glaring at me.

"So you don't give a damn!" she screamed.

A waiter passed by bearing a tray on which were two raw eggs. The excited girl picked up the plate containing those two egg yokes and sent them crash! right on my head.

I put my hands to my hair. A lot of yellow came down with them. At last I've had it, I thought, making it histrionic. My brains!

Four waiters jumped on her to pull the girl away from me and two gathered around me to clean up my wandering brains.

The headlines made merry of it all across the country: FLYNN LAID LOW WITH SPANISH OMELET.

Marge Eddington ran much of my life. She was in my employ as secretary and general factotum. One reason I had her around overseeing Mulholland was because she sided with me in any disputes I had with Nora.

She and Nora fought steadily.

Doubtless our sporadic marriage relationship could have done Nora no good. The uncertainty which she had as my wife transformed her and I couldn't blame her for losing much of the sweetness she originally had.

The fact is, I would never be a boon to any woman dreaming of domestic bliss, monogamy, serenity, composure, playing bridge and doing dishes.

I had, after all, met Nora during the rape trial and agreeably married her shortly thereafter. There was little in the situation to make me inwardly convivial to our marriage.

In 1949 we were divorced. Soon thereafter she married Dick Haymes.

A little later, while visiting with her and my youngsters, I talked to her about the strange turn of her temperament, for which I suppose I was in part responsible.

She said, "You and your friends gave me such a sense of inferiority, I rebelled against it. I suppose I should have gone along with it, but I couldn't."

It was one of those rare moments of self-revelation.

After work one evening my lawyer telephoned. "Nora wants full custody of both children."

"She does, does she?" I felt the blood rush to my face. "What can we do?"

"I don't know." He laughed a little nervously. "I just don't know." Lawyers always laugh nervously when they're in a quandary.

For a few seconds the conversation hung in pauses and uncertainties. "You're my lawyer, aren't you? What can I do?" I was frantic.

"I don't know—"

"Well, I know what I'll do!"

I slammed the phone with the kind of crash that a few vodkas can bring out in a man. I swigged another glass. Rage rose in me, working up from the pit of the stomach, and coming out in what must have been a face flushed from the neck up. This was too damned much! Get my dough? Throw me on the untender mercy of these California courts, which always ruled with the woman? So—Nora was fit to handle five kids and I none? Goddamit, no!

The Aussie was up in me. I rushed out the door. I jumped into my car, started backing out.

Ugh—What was that?

I felt the tire go over something.

I got out. There was my pet dachshund puppy, Grena, squashed flat. All of an instant my anger left me.

The rest of the night I spent in tears—burying her.

Grena may have prevented me from getting into the worst jam of my life, from doing the one thing to my little girls that I never wanted to do to them—hurt them in any way.

My affairs with Nora and Dick settled in other ways, in other days. Now all is well with Nora and me. Our girls are a powerful bond. As to Dick Haymes, whose marriage with Nora has come and has gone, I'd send him a new Cadillac every year for Christmas, if I could afford it.

But we were all younger then, and our passions were high. Since then Nora has put flowers sometimes on little Grena's grave and perhaps our feud was buried there.

I made *The Adventures of Don Juan, Montana, Mara Maru.*

My war with Jack Warner went on, this time a battle royal over wardrobe.

I had a running fight with the studio for years over the question of clothes. A regular bill had been coming to me for years from the studio. It got higher and higher. I kept ignoring it, because I couldn't understand why the bill was growing.

I discovered that the wardrobe people are the biggest thieves of all. They walk off with a gown, a suit, a prop, any piece from the wardrobe, and make the star the goat. They think that the big brass won't make a fuss if they know the star has taken some item of apparel for his or her own use. After they swipe the item they alibi, "So and so just wore it home, that's all."

They had been stealing from my sets and palming off the pilfered items to my wicked ways. At last the matter got to Jack Warner, who ordered some threatening letters sent to me.

My agent came to me and said, "Jack is really mad about two things, Errol."

"What now?"

"Your telephone bill and this wardrobe bill. What are we going to do about them?"

"How much?"

"The telephone is $300 and the wardrobe they calculate to be $1,400."

I let out a scream. "For God's sake! That's about ten minutes' production time and I was early all last week. Give me that bill!"

The pile-up of things charged to me went back about four years. I wrote on the bottom of the statement:

> DEAR JACK:
>   I am prepared to let this matter drop now, if you are.
>   Fondly,
>   ERROL

It couldn't have endeared me to Jack.

I was between pictures. A bachelor again, I was lonely.

Ordinarily, when I wanted a change, I flew to Jamaica. I had been there several times since my discovery of the place. I had even bought some acres of coastal real estate, in a brave effort to try to do something substantial with my earnings. I bought a residence on the north shore called Boston House, and I had my sailboat moored off Port Antonio.

But this time I felt I needed Paris and Freddie. He had a beautiful apartment in Paris, overlooking Auteuil, the race track. He hadn't been married long to his present wife. Late in 1949 I was best man at his wedding in Miami to a French-Algerian girl, Claude, whom he married for love. His two previous marriages were for money. Claude was pretty, blond, vivacious. She had warmth. I knew I'd be welcome at their place and I was.

On my very first day there, at Freddie's suggestion, I went to the Louvre to look at some paintings. Be back for dinner, he said. I knew very well he would have somebody there for me when I returned.

I walked in at about seven o'clock. There was Freddie, Claude, and a dream, sitting in a chair across the room. She had the biggest pair of dark eyes I ever saw, dark violet, with eyelashes that went straight down and gave her eyes a shaded look. She was beautifully dressed. She sat composedly, like a woman in a Goya painting.

I gaped.

Freddie was a bit pompous about the introduction. "This is the Princess Irene. May I present you?" He pretended to have forgotten my name. "Er—Flynn . . . Errol," I said.

I approached without a word, bowed, and kissed her hand. "Princess," I said. "Enchanted." I had had a couple of Pernods on the way back and ventured on. "I only wish I could find you a necklace of jewels like your eyes."

I was amazed at my own figure of speech. I didn't let go of her hand, which felt good in my palm. I said, "These little hands could only have come from the Caucasus." I took a shot in the dark. "Do you feel what I feel? I mean, with your little hand against this large Australian one?"

It was such crap that, recalling it, it's a bit sickening.

The Princess, of a famous European family known all over the world, was delightful. She floated, didn't walk, like a slight mist over an Irish moor; and she was broke.

I was, frankly, anxious to contribute to her delinquency at the earliest possible moment.

This wasn't easy. It was a long siege.

Yet, like the water that drops relentlessly upon a rock and eventually wears it away, I too persisted. . . .

Soon she was using my flashy white convertible Cadillac, the first seen in France. I dressed my chauffeur in white. I even tried to dress in white myself; it made such a contrast to the usually darkly clad princess. Crowds gathered, whether to see the car or its occupants I am uncertain.

For days, weeks, months, I courted her like a Caribbean hurricane. She was reluctant, and very clever about it. I never knew royalty could be so hard to seduce. There was no carnal contact at all. I was getting frustrated. I would take her home to her apartment at night. There she had a wonderfully slick manner with a door key. She had a way of holding the key out as if it were a pistol, before I could kiss her hand, and her slender body would slip through the door like the lady in a disappearing bit in a magician's act.

I was champing.

On the pretext of having a script to do in the South of France, I asked her if she would go there with me—and, master stroke—I persuaded her mother to let her accompany me.

We drove off in the big white car. Halfway there, as we neared a hotel, I said to myself, "Strike, Flynn!"

Again she sneaked into her own room. All I got was that mysterious look from below her long, straight lashes. I lay in bed that night plucking listlessly at the coverlet and staring at the ceiling.

We reached Antibes, a beautiful place, where we put up at the Roc. I hired a secretary to occupy an adjoining suite, making everything look as if this were a business trip.

But I was now at explosion point. I knew she was fully primed, like a hot pump. I could feel the rise and fall of her own emotions as she contemplated Whether, When—and perhaps even How?

Either she had to go back to Paris and kick me out of her life, or—

The day came when the Bastille fell.

I felt revived. Life again looked good. I had someone to care for. I felt steadied. I had written to Jamaica to have the *Zaca* sent here and finally the ship arrived. Good. We would continue our love affair at sea, where I have found life and love to be always the best.

Once we sailed near the Isle de Levant, visiting a nudist colony. I couldn't be a nudist, but astonishingly, the reserved, holding-out Princess Irene could.

We stayed about the colony for two weeks. These people were sun worshipers. There was nothing lascivious about their conduct or life. They lived in a primitive, simple but wholesome way. An old man living in a cave with his daughter. A Sorbonne professor and his children minus even fig leaves. A painter, frustrated by Paris, cave dwelling and painting.

At night, when we went ashore to visit them, they wore a G-string or a leaf. Larger and smaller leaves, depending on the size of the area needing to be covered.

I knew of part of the island where they made love in broad day. The princess and I and a couple of my sailors got into a speedboat and went around to this part of the island. The people rushed out, shouting in French that we had come there to disturb them and stare at them. They turned over the boat. They were outraged.

Women I have always found to be a funny race. Princess Irene, royal blood or not, was like the others. They hate to see you read, they hate to notice that you are thinking, and you dare not look at another girl. The princess was like that. If I strayed abstractedly for a moment, she would chastise me. "You are thinking again."

It grew on me that she was a melancholy person.

One night one of my sailors saw a trickle of blood coming from under her cabin door. He called me and we pushed our way inside. She had so many razor cuts on her wrist, it looked like a washboard.

We revived her, tried to get an explanation. It was not easy. I was reminded of Lili.

Still, I took her to America.

Irene liked to dress in the young-American style of blue jeans. She was no longer the lovely little sloe-eyed Roumanian princess with the drooping eyelashes I had met in Paris. Somehow she didn't look the same way in blue jeans.

I was making a picture in the Rocky Mountains for Warners, entitled *Rocky Mountain*. Though I took with me Princess Irene and was still much involved with her, I had grown dubious about our relationship.

I met my leading lady, Patrice Wymore, of the New York stage. She was attractive, warm, wholesome. She was shortsighted and wore glasses. The more time I spent with her, acting, conversing, courting in an odd way, the more it seemed that she typified everything I longed for, or thought I longed for. I was deeply impressed to see her pick up some instrument and dig a hole in the ground, place corn and potatoes in aluminum foil, and bake them in a fire under the bright Arizona stars. The Kansas home-baked food tasted fantastic and I looked at Pat with wonder. What she was doing around the theatre when she could cook like that—in the ground itself?

I still don't know what that dinner of baked corn and potatoes is going to cost me. Patrice and I have been separated for about two years.

But at that time it seemed to me that this down-to-earth life was what I wanted. Back to the soil, back to this, back to that, back to back.

The princess may have spotted my growing interest in Pat. I had just bought her some kind of coat costing $4,000. She decided she wanted to alter the coat. Could she? Certainly. When I got the bill it was for $7,000. A slight alteration in anybody's language. Then off she went to Europe.

The way was free for me again to return home and the lovely fireside.

I wanted to see a lot of Pat. I invented a role for her, that of home-body, hausfrau, sweet domestic thing. A stupid course. It is better to evaluate a woman for what her personality is, rather than invent one to take the place of what she really is. Pat was of the theatre, but I chose to fancy that she might truly be the mistress of a house.

The time came when I must level with Irene, if I were to marry Pat. I believed I badly wanted marriage; one special woman. Lonely, lost, never far from despondency, I waged the inward battle for self-discovery. Maybe the special woman could bring this about. Maybe there was a "husband-man" somewhere inside me, and I must ferret him out and let him live. It was all working up in me—like a new role.

I didn't have enough guts to pick up the transatlantic phone to Paris and tell Irene it was no go. But I did have an amanuensis who took care of such matters. Mrs. Marge Eddington was still my housekeeper. Listening to Marge talking with the princess I was astonished at her ruthlessness. Marge's iron feminine sweet hand in telling the princess that it was off made the cut clean and clear.

The way was clear for two lovers of a quiet home life to come together in blessed matrimony.

Patrice typified everything that I was not, and I presumed that she knew what my life was, since my life had been an open newspaper. She knew the kind of man she was marrying. She must know that the leopard can't change his spots, especially if he is full-grown, and if she knew that and wanted to take a chance with me, I wanted to take it with her. She had all the qualities I admired so much and had never found. She could cook Indian curry, she could dance, she could sing, she was reserved, she had beauty, dignity.

With all these homebody qualities that go toward making a sensible and lasting marriage—if marriages are sensible, which I question—I thought I would give it a try. Flynn determined at last to find out what other men have—a sensible marriage.

Although we didn't know each other very well, I asked her what she saw in me. Pat looked troubled.

"I feel sorry for you," she said.

Well—

We decided to marry in Europe. It seemed to me that for a girl who had never been abroad this should give her a great deal of pleasure and happiness.

It was wonderful to have a legitimate wedding for a change. So unlike Lili threatening to jump from a window.

First there was a civil ceremony at Monte Carlo. This was relatively quiet, with only the press of all of France there. My parents were on hand. At last I was doing something legal and it pleased them. Pat's parents were there. So was Fred McEvoy, many business associates, and representatives from Prince Rainer's court. The Mayor of Monte Carlo gave us a medal of honor.

That was only a preliminary.

On October 23, 1950, Pat and I were married at the French Lutheran Church of the Transfiguration in Nice. This was complete with flowers, canopies, appropriate congratulations from all over the world, and a cordon of French cops holding off a crowd of 3,000 outside the church.

The wedding cake was enormous. I even ate a piece myself and posed for a picture enjoying the first fruits of what truly seemed to me to be a first marriage. Patrice looked beautiful. Her dress had been designed by a stage and film specialist, and she was radiant throughout.

After the ceremony there was a mild earthquake of a reception at the Hotel de Paris in Nice. Outside, the French milled as if the Paris Opera House was burning down.

It was—for me.

In the midst of the hilarities, a friend came to me pale-faced and whispered, "There is a man at the door wants to see you. He has some kind of a warrant for your arrest."

"Look, pal, I'm getting married now. No gags."

"This is on the level."

"Go and take the papers for me if you mean it," I said. I still thought he was ribbing, as friends are apt to do.

He went to the door and brought the papers back to me. I read the charge. Sure enough. It appeared that I had lustfully, lasciviously, and carnally had intercourse with a young lady aged seventeen named Denise Duvivier. The crime had allegedly been committed on board my yacht the *Zaca* a year earlier. I must answer the charges at once in the Monaco town hall . . . where I had just been civilly married.

Ts-t. Ts-t. It takes some ladies so long to realize they have been raped. I couldn't place this girl or this situation at all. Another utter phony.

I looked around, the paper in my hand. Several ambassadors were present. I smiled at an admiral. I looked at my mother who stood a few feet away talking with someone. She would love this. My wife, beside me, looked gorgeous. She whispered, "You look troubled, Errol."

"No trouble at all. Just another rape charge."

"What!"

"Yes, my dear. This one is French and has seventeen summers behind her."

"I don't believe it!"

I kissed my wife. That's the kind of support a man needs.

At the front gate, the word was out. A newspaper pal rushed up to see me. He was a chap I knew and trusted and he asked what I intended doing about the charge.

I would answer it, I told him.

"You know what you're doing, don't you? In Monaco there's no such thing as bail."

"What?" I choked. "No bail!"

"If the rap is a bad one," said my friend, "you have nothing to worry about. But if not, don't be a dope. Don't go there."

"What if it's another frame-up?" I asked.

"Don't go there," he urged.

I continued to eat my wedding cake, wondering. Legally, if I didn't want to go back to Monaco I didn't have to. But for my own self-respect, I simply had to, much as I loathed another scandal. I decided, for the time being, to let the wedding reception go on.

After the reception Pat and I returned to the *Zaca* for our bridal night. The yacht was anchored, a few hundred yards out, at Ville Franche.

In the morning I heard a sound like sixteen claps of thunder. I thought an atomic bomb had exploded. I ran on deck and found the *Zaca* surrounded by the American Navy. They were firing guns and shooting rockets. From the loudspeaker a voice called out, "Hear this now!" repeated several times. Then, "Errol Flynn just got married. Hear this now: Leave him alone!" The laughing voice signed off with one more warning, "Hear this! Hear this now! Stay away from that hot yacht."

That was the signal for every boat to come around. As the Navy men went by in shore boats, about sixty sailors to a craft, they shouted, "Hi, Errol. How was it?"

I had sought a quiet refuge in the world aboard my yacht, and here was the fleet shooting off rockets—and mouths.

Pat came up on deck and waved. The sea churned up as only the American Navy could make it do. They kept shouting all kinds of funny and suggestive nonsense. "Anything new, Errol?" "How'd it go?"

I waved back weakly. "Never better, sailor!"

Last night a wedding reception and a charge of rape. Today the fleet, guns saluting.

I went ashore that night and took Pat to a quiet restaurant along the waterfront. We had hardly got through the *escargots* when in came the Navy again.

Once more salutes and congratulations, so that we hurried through our food.

It started to rain as we walked out.

We went to the launch, tied a few feet off, intending to board it and get away from the latest maelstrom of screaming jokesters.

No one ever believes I want some peace, quiet, the soft moments of life.

I was wearing a pair of rubber loafers. In my hurry, in the rain, I took a flying leap into the launch. My feet went up into the air higher than my body and the bottom part of my spine came down on a corner of the engine box. I felt a searing pain. That was all I knew. I passed out.

I didn't know it then but Pat, in a panic, got the Navy boys to take me out to one of the surface ships of the United States fleet. They had to get me into a breeches buoy and pass me from boat to boat. I was carried there practically unconscious. Faintly I could hear the sailors on the U.S. aircraft carrier saying, "Gee, what a night, Errol!" "Nothing like getting married, eh, kid?" "Bust your back, Errol? Some guys get all the luck." Etc., etc. All intended to be congratulatory, all intended as a compliment.

About a week later I became fully conscious—mostly of pain. It was agonizing. The third, fourth and fifth lumbar vertebrae were fractured, and the ilium, connected to these vertebrae, also was broken.

I was flat for at least a month, unable to move. . . .

That accident took much of the gusto, the bounce, the guts out of me. But not for long. I'm no longer able to take a long jump on a horse over a wall at full gallop. I don't feel like leaping from turrets over old castles. I've reached the age of caution—I think.

Often, since then, I have wished I were built like a squid, so I would have no trouble with my spine.

I returned to the *Zaca*. Pat nursed me back to some degree of mobility.

While I convalesced there was growing interest all over France in the charge of rape still waiting for me at the Monaco town hall. To make it look real dire for me the young lady announced that if she won her suit for a million francs, about three thousand dollars, she would give the sum to charity. *Charity?* Now really—

A photograph was published in the French newspapers which showed this girl in my arms, at the rail of the *Zaca,* as I held her in a passionate embrace. We were both clothed.

Where had this picture come from?

Letting the anchor come up on the *Zaca* and returning to Monaco was the only brave thing I ever did in my life.

We sailed into Monte Carlo harbor. Journalists from all over were on hand for a field day.

They have what they call a confrontation in Monacan law. If an accusation is leveled, the magistrate has the accusing party confront the accused.

I pushed my way through the crowd with Pat. When she put her hand in mine, I clung to it as if it were my last link with the outer world. The police, dressed in their blue and scarlet uniforms, looked big and sobering.

We walked into a dark hall near to where we had only recently been married. I saw the judge, a bald, lean, white-haired man. I had been told he was furious because of my remissness in getting around to answering the charge. I had a lawyer with me but he wasn't allowed inside. They asked me if I wanted an interpreter. I didn't, but I said yes. The charge was read. I was struck with one thing. It said that I had forced the girl into a shower and there wreaked my wicked ways upon her. I had pressed a button, it said, and an electrically operated door had swung shut behind her. Great idea, I said to myself—wish I'd thought of it. Except there wasn't anything like that aboard the *Zaca*.

The judge listened, neither friendly nor unfriendly, to my denial. He gave the order to bring in the accuser. The door opened slowly. I looked at the floor, wondering who was going to come in. I saw a policeman's boots and the cuffs of his trousers. Then—oh, shades of California . . . same scene seven years later—there was the same pair of flat heels, the same bobby socks! But those legs! Oh, no—not those long black hairy legs. Now I knew I was innocent. Drunk, sober, drugged, partly insane, these were not the legs that Flynn would have next to his. I looked up higher. Pigtails! Again!

Could lightning strike twice in the same place? My confidence returned. She looked shyly at the judge, but not at me. I had never seen her before. She repeated her story and said that was indeed she in the photo.

I played the part of my own lawyer-detective. I respectfully asked His Honor to come to the boat, purposely brought to Monte Carlo, for examination. I wanted him to see the shower, what a horribly cramped place it was to have your way with anybody. I wanted to ask, "But Your Honor, have you ever raped anybody standing up in a shower? Do you know what might be the difficulties?" I checked myself.

Outside there was the usual milling mob which generally attends my rape trials.

The judge, followed by a large entourage, went to my yacht. The judge was at my side as I asked the engineer, through the interpreter I didn't need, if there was anything to the story of the electrical shower. Of course there wasn't. Point One for Flynn.

I showed His Honor the shower. It is a funny little cubicle, slightly larger than an upright coffin.

The judge experimented. He turned a faucet and immediately got his suit wet with a stream of salt water.

Frowning thoughtfully, he stepped out of the shower and took a last reflective look at the cubicle. I knew just about what went through his mind. That was the instant of decision. Not even Flynn could have his wickedness in there.

Back in court he dismissed the case.

A grateful France applauded the decision. A grateful Flynn made some inquiries about that photograph and was able to reconstruct how and when it was made.

Sight-seers and visitors were always snapping pictures of me and of my yacht. This photo had been taken about a year earlier, apparently carefully planned. The girl had swum out to the boat, climbed on board, stumbled against me and thrown herself on my chest so that I caught her. On shore, by prearrangement, a camera snapped us at the moment when she appeared to be in my arms. A bit of pretty skillful work.

Shortly after that the girl's father, who was in financial trouble, went to jail, and the rest of the family was invited to leave Monaco.

As the French themselves say, "After all, what is there but justice?"

I was in Los Angeles when I received the stunning news that Freddie McEvoy lost his life trying to save his wife in a storm off the coast of Western Africa. I had warned him about these waters; they were dangerous. He had been sailing around the Mediterranean, but there is a big difference between that kind of seagoing and what it can be along the coast of Africa.

He had a single motor in a Dutch-built yacht. The spars and rigging were light. In order to turn a dishonest penny—or an honest one, according to your viewpoint—he had loaded his ship with a hundred and ten cases of Scotch whisky. On board he also had valuable papers of mine. His wife's furs and jewels were aboard. Just about all he possessed.

The crew of the yacht consisted of three German displaced persons, Freddie's wife, a maid, two dogs. One of the Germans was an engineer, the other two crewmen. I wanted to loan him a Cuban seaman in my employ, but my boy took a look at the rigging of Freddie's yacht and refused to go. Clearly this wasn't a boat intended to ride in high seas.

There was a big blow. When the storm broke it must have flooded the engine and knocked out the sail. No one quite knows what happened. Freddie lashed his wife and the maid to the mast. The boat ran up on a reef. Some Arabs on shore saw the distress, but could do nothing. Freddie decided to swim to shore for help. How he made it through those enormous seas I don't know. On shore he couldn't get any assistance or make himself understood. He decided to swim back to the smashed-up ship. He cut loose from the mast his wife and the maid. The maid went down immediately.

He and Claude started swimming for shore.

Freddie could have made it again, but he saw that Claude was behind him. He returned to get her. He tried to tow her to shore. The rollers were high. He was within a few feet of land and hands were actually outstretched to pick them up. Then a huge wash carried them back and they were never seen alive again.

I like to think of Freddie making that gesture. It was really unlike him. He was such a selfish fellow, not one to lay down his life for anyone. Not really heroic. And yet, as I have always said, you never can tell what people will do in special circumstances—especially when you love, truly love.

My friendship with Freddie was deep—a real sporting relationship. He made life appear a thing of gaiety. He dominated most situations in which he figured. When he was with the Olympiads, he even dominated their sessions. He was an international playboy. His profession? Anything. He made a fortune, he married wealth, he raced cars, he was a leader in his set. People like me had to work. Freddie didn't in order to live high. There was a certain gift which not many have. I had been close to him for twenty years and his passing was a hard blow to me. I could have understood if he went out like a cheat, a gambler, a ne'er-do-well—but not in that gallant way.

I was in the middle of a picture when I heard the news. I called the State Department in Washington to ask for an investigation. They cooperated. Searchers found his body. It was only recognizable by a belt I had given him. It had a gold buckle on it—which he'd swiped from me.

I completed *Adventures of Captain Fabian, Against All Flags, Master of Ballantrae.*

Whenever I finished a picture or drew a big paycheck, I flew to Jamaica and enlarged the Errol Flynn Estates. I was bound to try to salvage something from my earnings before people, friends, wives, mistresses, courts, took it away from me. I knew that if I didn't do this, soon I'd be on the bum again. I didn't know at this time how many millions I had made, or just where it had gone. I knew that I owned precious little in the way of real property, stocks, or anything else that would be of help in any emergency. I had a couple of valuable paintings stashed away, but mostly the cash was drawn from me by an unending retinue of lawyers, agents, servants, aides, flunkies and females.

When I landed at the Kingston airport my custom was to hire a limousine to drive me across the island to where Boston Estate now ran along the coast for about two miles. It was characterized by a blue fence. Wherever the blue fence ran, within was my property, and one or two signs along the way said ERROL FLYNN ESTATES.

Back in America, little was known of my life in Jamaica or my interest in the island. Columnists merely reported from time to time that I was on my way there or I had returned from there, or that a wife, or perhaps a young lady, went with me.

Once I arrived there I lapsed into a completely different life. It was a reversion to my New Guinea days. The native Jamaicans reminded me of the brown-skinned Melanesians, though there were great differences as to personality, education, and literacy. I was fascinated by the Jamaican language, a derivation of the English tongue, with its odd and colorful idiom. I cocked my ear to hear the special language that the Jamaicans spoke among themselves when they didn't want a white man, Yankee or English, to understand them. They took the traditional English and by shifting the beat of pronunciation, they produced a different tongue which sounded a bit like Gaelic.

I cut an imperial figure along the north shore of Jamaica. I formed certain habits during the periods of one to three months that I stayed there. Each day a ride over my ranch on horseback, or a walk on foot, watching the copra grow, as I had watched it in New Guinea. Then perhaps a rafting trip down the Rio Grande. You go down-rapids on bamboo rafts poled by a fleet Jamaican. As you glide down this river you look up on either side to the most magnificent skyline of hills that God or Nature has created. This was a four-hour jaunt in which you picnicked along the way, you swam in the river, or you took along your skin-diving equipment and went down thirty or forty feet looking for "the big Snook." Most Snooks are twelve or fourteen inches long—in my river they can come to forty inches. Then perhaps a trip in my motorboat around Navy Island or down the coast. At night, a stroll in the market place of Port Antonio. This is a town of eleven thousand. You get the feeling you have gone back one hundred and fifty years. The houses are built in an early English style. The more prosperous swains have bicycles, and in the evening a boy and girl court by riding double on a bicycle along the main street. Everywhere there is rum and calypso music. I had not been there long when a band of calypso musicians asked if they could become my band and bear my name. They dubbed themselves "Errol Flynn's Swamp Boys" and they play all over the north of Jamaica.

There is the beauty of the Jamaican females. Jamaica Royal, she is
Chinese and Negro, rare and beautiful. Jamaica Brown is the predomi-
nant female of the island, of middling bronze color. There is Black
Ebony Daughter and there is English-style white woman. And there
are a few Chinese and a few others, East Indian mingled with Jamaican.
Altogether a colorful, a diverse people—and those songs!

> Brown skin girl, go home and mind babee
> Brown skin girl, go home an' min' babee
> Your daddee gone on a sailing ship
> And if him don' come back
> Throw away the damn babee. . . .

The Jamaicans live in small one-room huts in the hills, in the towns
and along the shores, and most of all they live in fear of the hurricane
season.

I decided that I must make a moving picture of the sea world which
surrounded Jamaica. The film came to be known as *The Cruise of the
Zaca,* and in making it I made some enemies in Jamaica.

I had captured three crocodiles in the Savanna-la-Mar, an area of
clear water along Jamaica's shores. I took them on board the *Zaca*
over to famous Doctor's Cave, at Montego Bay, where the underwater
scenery is beautiful. I had in mind making this picture for my own
interest, an item just off the cuff, for amusement, and perhaps even
profit. I wanted to record the beauty of marine life on film.

For a week, while my cameraman ground away, I kept the crocs on
board, tied up. It wasn't easy on them. They weren't eating much, they
were in the sun, and they were on call occasionally as I needed them
in some underwater wrestling scene. The reptiles' jaws were sewed up
with wire. That was a piece of hemstitching that I didn't want to come
apart. We undid the wire when they ate, but then quickly reshut their
snouts: and so, I was able to work with them.

Once one of the creatures gave me a nasty cut across the leg with
his tail. I was under water with him at the time. I came up bleeding
and I swam for the side of the *Zaca* as fast as I could.

During all this time we were within sight of the vacationers who
came to Montego Bay. We could see the bathers on the beach, and
they didn't know that on board my ship were these ferocious, captive
sea lizards.

A storm broke. The crocodiles got loose, and though their dangerous
jaws were still wired, they started threshing around the deck. The *Zaca*

rocked at her anchor, the squall leaned the boat far over, and all hands took to the rigging—for the crocs were after us.

A wave came, caught one and he went over the side.

We turned on the two remaining ones. While they snapped at our heels we tried to re-lasso them.

Then, as the storm settled, the two crocs went over the side.

Word went out that they were free—in Doctor's Cave.

Like obliging fellows, the crocs stayed in the cove, their heads popping up out of the water, to the consternation of the people on shore.

Mr. Fletcher, a Montego Bay leader, and a crowd of business colleagues descended on me like a school of barracuda. We'll sue you, Flynn! . . . Get those things out of our waters—you and they—get out! . . . You want to destroy our business?—Let word of this get to New York, and who'll come here? Crocodiles at a resort!

We got the two crocs out of the water—itself a miracle of recovery—shot up the sails of the *Zaca* and got out of Montego Bay.

I returned to Port Antonio, deciding that back in home waters I would work on the far, or sea side of Navy Island. With a diving outfit and a cameraman I would go down there and complete the work begun at Doctor's Cave.

But the crocs were sluggish, worn out, perhaps even dying, and when they moved they showed no life, no savagery.

I couldn't think of a thing to get them to look alive. I tried poking them, pulling them on a wire. I injected them with adrenalin and digitalis. Nothing helped. I was fretful, because one important scene had to be shot—a death scene in which I killed one of them with a knife. I needed some opposition, but the crocs were fed up with the whole deal.

I remembered what I had seen years before when a frog in a certain picture had to jump. The frog was supposed to jump six feet but wouldn't go more than six inches. Everybody went mad. The frog was holding up the picture. But an ingenious prop man got an idea. He located an eye syringe, put some ammonia in it, and he stuck it up the frog's rectum at the right time. It then took the longest jump ever made by a frog, going about forty feet high, almost out of our studio, almost over to Paramount—and of course we didn't get the shot. But it was a matchless performance. Mark Twain could have made a wonderful bet on him.

I got the necessary materials, the syringe and the ammonia, and I prepared to press this thing to a finish, wherever it led. . . .

My cameraman went under water. I had another man on deck. I put the crocodile where I wanted him. I got into the water, in position. . . .

Camera . . .

"Okay, let him have it—"

My assistant stuck the syringe full of ammonia up the reptile's fanny —and my God, he looked like a torpedo that goes mad and comes back and sinks the submarine that sent it! The croc came around, gave me a good cut with his tail, went down, zoomed up, bumped into the cameraman, knocked out the equipment, went stark raving mad under the *Zaca* and scrammed out to sea.

We never did get the shot.

For a while I kept the other reptile in an aquarium I built at Navy Island.

The Cruise of the Zaca was a thoughtful little picture. People still talk about this film. They don't ask me about *Robin Hood,* they ask about *The Cruise of the Zaca.* It had tremendous public interest. I sold it to Warners, idiot that I was, for practically nothing. This film, in color, is still playing. There was only one heartbreaking incident in connection with it. There was a 1/200,000th inch aperture in the camera that took some beautiful underwater shots, and it destroyed about five thousand feet of film. That minute disorder became magnified so that on the screen a diagonal yellow streak three feet wide ran through the film.

To this day I am a little chary of finding myself in the Montego Bay district. Hotel proprietors there feel that I am not good for business. That is why, when I go over there to visit Noel Coward, Blanche Blackwell and other pals, I usually make the trip after twilight.

As a result of my newly arranged intermittent life in Jamaica, I was thrown frequently into contact with my mother—for the first time since childhood. She and my father came to live in Jamaica for long stretches, and they occupied the old slave-day place called Boston Great House. The home was surrounded with frangipani, hibiscus, pimiento trees, high palms, and the stubby grass of the island, and it overlooked the blue Caribbean.

But life with Mother never eased. I couldn't be with her for long, for more than an hour or two, without fierce tensions breaking loose. She and I were oil and water. The woman who, it was said, I took after physically and mentally—she and I continued our lifelong feud. It was tiger and lion in one cage when we were together. I didn't see how so many people could tolerate her and she couldn't conceive how anyone could put up with me.

It was hard to best her, and I rarely did. I think I never really will. It was hardly worth trying: knockdown affairs, terrible in the clinches. Such energy. If I had her energy I'd make forty more pictures, buy two more sailboats, be the first man to the Moon and have a mistress on Mars.

As she passes the seventy-year mark and I reach the halfway point, Father continues to referee a perfectly senseless war: one of attrition, where the causes, the purposes, and the values on both sides have been decimated and long since lost in the more grueling business of simply getting at each other at every opportunity and in any possible way.

She has regarded me for a whole lifetime, rightly or wrongly, as a complete dope, and I have conceived of her as a pain in the neck.

So, in Jamaica, not far from Navy Island, once earlier the scene of trouble between Spain and England, she got in her innings—and I tried in vain to get in mine.

As we entered into a semidomestic relationship in Jamaica our opportunities for tension increased. Mother didn't like it when I tossed a cat across the room and it knocked over and broke a lot of her prize crockery. But cats never seem to get hurt in a toss like that, and when this cat crawled all over my face as I slept, I simply reacted.

She nearly had a seizure when she heard I liked to go nude bathing at Boston Beach.

Not only would she insist on advising me in my motion picture affairs, but she took a hand in all my business activities, like the running of the Titchfield Hotel, which I owned for a time. I had a bellyful of Mother—there's a switch—after I bought the hotel and she set out to run it for me—her way.

For one thing, she believed that people who came to the hotel should be married. I believed people should mind their own business and not pry.

She thought the staff should be elderly and churchgoing. I thought they should be young and lively, and not waste time on Sunday sitting around on any hard wooden pews, when you could stretch out on a white sand beach.

There were church meetings in the place, which I frowned upon while downing good Jamaican rum.

Mother wanted to bring in the old English atmosphere—retired gents whose country had no use for them any more. And she found them: there are plenty such in Jamaica. I have nothing against old age per se—being not far from it myself—but the folks she brought to the hotel were so ancient they creaked. Mother, you felt, would have liked a bell captain around with an ear trumpet, his own pair of crutches, or a wheelchair which he hid in a corner when not in use.

Piously, she was opposed to a bar. Imagine a hotel without a bar! How did she expect people to be able to go to sleep at nights, drinking water? You might just as well convert the establishment into a morgue.

For a time, as Mother's views prevailed, the characteristic guests were about seventy. The gentlemen usually had a white mustache, except for that portion of it which was yellowed by age and soup. These folks were so decrepit that they could keep you awake at night dropping dead in the corridors and the rooms—thud! thud!

My dough was in this hotel, and I wanted young people around: vitality and music, the Mango Walk, calypso, be-bop and rock and roll; dancing and life; for we are here this once only—only this once—so let there be gaiety and joking and clowning, hoaxing and capering, romance and sport and rafting on the Rio Grande—and laughter and the good life till the eyes closed in sleep at night.

While I was in the States I received a letter from Mother saying that on the Boston property there was a beautiful old church bell. The bell needed to be restored to its proper place swinging and ringing in a belfry. The community needed to hear the bell on Sunday. It was my duty, she said. Would I therefore send the money to build it?

Mother has been bitten by religion in her declining years. She put by her own youth-time cavortings, no longer was interested in such distasteful goings-on. Now she was engrossed in reform, good works, deeds of heavenly import. The Boston Church was a tiny worn-out wreck through which cattle and goats wandered.

Though not much of a churchgoing man, it seemed to me that I could do this to placate Mother, my eternal will-o'-the-wisp pursuit of trying to please her. If people wanted to go to church and could find nothing better to do on Sunday, then let them. I said yes.

She sent a letter telling me how happy the local community leaders were at this gesture. I felt a surge of religion coming on.

I figured that this ought to come to about a hundred and fifty dollars. But when I got the bill I almost choked. It was for about five thousand dollars. There must be some mistake; this must be for the belfry of Notre Dame or of St. Paul's in London—not for the little old ruin on our estate.

I was so upset about this bill that I decided it was worth making a special trip to Jamaica to hassle it out. That—or I was willing to travel six thousand miles to fight with my mother, I wasn't sure which.

In my incessant quest for the dangerous way to do things, I bought a small Navion plane. I flew it with my associate, Barry Mahon, from California right across the American continent to Nassau, to Cuba, and down to Jamaica. This was, for a single-engine plane, a feat. Naturally, going across deserts, landing at little unfamiliar airports, passing over great expanses, was much to put a small plane through. Each time you lighted on some dinky airstrip and got up again, it was a hazard.

At one place I opened the door to get out. As I did, a bottle of vodka fell out and crashed at the feet of the airport officials. Drinking is against the rules for aeronautical people. It was a tense moment, but I explained that it was only water, and as vodka has no smell, I got away with it.

Barry and I, alternating at the controls, reached Cuba. He was an expert flier, a Spitfire pilot with World War II experience. Now came the flight from there to Jamaica. The plan was to land at Montego Bay, the western end of the island.

We started a little late, and as we made our way through the skies we could see the sun lowering rapidly, twilight setting in, with Jamaica still considerably distant.

It was my turn to pilot. I was flying on beam ADF. I couldn't get a signal, nor could I see the island. The sun was just above the horizon. That meant about ten more minutes of flying time before darkness. I didn't know the Montego Bay airport from a flying standpoint, neither did Barry, and the same thoughts hit us at the same time. Over the Caribbean in a single-motor job, no land in sight, no way of turning back, no automatic direction finder, no coast guard around. Below, the waters of the dreaded white shark. I began to sweat. Barry asked for a cigarette—and he doesn't smoke.

In that brief twilight that you have in the tropics, I saw a small dark blur far ahead. Minutes went by. Could we make it before it was dark? Obviously we couldn't. It would be a night landing in an unknown airport.

The sun settled swiftly, and there it was—night—though the island was big now and unlighted.

Barry smoked his cigarette so far down it burned his fingers, and he lit another. We speculated what to do.

"Any idea where this airport is?" I asked, my voice overloud.

"Me? No. Let's go on and see what we can do."

Over Montego Bay I should have been able to see the landing field, but there was no light. I thought I recognized some of the promontories, vague outlines of the depot structures.

We circled, but dared not go too low.

Again we went around.

Barry, on the radio, tried to reach Kingston or Montego Bay. Not a word, not a sound, no reply back. No radio, pitch darkness, silence.

"For Christ's sake," said Barry, "we're out of gas, too!"

In a minute or two we'd have to go down anyway, one way or the other.

"We'll ditch in the water," I said, "our best bet, sport. Maybe we can swim to shore."

At that instant there was a blaze of lights all over the airport.

I took a bit of altitude, looked down.

They were rebuilding the airport, and there were three big bulldozers right in the place where I had to land.

Even so, I must come in.

We zoomed down, the buildings zoomed up.

I put the plane down, the wheels just skirting to the side of those bulldozers. We climbed out pretty shaken.

"What's the use kidding ourselves?" Barry said. "I got out of three rough spots in my Spitfire, but this was worse."

It appeared that we had been circling—and by the grace of God, or the help of Lady Luck—an old colored man saw us, and, though the airport was closed for the night, he figured there was a plane in trouble and took it on his own responsibility to switch on the lights.

I send this old boy a present every year.

We stayed in Montego Bay that night, never expecting that the following day there'd be a sequel even more frightening. . . .

Months earlier I had written to my father in Jamaica to build an airstrip on the race track on our ranch. He wrote back that the job was going along fine, he was following my directions about wind, leveling the strip, and it would be a thousand-foot run. There was a bulldozer on the estate and it had been put to work. He wrote, *You can land a plane now any time you want to.*

We took off from Montego Bay, with me at the controls and Barry enjoying the scenery of the north coast of Jamaica. You can find nothing more beautiful: it is a wondrous sight. You zing along low over the water and see the royal palms, the coconuts, the beaches, the incessant green as if one huge leaf covers the whole land. You can almost smell the frangipani trees, and the hibiscus is everywhere. The idyllic way to go to your own ranch.

We reached the region over Port Antonio. Below, in the harbor, lay the *Zaca,* and I said to Barry, "Let's buzz it."

"Do you mind if I hang on? Don't want you to go flying between the mast and showing off."

"I've no idea of showing off, especially after last night at Montego."

I circled about three times over the top of the *Zaca.* Below, on deck, was my faithful crew, arms waving. There was the Titchfield and people were out in front, staring up, waving. It was a real homecoming.

There were only a few miles more to go to the airstrip at Boston. There would be another welcoming and then a dinner, music, the gaiety of the tropics. . . .

I steered for the Flynn Boston House.

In a few minutes we were over the race track, part of which was supposed to be converted to an airstrip.

Airstrips are supposed to be level and they are always in a straight line. But the strip that my father built was like none that Barry and I had ever seen. Peering down at it, it was shaped like a dog's leg: it made a kind of triangle. If it was a thousand feet long, it was laid out in three contraposed directions so as to measure that distance.

At one corner of this triangle there was an enormous tree. Beyond that tree, the strip went off at a different angle.

I looked at this lightning-shaped strip aghast. There was no possible way to get in. Over the tree? Into it? Beyond it?

Below, as we closed in, looking for a way to get at the field, the angles enlarged: the tree was right in my way.

"Barry, there isn't a chance here in a tonload. Our best bet is to go to Kingston—fly twenty-five minutes more."

"The hell you say, Baron—look there—!" The gas gauge again, it was empty! We hadn't put much in at Montego Bay because it was only a short run to Boston.

We headed out over the water. Again cigarette smoking.

"Barry, what do you think we ought to do?"

"Guess you better take another turn."

"If we take another turn we'll never make it anywhere else. Barry, I can't make it—impossible—you want to try it?"

"I'm thinking," he said.

"What?"

"What I've been thinking is no."

"Barry, you're a better flier than I. You want to have a go?"

"Okay, move over."

We switched and he said, "Get that seat belt fastened mighty quick. If we're going to crack we're going to go over on our front, and we're going to roll over. So I'm going to cut the motor as soon as we get down." That would lessen the danger of fire from a crack-up.

We were convinced we were headed for a smack, but this was the last instant for action. Barry moved in toward the airstrip.

He came in high, aimed straight down for that damned tree, plummeting like a hawk on a chicken, and he plumped the plane in the first possible space behind the tree. He slid the plane down, almost sheer.

He pulled her up, straightened out, and the plane careened along this horrible slanted rutty strip.

The coconut tree at the end of it came closer and closer. Next to it was a brick wall. It was hit one, or hit the other.

We were on one wheel.

The plane moved like a tightrope walker over the field, these obstacles magnifying, and then we stopped exactly in front of the brick wall—with no more than two inches between our propeller and that barrier.

I looked at Barry. His complexion is normally gray, but this time it was like Bela Lugosi's before a draught of blood. My heart hammered and I couldn't move.

People came running: my father and my mother, my son Sean, who was visiting his grandparents, the neighbors, the workers on our ranch.

I kissed my mother's hand.

I hugged Sean.

I embraced my father.

I said hello to others . . . then promptly, in front of everybody, I threw up—

When I began to recover, rage worked up in me. I hissed into my father's ear, "Dad, what in the friggin' world ever made you build an airstrip like this? . . . You must be mad. We almost got killed."

He salved me in his usual way: Now, now, old boy, don't be silly, let's have a drink, you'll feel better.

"Bugger off, Dad! I feel lousy. I almost broke my neck. Whoever heard of a crocked airstrip with a hundred-feet—I mean foot—high tree in the middle of it, for God's sake!"

"Now, now, son, not in front of your dear mother."

We went up to the house, ancient, comfortable Boston House, since burned down but then looking homey.

At the house Mother offered me some tea. Tea of all things. How un-understanding can a person be—at a time like this—when Barry and I needed restoratives of the sternest sort.

· I spoke to my father in a way I rarely did: for normally Mother and I had an option on all major family entanglements.

"Dad, how in hell *could* you do this? I sent you the plan. You know how an airstrip is supposed to be built—or you ought to know."

"My boy," he said, "please let's not discuss it—"

"Yes, let's. I want to know. Must I believe that a man of your supposed intellect in the world of science is ignorant of the shape of an airstrip?"

"If you must know, son, your mother has always been fond of that tree. She likes to see the little calves gambol under it of an evening. She wouldn't let me cut it down."

Ah, my mother! I should have known!

I waited till dinner time the following night before I nailed her to her own cross. I'd teach her how to spend my money on church belfrys.

Dinner was cheerful, gay. Despite all, Mother is a fabulous cook. We went out to the veranda for tea!

Finally I said to my son, "Listen, sport, mind if I have a little talk with Mother?"

She sat up stiffly, the Duchess of Boston.

Sean went out, around the house, just out of sight, where he could listen cleanly and honestly.

I pulled out the statement on the belfry costs. "Mother, there are a few items—"

She interrupted. "Errol, what items!" It wasn't a question at all—it was a frontal attack.

"A few things here I would like to have you explain. For instance, I don't understand why our launch, our boat—"

I got about that far. She said, "What else?"

"Here is what I really want to talk about." My nerves had rallied. There must have been a bit of rasp in my voice. "I would like to know how you could put up a belfry for an old bell and have it cost me five thousand smackeroos! Don't you think we could halfway rebuild the whole cathedral for that? And besides—"

That was as far as I got. She turned from me and stabbed a finger at my father. "Theodore, I told you! I told you that Errol would take this attitude."

Father rose. He said, "I don't know much about it, my darling," and looked vague, as is his habit under fire.

"Of course! You don't know anything about anything, but Errol is always like this, Theodore. He has no sense at all!"

My father paused in the doorway as he made ready to enter the house.

"How," she addressed him, calling upon logic—mother's logic— "does he expect"—pointing at me—"that you can put up a belfry with no church under it? Does he want to see this belfry hanging up in the air just with a bell and with no church under it to support it?"

My father beat it then, leaving me trying to envision a belfry defying gravity, sitting in mid-air, with a bell and no church underneath it. They'd have a helluva time with that one even in the special effects department of Warners.

Around the other side of the house I heard a steady snickering. It was Sean, getting his usual rise out of these things that went on between Mother and me. I was glad somebody was happy.

She turned on me. She didn't see how I could be this unreasonable. Didn't I see? Didn't I understand? Well, that was where the money went!

No, I didn't see!

"Well, I didn't expect you to," snorted mother, mollified.

She rose from her chair on the veranda. She pointed across the Errol Flynn Estates, five thousand acres into which I put my life, my money, my time, my interest, my years.

My own property. My new home, where I was looking for peace.

"Go out for a walk, Errol, and come back when you make some sense!" she rasped, tossing me out of my own house. My son Sean thought it was all slightly hilarious and I felt like giving him a clip over the ear.

Sean and I took a long walk in the frangipani, a long cool stroll through the paths between the palms, into the green-stalked meadows, beyond the chicken coops, and higher to where the goats scampered, then far over the knolls where the green lime grew, beyond to the houses where the farm hands lived, then up, up, up to a high point that looked serenely across the long, quiet waters of the Caribbean.

At the outset I told how my eighteen-year-long affair with Warner Brothers came to an end. The hassle I had with Jack Warner at the time was one of the worst, although we laugh at it today.

Most people who work for a company for so long a time get some recognition. My recognition, in 1952, when I was ending my service with Warners, came in the form of a letter accusing me of a breach of contract, holding up the company, and general bad behavior.

They were trying to get rid of their star roster, and this by trying to force the stars to break their contracts. Maybe they wanted to build new people who would cost them less. Perhaps they hadn't been making money enough of late on some of us. Television was making inroads. A time of change was at hand and the tensions were high at Warners between the front office and several of their traditional big drawing cards. They got rid of Bogart—the hard way for him. They bluffed him skillfully, sending him four bad scripts. They did the same to Bette Davis, the same to me. We were the three people on the lot who counted the most to them. Bogy wound up paying $100,000 to get out of his contract. At least that's what he told me. I don't know what the settlement was with Bette Davis, but I think she had to pay too.

When it came my turn, I met Jack in his offices.

He was smiling, cheerful, his usual gay manner but with wariness underneath.

The talk went something like this:

"I think, Baron," he said, "we settle with you the same way we did with Bogart."

"What is that?"

"He paid us $100,000 to buy up his contract."

I smiled at Jack. "Don't you think it's a good idea we do it the other way round in my case? You pay *me* $100,000."

He got up, to break off the interview."What! Are you crazy?"

"No, just want to break my contract."

Actually I was anxious to get out of it. But I said, "I'm happy after being here so long. I like it."

"What would you prefer?"

"Just what I said. You pay me."

He laughed now a friendly laugh. "Come on, let's talk sense." He offered, "I tell you what. You pay us $50,000 and we will let you go."

I imitated his laugh. I had had some acting experience.

There was an impasse. We parted.

A week later I was shown into Jack's quarters again. Once more he asked, "What do you propose to pay us?"

"Pay you? Nothing!"

"You know what this can lead to? This is no threat. We can cast you in any kind of role that we want—under the contract. We don't have to star you. You know your contract."

I said I did. "I will tell you something, Jack. If what you are implying is you have me play the chauffeur who comes in and says, 'Your car is ready, sir,' and goes out—I will do it. As a matter of fact you call me to work and I will even go further than that. I will sweep out the men's room. But I'm paying you nothing!"

That must have been what Jack was waiting for. "In that case why not just let's call the whole thing off right here and now?"

"It's a deal."

That was how I left Warners.

Through with films, facing the future not knowing how I was going to make a living, with most of what I had tied up in Jamaica real estate, and determined not to part with that, I now had the biggest problem of my life.

What to do? Stay in the United States without earning money and try to maintain the regiment of interests that drew on me for subsistence? How could I do it? I had children, ex-wives, aides, a new wife. I even had a new child, Arnella, by Patrice.

Most of all there was always my nemesis, Lili. She was constantly taking, in alimony, a bigger and bigger sum every year. Courts stood by her, and there were always my earnings at Warners that she could attach.

It was this that shook me more than anything else and is still today a very raw exposed nerve.

So what?

A generation after that first hot love of ours I was still paying and paying and paying.

I remember Lili Damita fondly. She did not rob me of my best years, as the saying goes—usually said by women. She merely took my creativity and about a million bucks, but her memory is forever fresh when I feel the holes she left in my head.

Lili taught me more than I wanted to learn. The workings of a woman's mind are not as tortuous as some think. Novelists make some great mystery about female psychology; but maybe these novelists have had only some piddling experience with women so that they have not had enough to go on, so as to speculate or draw conclusions. It is true I got a late start with the feminine mentality, but Lili had engine power enough to put me out ahead of the rest of my brethren in the opportunity to learn something.

Any time you have an experience with a woman which costs you a million dollars—especially if you began life as a bum and mostly broke—you will do some thinking about women, draw conclusions, and come out wiser about the so-called "mystery" of the human female. There is no mystery. As I said before—based on my experience —women go for a million bucks faster than a man.

In the same breath I want to say, a woman friend is the best friend you can have. In my early days I was brought up to hear it said that you can never have a real woman friend, that male friendship is deeper, like Damon and Pythias. That is not true—not in my book. I have had two great friends: I still have them. They are so far superior to male friends, so much more understanding, so much more generous in feelings.

Solid friends—both women.

I learned, when the cards were down, who were my friends and who were not—and these were. Women make better friends than men: good, really honest friends. When the going is tough, give me a woman for a friend. If they happen to care for you they will go farther than any man. Half the world will disagree, but that has been my experience, and it is useless to generalize unless you can speak from the empirical.

The situation I faced after I was through with Warners was this: I would never be able to make the annual payments which the court called for me to make to Lili at this time. The sum had become astronomical. The tax on the tax on the tax had become impossible.

Lili was gradually breaking me and by this time, when the main part of my picture-making career was ending, she, her lawyers and my lawyers, and the California court broke me.

It worked on me that a man could be forced to risk life and limb in my type of action picture, and wind up with nothing or very little. A little was left over for me to put into Jamaica real estate.

Now, with no more money coming in, I decided to put in a call and ask her to get her teeth out of my neck.

I telephoned her at Palm Beach.

"Hello, Lili?"

"Yes."

"This is Errol."

"Yes."

"I can't keep up those payments to you any longer. You'll have to do something to make it easier."

"I don't know what you're talking about."

"I'm wound up at Warner Brothers. My earning power is over. You'll have to get off my back."

"Fleen, you better talk with my lawyers." A familiar noise.

"I've given you a million bucks and it has to stop! What do you want? Do you want me to put my blood in bottles and have them send it to you and you drink it at mealtimes?"

"I don't understand, Fleen!"

"Well, I'm through, Lili! You're not getting any more!"

"Fleen, talk with my lawyers!" She slammed the phone.

I said to myself, To hell with California! To hell with America! I'll live on the *Zaca!* Sail the seas! Beat it!

I had to do this, or kill myself with this burden, or go crazy. I decided I would do nothing of the sort.

I will leave this adopted country for good! Let them chase me through the world! Let every leech try to collect! Let Lili hire more lawyers and cops and collectors and let them all pursue me through Europe!

I had gotten mighty goddamned tired of hearing people say, "It's Flynn. Take the sonofabitch for all you can while the getting's good!"

With my wife Pat, and my daughter Arnella, I took flight for Rome.

Our apartment in Rome was an open house. The wanderers of Europe, ex-kings, floating celebrities, moving picture people, came and went like breezes through a screen door. Prince This and Prince That. The *Anschluss* between the royalty of Hollywood and the royalty of Europe. I had been deposed by Warner Brothers, and one deposed king, Farouk of Egypt, came to my place frequently.

Farouk is a tremendous eater. He loved my larder. He would hardly say hello before he headed for the icebox. If I happened to have some *fois gras,* carefully preserved, it was gone instantly, one gulp down his gullet like a shark swallowing a bluefish. Caviar disappeared as if a magician arranged it. One spoonful and whaff! the whole jar would slide away. He didn't even allow the eggs to explode on the roof of his palate—they short-circuited straight to his belly.

He never thought of replacing this food. Maybe he thought it was a royal prerogative. After he wiped out the contents of the refrigerator his eyes turned appraisingly to whatever might be around the place in a feminine way. He was a pincher. A pinch for any lady present. Some didn't go for it. Once a little lady from Texas, pinched by him, hauled off with a swing taken from the floor and caught "His Majesty" a clap behind the ear. The descendant of the Pharaohs descended fast—to the floor. Since he weighed more than 250 pounds, there was a respectable thud like a kettle drum.

He wanted to know all about the female stars and starlets. He had a particular interest in Anne Sheridan. He had seen me in a picture with her. I think that he had me in mind for a special post, in case he ever returned to the throne of Egypt—Royal Procurer.

Toward the end of our relationship he phoned before he dropped by. This gave me a chance to clean out the icebox pretty well myself before he blew in. I don't recall a single thing he ever said that could be quoted, remembered or noted. He came to be entertained, to be fed, to look on, and to belch.

Jack Warner came to Italy at this time. One day I was in one of Rome's most noted restaurants with Jack when Farouk came in.

I said, "Jack, you know 'Big Jim' Farouk, don't you? May I introduce you?"

Jack paled visibly.

He stood to his feet. I was flabbergasted at what I saw. Jack Warner, who has had ten times the power and influence of Farouk, a man who has justified his existence a thousand times over, bowed at the waist. He was that impressed.

Jack was taking Farouk at his face value, apparently. They reminisced about their experiences at mutual gaming tables.

One thing I knew, the ex-King wouldn't pick up the tab.
Royalty ain't all it's cracked up to be.

Not long afterward, groping for film work, for a production of
my own, I dealt with another royal personage.

Prince Ranier of Monaco is a distinguished man with a distinguished
mind. My boat used to be in Monte Carlo, so that I saw him from
time to time, and I may say, he is the exact antithesis to "Big Jim"
Farouk. Ranier is a man who takes his responsibilities seriously and
does a job and a very good one, in my opinion.

We were drawn together by mutual interests in the world of oceanography. Ranier's grandfather had done a great deal for marine exploration, and he built the fabulous aquarium and marine museum in
Monte Carlo. I can recall, even when I was a youngster in Australia, my
father singing his praises, calling him another Darwin. So when I
went to see young Ranier in Monte Carlo, we had a common bond.

I proposed a favorite project of mine, an underwater film, for
which I wanted to borrow the famous Monte Carlo aquarium. Also I
brought up the idea that perhaps the government of Monaco might
like to kick in a bit of finance.

His Highness was very interested. His eyes lit up as I outlined the
film I proposed to do. It would be in color, shot underwater.

As I went along describing it, I said, "Of course, you see, we can't
get a big octopus. I will make one out of rubber, and we will put it
in the aquarium and use special effects."

He looked startled. "You mean you are not going to use a real
octopus? You mean you are going to fake these things—the sharks
and the octopus?"

"Look, Your Highness, what do you want me to do? Sit on the
bottom of the ocean for two weeks waiting for an octopus or shark
to come along so that we can catch it? You get cold down there."

He wanted everything to be real. He didn't know that plenty of these
filmed things are impossible. I had to explain. "A rubber octopus on
the scene looks far more effective than a real octopus ever can. The
same goes for a rubber shark."

He looked skeptical. I argued, "It looks far more ominous on the
screen too, Your Highness. Besides, you can't get bitten."

"But the reality of this?"

"The audience doesn't know whether it is real or not, or how it is done. Look, Prince—" I was pleading hard now. "You can't find a live octopus which will co-operate with you, especially a big-enough one. The same goes for sharks. They are very unco-operative."

Sometimes there is such a thing as too much integrity.

We never made the picture. But possibly little Grace Kelly has put His Highness wise by now.

I moped, I drank, I sailed, I went deep down underwater.

While the *Zaca* was anchored at Majorca I bet a friend, Emanuel Cervantes, I'd dive off the crosstrees of my ship. It was the kind of bet you would make if you weren't exactly stone cold sober.

The *Zaca*'s mast is 110 feet high. It doesn't look like much when you look up—but when you are aloft, the deck below looks small like a sardine. The height is equivalent to ten or eleven stories of a Manhattan building. When you're up there and the mast sways, you hang on like death. Unless you've climbed a mast, you can have no idea of the anticipation, the fear and sometimes the terror, to get up that rig; no idea what it is to go up and examine some blocks which might be a danger to the ship's safety. But if you're the captain, you have to put up a front: "I'll go aloft and take a look myself." You could look up from the deck with the binoculars and see the same damn thing, but you have to prove yourself.

Emanuel pooh-poohed my drunken suggestion that I would dive off the crosstrees. "Impossible, Flynn."

I said casually, "For a thousand bucks I will do it tonight." There were people around listening to this bravado. I may have had a quart of vodka in me.

"A thousand bucks?" he echoed. "Agreed! You are on!"

Now I was confronted with this awful thing. Just because I didn't like this guy and wanted to take some of his dough, I was hooked. I had to do it. I put the glass down.

Using the old tactic of stalling while you think, I got my valet and I sent him down to the engine room for some grease. I said, "Put a mat on the deck. I don't want to get it greasy."

I hoped I wore a fairly easy smile, as if it was a cinch. I said, "Cover me with grease because if I go in the water from that high, I don't want to break my skin."

Cervantes watched the operations. Of course I didn't know what the hell I was doing, but I was stalling like a financial wizard. "Now bring up the rubber sole slippers because when I go up to the top I don't want to cut my feet on the rig. . . . Ah yes, another thing—I think I will wear a sweatshirt."

This was taking a lot of time, while crewmen took care of these details.

I looked up at the crosstrees from time to time, as if assaying the wind, or how I would jump. "By the way, bring me a little brandy. Anybody else care for a little brandy or anything?"

How the hell did I get into this? Then, nonchalantly, I said, "Take this grease off. I'll just wear the sweatshirt." It was getting darker, the bet was on, heavier than ever. Cervantes stood around and looked. I was hoping the fellow would think it over one hundred times. All of this was a war of nerves.

Cervantes said, "You are not really going to do that?"

"Of course I am. Give me the thin white sweatshirt!"

"You are going in headfirst?"

"What do you expect me to do, go in feet first? What do you want to do?—Pull out of the bet?"

"No, no, Flynn."

"Then put up or shut up!"

I turned to the crew, "Come on, boys, let's get this over with."

I pulled off my shoes, taking much time. I said, "Ready, here we go, boys"—and I began the slowest climb up the rig that sea annals have ever known.

I got about forty feet, and Emanuel was on deck, looking up, and the others all craned their necks, watching me go up foot by foot, slow step by step.

Now Cervantes yelled up, "Errol, you don't want to do this? You will hurt yourself—"

"What's—that?" I called down, as if I didn't hear.

He howled up to the sky. "Why—don't—you—settle?"

I shouted down, "What—for—?" And I took a few more steps. I was near the top. I screamed down, "Are—you—kidding—?"

I was nearly at the crosstrees and my heart swayed like the mast.

He cupped his hands and offered up the ropeline, "Why—don't—you—settle—for—half?"

I roared down, "*Booked!* You've got a deal!"

Nobody ever hit the deck quicker. I still thank God he offered to settle for half before I made the jump, because I would have had to do it.

I was skin-diving off the coast of Spain, off the Balearics. I was with one of the most skillful divers I ever met, Paul Buttles. He is a one-legged fellow, a great athlete. We knew of the existence of a sunken ship off of these islands. Buttles went far down and he saw a huge ancient leaden anchor. He figured there must be a ship somewhere around. He came up and told me. Then we went down together.

In making a foray like that you use what is called an underwater sled. This is a device which lets you cover a lot of territory. You board this contrivance from a launch. The sled operates so that by making huge circles, which diminish in size, you can do much exploration as the circle narrows. Inside that circle you may spot something. If you do, you surface and place a marker over what you think you have seen. Then you make your descents at that point.

Buttles and I were searching for days in this area without finding the ship. Meantime, as we explored, we ran out of fresh meat and relied on the fish we caught. Many fish of a variety called the *meru,* a delicious grouper fish, were deep down in the water hereabouts and I went for one this day.

I was down about a hundred feet and I saw a big one weighing perhaps forty pounds. I took a shot at him and missed. Off he went, downward. I saw him disappear below into a hole. I should have looked at the gauge on my wrist to see how far below I was, but I didn't. I went down, peered into the hole. There, in the darkness, I could see the movement of gills.

I figured if I could edge my way down there quietly I could get a shot at him. I worked my way very quietly, because if you touched a tank against a rock the fish would take off. It was like going down a chimney. The tunnel I was going through was about big enough to admit my body with the tanks. I got closer.

As I was about to pull the trigger he gave a swish of his tail, whipped up the sand on the ocean floor, and was gone. I was now a hundred and fifty feet down—the deepest I had ever been. As the sand settled I saw what might have been bits of lead or some other metal or substance not looking like rock or weed. I paddled my flippers, went down a few feet, picked up the shiny pieces.

I looked at my wrist gauge. It said 42 meters. I felt my air getting short. I pulled the emergency on the air tank. There was a wonderful fresh flow of air. I had three, at most four, minutes between me and the surface.

But I had grown faint, or engrossed, or slowed. I didn't know at the time that I was upside down. I felt a bit of blood on my mouth. I had gone too deep, too fast, in the tunnel. I felt a little drunk. A fish passed by. I wanted to give him a cigar, but I had none. Then I wanted to take my mouthpiece off and give that to him. Changes were taking place in my metabolism. I was experiencing the Rhapsody of the Depths—a dangerous thing because it may be the last rhapsody you will hear. You are drunk, your metabolism is awry, you do not know whether you are right side up or where you are. It is like having a shot of dope in you. You have to get out of that, or you are done for.

I wiggled my way out of the tunnel, like a snake backing out of a hole. I didn't want to go up too fast. But my head was ringing as if a steel band were around it. You have to be in particular training to dive down to even two-thirds of this depth, and I was not. I had been training regularly on a quart of vodka a day and it didn't help. Up I came, like a speck at the surface. I didn't know how much emergency air was left, and I hurried.

My hand went over the gunwale of the launch and I tossed into it the things I held in my hand.

I was pulled into the boat and I lay there exhausted.

The items I had emerged with were broken bits of porphyry shattered but still painted so that the centuries hadn't done as much damage as you might suppose.

We were excited. We decided to go down there again and have a further look. But not me. Buttles and a French boy we had with us went down, scooped up the sand in the spot where I had been, and they came up with a half-dozen curious little art bits which I still have in Jamaica. Among the items was an almost perfectly preserved little Phoenician head done in some material that had outlasted many centuries. At the Spanish Museum this and the others were identified as Phoenician carvings, in age probably three or four centuries before Christ. The reason they had not been crushed by the ocean was that the cave I had gone into had protected these bits from wind, current, mistrals.

I was petrified about having to take them out of Spain, because in Spain you might get off with a life sentence for murder, but try taking art objects out of there and you might get shot.

Every time I go underwater for a deep dive I am petrified. Outwardly I try to appear nonchalant. Light a cigarette, to stall. I take a drink. Underwater you can't do this. Why do I challenge the depth of the sea as I have been doing for twenty or more years? As I have done hundreds of times? In my normal senses I wouldn't take such risks, in other matters, for anybody in the world. On scores of professional and personal hazards, where I might appraise a situation and figure my chances weren't good for coming out alive, I would say no. But not skin-diving.

There I throw caution to the skies—or seas. I know that I have a deep fear of it and that I am in rebellion against my fear. I know I am going down into an element I don't know—nobody knows. Once I get into the water I don't feel so badly. But I must go down. Next to this sport all others are childish: the thrills of baseball, tennis, football, golf, they are nothing compared with being a hundred feet below, with a great stone sea wall about you, the sunlight shining down through the green illuminating an underwater seascape, and the fish moving by.

The lure of the sea, in all its forms, is probably the strongest urge in me. It is a silent world. I am always fascinated, as one is with a favorite poem. It is the indescribable beauty down there that makes you want to go to it and hold it. It is an exercise in quick reflexes. Your mind sharpens, it snaps, it works like an automatic pistol. It is an exercise in self-control too, for you have to breathe half the number of times you do normally. The oxygen tank is on your back. It is a new, a different, a fallible lung, and you go with dread and expectation and a sense of danger, and you hope you'll live.

This sport keeps me alive, but there are those who know me who say I am trying to kill myself this way. I wouldn't say no. I just don't know. I know that when I get down a hundred feet or so, and the air in the tank is gone, and I have only a two-minute or three-minute reserve supply left, and I pull the lever that sets this free, and I start my swim back up to the surface—then I am living—and if not, I am dying as one who has, just before, been living intensely.

Throughout the period of my decline, 1952 to 1956, I went skin-diving, if not daily, then two or three times a week—off Spain, in the Mediterranean, and at a dozen points in the waters of the Caribbean.

When you are down and out and you need a lift for your spirit, you will do something that you might not at another time. At this time, when I was moping, becoming a master mariner in a liquor bottle, I got an invitation from the Northampton Repertory Theatre, in England, to come back and see them. A sentimental journey. Local boy makes good. They wanted to claim one of their own.

They had very little money. I had much more. So I chartered an airplane and went.

I found myself mentioned again in *Spotlight,* the same publication in which twenty-five years earlier I had lied to get myself a job.

I got up before an appreciative audience of the same type to which I had played almost a generation earlier. I had been away a bit, I said, since I played the Wicked Prince Donzil. I was now playing the Wicked Flynn. (Great laughter.)

I called back the memories of the year and a half I played there. I told them how I ran through the streets of London from show to show. (Laughter.) Of the gun that didn't go off. I joked about girls. Then I said something that drew the top laugh of all. "The happiest days I have ever spent anywhere that I can recall in my life were spent here at Northampton."

I didn't realize I was saying this to an audience of people who dreamed of getting away from the dreary place, an audience that went to the theatre to escape. I didn't realize they knew how much of the world I had seen and how odd my words must have sounded to them: Flynn, who had been in the Court of St. James, the courts of California, the courts of love, the tennis courts, the court-esans.

So they laughed heartily and I joined them. It was wonderful, refreshing to be there again, even to see one or two old familiar faces backstage. I needed a lift very badly at this time and I got it in the town where—as I told them truthfully—I had spent the happiest days of my life.

On this trip to England I happened on an old pal, Clark Gable. We stayed at the same hotel and spent two or three days together.

If anyone should ask, "What do two actors talk about when they meet?" the answer is, "Themselves."

But Clark also discussed ranching, women, the peculiarities of our mutual friends. No profundities, though I guess we didn't get around to them. I said to him, "Listen, sport, I have a great story about two brothers. Why don't you and I make it."

Clark laughed his head off.

"Me? Do a picture with *you?* Are you kidding?"

He laughed again.

I must have looked befuddled. "Why not? This is a good yarn. Look what you did in *Boom Town* with Spencer Tracy."

He laughed more. "I would do a picture with him any time—but you —you sonofabitch—you're too young!"

On board the *Zaca,* Pat cooked and comforted me. I frolicked with Arnella. Occasionally friends came on board for a meal or a short cruise. I saw my pal John Hertz, Jr., from time to time. His yacht, the *Ticonderoga,* was at Palma de Majorca. I read. I dreamed. I tried to think who I was. I got paunchy, mottled in the face; still I stayed in the sun and the water, and didn't let myself drift as badly or as far down as people thought I had slipped.

I asked myself some fundamental questions. What did I believe? What had I learned? How did I feel? What were my strengths and weaknesses?

During the next few years, at Majorca, in Rome, wherever I went, I kept a diary of reflections, an irregular chronicle, and some of the answers came out like this:

Naples, Jan. 19, 1952:

It is all very well for philosophers to tell you that Work is an end in itself. But there are great questions here. I am only angry that I haven't been able to find out what makes a man want to work. What makes primitive people on primitive islands build statues twenty or thirty feet tall, as on Easter Island? Isn't this a visual example of the mysterious urge of mankind to do some memorable work? There is an innate urge of creation here that man doesn't understand about himself. Always urges: to procreate, to get drunk, to sleep. What is it that makes a man want to make a motion picture, or become a doctor, or work night and day? I do know it's not just money. Money has flowed through my fingers like water. The urge to work keeps waking in me no matter what my physical condition, no matter what I have gone through, and despite two or three very low ebbs in my life. It is something deeper, more profound. The urge annoys and upsets you, interferes with a genuine desire to be a perfectly happy bum. I don't like the urge to work because I don't think it's worth much. Yet I fear it is stronger than most of my other impulses. Except sex.

Naples, Jan. 23, 1952:

Alcohol is a far greater killer than all opiates. You can buy alcohol on any street corner throughout the world. It gets your brain, your liver. It destroys your morals, destroys your vitality, kills the sexual potential, and you become sluggish. It is a great pity that Prohibition failed. The experiment was too radical. Instead of barring it altogether, the dispensation of alcohol should have been under prescription, or some other control. Prohibition was one of the worthiest attempts of a group to impose their will upon the rest of the people. But of course if you prohibit something you deprive people of an essential liberty; when you deny the right of choice you oppose the greatest gift in the world. People will not stand for it. Alcohol makes man mad, leads to such strange behaviorism. Yet beer and liquor ads maintain newspapers, television, some huge portion of the national and the world economy. Drinker that I am, I think essentially I am the victim of an addiction that is here in the world, revealed to all, exposed to all. It is there. We who are weak take to it and are destroyed by it, but it is essentially a weakness of governments everywhere to allow this poison to circulate like a river through the bloodstream of the human race. As one of the heartiest drinkers in the world, I speak with a voice of authority.

Naples, Jan. 26, 1952:

I have no fear of the Hereafter because I believe there is no such thing. I have been afraid of dying before my time, or dying violently, or of having some unpleasant method of leaving, but as I am a complete agnostic this leaves me philosophic. Why be afraid of something I have no control over?

Naples, Feb. 2, 1952:

A traveler's conclusion: The words human nature, human being, humanity, are the most misused words in our vocabulary. The human as a species is the same universally. But his behavior varies in different places. I behave differently in the South of France than I do in England. You behave according to the customs of a country, or try to adapt yourself. But when or where you find what they call humanity, that is a question. Man's indecency to man all over the world rules out the idea of humanity as an actuality. It is a dream of young idealists. In practice it is a misnomer. Man is at man's throat, as in the sea the fish swallow one another.

Naples, Feb. 5, 1952:

On ubiquitous knowledge: After thirty years of circling the globe I can shed no light on the cosmos. But what makes people tick, that is clearer in mind than it was when I was young. I have learned that you can never trust a human being to behave as you would have expected in a given circumstance. You can never rely upon it. Men and women are both very unpredictable. You can only guess what people will do.

Rome, Feb., 1953:

I keep returning here, trying to salvage my lost fortune, still hoping to make my film *William Tell.* Yet I am drinking more than ever.

I seem, these days, filled with reflections, on so many things—

On narcotics: I have taken many and most drugs but I am not an addict. The only drug I have never taken is heroin. Take it once, you are hooked, done for. So it is not for me. I have found that opiates take away the male sex impulse. A male is too busy dreaming. On the contrary, opiates stimulate the female. I am talking empirically. I will accept any challenge from medical sources to refute this. I probably have had a lot more experience with narcotics and females than most doctors. If medicine knew more about the efficacy of opiates on females they would probably do more with narcotics in the menopausal stages of a woman's life. I am now listening for the howl from the A.M.A. and the screams of glee from my traditional female audience.

My greatest addiction: Not drink, not drugs, not sex. It is curiosity. This has gotten me into all my troubles, successes, failures.

I cannot resist looking into a garbage can or a good book, a new or an old bottle, a bar, an empty or a full paper bag. I cannot resist anything that holds out an antenna toward me, or looks alive or dead, or scarlet or putrid or beautiful. I am drawn toward light, toward darkness, toward brilliance, stupidity, monstrosity.

My greatest fear: The fear of mediocrity. This is an innate and inborn fear. It is what has impelled me to challenge anything I recognized as terrifying to me. As to my own accomplishments, I have a very realistic view of what other people think are accomplishments. I know that my so-called fame or fortune is truly a matter of luck. I don't put a great deal of emphasis on acclaim. I recognize that while I might be mediocre to myself, that I have done the best I could about it. That is not a fear, that is a regret. I think I could have done more. There is only a regret for opportunities lost or missed.

On the stimulation of challenge: When disaster hits me worst I am at my best. I feel a surge of spirit. When I am having it good, I'm no good. I like to have a barrier. I like to have a definite challenge. Yet right now I have the greatest challenge of my life, and I can't seem to do anything about it—but drift.

Rome, Oct. 19, 1953:

I seem to be out of the picture now, and it doesn't seem to matter. Or does it? Why is it a man will lose so suddenly his will to work and instead of doing something he thinks worth while, will start to procrastinate with himself?—And in this condition the edges of his perceptions become dulled, lethargic. Alcohol? Sure, but not this much. This sluggishness is the beginning of some sort of disintegration inside. I sense somehow a great danger. It could be a sort of moral gangrene. It is a mistake to think you can't be hurt if you don't care. You can be hurt very much even if you don't care.

Rome, Oct. 23, 1953:

What do you know about yourself, Flynn? How do you stand on a variety of the little human qualities?

My own talents: It is a habit for me to discount myself before somebody else does it for me. Better to get in the first lick. You toss away your pictures. That one stank. This one was no good. I didn't care for the others. I don't even like to discuss them. Yet there is a certain hypocrisy in this. Because I know I have done a few things I can take a bow for. I am embarrassed if somebody tells me I have done something good, even though I may secretly believe it.

On ego: I have never had any problem with my ego. On the contrary, I have developed it. Nonetheless I am not usually regarded as an egotist, as an obnoxious or too-important person. I do not carry myself that way. But I don't tell myself I don't have the goods. I may be finished in films now, but I did make them for a long long time.

On envy: I don't envy anyone. That is not one of my sins. I am not an envious man. I didn't envy anyone when I was having it good, and I don't envy anyone now. I can't remember envying a guy, not with animosity, but I wished I could have done what he was doing. It therefore always comes as a shock how many people there are in the world who hate you because of success. I can never get over that. Everybody will recognize it as a very human trait: "What the hell has he got I ain't got?"

The best life: I am resigned to the fact that the primitive life of the simple South Sea Islanders is the best, but it is not for me. I have become too much a cosmopolitan, I have gotten too far away from that time, that world. Now I belong to Rome, Paris, New York—and Jamaica.

The greatest city: Paris. Because of the sense of freedom. No Parisian is surprised at any costume you wear, how you wear your hat, how flat your feet, how ragged your jacket—as opposed to New York and London. There you are stratified by class almost at once by your dress. In Paris there are so many oddballs. I have a sense of freedom there that I have never found in any other city, with the possible exception of Rio de Janeiro. In Paris you are left to your own devices, to live your own life. I know what is good for me. It is Paris.

My greatest regret: That I never learned to play the piano. I think if I could have learned to play the piano, practicing would have permitted me to reflect and imagine and drift and think and develop. I have never found a substitute for this kind of creativity and re-creativity that I know the rambling reflective pianist to be able to enjoy.

Port Antonio, March, 1954:

I am in my mid-forties. They say I am a sight to behold, compared with my looks a few years back. I can hear them a few feet away . . . "My God how he's changed." People don't like or envy the way I live.

It seems absurd, ridiculous and laughable that somebody should tell me how to behave during my brief span here on this earth. I feel like rebelling every time I think of it. A rough, bemused, rugged individualist, I was born this way and that is the way I will die. I have no clear-cut system of philosophy. I want none. I want no design for living, I want no one to tell me how to live. I will take it from day to day. I follow no leaders, no set of rules, and don't anyone lay down rules for me.

Boston Estate, Jamaica, April 4, 1954:

My dream of happiness: A quiet spot by the Jamaica seashore, looking out at the activity in the ocean, hearing the wind sob with the beauty and the tragedy of everything. Looking out over nine miles of ocean, hearing some happy laughter nearby; sitting under an almond tree, with the leaf spread over me like an umbrella, that is my dream of happiness.

Unfortunately, an hour later, I might not be happy with that.

Palma de Majorca, Oct. 8, 1955:

Has anything changed? As I have gotten older, as I move toward the halfway mark, I find nothing has changed. I think a man's pattern in life very seldom changes. But the chances I take may be of a very different character. I don't want to go jumping over cannon or horses any more. I have been there and I know what it means.

On archaeology and what have you: There is nothing I can think of I would like better than to spend the hot days digging up something, like opening a tomb in Java or going down to the Yucatan to look at the ancient Incan ruins to try to figure out the hieroglyphics, and being able to come back, sweat pouring off, burnt by the sun, tired, exhausted and very happy and in the sure knowledge that you can take a bath, clean up and hop over to visit some madam of integrity. . . .

A man at his best: The quality I most admire in a man is his capacity to level.

Personal defects: Probably my greatest defect is that of a habit of sudden withdrawal, not in a very obvious way, from intimate relations with friends. I know this has aggravated many friends when I just pull out, withdraw and pull down my own personal shade. Then I develop a deep suspicion of any offer of friendship: perhaps it's a caustic and over-cynical appraisal of their motives in proffering friendship. At that time I have a nasty habit of trying to get at their true motives by the exploratory system, which sometimes takes the form of practical jokes.

On being amusing: I think I contribute certainly not only to the amusement but the fundamental being-alive sense that some humans can supply to those they like. In other words, you make their day perhaps a little more happy than it might have been if left to their own devices. I know I do this. I am one of the last holdouts against the modern distractions, radio, television—better not mention movies. I have held steadily to the art of conversation. I don't know what I have to offer a companion beyond that, unless it is a desperate effort to be frank and honest, not only with myself but with others. You don't have to tell others but yourself. I level with me. I love all of the simple things of life: breathing, eating, drinking, frolicking, fishing, all the f's. I love fundamental excitement. A baked breadfruit can be as exciting to me as a visit to see a Rembrandt.

Favorite occupation: A prolonged bout in the bedroom.

The greatest calamity: Castration.

What would I like to be at seventy? At seventy I confidently hope I will have had at least eight more wives, have grown a stomach that I can regard with respect, and can still walk upstairs to the bedroom without aching or groaning.

Palma de Majorca, Oct. 9, 1955:

Reflections:

If I had a pen that would write with Spanish ink, I might feel like starting my memoirs now. But a hiatus, a mental-moral block in my marriage with Pat would, at this time, probably emasculate anything of value. A case history of any marriage, with rare exceptions, could only culminate in boring, spiteful recriminations.

I am not biased against the rich because they are rich, but the most lively people are those without money who would like to have some.

What about love-making as dished up by the diverse ethnic types and nationals? Are they alike? Is woman a universal creature? Does a man take all women to bed when he takes one to bed?

I question straight from the boudoir: Has every oyster a different taste?

My chief delusion, if it is a delusion, is that I have learned as much about sex as Freud. Don't let anybody tell you sex isn't the most important drive in life—except hunger. Otherwise there would be no humans on earth, no other life of any kind. I pretend to be nothing but realistic.

American women are better than the French, but the French cost you less. The American women have learned to love the specific center of gravity of a man. European women have an inherent, built-in antipathy toward this sort of thing. Why this should be I have no idea. The clean-cut American sophomore begins her sex life while still a virgin with this same sexual process. There have been many virgins whom I have met who have told me that formal coition is bad, whether for moral reason or because they may become impregnated, I can't say. You look at their ear lobes and you see they are very long. I know that Kinsey only touched part of the truth. He was a boy scout and came very innocently in the country.

Palma de Majorca, Oct. 14, 1955:
John Hertz keeps pestering me about going back to work.

I know I am contradiction inside contradiction. I know that truth is sometimes an octagon and that I am one. I can love women and hate them and this may seem a contradiction. Contradiction is a cardinal element of life and of itself it may be no contradiction. You can love every instant of living and still want to be dead. I know this feeling often. Don't tell me that contradiction is wrong. Some people say, "That is a contradiction," as if something defies logic or understanding and is therefore not true.

I might be quite famous, but not feel famous, only feel sometimes like a heel. I can be worth a million or two million and feel like a bum and be a bum and live like a bum.

Tell me of paradox. Is there not some percentage of woman in each man, and some man in each woman, and if so, is this not contradiction and is it not true?

My awareness of my own paradox does only one thing to me: it makes me laugh. When I see and sense myself doing something inconsistent, opposite to what I think I believe, I realize it and I laugh. What else can you do when you're all rolled up in the same package of personality? Here is duality and singularity at the same time. I know that it is possible to say something at one time and believe it and know it is true and to say its opposite at another time and it can, in other circumstances, be just as true.

I know that there are two men inside me. One wants to ramble and has rambled around the globe more than once, in the sky and below water. The other man is a settled fellow, who thinks sometimes he is or should be a husband-man, and that he should sit settled in a house by the side of the road or by the side of the sea. Both are inside of me. Each is true.

No, contradiction has a place in human nature, in social values, just as it has in mathematics. Contradiction is neither true nor false. It *is*.

If they say I am inconsistent let them say it, for it is true, because inconsistency is a part of living nature.

I am the epitome of the twentieth-century cosmopolitanism, but I should have been born an explorer in the time of Magellan.

I am sour on women but cannot do without them and I need them incessantly so as to feed my sourness.

I could have killed Bruce Cabot but I can forgive him.

I am bitter about what Lili Damita did to me, but I also laugh about it.

I crave the indulgence of my senses but this is countered by an interior desire that is even keener than my senses to know the meaning of things.

I want to be taken seriously. I feel that I am inwardly serious, thoughtful, even tormented, but in practice I yield to the fatuous, the nonsensical. I allow myself to be understood abroad as a colorful fragment in a drab world.

I have a zest for living yet twice an urge to die.

I have a genius for living, but I turn many things into crap.

I am dangerous to be with because, since I live dangerously, others are subject to the danger that I expose myself to. They, more likely than I, will get hurt.

I will do a great deal for a buck; then when I get it I will throw it away, or let it be taken from me.

I am very tough, but also I am a patsy.

The pursuit of gold, pleasure and danger motivate most of my springs.

I am alternately very kind, very cruel.

I love art but finance may be my forte.

I want faith and I am faithless.

I look for causes, and they wind up with me a romp.

I love myself and hate myself.

I want to be loved but I may myself be incapable of really loving.

I hate the legend of myself as a phallic representation, yet I work at it to keep it alive.

I despise mediocrity above all things. I fear it, yet I know some of my performances have been mediocre.

I generally deny that I was ever a good actor, but I know I have turned in a half-dozen good performances.

I call myself a bum but I have been working hard most of the days of my adult life.

I portray myself as wicked, hoping I will not be regarded as wicked. But I may really be wicked in the Biblical sense.

Women do not let me stay single. I do not let myself stay married.

Cheers for Mama. Damn her too.

Give me the artistic life, except when I'm producing, directing, organizing, banking, playing the stock market and in other ways being a businessman.

I hate the law and spend too much time with lawyers.

I have been called the eternal sophomore, the perennial youth. I can do nothing to alter this. I am hung with it. The stamp is upon me. It is too late for me to become a scientist, saint or messiah. If I symbolize anything it is that I am the eternal *sempervive*.

I laugh a lot, and I weep secretly more often than most men.

I have quested all my life for truths and I wallow in bromides. The bromides themselves wallow in truth.

I live polygamously but I am fascinated by people who appear to live happily monogamously.

I am on the side of the underdog, except when I am on the side of the rich.

In me contradiction itself, as a principle, finds its own *raison d'être*.

I am convinced of the validity of contradiction. There are many worlds. Each is true, at its time, in its own fashion.

For three years or so I aged in the ports and capitals of southern Europe, though chiefly living on the *Zaca* at Palma de Majorca. I made several trips to Jamaica to see how my holdings were doing. My mother and father continued to spend time at the island intermittently. My big operation was to try to hang onto my property. Values went up. The land I had bought there in the late 1940's had trebled and quad-rupled in value, but I had a hard time hanging onto the real estate. While the coconut trees grew, I borrowed and clung precariously to what was left.

I steered clear of the United States. Let them clamor for money. I had none. Lili took over my beloved Mulholland House—my last possession of consequence.

My son Sean, now about fifteen or sixteen, was on his summer vacation in 1955, visiting Pat, Arnella and me aboard my yacht.

We invited a number of friends to celebrate a farewell party. We were on our way to the Cape Verde Islands, where few people go nowadays. It was off the beaten track. I intended heading directly south to Gibraltar, and perhaps put in at some of the little Spanish towns along the coast which I hadn't seen since the Spanish Civil War.

The party aboard ship was exceptionally pleasant and amusing. It broke up at three or four o'clock in the morning, with all of us in the best frame of mind.

Usually my wife and I had separate cabins but this night we didn't. We were in bed together. The silence of the night was suddenly broken by raucous voices on the deck. Who could it be? Were my friends returning?

I heard footsteps in the corridor leading to our room.

The door was flung open.

There was I, in bed, not a stitch of clothes on. Neither had Pat. And completely strange people saying, "Where's your party, Errol? Where's the party?" Two men and two women. The men were Spanish. One woman was French and the other was American. They said, in various languages, "We thought we would just drop in on you for a few jolts."

I had always been indignant about people who figured my yacht to be a public museum and open to all. In fact one reason for living aboard ship is because you can have some privacy.

"The party is over. Who are you? Hasn't it occurred to you that you mustn't set foot on a foreign boat without asking for permission?" I said this lightly, hoping to dispose of them genially.

The American woman said, "Oh come on, you old stick in the mud, the least you can do is offer us a drink."

I kept myself under control. "Besides, madam, busting into my private quarters is even worse."

They laughed uproariously. I felt like a damned fool, in bed with my wife, both of us nude, a sheet only partially covering us.

"Party pooper," yelled the girl.

Pat spoke up, addressing the American woman. "Get off this ship, you bitch. How dare you disturb us like this. There's a baby in the next room too."

The Yankee lady retaliated, "Who the hell are you?"

That did it.

I grabbed a towel and wrapped it around my middle. "I'm sorry, I'll have to ask you to leave."

I started to get out of bed. This woman said, "Who's leaving? We came for a drink."

"Lady, you do nothing of the kind. You know how you got down here?—That's the way out!"

I hustled them up the companionway, still trying to keep the towel around myself.

On deck the Spanish fellows cussed steadily. Abusive cracks floated forward and aft in three different languages. It was like a United Nations meeting.

I rushed them to the end of the ship, toward the shore.

One of the Spaniards, who had an even better vocabulary of Spanish abuse than I ever heard, riled me a bit. I took him by the arm to hurry him along.

He made the error of pushing me in the chest.

I now stood in the nude, and the starry light of early morning displayed Flynn in all his valor but no armor. I hauled off for a long punch. I aimed for his chin, but I hit him in the teeth. At the same instant I felt a horrible blow behind my head. His pal had hit me behind the ear. I took after him, chasing him around the wheelhouse. Ordinarily, since the accident to my back, I had trouble lifting up even a chair. But I got hold of him, lifted him above my shoulders, and tossed him into the Atlantic. I didn't know he couldn't swim.

The girls were flying after me. Pat was flying after them. I took the other fellow and tossed him over the side.

Mike Curtiz couldn't have staged a better deck fight.

It is amazing what you can do when you are provoked.

There is a point where my gallantry runs right out. I took after the dames and was going to serve them the same, but having heard their two friends leave, they got ashore. There they stood on the shore hurling abuse, more French and American. The American four-letter words, by the way, are usually five letters in French.

I could feel the back of my head swelling up where I had been conked. The visitors now went off, up the street, three of them carrying one near-drowned guest.

After the tumult settled and the shouting died down, Sean poked his head out of the ship's companionway with a big revolver. "You didn't have a thing to worry about, Pop. I had them covered all the time."

That broke me up—anything funny can turn my black anger from hot to cool in a hurry.

He probably would have shot me in the back.

At daylight I was on deck. I looked at my right hand. There was a nasty gash and remnants of teeth were in it. One of my seamen found two teeth on the deck. There was blood, which was neither Pat's nor mine. I stuck my hand in some salt water, put Band-Aids on it, and decided to forget about it.

We upped anchor and began a glorious sail.

Next day or so the hand began to swell. It was obvious that blood poisoning set in. Stupidly I paid no attention to it. I had been cut in all sorts of places, all my days, and I'd never had any serious infection. My hand and forearm were taking on the dimensions of a small suckling pig, very red and angry-looking.

We made our first port two days later, a southern island off the coast of Spain, near Ibiza. I headed for a doctor and he gave me penicillin.

Although the arm throbbed with pain, the sea was glorious, the ocean breeze was fine, my vodka supply was high, and I enjoyed the seascape. But you shouldn't drink when taking antibiotics for a chaser. I was in poor shape when I got to a hospital in Gibraltar. By then I couldn't move my arm. Violent pains shot up to my shoulder. I headed for Tangiers so as to get into a French clinic as fast as possible.

They took blood tests. The French doctor explained to me that the most poisonous thing in the world, after rattlesnake bite, was the human teeth.

Samples of the poison in my blood were sent to the Pasteur Institute in Paris. They couldn't identify the type of germ that was in the blood. I became delirious, and was in a coma that lasted for four days.

The doctor said if there were no improvement within twenty-four hours my arm would have to come off at the shoulder. "Perhaps," he said cheerfully, "I can save a bit of the stump."

A fever raged. I was tossing in bed but I wasn't going to have that arm off. He said, "It's your decision. We won't answer for your life if you won't follow the best advice you can get. You have a choice— to lose your arm or to have a nice flowerpot six feet by two."

This was the third time I was supposed to die. The other two were in Italy, when I had hepatitis, and in New Guinea, when I had black-water fever.

Just when I reached a crisis, the Arab riots were getting under way. Arabs and Frenchmen had been massacred. Houses had been burned. You could hear the excitement outside the hospital.

There was a private lawn outside my room. The Arab gardener chewed hashish as he cut down the weeds. Every now and then he would be kind enough to give me a touch. My arm was still massively swollen, but I was holding my own.

I was there a month. Each night I heard the chant of ten thousand Arabs vowing hatred of the French, screaming in Arabic for the death of all Frenchmen.

The doctor now said he would only cut off the arm at the elbow. "Wait," I told him.

The riots got worse. There was all kinds of violence. Houses were broken into. Reports of what was going on came in from gardener, orderlies, Pat, the doctors.

I gained a little more ground. I would now have only to cut it off at the wrist, I was told.

"Not yet," I said.

A riotous night occurred that was the worst yet. Thousands of people milled about the clinic. Nobody gave a damn that Flynn was there. I knew what would settle their hash and save the day for France. If Lili were there, with plenty of portable materials about, she would have settled these Arabs in ten minutes.

The doctor came in with a gun and he said, "We've issued revolvers to everybody here. We've barricaded the doors. Here's a gun for you."

"Good God, take it away! I hate using them even in my Westerns. If those fellows bust in here I don't want to have any gun around. I would be the first one to get knocked off."

"I would advise you to sleep with it under your pillow."

"There are better things to sleep with than that. And that reminds me, where's that nurse with my shot? The 36-23-36 with the dark brown eyes."

When I recovered we headed back to Palma de Majorca. We never did get to the Cape Verde Islands. I continued under treatment for a long time. Altogether that Spanish tooth had cost me six months of time, apart from such considerations as money.

It was around this time that I was visited by the Hollywood agent who suggested I quit beachcombing and go back to films.

A wire came from Paris about a moving picture.

Friends saw me off on a trip to Paris which, they hoped, might re-open for me my moving-picture career.

The plane had taken off and I settled down to a mild drink of brandy and a book.

A hostess asked, "Mr. Flynn, would you care to go up and see the cockpit?"

Rather reluctantly—I had seen so many cockpits—I rose and went up front, wearing a big, broad smile—which immediately froze.

The pilot had no teeth in front. The rest of his face looked startlingly familiar. It was the guy I smashed in the teeth on board my boat six months earlier!

A glint of recognition and remembrance came into his eyes. *"Que malo noche,"* he said. What a bad night.

The first thing I could think of was, Sonofabitch, he's got me! Then, no, we're both in the same plane.

At the Napoleon Hotel in Paris I waited for a certain studio manager from Universal-International. He was on his way back from Turkey.

Up came the gentleman, with a ready smile and a handshake. He asked me if I didn't remember him. I said I did, not having the least idea who he was. I don't even know now. I noticed he was eying me curiously, appraising me. I didn't know I was supposed to be a lazy wreck. He told me that I looked exactly like Kemal Ataturk, the hero of Turkey, whose life they were about to film. After this surveyor went I sent out for a picture of the Turkish dictator, and I saw that he looked like a mixture of Mickey Rooney and Humphrey Bogart.

A report went to Universal-International that I was amenable and capable. Cables went back and forth and I was all set to go to Turkey. I was prepared to sail the *Zaca* through the Mediterranean. I could see it all clearly as the blue sky: a return to films, and besides this, minarets, old mosques, temples, veiled ladies in a harem. A place I had never seen before. The deal, $160,000. I planned to get an old house. I'd wear those big baggy white or purple trousers that the Turks wore— and I would have about me seventeen lovely Turkish ladies. Black eyes flashing. Do the picture up right. All the trappings, trimmings.

I was going to live again. Then a cable came.

Suddenly I learned that I had to go back to Hollywood to make this picture. It appeared that I wasn't wanted for Kemal Ataturk at all, but there was a picture called *Istanbul* to be made on the back lot of the studio.

In Hollywood, even though contracts may not be signed, you can't back out. A deal is a deal and you go through with it. Anybody who tells you that Hollywood is any different is out of his mind. It is a place where a man doesn't dare back out of a handshake, even though there is a misunderstanding.

At least that is my code.

I had no desire to go back there, but back I went to Istanbul, Turkey, via Beverly Hills.

It was the beginning of my return to films.

Ben Hecht, the screenplay writer, has said that only six or seven out of the hundred or so screenplays he has written had any validity, that there were only these few that he might take any pride in. If so, he was lucky. I can't speak that well of as many pictures that satisfied me, as compared with the fifty or so films I made.

The screenwriter is in about the same position as the actor. As you know, the writer is hard put to it to recognize his own work. It is the same with the actor. A screenplay is never, regardless of what anybody tells you, the work of one man. It is hashed, rehashed, rewritten. The actors change the lines. So does the director on the set. The final cutting and editing is in the hands of the producer. The actor may have a bit more prerogative than the writer in so much that he—if he is in a position, and given the material, to do so—can give his own interpretation of it.

But film-making is not solo work—like doing a novel, or playing the violin at Carnegie Hall, or writing a poem, or being your own exclusive creator—insomuch as it is anyone's perquisite to be entirely himself. It is an assembly-line operation.

The effect this has on you is: You always feel you could have done better *if*—if you had been left alone, if you had worked harder, if you had been more artistic—a constant series of ifs, which leads to regret. The incessant reproach, if you have done an interesting picture, is "My God, I wish I could do it all over again."

Nowadays when I am cast as a drunk I am said to do it rather effectively. In my earlier days, when I played the part of a drunk opposite Bette Davis in a film called *The Sisters,* I must have made the worst lush.

In those days I would pick up a script, or a script would be sent to my home and a description of the male lead would say: Spike Rudling; lithe, lean, handsome, piercing-eyed, a man not to cross. That would be me.

Today it is so refreshing. I don't have to look any further than the description, of say, Pete Anderson—a once-handsome man, now decadent, a shadow of his former self and who has taken to the bottle and . . .

Then I know that must be me.

It is better than riding around on a horse, with a sword dangling at my side with which I might accidentally plunge out a friend's eye, or castrate myself.

I have a dream that wakes me up, a nightmare that sets upon me from time to time. I am falling. I feel something go up my calf, it always begins in my calf, and it crawls up my limbs; it is almost a physical dream that works through the nerves and the muscles of me. I wake up with a yell—a yell that will shock any possible head next to me, or bring the house detective—because somebody has told me to look down from a cliff, and I can't do it. . . .

In the early days of movie-making, when I first found out I had vertigo, that I was made dizzy by heights, it never seemed important to me. It was my life to be up on high levels, to fight on parapets of ancient castles, to climb, jump over horses, take a chance on everything there was.

Until one day, a few years back, while making *Crossed Swords* in Italy.

I found myself on the side of a hill in Catalina, the camera grinding, a scene being shot. I looked down and there were rocks and waves. I stared. I threw my gun down. I clung to that rock and just held on. Blood came out of my nails.

My pal Archer Hill was amused. "Come on, Flynn, what are you stalling for?"

You couldn't have pried me loose with an ice axe. I was absolutely frozen, digging into the rocks on the side of the cliff. Down below, three hundred feet, were the deadly rocks and the rushing water. I was in that position for what seemed an eternity. Finally, Hill realized I was absolutely rigid.

All I could say, faintly, was, "Come and get me . . ."

He stopped laughing.

A little later, when I recouped, I found the director saying, "Now we are going to stage a duel up here, and what do you think, Errol?—I think you ought to jump across this tower on the ancient castle, to the other one; then, as you jump down, you go into the sword fight, you fight along this parapet that looks spectacular . . ."

I looked down. I knew I couldn't do it.

The best thing is to level, I said to myself, so I went to him. "Frankly, chum, I can't do that."

"Come on, stop kidding. Why not?"

"Frankly, I'm just scared."

I didn't tell him why, because I didn't quite know myself. I only knew that if I got up on a height and looked down, something might happen.

So they shot something else, and I thought it over while they kept busy for the next couple of hours. Nobody seemed to understand; maybe they thought I was holding out for more salary.

I saw they were upset, so I took a deep breath. "Well, I'll try it."

The scene called for me to jump a few feet, not a large jump. But this time—unlike the early days when I used to do such a stunt without thinking about it—it looked about a hundred feet across.

I just have to do this. I must.

I pulled on the old boots; the sword was there. I figured the distance.

If you look down, Errol, you have had it.

I went to measure it again—and I did look down.

Sure as hell, I couldn't do it.

Looking back on a career where I have had guns firing at me, explosions behind my head, horses falling from under me, falls of earth collapsing around me, big leaps to make, it is amazing to me that I am all in one piece. I still have two ears, my nose, all my limbs, and my eyes. Slightly astonishing.

Fear is a very curious thing. It's so relative. What will scare you won't scare me.

You are afraid, every day, of something. It might be anxiety, economic trouble, or anticipation of something you have to do: but I defy anybody of mature years to say there's not some kind of fear in his or her head.

Joshua Logan, who, if anybody, should know more about actors, theatre and direction than most people, had something to say on fear recently which I found very interesting. He was talking, in a printed piece, about William Holden. Holden is a lad I met when I was making *The Sea Hawk*. He was then a fine-looking boy playing small parts, and quickly afterwards married my leading lady, Brenda Marshall, and they lived happily ever after. I liked Holden very much, although up to that time he had done nothing much. I was the big star and Bill was beginning.

Logan said that he was going to make a picture which called for Holden to be an acrobat, and he wondered whether Bill could qualify. At this meeting, Holden said, "What do you mean, be an acrobat—look!" And he opened a window with a six-floor drop and did a handstand on the window sill. Logan took one horrified look, retreated out of the room, and refused to come back till Holden re-entered the window, "Now, do you think I am okay?" he asked the famous director.

Holden explained that when he was a small boy it was a kick for him and his brother to see who could do a handstand off the highest place. His brother was rescued off the Brooklyn Bridge doing just that.

That incident between Logan and Holden was about ten years ago. I wonder how Holden would feel if he had to do that handstand today?

The funny, odd part is I know that William Holden is petrified of getting onto a dance floor. I know he stayed away from the studio one day when he had to do a dance scene. So, there is fear for you. Not afraid to do the handstand on the window ledge, Holden flips and folds on a dance floor. I wonder now if he has overcome his terror of getting up and pointing the toe doing an ordinary dance, whatever the hell that is these days.

In making *Too Much, Too Soon,* it would have been easy for me to simulate Jack Barrymore's physical characteristics. For I can do, with the lifted eyebrow, an imitation about as good as anyone else's. In fact I have often, at gatherings, told stories of him and mimicked his motions, such a fabulous human figure the man was.

Jack turned himself into a burlesque of himself at the end, and many who had known him and his work were distressed to see this, because he typified to them the greatest actor they knew or heard of in their lifetime; the public remembered this final phase of his and they may have come to look upon Jack as a clown, and perhaps they expected to see that in my portrayal.

When I started to try to get Jack into focus, I wanted to delve into his inner self, not to imitate him—that was too easy. I wanted to show a man with a heart, a man eaten up inside—as I knew him to be in those final days when I was close to him—a man full of regrets and all ready to die, but with one last thing to live for, the love of his daughter, Diana, his desire to get back her love.

I determined that I would stay away from the least suggestion or imitation of manners. That would have been deadly wrong. The only concession I made to that was to try to look like him. To facilitate that, the studio put a tip on the end of my nose which aided in conveying his profile.

There was much controversy about my playing him. Some said I was the only one who could do it, others said I'd foul it up. It was a challenge, because it was almost impossible to be right, whatever you did.

I determined I would show the inner Barrymore as I knew him: right or wrong. I would win, lose or get a draw. For once in my long career I worked hard at the characterization that I thought should be presented. I tried hard to remember him, to underplay, to underemphasize, and in this way to get nearest to the recesses of the mind and heart of a great human being.

For many reasons the favorite picture in which I played was *The Roots of Heaven.* This story by the Frenchman, Romain Gary, was one of the most unusual I ever read.

When you pick up a book that some director or producer has asked you to read, you never know what the screenplay is going to be, or how close it is going to stick to the original. But first, here was a wonderful work to begin with, a story that interested me—contrary to so many vehicles I have had to appear in. Add to that, you have a master showman who wishes to produce it: Darryl Zanuck, and he asks you to be in this picture. Here is a man with all the gambling guts in the world. How he can sit down and decide to spend four million dollars—with me heading the cast—naturally I was fascinated and enthused.

The sources of interest in this picture piled up. I had top billing. That was very funny because William Holden was supposed to do this, and I was going to co-star with him, but Holden got into some kind of beef with Paramount, to whom he is under contract—and Zanuck switched to another just as brilliant actor, Trevor Howard. However, when Holden bowed out, I had to take star billing. This was strange because the main burden had to be carried by Howard.

Now, add to these factors the point of the story itself. We are organized and there is Zanuck with the guts and convictions to sink a fortune into a picture which uses elephants as a symbol of the survival of life. Then we go off to French Equatorial Africa to shoot the film.

It was a fascinating six months, in some ways the most astonishing period of my life: whole new worlds of interest in people and lands opened up.

Everybody, almost everybody, got sick. There were 164 people, an English camera crew comprising about a third, about another third were Americans, and the final third French and Italian. This led to a lot of excitement when it came to eating. The French wouldn't eat spaghetti, the Italians wouldn't eat French food, and the Americans wouldn't eat either. It was amusing to sit down with these groups all seated at different tables, with their varying cultures, manners, beefs, contrasts.

French Equatorial Africa is a place anybody can leave off their world itinerary when they take their next vacation. One hundred thirty-two in the shade. We would run short of ice and that was really torture because we were all absolutely parched.

Out of our entire crew, the casualty list—I think I am right about this—was twenty-two or twenty-four who got sent back to Rome or to Paris or to London or the United States. The conditions were as fine as Zanuck could make them but this didn't mean that he could get rid of malaria mosquitoes. This didn't mean that the fresh water you had to get flown down from France would arrive on time. If it didn't, you had to drink the local water. I refused to do that on principle—which may be the reason why I was practically the only one on the set who didn't get sick. I stuck with vodka, and fruit juices liberally laced with more vodka. Even the ice was made of bottled fresh water, great big cans of sealed pure water.

As a result of these conditions, the planes kept flying out with the critically ill. The medical problems ranged from a cut toe to amoebic dysentery, gonorrhea, malaria. But not in that order.

One Italian didn't take his anti-malaria pills and caught the most virulent type of African malaria, the mortality rate of which is so tremendously high, and he died. Darryl's son-in-law, a most wonderful-looking young man in the prime of youth and good shape, had taken his pills regularly—even so, he was shipped back, out of action, with this malaria, because it was really nothing to fool with. There were about eleven cases of that disease alone.

Dysentery accounted for about five, and almost everybody had a form of that, except me. I would attribute my staying in good health to Smirnoff's (if they promise to send a case a month). There were some rather strange cases of gonorrhea that accounted for about four. When the company arrived, and before the shooting began, some of the fellows prowled in the villages and got the bug from the local girls. One fellow got a strange African disease, for which he was returned to Paris, and even the Pasteur Institute there couldn't identify it.

You ask, Well, what was so fascinating about all this? Only that it was a challenge in a variety of ways. Things like how to be the last one to get sick, or how to make a horrible experience look like fun, were very important. Personally, I made it fun. I went there mentally determined whatever kind of hell it was going to be, I was going to make it merry for myself and for everybody else, if I could. Yet perhaps I had some preparation for all this. I had been through the New Guinea jungles, worse even than French Equatorial Africa, so probably I had a gearing for this that the others didn't.

The roads were the most primitive in the world. The French Equatorial people were the most colorfully dressed people I have ever seen. They have a natural capacity, it seems, of merging colors. We bounced around, examining the wonderful colored garb of the Africans wherever we saw them. The materials they used came from France.

Johnny Huston has a lust for the outdoors. He lets nothing get in the way of his love for it. I knew about this and it took a bit of skillful conniving to figure a way for some outdoor action with him. One time the company had to move from Central Africa down to the Belgian Congo. Huston and I arranged, while this move was taking place, for a private safari. I shall never forget it. I didn't shoot anything. Frankly, I don't like to kill. Beyond that, I don't even like to photograph animals. I just want to look at them. We saw everything, great surges of elephants, the African fauna with their strange names; the very rare giant eland; a beast said to be the most ferocious in the jungle—the water buffalo. Huston got one of the largest pairs of horns for a trophy, and he was like a kid with his first lollipop. He was obviously very good in the jungle. I thought I was pretty good, on foot, but this fellow Huston, no youngster, leaped along like a big spider swinging through the trees.

Then, the making of the movie itself: you can imagine everybody having to make up properly, sweating, then making up again. All except me. I didn't have to make up. I didn't have to have any beads of sweat put on me. It was there when I woke in the morning, the vodka, the heat, the Flynn sweat all the time. I would get up later than the others, able to save on this make-up time when a half hour meant something. It was tougher for the leading lady, Juliette Greco. They had to take sweat off of her, put sweat on others. Howard had a brick-red complexion which, in color, didn't photograph right, so he had to use make-up, a tan, and of course he was sweating like everybody else. So that went on all the time, make-up, take it off, put it on, sweat, sweat sweat. Then a shower of water over your head to cool you off, put the make-up on again, and five minutes later repeat the same thing.

Finally you play your part, the camera is working, so are you. Naturally, when you pick up a novel and read it, you never know what the screenplay is going to be or how close it is going to stick to it. I had my eye on a special part, the role of Forsythe, and now I was doing it. But as is generally the case, the character is developed on the set. When the camera starts to grind, you hope you strike the right tuning note—you hope, because you don't know if you will be right. Maybe—it sometimes happens—your performance picks up in the middle of the picture.

Now you are on your own—excepting the help you get from a top director like Huston and your fellow actors. Each actor or actress has an independent approach. There is no standard set of rules, so I can only take myself as an example. Because other people, I am sure, if they are outstanding personalities of the screen or stage, have their own approach. The stage is a different technique. You have three or four weeks to rehearse, so that when you come to opening night you have a fair idea, you hope, of what you're doing.

Not so with the screen.

Every day the script changes on the set. So too the location.

I was even up to my old tricks, doing my own Fearless Flynn stunts when a double might have done just as well. I found myself singing a bawdy Australian song while pretending to be drunk, swimming in an African river, and hanging onto a horse's tail, the horse kicking me in the crotch. I was singing:

> "So you swim to the shore, boys,
> And I'll save me life
> I got to get back by 7 o'clock
> To get a divorce from me wife."

A song my grandmother used to sing to me when I was knee-high, in Sydney.

I had to continue with the song after swimming this jungle river at Port Archambeau. I didn't know that only a week before a captain in the French Army had been seized by a crocodile just a few hundred yards up this African stream.

And so, things still interest me when they interest me. When there's a chance to do a job, a picture worth doing, a scene worth shooting, I still steal a march on the worriers about insurance.

Since we never had a chance to rehearse in Africa, you just take your best intuitive hold and hope that you are right. If they "shoot" in continuity, that is, from beginning to end, that is one thing: but it is a very bad thing when they shoot the ending first.

This is done because there are so many well-paid people on salary, and the directors and producers must get rid of them fast. Shoot their scenes and get them off the lot. Maybe these people only have a week. I don't think I have ever been in one picture which was shot in continuity. Those people are blessed who have had this happen. It is rare.

It may be hard to pick up the next day's shooting because of the change of tempo, the disjointed planning, the need to get the whole thing done and out of the way, regardless of time and order.

You are given a scene to do and you must do it. The director doesn't know for sure what is going to happen. He may have an over-all scheme in his mind, but he doesn't know how his people are going to behave, or how his camera is going to be, or even where it is going to be. Everybody is in a dark, obscure cloud.

It is uncertain and frightening to make a scene where you may have been in the jungle of Africa for three days or a week. It may occur to the public, "That's very funny. He is clean-shaven. Why doesn't he have a beard? Does he carry a razor and blades during these horrible things he is going through?"

All these details are wearing, trying, nerve-wracking. What boner is being made that the public will see through? Watch it, watch everything, very closely. Watch yourself because only you can take care of yourself, finally. Everybody else has himself to watch out for. I don't think people realize the effort involved to take care of these apparently minor details.

You also don't know what's in the director's mind or the producer's. You must say, "This is the way I see it and this is the way I am going to do it. If I am wrong, then I hope I will get corrected soon enough, so I can correct it." It is like a tuning fork. How many of them are there? If you hit one of these chords in the beginning, fine! But supposing you don't?

Finally, the artistic slant, the way I do it, is to say to myself, "Who is this man I am trying to play?" Let's suppose the shooting script goes along more or less—but only more or less—the way it is down on paper. Then you say to yourself, "The most important thing is for me to keep in character." Since I will have no control over what stage of the story will be shot first, I can only conclude, "Here is the way I imagine him."

Imagination is the big thing to try to get over on the screen—your imaginative process.

Without this you are lost. It is the most essential thing.

So much for *The Roots of Heaven,* the roots of an actor.

I was on my yacht at Majorca, between pictures, when the *Confidential* trial got under way. I returned to offer battle to this scurrilous outfit. I knew that others who were suing, or had been maligned, were not offering real resistance. Some did not press their suits. Others didn't want to go into court.

The press gave me a royal welcome. My new pictures were beginning to be shown, and the boys met me on board ship as we landed.

"Hello, fellows."

I was greeted with a most unexpected warmth. They were delighted to see me home again. At last, they said, Hollywood will be Hollywood again. There'd be news and color and copy. They wanted to know what I was up to and what I was going to do.

I said, "Boys, what do you expect me to do? Poke somebody in the nose? Pull a knife on someone, just to lighten the troubled air?"

They laughed, and insisted all was well again. Flynn was back and gay stories of vodka, night clubs and new blondes could start again. I told them all I wanted was peace and that I had found much of it aboard the *Zaca*. I came back this time on business—*Confidential* business—then I'd be going to work again.

The magazine *Confidential* had been running stories about me. I, like the rest of Hollywood, was the object of its disaffections. In Europe, reading about the perfidies of this so-called exposé publication, I rankled. They had published accounts about me which were false, and I brought suit for a million bucks. Mine was a small one compared with a few of the astronomical suits brought by others. I read with disgust how this outfit libeled Maureen O'Hara, Ava Gardiner, and others, and I decided: Whatever the others do, I must fight.

They printed a story that said that on my wedding night, after I was married to Patrice Wymore in Hollywood, I walked out on her to keep a date and spend the night with a call girl.

The magazine settled on the courthouse steps. They paid me $15,000. That's a large settlement for libel under American laws. It wasn't really the dough I was after, on this, but I was angry that such a phony story could get into print and that such a scandal sheet should be allowed to publish.

Not that I have been a paragon of the conventionalities. I have not, and the world knows it. I acknowledge my own peccadilloes, and if and when there are real incidents, I make no denial, no apology, and I even stand by them. But I resented such a gross mismanipulation of the legend around me.

At the same time I hasten to affirm the truth of another *Confidential* report that I had a mirror over my bed. The publication reported that it was a two-way mirror. You could be on the other side of that mirror, in a room above, and look down and see what was going on. From the bed below, looking up, you could see nothing.

Alas, as they used to say when proprieties were broken in Victorian times—this was true. With the exception of once in the case of Freddie McEvoy, this gadget never got to be used. The architect who built the house arranged this on his own. I thought it amusing and let it be completed. It was a magic mirror, all right, but when the word of this got out, nobody wanted to be caught in that annex of the apartment.

I am not trying to cover up anything about myself. What's true is true and I make my own admissions, but what is false will cost my accusers their hard-won, or hard-earned, or hard-stolen money.

By 1958, I was no longer living with Pat.

Nobody ever tried harder than Pat to make me happy.

We tried hard to adapt ourselves to roles which we both found desperately hard to fulfill. I think some enterprising dramatist could find a fine story in that. Two show people try hard to invent a quiet life for themselves, to live the way others are said to live; they work at this while being deeply involved in the business of being famous and busy in the insane world of the theatre. Naturally it cannot work.

I struck up with the wealthy and cultured playboy, Huntington Hartford, to do something in the legitimate theatre. Hunt, as he is usually called, had written an adaptation of *Jane Eyre*. I signed to do the male lead.

Huntington is tall, sallow, with a native charm when he wants to put it on. He has great power in the community, as money always gives a man power, and he has tried to do something constructive with his wealth. Apart from what he has done in the theatre and in other arts, he is a fine athlete. Beyond the arts, he and I had much else in common: we never fell out over the sight of a figure 35-23-34, or some other even more vital statistic.

I wasn't happy in the play, much as I wanted to do something in the legitimate theatre. I thought the play in its present form was too archaic. My problem was to utter lines that were unbecoming to me. A love line like: "Now, my little sparrow, I'll never let you go." It hurts. I just can't call a woman my little sparrow—not even for money. In this play you had to utter a line like, "Stop—cease this farce." That kind of language belongs to Victorian England. I wanted to change the language—and I couldn't. Huntington and I fell into litigation.

But the play got a tryout in Cincinnati. One cold night, after the performance, I left the theatre disgruntled. I disliked the play, wondered what I was doing out here, in this town, in this unconvincing drama.

I felt like a dog who has had his day—that it was late in the afternoon professionally. Dejection had really set in.

As I walked out of the theatre a crippled old lady in a wheelchair blocked the stage entrance. I excused myself and tried to get by. She took me by the arm. Gently she said, "Thank you. Thank you so much."

What had I done? Maybe I had given her a couple of tickets to the show and didn't remember, or what?

She said, "Thank you for all the wonderful hours of happiness. If you knew what my life had been you would know what I am saying."

I was embarrassed. She kissed my hand and said, "Go home to bed now."

I walked off thinking, Maybe I haven't been such a loss after all. Anybody who can bring a few moments of happiness to another human life certainly can't be wasting his time in an otherwise fear-ridden and very often drab world. Maybe it hasn't all been so futile. Maybe it wasn't all a waste.

Maybe all that I am in this world and all that I have been and done comes down to nothing more than being a touch of color in a prosaic world. Even that is something.

I hope I haven't given the impression that the foregoing is anything like a definitive account of the women I have known, the brawls I have been in, or the incidents of motion picture making. Nothing of the sort. But even the Mississippi comes to an end. I don't want to be redundant. I could mention more rows, more litigations, more hoaxes, more drinks, more kicks, perhaps more thoughts. Nor have I touched on my sea experiences. But who wants to get drowned in words?

Women? Could I present a gallery of women I have known, loved, been loved by, or just taken by?—I could not. It is impossible. I remember the first—the maid that worked for us in Australia—and I remember the last. No mention of names. But in between I have done a lot of traveling. Since my teens I have gone to bed twelve or fourteen thousand nights. And I don't want to enter into competition with any of these computers they are working with up at Harvard. I would lose out—to a computer.

Living I have done, enormously, like a gourmand eating the world, and I don't suppose it is egotism, but only fact, to suggest that few others alive in the present century have taken into their maw more of the world than have I.

On the sea, beneath it, in the air, and in all the parts of most of the lands, I have gone a-hunting in quest neither of fame nor of fortune, but the vindication of the act of living. But I have found my Holy Grail.

I have seen the structures of this century and been within them and I am of them. I have had my fun, my kicks, my vodka, my affairs and my fights and my pictures, at one place or another, and at all of them. I rather suppose that not since Ulysses has anyone roamed more than I, waged more of a war with and against the sirens and the siren songs of our time. I have slain the lensed, one-eyed, single-focused cinematic Polyphemus of our time, as the earlier wanderer slew the Cyclops. I have had my women, felled the suitors, wielded my sword for the world to see, have had fun and action, romance and sport, and looked hard for the deeper meanings of it all. I have tried like a warrior in a cause to find meanings in the meaningless, life in death, death in life, joy in anger, laughter and love, and I have found hardship, money and fame and riches, and wretchedness and pain and unhappiness. I have had wives, loves and children.

All my life I have tried to find my mother and I have never found her. My father has not been Theodore Flynn, exactly, but a will-o'-the-wisp just beyond, whom I have chased and hunted to see him smile upon me, and I shall never find my true father, for the father I wanted to find was what I might become, but this shall never be, because inside of me there is a young man of New Guinea, who had other things in mind for himself besides achieving phallic symbolism in human form.

I am living with this brand—even relatively happily—but I wish it hadn't happened. I do not know whether I have conveyed it—or tried not to convey it—but I have been cut by my own sword so deeply that I am ready for whatever befalls. Flynn is not always In. Sometimes he is far far out—at the bottom of the chasm, at the bottom of the cleft.

There is my life, a picaresque painting. Not like a Van Gogh, with its thick crazy beauty on a small canvas; not like a Gauguin, with its placid skies and its serene folk and its bronzed splendor; not like a Rembrandt, conservative and model and burgomaster; not like a Michelangelo, vast and religious, with truth and strength in the limbs. Mine is more like some Toulouse-Lautrec, with its high-colored panties and a wild abandon; more like a Dégas, with its endless dancing girls, its theatre, its burlesque, its vodka haze; more like the dappled obscurity of some surrealist painter of today's small gallery, where you have to peer hard to find meaning, where the color splashes endlessly, losing itself in a mosaic of insane design, mayhem-like wild stroking of the brush, drunken sprawls of oil laid on heavily in the wrong places.

I have tried to paint it in words, for I could not possibly do it in plastics. But no matter, there I am, unable to understand myself. Still not knowing who I am. Still hunting for my soul. Laughing boy—who tried to knock himself off from time to time, and even failed at this as at other things.

Oh, I have seen enough and done enough and been places enough and livened my senses enough and dulled my senses enough and probed enough and laughed enough and wept more than most people would suspect.

Where am I now?

On June 20th of this year I turned fifty, so I gave myself a birthday gift. A big stone house on the north side of Jamaica, overlooking the Caribbean.

As I read the galley proof of this book I am seated on the front piazza—I shall have to find a fancier name for the porch—it is a long stretch of stone. I stare out nine miles at the green Carib. It is quiet out there and quiet up here, a few hundred feet above that sea. I can be relatively happy now. I have the sea for a sister, a brother, a father and a mother.

There is a swimming pool within a few feet of where I sit. It is forty feet across and it takes a nice curve, fitting the loop of the hill on which the house is built. There is a wingspan of a hundred and fifty feet to this little chicken shed. I suppose it is rather baronial, as befits Baron Flynn, formerly of the Court of Hollywood, Regent to His Majesty Jack Warner, King of Cinemania.

I came here recently after finishing a picture in Cuba, *Cuban Rebel Girl,* based on the days I spent with Castro just before the fall of Batista.

My children are with their mothers back in the States. My own parents are in England. My war with Mother drones on steadily, toward a silent truce.

I am alone, except for my four dogs, Jamaica pups, one that looks like a spotted shadow and barks hastily and may bite hastily, and they are good company.

Not far away is the small house of my caretaker. He oversees the farm hands who grow the palms and pick the citrus and carry down the limes and lemons and breadfruit. All around me is the frangipani with its sweet smell of jungle, erasing for me what lies beyond in the great cities. There is a carefully groomed yard around this new house. Tall coconut stalks, with their monstrous yet beautiful spider-web branch design, shade me from the view of screwballs, beatniks and other forms of predators.

A mile below, at the water's edge, is another swimming pool, except that this one is formed out of a natural shore formation. I go there occasionally and take a dip in the blue salt water I love so very much.

The second half-century looms up, but I don't feel the night coming on.